to NORAH BARTLETT

for much generous advice, encouragement

and technical instruction,

my most grateful and affectionate thanks

Where's that Poem?

Where's that Poem?

*REVISED
AND ENLARGED EDITION*

AN INDEX OF
POEMS FOR CHILDREN
Arranged by Subject, with
a Bibliography of Books of Poetry

HELEN MORRIS

*Principal Lecturer in English
Homerton College, Cambridge*

OXFORD · BASIL BLACKWELL

Text set in 10 pt. Photon Times, printed by photolithography, and
bound in Great Britain at The Pitman Press, Bath

Contents

Foreword

The first *Where's that Poem?* was produced because I was so often asked by students in a College of Education, 'Do you remember that poem about . . . about badgers, or bagpipes, or baking, or Balaclava? And where can I find it?' I began to list poems and keep references, and the list became a book which I believe has proved useful to teachers of poetry. Since 1966 many new anthologies for children have appeared, and poems from them have been included in this much enlarged edition. I have also added many more subject-headings, including such abstractions as *Choice*, and since so many children enjoy attempting 'haiku', some examples under ORIENTAL POEMS, BRIEF.

The poems have been chosen for children of approximately seven to fifteen years. Children of five and six are usually best suited by nursery rhymes and jingles, of which there are several admirable collections (see particularly *Puf.N.R, Ox.N.R, M.G.E, M.G.B, M.G.R* at the end of this book). But many other poems mentioned here can be read to and with even the youngest children in the infant school. The teacher of children of fifteen upwards will naturally use a wide selection of adult poetry to suit both his own tastes and that of each of his classes. But how arbitrary and how artificial such divisions are! Much great poetry can be apprehended (admittedly at different levels) both by small children and by adults; parts of *The Ancient Mariner*, Robert Frost's *Stopping by Woods on a Snowy Evening* and some of Blake's songs are cases in point.

To classify poems as suitable for a particular age-group is to err in two ways: it is to expect a poem to speak exclusively to children at a certain stage of development, and to assume that children of a certain age are all at the same stage of poetic education and appreciation. The appreciation of poetry to any sophisticated degree has to be learnt, as much as the appreciation of music or art. Even though certain poems—like certain tunes and paintings—may at first hearing or sight be simple enough to appeal to the un-educated, yet it is the teacher's business to foster real enjoyment and appreciation of more difficult poetry by a careful and sensitive choice of poems for each individual class—and if possible for each individual child. Some teachers still invariably demand that every child turn to the same poem in the one available anthology, and that the whole class concentrate on that poem. But—once poetry is established as worth reading, because interesting or even exciting—each child should be given time to browse in different books of poems, while the teacher circulates with quiet words of individual guidance. Thus the child learns to choose for himself a poem that has something to say to him personally, to copy the poem into his personal anthology, or to read it aloud to the teacher or to the class. To say that a particular poem is suitable for a child of a particular age is to try to cram every child into a teacher-designed and teacher-enforced scheme of development which bears no resemblance to real, personal, individual growth.

Since grouping by age seems impracticable, the poems have been grouped under subject-headings, with ample cross-reference. A few 'kinds', such as limericks and riddles, are included (see p. xiii) simply because this seemed useful. Carols, ballads and nursery rhymes are not listed as such, but many appear under subject-headings. Some songs by Shakespeare are here, and often children also enjoy snatches from the plays; but very few of the latter have been included, lest the work swell beyond all bounds. Every teacher must have a fund of his own favourite Shakespearean passages, a line or two to quote at an appropriate moment; children may remember these, though not wholly understanding them, and grow later to full appreciation.

Sometimes a group of poems on the same subject is divided into two sections, 'Lyric and Descriptive' and 'Narrative', so that the teacher looking for a few vivid lines will not find a long story, and vice-versa.

Reference is given to a wide variety of sources—pp. 239 to 272 list 169 titles, comprising 309 volumes—since different schools possess different books. It is hoped that every teacher will procure as many different books of poetry as possible, and thus give every child the opportunity of browsing widely. In the index, each book is indicated by a symbol—a group of letters which indicate its title if an anthology, and its author if it is by a single poet. These symbols are explained on p. 239 and arranged alphabetically on pp. 239 to 272 for easy reference and identification. A few words of comment on each may, I hope, assist the teacher who is building up a library of books of poetry, for personal use or for the class, to decide whether any particular book is worth closer inspection.

This index is by no means comprehensive, but highly selective and personal. No poem is included that I would not, in particular circumstances, be happy to offer to a class. No one person can choose poems for another to teach with any *certainty* of success—though many poems are widely popular with a majority of teachers and children. No teacher should ever give a class a poem, no matter how highly recommended, unless he himself receives genuine pleasure from it.

In laying such emphasis upon the *enjoyment* of poetry I find myself in good company. Sir Philip Sidney wrote that the end of poesie is 'to teach and delight'; Dr Johnson declared that 'the end of poetry is to instruct by pleasing'; Robert Frost said that a poem 'begins in delight and ends in wisdom'. I hope that this book may help teachers to find poems which will both delight and enlighten their classes.

I should like to thank those of my friends who have helped me in the confusing work of compilation, particularly Wendy Lachman, Sue Toye, Pat Woodcock, Sally Boulter and Helen Harrison. Without the hard work, helpful criticism, constant encouragement and remarkable memory of Isabel Burn, the book would never have been completed, and I am deeply grateful.

Cambridge 1973   *Helen Morris*

The Grouping of Poems

The poems are grouped according to their subjects, but certain *kinds* of poems will be found under the following headings: COUNTING RHYMES, COUNTING-OUT RHYMES, CUMULATIVE RHYMES, FABLES, LIMERICKS, NONSENSE, ORIENTAL POEMS (BRIEF), PARODY, QUESTION & ANSWER, RIDDLES, TALES (CAUTIONARY), TALES (TALL), and TONGUE-TWISTERS.

The poems are arranged alphabetically, by title, under each heading. The articles 'A', 'An' and 'The' have been ignored. When only part of a poem is cited, the title is followed by the word '(part)'.

Explanation of the letters and numbers following each poem will be found on page 239.

1

ACCIDENTS (ROAD)

Ambulance (Miles Gibson)

they threw it/in a blanket
Drag 60

At any rate (James Michie)

'He's dead,' they shouted as he left his
motor bike
D.P.R IV 138

Auto Wreck (Karl Shapiro)

Its quick soft bell beating, beating
*Chal II 45; Flock 131; Way 82; Yim III
15*

The Diverting History of John Gilpin
(William Cowper)

John Gilpin was a citizen
*Ch.Gar 158; D.P III 119; D.P.R. III 88;
Min IV 71; P.Bk 226; Plea III 55; Puf.V
66; Ver II 13; V.F 39; Weal I 47*

Interruption to a Journey
(Norman MacCaig)

The hare we had run over
Drag 60; J.Vo IV 6

Mid-Term Break (Seamus Heaney)

I sat all morning in the college sick bay
D.P.R III 4; Liv 51; Spir.R 78

*The Strange Case of the Cautious
Motorist* (Ogden Nash)

Have you read the biography of Mr
Schwellenbach? You can miss it if you
try
Tell II 18

Street Accident (Richard Church)

In the road ahead of me
Sev 85

Travelling through the Dark
(William Stafford)

Travelling through the dark I found a
deer
*Cent 103; Flock 225; Song IV 161;
Them I 48; Voi II 65; Yim II 77*

Without Due Care (A. P. Herbert)

Old Mrs Alice Bird is dead—
Sto III 115

ACCIDENTS (WORK)

Butch Weldy (Edgar Lee Masters)

After, I got religion and steadied down
D.P.R. IV 140; Ev.M 34

The Stone (W. W. Gibson)

And will you cut a stone for him
Make III 145; T.C.N 78

ACROBATS

See also Trampolines

Blondin (Walter de la Mare)

With clinging dainty catlike tread
R.R 27

The Man on the Flying Trapeze
(Anon)

Oh, the girl that I loved she was
handsome
M.M.A 92

ADAM

See also Eden, Eve

Adam and Eve and the Serpent
(Negro Spiritual)

The Lord He thought He'd make a
man—
Tell II 3

Adam lay Ybounden (Anon)

Adam lay ybounden
Puf.V 255; Song IV 200

ADMIRALS

See Benbow, Columbus, Drake,
Grenville, Nelson

ADOLESCENCE

See also Exp I

Black Jackets (Thom Gunn)

In the silence that prolongs the span
Cent 73; Them IV 9

The Boys (Anthony Thwaite)

Six of them climbed aboard
D.P.R. IV 112; Them IV 10

The Cocky Walkers (Mervyn Peake)

Grouped nightly at the cold accepted wall
Peg V 99; Them VII 11

Life in our Village (Martei Markwei)

In our little village
Chal II 36; Nev 40

Mother and Son (R. S. Thomas)

At nine o'clock in the morning
Chal II 37; Exp I 7; Liv 25; Them IV 40

The Picnic (John Logan)

It is the picnic with Ruth in the spring
Act IV 22; Exp I 40; Read III 21; Them IV 15; Voi III 71

Protest of a Sixth Former
(Robert Hayes (aged 17))

Oh Father can cease to exist
Them IV 38

On the Move (Thom Gunn)

The blue jay scuffling in the bushes follows
Ev.M 70; Ver III 78

Twice Shy (Seamus Heaney)

Her scarf à la Bardot
Liv 40

The Young Ones (Elizabeth Jennings)

They slip on to the bus, hair piled up high
Bird III 51; Them IV 9

ADVERTISING

Advertising (A. S. J. Tessimond)

You, without gleam or glint or fire
D.P.R II 34

Attack on the Ad-Man
(A. S. J. Tessimond)

This trumpeter of nothingness, employed
Sev 119

Girl, Boy, Flower, Bicycle
(M. K. Joseph)

This girl/waits at the corner
Drag 42

AEROPLANES

See also Flying, Gliding, Parachuting, Wars: 1914–18 (Air), Wars: 1939–45(Air), (Blitz) (Bombing)

Above the Storm (W. W. Gibson)

Sheer through the storm into the sun the plane
Sphe 190

The Landscape near an Aerodrome
(Stephen Spender)

More beautiful and soft than any moth
Man II 28; Pers 95; P.F.P II 157

On the Wings of the Morning
(Jeffery Day)

A sudden roar, a mighty rushing sound
Peg V 3

A Time to Dance (part)
(C. Day Lewis)

Sing we the two lieutenants, Parer and McIntosh
Peg V 6; P.Tong II 128; Sto III 29; T.C.N. 40

AFRICA, SOUTH

See Ver III 242–275

Afar in the Desert (part)
(Thomas Pringle)

Afar in the desert I love to ride
Ark 168

'Barricadoed Evermore' (George Miller Miller)

Sophiatown's not far away
Ver III 258

Drought (David John Darlow)

The burning skies are steel
Ver III 253

Drought (part) (Francis Carey Slater)

The sky is a blue, coiled serpent
Ver III 248

Pass Office Song (Anon) (trans. P. Rutherford)

Take off your hat
Voi III 44

AGE

See Old Age, Youth and Age

AGINCOURT

Agincourt (Michael Drayton)

Fair stood the wind for France
*By 18; Fab.C.V 237; Iron II 7; Kal 90;
P.F.P II 67; P.W 58; P.W.R 52; Riv III
91; Trea 5; Ver II 107*

Henry V (before Agincourt)
(William Shakespeare)

From camp to camp through the foul
womb of night
*Prologue IV; Cher 337; Prem 133;
Wheel IV 50*

O that we now had here
*IV iii 16–66; Kal 92; P.W 71; Sto III
99; Wheel III 62*

This day is called the feast of Crispian
*IV iii 40 ff.; D.P.R IV 53; Mood IV 7;
Peg III 96; Rain 108; Spir 80; Spir.R
63*

Henry before Agincourt (John
Lydgate)

Our king went up upon a hill high
P.Tong I 110

*King Henry Fifth's Conquest of
France* (Anon)

As our King lay musing on his bed
Bal 464

Song on the Victory of Agincourt
(Anon)

Our king went forth to Normandy
P.Tong I 20; Riv III 95; Song IV 63

ALE

Back and side go bare (Anon)
(?William Stevenson)

I cannot eat but little meat
*Plea VIII 17; P.W 54; P.W.R 46; Wheel
III 52*

Bring us in good ale (Anon)

Bring us in good ale, and bring us in good
ale
Chor 64; P.Tong II 12; Wheel III 50

In Praise of Ale (Thomas Bonham)

When that the chill Charocco blows
Fab.C.V 114; Man I 30

ALEXANDER THE GREAT

Alexander the Great (Anon)

Four men stood by the grave of a man
P.W 30; P.W.R 26

ALPHABET RHYMES

See also Ox.N.R 105–109

A was once (Anon)

A was once an apple-pie
*Fab.N.V 186; M.G.B 136; M.G.R 45;
Ox.Dic 47; Ox.N.R. 108; Puf.N.R 12*

The A.B.C. (Spike Milligan)

'Twas midnight in the schoolroom
Mill.S.V 65

ABC of Names (Anon)

A is Ann with milk from the cow
Fab.N.V 96

*Alliteration, or The Siege of
Belgrade* (Anon)

An Austrian army, awfully arrayed
Cher 336; Key III 43

Alphabet (Anon)

A B C D E F G/Little Robin Redbreast
sitting on a tree
B.L.J I 21

Tom Thumb's Alphabet (Anon)

A was an Archer who shot at a frog
*Fab.N.V 43; Mer 232; Mer.Puf 170;
M.G.B 214; M.G.E 181; M.G.R 29;
Ox.Dic 48; Ox.N.R 106; Rhyme I 1*

ANEMONES

Anemone (Kazumasa Nakagawa)

When I paint you
Shep 75

ANEMONES (SEA)

The Anemone (John Walsh)

Under this ledge of rock a brown
Man I 41

4

ANGER

Anger (Yvonne Lowe) (aged 8)

I was angry and mad
J.Vo I 9

Give me back my Rags (Vasko
Popa—trans Anne Pennington)

Just come to my mind
J.Vo IV 44

A Poison Tree (William Blake)

I was angry with my friend
*Bla.Gr 47; Chal II 28; Choice 50; Eye
19; Mood IV 57; Prem 177; P.Tong II
55; P.W 141; S.D 77; Voi II 86; Wheel I
62*

ANIMALS

See also Animals Fantastic, Birds,
Fishes and Sea Creatures, Hunting,
Insects, Noah, Pets, Reptiles,
Spiders, Traps, Zoos

*See throughout Ark, B.B.F, Bro.B,
F.Feet, Peng.An*

See also Apes and Monkeys, Asses
(See Donkeys), Baboons, Badgers,
Bats, Bears, Boars, Buffaloes,
Bullfrogs, Bulls, Camels, Cats, Cat-
tle, Cheetahs, Crocodiles, Coyotes,
Deer, Donkeys, Dogs, Dromedaries,
Elephants, Fawns, Foxes, Frogs,
Giraffes, Goats, Hares, Hedgehogs,
Hippopotami, Horses, Jaguars,
Kangaroos, Kittens, Lambs,
Leopards, Llamas, Martens, Mice,
Moles, Monkeys (*See* Apes), Moun-
tain Lions, Otters, Oxen, Oxen Arc-
tic, Panthers, Platypuses, Pigs,
Ponies, Rabbits, Rams, Rats, Seals,
Sheep, Sloths, Squirrels, Stags,
Tigers, Weasels, Whales, Wolves,
Worms, Yaks, Zebras

Allie (Robert Graves)

Allie call the birds in
*B.P II 30; Dawn 46; Go.Jo 81; Mer 252;
Mer.Puf 185; Ox.V.J I 50; Pat 64;
T.P.W 62; Tree IV 26*

Animals' Houses (James Reeves)

Of animals' houses
Puf.Q 75

Auguries of Innocence
(William Blake)

To see a world in a grain of sand
*Bla.Gr 50; Choice 48; D.P IV 24; D.P.R
IV 13; Fab.C.V 63; Iron III 66; My 180;
Plea VII 53; R.R 174; Shep 80; Ver II
183; Wheel III 102*

A robin redbreast in a cage
*B.B.F 25; P.Bk 47; Peng.An 75; Weal II
170*

He who shall hurt the little wren
Start 35; Sto I 118

The Bells of Heaven (Ralph
Hodgson)

'Twould ring the bells of heaven
*By 223; D.P I 22; D.P.R I 11; Go.Jo 20;
Mood I 39; P.F.P I 95; Plea IV 71;
Rhyme IV 116; Sphe 96; Spo I 123; Ver
II 202*

Caring for Animals (Jon Silkin)

I ask sometimes why these small animals
Drag 30; J.Mod 78

Circus (Margaret Stanley-Wrench)

Saucer of sand, the circus ring
Rhyme IV 115

Eddi's Service (Rudyard Kipling)

Eddi, priest of St Wilfred
*Key III 148; Mood III 100; Plea IV 55;
Speak I 132*

The Human Attitude (Geoffrey
Dearmer)

When I catch myself agape
D.P IV 26

Jigsaw III (Louis MacNiece)

The gulf between us and the brutes
M.Ver 92

The Law of the Jungle (Rudyard
Kipling)

Now this is the Law of the Jungle, as old
and as true as the sky
Peg II 88

Little Things (James Stephens)

Little things that run and quail
Go.Jo 19

Rattlesnake (Anon)

Rattlesnake, O rattlesnake
J.Vo II 44

Shepherd Song (part) (Sir Philip Sidney)

The lion heart, the ounce gave active might
Ark 38

The Sixth Day of Creation (John Milton)

When God said
B.B.F 16

Song of Myself (part) (Walt Whitman)

I think I could turn and live with animals
Bat 28; B.B.F 14; Drag 17; Kal 1; Mood IV 89; My 129; Peg III 45; Peng.An 15; P.W 201; P.W.R 231; Riv IV 129; Shep 102; Six VI 6; Sphe 96; Them I 52; Ver II 194; Yim III 149

ANIMALS, FANTASTIC

See Bel.C.V 94–131

See Dragons, Nonsense (Lear), Sea Monsters, Unicorns

The Adaptable Mountain Dugong (Ted Hughes)

The Mountain Dugong is a simply fantastic animal
Start 141

Behemoth and Leviathan (The Book of Job)

Behold now Behemoth, which I made with thee
Key IV 114

The Chickamungus (James Reeves)

All in the groves of dragon-fungus
G.Tr.P 222

The Common Cormorant (Anon)

The common cormorant or shag
Act I 41; A.D.L 227; Cher 21; Fab.C.V 88; Fab.N.V 82; G.Tr.P 223; Min IV 32; My 158; P.Tong I 123; Sphe 251

The Derby Ram (Anon)

As I was going to Derby, all on a market day

See Rams

The Doze (James Reeves)

Through Dangly woods the aimless Doze
G.Tr.P 223; Mood I 18

The Hippocrump (James Reeves)

Along the valley of the Ump
Chor 49; Hap 45; Tree III 92

The Magical Mouse (Kenneth Patchen)

I am the magical mouse
Say 118

Oliphaunt (part)
(J. R. R. Tolkein)

Grey as a mouse
J.Vo II 49

The Snitterjipe (James Reeves)

In mellowy orchards, rich and ripe
Six VI 54; T.P.W 110

The Wangsun (Chinese— trans Arthur Waley)

Sublime was he, stupendous in invention
Hap 52

Welsh Incident (Robert Graves)

But that was nothing to what things came out
Com 121; Ev.M 22; J.Mod 48; Nar 51; Peg IV 22; Pers 66; P.F.P II 222; R.R 178; Six II 33; Song III 133; Them II 50; Voi II 11; Weal II 114

The Wendigo (Ogden Nash)

The Wendigo, the Wendigo
Fab.N.V 80; Key IV 59

ANIMALS (FOR EXPERIMENT)

A Black Rabbit Dies for its Country (Gavin Ewart)

Born in the lab, I never saw the grass
Them I 66

ANIMALS (PREHISTORIC)

The Dinotherium (Hilaire Belloc)

The Dreaded Dinotherium, he
Key IV 147; Start 18

Next! (Ogden Nash)

I thought that I would like to see
Key IV 146

ANTS

The Ants (John Clare)

What wonder strikes the curious, while he views
B.B.F 125

The Termite (Ogden Nash)

Some primal termite knocked on wood
Key III 26; Peg III 45

The Termites (Robert Hillyer)

Blind to all reasoned aim, this furtive folk
Ark 159

APES & MONKEYS

See also Baboons

At Woodward's Gardens (Robert Frost)

A boy, presuming on his intellect
Bird IV 2; Exp III 9

Au Jardin des Plantes (John Wain)

The gorilla lay on his back
Exp III 14; Flock 220; Make IV 217; Sphe 119; Them I 71; Yim III 58

The Black Ape (Leo Aylen)

The black ape's principal food is fruit
Make IV 197; Yim II 78

Road-Song of the Bandar-Log (Rudyard Kipling)

Here we go in a flung festoon
Plea V 43

The Ship of Rio (Walter de la Mare)

There was a ship of Rio
De la M.Col 94; De la M.P.P 26; Ex.Ch 76; Fab.N.V 242; Min IV 49; Ox.V.J I 66; Plea III 70; P.Life III 19

The Signifying Monkey (Anon)

The Monkey and the Lion
J.Vo II 39

APOLOGIES

This is Just to Say (William Carlos Williams)

I have eaten/the plums
Bits p; Go.Jo 211; Flock 232; Prel IV 24

APPLE-PICKING

After Apple-Picking (Robert Frost)

My long two-pointed ladder's sticking through a tree
Bird IV 47; Cent 41; Choice 279; Ev.M 40; Fro.You 94; Pers 72; Say 150; Ten 79

APPLE PIES

A—Apple Pie (Walter de la Mare)

Little Pollie Pillikins
De la M.C 231; De la M.S 93; Patch 8

APPLES

The Apple Tree (Oliver St. John Gogarty)

Let there be light!
A.D.L 81

Apple-Tree Rhyme (Anon)

Here stands a good apple tree
B.P I 13; Tree II 44

Here's to thee old Apple tree!
Fuji 100; M.G 191; Ox.P.C 139; Ox.V.J I 21; Puf.N.R 29

Apples (Laurie Lee)

Behold the apples' rounded worlds
Act III 29; Drag 50; Man I 64; Quest IV 7; Shep 71; Song II 17; Weal II 48

Unharvested (Robert Frost)

A scent of ripeness from over a wall
Drag 50

APRIL

April Day: Binsey (Michael Hamburger)

Now the year's let loose; it skips like a feckless child
Dawn 96; Drag 42

April Rise (Laurie Lee)

If I ever I saw blessing in the air
A.S.L.A 47; Com 203; Drag 42; Flock 13; Mod.P 48; Pat 34; Peg IV 50; Song III 34; Sphe 9

Home-Thoughts from Abroad (Robert Browning)

O to be in England
B.P IV 96; By 173; Ch.Gar 83; D.P IV 50; Fun II 100; Mood IV 6; Peg IV 55; P.F.P I 117; Plea VI 18; P.Life IV 71; Puf.V 177; Rain 82; Song II 41; Sphe 11; Spo I 99; Sto I 83; Trea 111; Ver II 243; Vic 82

AQUARIA

At the Water Zoo (E. V. Knox)

Today I have seen all I wish
Dan 37; Peg IV 18; Ver II 219

ARITHMETIC

See Numbers

ARK, THE

See Noah

ARMADA

The Armada (Lord Macaulay)

Attend, all ye who list to hear our noble England's praise
Fab.C.V 243; P.Bk 288; P.F.P II 55; Plea VI 29; Trea 49

Armada (Anon)

Some years of late, in eighty-eight
D.P II 104; D.P.R II 57; Fab.C.V 241; Plea VII 9; P.Tong I 117

Armada (John Masefield)

The wind and seas were fair
Fun II 161

ARRAN

Arran (Old Irish—trans K.Jackson)

Arran of the many stags
Cher 238

(trans Kuno Meyer)

Arran of the many stags
Fab.C.V 133

ARTHUR, KING

Morte d'Arthur (Alfred Lord Tennyson)

At Francis Allen's on Christmas Eve
P.Rem 167

So all day long the noise of battle roll'd
Peg III 108

ASPENS

Aspens (Edward Thomas)

All day and night, save winter, every weather
Choice 176; Ten 129; Tho.Gr 46

ASSES

See Donkeys

AUGUST

August (Andrew Young)

The cows stood in a thunder-cloud of flies
You.Qu 24

August Weather (Katharine Tynan)

Dead heat and windless air
Peg II 1

AUSTRALIA

See also Ver III 278–306

See also Aborigines, Bunyip, Bushrangers, Drovers, Kangaroos, Kelly (Ned), Swagmen, Transportation

Billy Barlow (Anon)

When I at home was down on my luck
All 14

A Bushman's Song (A. B. Paterson)

I'm travelling down the Castleragh and I'm a station hand
Song III 112

Drought (Flexmore Hudson)

Midsummer noon; and the timbered walls
Ver III 304

The Flying Gang (A. B. Paterson)

I served my time, in the days gone by
Sto I 63

The Geebung Polo Club
(A. B. Paterson)

It was somewhere up the country, in a land of rock and scrub
Them V 12

H.M.S. Glory at Sydney (Charles Causley)

Now it seems an old forgotten fable:
Song IV 86

The Man from Snowy River
(A. B. Paterson)

There was a movement at the station, for the word had passed around
Sto I 16; Weal II 91

The Sick Stockrider
(Adam L. Gordon)

Hold hard, Ned! Lift me down once more and lay me in the shade
Spir 35; Spir.R 28

The Stockman's Last Bed (Anon)

Whether Stockman or not, for one moment give ear
J.Vo III 95

The Tantanoola Tiger (Max Harris)

There in the bracken was the ominous spoor mark
Ris 68; Tell II 21

Wallaby Stew (Anon)

Poor Dad, he got five years or more, as everybody knows
Eye 14; Read II 60

When the Children come Home
(Henry Lawson)

On a lonely selection far out in the west
Tell II 58

AUTUMN

See also Bonfires, Months

Autumn (or *November*) (John Clare)

I love the fitful gust that shakes
Fuji 92; Key I 74; Mood I 51; Peg II 7; P.F.P II 31; Read I 131; Rhyme III 57; Say 51; Six I 14; Sphe 21; Spo II 72

Autumn (Roy Campbell)

I love to see when leaves depart
Peg IV 43

Autumn (Vernon Scannell)

It is the football season once more
Mod.P 170

Autumn (John Clare)

The Thistledown's flying, though the winds are all still
Key III 16; P.Tong I 142; P.W 186; P.W.R 207; Riv III 18; Song II 18; T.P.W 88

Autumn (T. E. Hulme)

A touch of cold in the autumn night
Act II 39; Fla 40; My 10; P.W 252; P.W.R 297; Shep 64

Autumn Change (John Clare)

The leaves of autumn drop by twos and threes
Iron I 46; Song III 37

Autumn Evening (John Clare)

I love to hear the autumn crows go by
This W.D 128

9

The Autumn Wind (Arthur Waley)

Autumn wind rises; white clouds fly.
Man I 30

The Coming of the Cold (Theodore Roethke)

The ribs of leaves lie in the dust
J.Vo III 100

The Cranes (Po Chu-I—trans Arthur Waley)

The western wind has blown but a few days
Act II 39

A Day in Autumn (R. S. Thomas)

It will not always be like this
A.S.L.A 55; Six V 50; Weal II 134

The Faerie Queene (part) (Edmund Spenser)

Then came the Autumn, all in yellow clad,
Ch.Gar 93

Fields of Autumn (Laurie Lee)

Slow moves the acid breath of noon
Drag 73; Read II 72; Shep 67; Sphe 22

The Georgics (part) (Virgil—trans C. Day Lewis)

Am I to tell you next of the storms and stars of autumn
Flock 261

Late Autumn (Andrew Young)

The boy called to his team
Key IV 38; M.Ver 30; Ten 168; You.Qu 29

Pendulum Poem (Norman Nicholson)

Leaves fall/The air is full
A.S.L.A 54

Puk-Wudjies (Patrick R. Chalmers)

They live 'neath the curtain
P.Bk 24

Rich Days (W. H. Davies)

Welcome to you, rich autumn days
Act II 84; Peg III 17; P.F.P II 29; Song I 18

Shortening Days at the Homestead (Thomas Hardy)

The first fire since the summer is lit, and is smoking into the room
Har.Ch 20

Something told the Wild Geese (Rachel Field)

Something told the wild geese
Chal I 28; Cor 148; My 114; Rhyme IV 13; T.P.W 87

Song (Richard Watson Dixon)

The feathers of the willow
B.L.J IV 12; B.P IV 54; Fab.C.V 55; First III 31; Fun II 130; Ox.P.C 134; Plea VI 9; Riv II 2; S.D 135; This.W.D 61

To Autumn (John Keats)

Season of mists and mellow fruitfulness
Bird III 45; By 140; Ch.Gar 95; Choice 66; D.P IV 58; D.P.R IV 33; G.Tr.P 279; Iron IV 117; Mood IV 44; Pat 54; Peg III 18; P.F.P II 30; Plea VIII 60; Prel IV 4; P.W 186; P.W.R 211; Rhyme IV 10; Riv III 16; R.R 87; Say 132; Sphe 24; Song III 38; Trea 215; Ver III 141; Weal II 34; Wheel IV 112

BABIES

Infant Joy (William Blake)

"I have no name:
By 112; Com 92; Go.Jo 132; G.Tr.P 10; Pers 7; This.W.D 52; T.P.R 31

Infant Sorrow (William Blake)

My mother groaned! My father wept
Bla.Gr 35; Choice 46; Pers 7

Johnnie Crack and Flossie Snail (Dylan Thomas)

Johnnie Crack and Flossie Snail
Act II 62; Dawn 18; Go.Jo 150; J.Vo I 21

BABOONS

The Big Baboon (Hilaire Belloc)

The Big Baboon is found upon
Riv I 92

BADGERS

Badger (John Clare)

When midnight comes a host of dogs and men
Act I 20; Cla.Wo 82; D.P.R IV 10; Key IV 68; Make I 94; P.W.R 207; Riv III 20; Song IV 162; Them I 61; Wheel II 85

Badger (?) (Riddle) (Anglo-Saxon—trans K. Crossley-Holland)

Whereas my neck is white, my head
Rid 22

The Badger (John Clare)

The badger grunting on his woodland track
Read I 140; Voi I 102

The Badgers (Eden Philpotts)

Brocks snuffle from their holt within
B.B.F 105 D.P III 16; D.P.R II 14

The Six Badgers (Robert Graves)

As I was a-hoeing, a-hoeing my lands
Fab.N.V 22; Go.Jo 76; J.Vo II 59; Mer 141; Mer.Puf 106; Say 24

The Combe (Edward Thomas)

The combe was ever dark, ancient and dark
Key IV 67

BAGPIPES

See also Pipers

Bagpipe Music (Louis MacNiece)

It's no go the merrygoround, it's no go the rickshaw
Liv 64; Mod.P 7

Pibroch of Donald Dhu (Sir Walter Scott)

Pibroch of Donald Dhu
D.P III 104; Fab.C.V 231; J.Vo III 78; Song II 126; Spir 79; Trea 81

BAKING

Baking Day (Rosemary Joseph)

Thursday was baking day in our house
Bird III 25; Make II 90; Mod.P 137; Sto III 60; Them IV 44

BALAAM

Balaam (Charles Causley)

King Balak sat on his gaudy throne
Cau.Nar 15; Tell I 20

Balaam's Asses (The Bible)

Now he was riding upon his ass, and his two servants
Numbers 22; B.B.F 161; Ch.Gar 108

BALACLAVA

The Charge of the Light Brigade (Alfred Lord Tennyson)

Half a league, half a league
All 102; Look 79; Mood III 40; P.Bk 316; Peg II 50; Prem 83; Rain 105; Six IV 42; Spo I 155; Trea 106; Ver II 148

BALLOONS

As when a man (Alfred Lord Tennyson)

As when a man that sails in a balloon
J.Vo III 90

Balloons (Sylvia Plath)

Since Christmas they have lived with us
Mod.P 93; Prel II 31; Yim II 129

Les Ballons (Oscar Wilde)

Against these turbid turquoise skies
Look 337; Ox.V.J IV 69; Peg V 24; Yim I 82

BANANAS

Song of the Banana Man (Evan Jones)

Touris', white man, wipin' his face
Mod.P 162

BANDS

The Ceremonial Band (James Reeves)

The old King of Dorchester
Chor 18; Mood I 5; T.P.R 107; Tree II 78

BANJOS

The Song of the Banjo (Rudyard Kipling)

You couldn't pack a Broadwood half a mile
Fab.C.V 37

BANNOCKBURN

Scots wha hae (Robert Burns)

Scots wha hae wi' Wallace bled
Fab.C.V 143; Peg II 58; Wheel I 66

BARBERS

Alex at the Barbers (John Fuller)

He is having his hair cut. Towels are tucked
A.S.L.A 37; Hap 42; Quest III 9; Sev 18; Six IV 62; Them VI 53

The Barber (C. J. Dennis)

I'd like to be a barber, and learn to shave and clip
Puf.Y 40

The Barber's (Walter de la Mare)

Gold locks and black locks
De la M.Col 39; De la M.P.P 32; Ex.H 92

The Barbershop (Charles Reznikoff)

The barbershop has curtains
J.Vo IV 28

BARLEY

(Sir) John Barleycorn (Anon)

There came three men (kings) from out of the west
B.B 182; Broad 97; Chor 65; Com 29; Fab.Bal 156; Fab.C.V 197; Iron II 70; Key II 92; Mer 326; Mer.Puf 246; Rain 22; Read I 114; Riv II 63; Song II 12; Voi I 70

John Barleycorn (Robert Burns)

There was three kings into the east
D.P.III 133; D.P.R I 85; Peg IV 39; Plea VIII 33; P.Tong I 153; Sto III 129; Wheel II 74

The Ripe and Bearded Barley (Anon)

Come out, 'tis now September
B.P III 95; Cher 313

Wind through Barley (D. O. Pitches)

The wind is green
Man I 38

BASKETBALL

Foul Shot (Edwin A. Hoey)

With two 60s stuck on the scoreboard
Chal II 71

BATHING

East Anglian Bathe (Sir John Betjeman)

Oh when the early morning at the seaside
A.D.L 75; Prel II 39; Speak II 31; Ten 35; Them V 36

Sunday Dip (John Clare)

The morning road is thronged with merry boys
Mood III 25

BATS

Bat (D. H. Lawrence)

At evening, sitting on this terrace
Bird III 30; Dan 65; Kal 16; Look 235; Peng.An 30; P.F.P I 125; P.Tong I 9; P.W 255; P.W.R 300; Sphe 124; Them I 45; Under 88; Ver II 211; Wheel III 155

The Bat (Theodore Roethke)

By day the bat is cousin to the mouse
Bird I 57; Cor 166; Eye 6; Flock 209; Go.Jo 80; G.Tr.P 56; J.Vo III 13; My 125; Them II 33

The Bat (Ruth Pitter)

Lightless, unholy, eldritch thing
A.D.L 162; Dawn 67; J.Mod 97; Look 214; Shep 96; Song II 54; Sto I 117; Weal II 44

The Bat (Ogden Nash)

Myself, I rather like the bat
Act III 148; Tree IV 49

Bats (Randall Jarrell)

A bat is born/Naked and blind and pale
Ark 10; Chal I 25; Mod.P 152; Voi I 99

Bats (George Macbeth)

have no accidents. They loop
Drag 26

Childhood (part) (John Clare)

On summer eves with wild delight
Ark 77

Man and Bat (D. H. Lawrence)

When I went into my room, at mid-morning
J.Mod 90; Law.S 24; Start 26

'Noah and the Bat' (George Macbeth)

bat/flies next like a broken
Say 30

BATTLES

See Agincourt, Balaclava, Bannockburn, Blenheim, Calais, Chevy Chase, Corunna, Culloden, Flodden, Harfleur, Hohenlinden, Killiecrankie, Maldon, Naseby, Otterbourne

BAUCIS & PHILEMON

Baucis and Philemon (Jonathan Swift)

In ancient times, the story tells
Tell II 84

BEAGLES

Beagles (W. R. Rodgers)

Over rock and wrinkled ground
Them I 62

BEANFIELDS

The Beanfield (John Clare)

A beanfield in blossom smells as sweet
Peg IV 51

BEARS

The Bear (Frederick Brown)

His sullen shaggy-rimmed eyes followed every move
Ev.M 21; Exp III 16; Yim II 112

Furry Bear (A. A. Milne)

If I were a bear
F.Feet 189; Mil.N.S 46

Grizzly Bear (Mary Austin)

If you ever, ever, ever meet a grizzly bear
Go.Jo 4

The Lady and the Bear (Theodore Roethke)

A Lady came to a Bear by a Stream
Go.Jo 151; J.Mod 52; Quest II 75; V.F 129; Voi I 95

My Mother saw a Dancing Bear (Charles Causley)

My mother saw a dancing bear
Cau.Fig 94

BEDTIME

At Night (Elizabeth Jennings)

I'm frightened at night
Quest I 33

Bed in Summer (Robert Louis Stevenson)

In winter I get up at night
Go.Jo.100; Min I 13; P.Life I 67; Puf.V 137; Rain 121; Rhyme 22; Ste.C.G 17; Tree I 18

Bedtime (Eleanor Farjeon)

Five minutes, five minutes more, please!
Puf.Y 46

Bed Time (Ruth Squires—aged 11)

I am in bed
Prel IV 28

The Country Bedroom (Frances Cornford)

My room's a square and candle-lighted boat
B.P IV 72; J.Mod 72; Ox.V.J III 55; Quest III 28; Shep 147; Them VII 36

Good Night (Thomas Hood)

Here's a body—there's a bed!
J.Vo I 84

The Land of Counterpane (Robert Louis Stevenson)

When I was sick and lay abed
B.P I 36; First 41; Min I 22; Rain 95; Six II 40; Ste.C.G 33

No Bed (Walter de la Mare)

No bed! No bed! we shouted
A.D.L 267; Cor 14; De la M.Col 31

BEES

The Arrival of the Bee Box (Sylvia Plath)

I ordered this, this clean wood box
Say 154

Bees (Lo Yin—trans R. Kotewall)

Down in the plain, and up on the mountain top
D.P.R I 14

The Bees' Song (Walter de la Mare)

Thousandz of thornz there be
De la M.Col 113; De la M.P.P 109; De la M.S 23; Plea V 26; Rhyme II 30; V.F 51

For so work the honey-bees (William Shakespeare)

For so work the honey-bees
Henry V I ii 187; F.Feet 79; Speak II 17; Wheel I 46

The Georgics (part) (Virgil—trans C. Day Lewis)

Next I come to the manna, the heavenly gift of honey
Flock 113

How doth the little Busy Bee (Isaac Watts)

How doth the little busy bee
G.Tr.P 69; Mer 275; Mer.Puf 206

The Land (part) (V. Sackville-West)

In February, if the days be clear
F.Feet 77

Forget not bees in winter, though they sleep
M.Ver 80

Wild Bees had Built (W. W. Gibson)

Wild bees had built, while we had been from home
F.Feet 168

BEETLES

I knew a Black Beetle (Christopher Morley)

I knew a black beetle who lived down a drain
Fab.N.V 172

A Midday Rest (part) (Robert Bloomfield)

The small dust-coloured beetle climbs with pain
B.B.F 119

Rendez-vous with a Beetle (E. V. Rieu)

Meet me in Usk
Puf.Q 114

Worlds (Wilfrid Gibson)

Through the pale green forest of tall bracken-stalks
Way 45

BELLS

Bells (James Reeves)

Hard as crystal/Clear as an icicle
B.P.IV 72; Speak I 11

The Bells I & II (John Keats)

Pancakes and Fritters
Tree IV 34

The Bells (Edgar Allen Poe)

Hear the sledges with the bells
Ch.Gar 175; Puf.V 29; Trea 93; Tree IV 65; Ver II 54

The Bells of Aberdovey (Duncan Young)

Gaily ringing o'er the dales
Puf.S.B 60

The Bells of London (Anon)

The bells in London all fell wrangling
Mood I 62

Bells of London
Oranges and Lemons (Anon)

Gay go up and gay go down;
Oranges and lemons/Say the bells of St
Clements
*B.P.I 74; Cher 296; Ex.Tra 14; Fab.N.V
116; Fun I 4; Mer 60; M.G.B. 138;
M.G.E 16; M.G.R 84; Min II 80; Ox.Dic
337; Ox.N.R 68; P.Tong I 35; Puf.N.R
46; Puf.V 178; S.D 132; Tree I 46*

The Bells of Northampton (Anon)

Roast beef and marshmallows
Puf.N.R 47

The Bells of Shandon (part) (Francis
S. Mahony)

With deep affection
*Cher 34; D.P II 13; Plea VI 33; P.Tong
II 204*

The Bells of Shropshire (Anon)

A nut and a kernel
Puf.N.R 47

Bell ringer (Leonard Clark)

Carswell, George, is the name
Sev 22

Bredon Hill (A. E. Housman)

In summertime on Bredon
Song IV 18; Sphe 439

The Children's Bells (Eleanor
Farjeon)

Where are your oranges?
B.P II 21; Speak I 11

Great Tom (Anon)

Great Tom is cast
Puf.S.B 63

Gwalia Deserta (part) (Idris Davies)

O what can you give me?
S.D 133

Jingle Bells (Anon)

Dashing through the snow
Puf.S.B 70

New Year (Alfred Lord Tennyson)

Ring out, wild bells, to the wild sky
D.P.R I 20

School Bell (Eleanor Farjeon)

Nine-o'clock bell!
Quest I 4

BENBOW

The Death of Admiral Benbow
(Anon)

Come all ye seamen bold, and draw near,
and draw near
*Fun I 147; Iron III 19; Mer 260;
Mer.Puf 192; Ox.P.C 44; P.Tong I 18;
Rhyme III 35; Riv I 72*

BICYCLING

The Cyclist (Louis MacNiece)

Freewheeling down the escarpment past
the unpassing horse
Sphe 174; Them V 47

Mulga Bill's Bicycle
(A. B. Paterson)

'Twas Mulga Bill from Eaglehawk, that
caught the cycling craze
Chal I 19; Fun I 78; Mood II 93

BIRCHES

Birches (part) (Robert Frost)

When I see birches bend from left to
right
*Bird II 33; Choice 281; D.P.R IV 28;
Fro.You 36; Hap 55; M.Ver 35; Sev 20;
Six V 44; Ten 81*

A Young Birch (Robert Frost)

The birch begins to crack its outer sheath
Fro.You 38

BIRDS

See also B.B.F throughout
See also Cages

See also Blackbirds, Blue jays, Blue-tits, Bullfinches, Choughs, Cockatoos, Cocks, Condors, Corbies (*see* Ravens), Cormorants, Cranes, Crows, Cuckoos, Doves, Ducks, Eagles, Flycatchers, Geese, Goldfinches, Gulls (*see* Sea-Gulls), Hawks, Hens, Herons, Humming-birds, Jackdaws, Kingfishers, Kiwis, Landrails, Lapwings, Larks, Linnets, Magpies, Mallard, Martins, Missel-thrushes, Nightingales, Ostriches, Owls, Parrots, Penguins, Pewits, Pheasants, Phoenixes, Pigeons, Quails, Ravens, Redwings, Robins, Rooks, Sea Birds, Sea-Gulls, Shags, Skylarks (*see* Larks), Song Thrushes, Sparrows, Starlings, Stockdoves, Swallows, Swans, Thrushes, Titmice, Turkeys, Vultures, Wagtails, Woodlarks, Woodpeckers, Wrens, Yellowhammers

Allie (Robert Graves)

Allie call the birds in
B.P.II 30; Dawn 46; Go.Jo 81; Mer 252; Mer.Puf 185; Ox.V.J I 50; Pat 64; T.P.W 62; Tree IV 26

Autumn Birds (John Clare)

The wild duck startles like a sudden thought
Ark 182

Birds (Ray Fabrizio)

A bird flies and has wings
A.S.L.A 59; My 137

Birds (Elena Fearn)

The peacock is silver
Mer 167; Mer.Puf 127; Quest I 8

The Birds (Anon)

From out of the wood did a cuckoo fly
P.P 58; Song I 50; Speak I 139

A bird came down the walk (Emily Dickinson)

A bird came down the walk
Cor 171; Fuji 49; Go.Jo 77; Hap 35; Iron IV 71; Key IV 158; Ox.V.J II 58; Shep 105; Sto I 113; Them I 40

Bird Language (W. H. Auden)

Trying to understand the words
Prel IV 30

Birds' Nests (Anon)

The skylark's nest among the grass
Rhyme III 50

The Birds of the Air (Anon)

I went into the woods
Ones 109

Caught by Chance (T. W. Ramsey)

I found you fluttering
Drag 29

Children of the Wind (Carl Sandburg)

On the shores of Lake Michigan
Weal II 41

Milton Bk II (part) (William Blake)

Thou hearest the Nightingale begin the Song of Spring
B.B.F 226; Say 144

Feel like a Bird (May Swenson)

Feel like a bird
J.Vo II 52

Field Glasses (Andrew Young)

Though the buds still speak in hints
Pat 26; Peng.An 267; Prel IV 5; Ten 165; Them I 39; You.Qu 11

The Flight of Birds (John Clare)

The crow goes flopping on from wood to wood
B.B.F 76

How to Paint the Portrait of a Bird (Jacques Prevert—trans Paul Dehn)

First paint a cage
A.S.L.A 58; Ev.M 94; Flock 96; Hap 23; My 138; Song III 71

A Living (D. H. Lawrence)

A bird/picks up its seeds or little snails
F.Feet 196

Matin Song (Thomas Heywood)

Pack, clouds, away! and welcome day!
B.B.F 169; By 29; Ox.P.C 42; Peg IV 112; P.F.P II 125; P.Rem 49; Spo I 122; Trea 12

The Manciple's Tale (part)
(Geoffrey Chaucer)

Take any bird, and put it in a cage
Ark 17; B.B.F 26; Key I 72

Michael's Song (Wilfrid Gibson)

Because I set no snare
D.P.R I 9; Key II 38; P.Life IV 19

No Shop does the Bird Use
(Elizabeth Coatsworth)

No shop does the bird use
F.Feet 185

Polyolbion (part) (Michael Drayton)

The Duck, and Mallard first, the
falconers' only sport
Cher 95

Proud Songsters (Thomas Hardy)

The thrushes sing as the sun is going
Flock 90; Song III 79

The Seasons (part) (James
Thomson)

Up-springs the lark
Com 47

Spring (Thomas Nashe)

Spring, the sweet spring, is the year's
pleasant king
*By 26; Com 206; Flock 6; Fun II 122;
Key I 51; Mer 331; Mer.Puf 251; Min
IV 25; Mood IV 47; Ox.P.C 102; Pat 31;
P.Bk 23; P.F.P I 117; Riv I 1; Trea
157; Wheel III 67*

Stupidity Street (Ralph Hodgson)

I saw with open eyes
*B.B.F 27; D.P II 14; D.P.R II 10; Mood
III 61; P.F.P I 95; Sphe 101; Ver II 202*

*To Boys not to kill the Sparrows on
his Roof* (John Clare)

Sure my sparrows are my own
B.B.F 27

What bird so sings (John Lyly)

What bird so sings yet so does wail?
By 17; Ox.P.C 67; Ths.W.D 70

BIRDSNESTING

The Firetail's Nest (John Clare)

The firetail tells the boys when nests are
nigh
B.B.F 82

The Ruined Nest (Christina
Rossetti)

Hear what the mournful linnets say
*F.Feet 43; Key III 111; Rhyme II 29;
Tree III 57*

Wild Duck's Nest (John Clare)

As boys were playing in their school's
dislike
Prel II 19

BIRDS' NESTS

See also Linnets, Ravens

Birds' Nests (Anon)

The skylark's nest among the grass
Cor 174; Min III 42

Birds' Nests (John Clare)

How fresh the air, the birds how busy
now!
Cla.Wo 56

Birds' Nests (Edward Thomas)

The summer nests uncovered by autumn
wind
*Bird II 34; Cor 16; Iron II 73; Prem
60; T.P.W 89*

The Exposed Nest (Robert Frost)

You were forever finding some new play
Day 114

The Groundlark (John Clare)

Close where the milking maidens pass
Make II 31

House Hunters (Eleanor Farjeon)

Birds will be house-hunting
Tree IV 31

The Lark's Nest (John Clare)

From yon black clump of wheat that
grows
B.L.J III 55; Key III 111; Wheel I 77

The Pettichap's Nest (John Clare)

Well! in my many walks I've rarely
found
Iron I 36; Song III 76

Quail's Nest (John Clare)

I wandered out one rainy day
B.B.F 83; B.L.J III 36; Ex.Ch 16; Sto I 115; T.P.R 78

The Seasons (part) (James Thomson)

Now 'tis nought
B.B.F 33

Starlings (David Sutton)

My father got up determinedly that Sunday
Drag 15

Thistles (John Clare)

The yellowhammer, often prest
Fun I 48

The Thrush's Nest (John Clare)

Within a thick and spreading hawthorn bush
A.D.L 171; B.B.F 34; B.P III 46; By 153; Cor 168; Cla.Wo 64; F.Feet 42; Flock 12; Go.Jo.91; G.Tr.P 64; Man I 32; Mood III 57; My 118; Ox.P.C 67; P.F.P I 121; Riv II 8; Song I 52; Sphe 153; This W.D 117

The Yellowhammer (part) (John Clare)

Rude is the tent this architect invents
B.B.F 83

BIRMINGHAM

Birmingham (Louis MacNiece)

Smoke from the train-gulf hid by hoardings blunders upwards
D.P.R IV 88

BIRTHDAYS

Monday's child is fair of face (Anon)

Monday's child is fair of face
B.P I 18; G.Tr.P 22; M.G.B 16; M.G.E 30; M.G.R 79; Min III 10; Ox.Dic 309; Ox.N.R preface

BLACKBERRIES

Blackberry-Picking (Seamus Heaney)

Late August, given heavy rain and sun
Drag 51; Quest II 41; Read II 69; Them IV 6; Voi II 10

BLACKBIRDS

The Blackbird (Humbert Wolfe)

In the far corner
Bits p; Ex.Tra 23; F.Feet 51; Fun I 20; Go.Jo 75; Puf.Y 95; T.P.W 91

A Blackbird Singing (R. S. Thomas)

It seems wrong that out of this bird
Song III 77

BLACKSMITHS

See also Cyclops

The Blacksmiths (Anon)

Swart swarthy smiths besmattered with smoke
Kal 41; P.Tong I 119; Wheel III 39

Felix Randal (Gerard Manley Hopkins)

Felix Randal the farrier, O he is dead then? my duty all ended
Camb 7; Choice 114; Fla 28; Make IV 158; Pers 62; P.W 228; P.W.R 265; Voi III 171

The Forge (Seamus Heaney)

All I know is a door in the dark
Read III 70

Twankydillo (Anon)

Here's a health to the jolly blacksmith
Puf.S.B 143

The Village Blacksmith (H. W. Longfellow)

Under a spreading chestnut tree
Fuji 86; Fun I 44; G.Tr.P 96

BLENHEIM

After Blenheim (Robert Southey)

It was a summer evening
By 143; G.Tr.P 146; Key III 68; P.F.P II 82; Song II 112; Riv III 106

BLESSINGS

See also Graces, Prayers

The Bell-Man (Robert Herrick)

From noise of scare-fires rest ye free
Plea II 63

The Robin Song (Anon)

God bless the field and bless the furrow
B.B.F 233; Rhyme II 65; Sto I 141

BLIND MAN'S BUFF

Bhnd Man's Buff (Eleanor Farjeon)

Blindman! Blindman! Blundering about
Prel IV 12

BLINDNESS

The Astigmatic
With Half an Eye
(Philip Hobsbaum)

At seven the sun that lit my world blew out
Bird IV 31; Hap 92; Man II 44; Way 49

Blind Man (Michael Hamburger)

He can hear the owl's flight in daylight
Prel IV 16

The Blind Man (Andrew Young)

How often it comes back to me
You.Qu 13

The Blind Rower (Wilfrid Gibson)

And since he rowed his father home
Tell I 73

The Fog (W. H. Davies)

I saw the fog grow thick
B.L.J III 5; D.P III 93; D.P.R I 17; J.Vo III 98; Key IV 128; Make I 58; Man I 61; Peg I 103; P. Life IV 28; Song III 126; Ver II 199

On his Blindness (John Milton)

When I consider how my light is spent
By 72; Cher 434; D.P IV 180; Flock 181; Riv IV 67; Sphe 396; Trea 186; Ver III 92

On my Short-Sightedness (Prem Chaya)

To my short-sighted eyes
Flock 179

Sight (Wilfrid Gibson)

By the lamplit stall I loitered, feasting my eyes
Tree IV 59

The Six Blind Men (John G. Saxe)

It was six men of Hindostan
Bird I 54; Cor 59; D.P I 26; D.P.R I 21; Ex.Tro 49; Fun II 60; G.Tr.P 200; Key III 40; Min IV 55; Ox.V.J II 63; Speak I 50; Sto I 108

BLUEBERRIES

Blueberries (Robert Frost)

"You ought to have seen what I saw on my way
Fro.You 23

BLUE-JAYS

The Blue-Jay (D. H. Lawrence)

The blue-jay with a crest on his head
Law.S 50

BLUES

See also Jazz

The Weary Blues (Langston Hughes)

Droning a drowsy syncopated tune
S.D 126

BLUE-TITS

Blue-tits (Phoebe Hesketh)

Bobbing among the fleecy willow-catkins
J.Mod 135

BOARS

See also Pigs

The Boar Hunt (The Odyssey)
(Homer—trans R. Fitzgerald)

When the young Dawn spread in the
eastern sky
Flock 230

The Wild Boar (William
Shakespeare)

On his bow-back he hath a battle set
*Venus & Adonis 619; B.B.F 90; Tree IV
113; Wheel I 47*

BOATS

See also Canoes

Boat Poem (Bernard Spencer)

I wish there were a touch of these boats
about my life
Under 118

Paper Boats (part) (Rabindranath
Tagore)

Day by day I float my paper boats one
by one
A.D.L 159

Sampan (Tao Lang Pee)

Waves lap lap/Fish fins clap clap
Kal 61; Speak I 103; Weal I 1

Where go the Boats? (Robert Louis
Stevenson)

Dark brown is the river
*A.D.L 158; B.P I 60; Ex.Tra 64;
Fab.C.V 99; First II 28; Go.Jo 177;
Ox.V.J I 68; Start 77; Ste.C.G 32;
Ste.Ho 22*

BODIES

See Feet, Fingers, Legs, Toes

BONFIRES

See also Guy Fawkes Night

Autumn Fires (Robert Louis
Stevenson)

In the other gardens
*B.P III 104; First III 45; Mood I 52;
Ox.V.J I 46; P.Life II 57; Scrap 39;
Ste.C.G 103; T.P.R 106; Tree II 45*

For Bonfires (Edwin Morgan)

The leaves are gathered, the trees are
dying for a time
Drag 79

The Burning of the Leaves
(Laurence Binyon)

Now is the time for the burning of the
leaves
Act IV 107; Peg IV 42; Shep 68; Six I 8

BOOKS

Commercial Candour (G. K.
Chesterton)

Our fathers to creed and tradition were
tied
Wheel IV 148

There is no frigate like a book (Emily
Dickinson)

There is no frigate like a book
Go.Jo 218; Peg II 31

BOOTH, GENERAL WILLIAM

*General William Booth enters
Heaven* (Vachel Lindsay)

Booth led boldly with his big bass drum
Spir 97; Spir.R 73

BOUNCING BALLS

Child's Bouncing Song (Tony
Connor)

Molly Vickers/Wets her knickers
Prel I 31; Voi I 23; Yim I 7

Song for a Ball-Game (Wilfrid
Thorley)

Bounce ball! Bounce ball!
Ex.Tra 52; Min I 29; Rhyme II 25

BOXING

The Fight (John Masefield)

From the beginning of the bout
Sto II 21

First Fight (Vernon Scannell)

Tonight, then, is the night
Make III 48; My 72; Them V 15

Bite on gumshield/Guard held high
Chal I 60

Peerless Jim Driscoll (Vernon Scannell)

I saw Jim Driscoll fight in nineteen ten
D.P.R II 49

Randolph Turpin v. Sugar Ray (Anon)

Come all you sporting citizens
Song IV 163

BOYS

See also Tales (Cautionary) (Belloc)

BOYS (LYRIC & DESCRIPTIVE)

All over the World (Geoffrey Johnson)

Noisy now are the sparring sparrows, but noisier
M.Ver 118

Boys (S. Robinson)

Boys are nasty, dirty and mean
Prel II 7

Boy at the Window (Richard Wilbur)

Seeing the snowman standing all alone
Prel II 32; Say 92

A Boy's Head (Miroslav Holub)

In it there is a space-ship
Man II 46; Voi III 167

The Return Journey (part) (Dylan Thomas)

Oh yes, yes, I remember him well
Act V 39; D.P.R II 6; Man III 20; Quest V 58

Farm Child (R. S. Thomas)

Look at this village boy, his head is stuffed
Choice 304; Cor 154; Dawn 78; Flock 77; Key IV 125; Pers 49; Weal II 134; Wheel IV 187

Farmer's Boy (John Clare)

He waits all day beside his little flock
D.P III 18; D.P.R II 26

The Herdboy (Lu Yu—Chinese trans Arthur Waley)

In the southern village the boy who minds the ox
Cher 114; Flock 76

The Hero (Robert Graves)

Slowly with bleeding nose and aching wrists
A.S.L.A 22

His Life (Jennifer Webb)

Dirty, damp, dark/Cold, miserable, dull,
Man III 44

Johnny's Pockets (Alison Winn)

Johnny collects
Puf.Y 37

The Naughty Boy (John Keats)

There was a naughty boy
A.D.L 200; B.P.I 19; Fab.C.V 284; Fab.N.V 97; Fuji 77; Mer 204; Mer.Puf 155; Min II 82; My 107; Ox.V.J I 32; P.Bk 121; Plea V 14; P.Life III 37; Puf.V 122; Tree II 36

Portrait of a Boy (Stephen Vincent Benet)

After the Whipping he crawled into bed
Act I 94; Peg III 87; P.F.P II 7 Way 19

A Schoolboy Hero (Phillip Hobsbaum)

Your rapid motion caught the eye
Sev 19

Schoolboys in Winter (John Clare)

The schoolboys still their morning ramble take
Riv III 5

Timothy Winters (Charles Causley)

Timothy Winters comes to school
A.S.L.A 11; Chal I 73; Com 171; Mod.P 67; My 100; Read II 66; Sev 17; Them IV 43; Under 59; Voi II 90; Wheel II 167

Truant (Phoebe Hesketh)

Sing a song a sunlight
Prel II 4

BOYS (NARRATIVE)

A Boy is a Boy (Ogden Nash)

There once was a dog, he was really just
a pup
B.P II 24

Legend (Judith Wright)

The blacksmith's boy went out with a
rifle
Flock 192; Rain 91

The Rescue (Hal Summers)

The boy climbed up into the tree
*Bird I 18; Chal I 32; Cor 104; Dawn 58;
D.P.R I 42; J.Mod 26; Make I 102; Prel
I 16; Quest V 15; Six VI 62; Song I 64;
Sto I 11; Tell I 10; T.P.R 64*

Rhythm (Iain Crichton Smith)

They dunno how it is. I smack a ball
Mod.P 169; Prel II 6; Sev 16

Windy Boy in a Windswept Tree
(Geoffrey Summerfield)

The branch swayed, swerved
A.S.L.A 21; Quest IV 22; Them V 51

BREAD

Crusty Bread (E. V. Lucas)

The country is the place for milk
Mood I 64

BREAKFAST

The King's Breakfast (A. A. Milne)

The King asked/The Queen, and
*B.L.J I 57; B.P.I 53; Ex.Tra 70;
Fab.N.V 266; Mil.V.Y 55*

BROOKS

The Hurrying Brook (Edmund
Blunden)

With half a hundred sudden loops and
coils
Bird II 26

BROTHERS

Brother (Robert Graves)

It's odd enough to be alive with others
D.P.R I 35

BROWN, JOHN

John Brown's Body (Anon)

Old John Brown's body lies a-mould'ring
in the grave
B.L.A.F 120; Iron II 39

BUCKINGHAM, 2nd DUKE OF

Absalom and Achitophel (part)
(John Dryden)

Some of their chiefs were princes of the
land
Trea 184

BUFFALOES

Buffalo Dusk (Carl Sandburg)

The buffaloes are gone
Ark 29; Yim I 71

Buffalo Skinners (Anon)

'Twas in the town of Jacksboro in the
year of seventy-three
*Bal 773; Bird IV 25; B.L.A.F 174;
Make II 62; Tell II 81*

It happened in Jacksboro in the spring of
seventy-three
Song IV 126

The Flower-fed Buffaloes (Vachel
Lindsay)

The flower-fed buffaloes of the spring
*Cher 124; Go.Jo 203; Liv 125; Look
194; Peg V 19; P.F.P II 232; Six VI 58;
Them VII 62; This W D 123; T.P.R 44*

BUGLES

No one cares less than I (Edward
Thomas)

No one cares less than I
Liv 93; Tho.Gr 84

The Splendour Falls (Alfred Lord Tennyson)

The splendour falls on castle walls
A.D.L 216; By 166; Cher 444; Ch.Gar 28; Choice 83; D.P III 95; D.P.R III 65; Fab.C.V 36; Go.Jo 139; Man I 24; Ox.P.C 142; Ox.V.J II 88; Pat 194; P.F.P II 132; Plea VII 55; Prel IV 40; P.W 191; P.W.R 217; Riv II 22; Song I 103; Spo II 142; This W.D 86; Trea 105; Ver III 33; Vic 49; Voi I 120; Weal I 106

BUILDERS

See also Construction

The Builders (Hugo Williams)

A cage flies up through scaffolding
Drag 41

Thaw on a Building Site (Norman MacCaig)

The strong sun changed the air
Drag 40

A Truthful Song: I The Builder (Rudyard Kipling)

I tell this tale which is strictly true
Plea V 86

BULLDOZERS

The Chant of the Awakening Bulldozers (Patricia Hubbell)

We are the bulldozers, bulldozers, bulldozers
J.Vo I 44; Them VII 49

BULLFIGHTING

Bullfight in the Sun (Dannie Abse)

The public matador in his arrogant yellow suit
Them I 66

Novillada (James Kirkup)

Madrid is on the Manzanares
Peg IV 6; Them V 20

BULLFINCHES

The Bullfinch (Betty Hughes)

I saw upon a winter's day
F.Feet 75

BULLFROGS

Bullfrog (Ted Hughes)

With their lithe long strong legs
Bird II 46; Dawn 65; D.P.R II 8

BULLS

The Bull (Ralph Hodgson)

See an old unhappy bull
Ark 122; P.F.P II 92; Spir 47; Spir.R 39

The Bull Calf (Irving Layton)

The thing could barely stand. Yet taken
Peg IV 12; Yim II 69

Bullock (Riddle) (Anglo-Saxon—trans K. Crossley-Holland)

I saw a creature: masculine, greedy
Rid 59

BUNYIPS

The Bunyip (Douglas Stewart)

The water down the rocky wall
Ark 66

The Bunyip and the Whistling Kettle (John Streeter Manifold)

I knew a most superior camper
Sto III 15; Ver III 299

BURGLARS

The Burglary (Tony Connor)

It's two o'clock now; somebody's pausing in the street
Them III 6

BUSES

Bus to School (John Walsh)

Rounding the corner
Cor 82; Key II 18; Mood I 24; Prel II 2

23

BUSHRANGERS

See also Kelly, Ned

Ballad of Ben Hall's Gang (Anon)

Come all you wild colonials
Ver III 279

Bold Jack Donahue (Anon)

Come all you gallant bushrangers that gallop on the plain
Bird I 52

The Bushrangers (Edward Harrington)

Four horsemen rode out from the heart of the range
Act III 39

Conroy's Gap (A. B. Paterson)

This was the way of it, don't you know
Tell II 37; Sto III 34

The Death of Ben Hall (Anon)

Ben Hall was out on the Lachlan side
Act I 56; Them III 12; Yim II 13

How Gilbert Died (A. B. Paterson)

There's never a stone at the sleeper's head
Act I 59; Make II 41; Nar 116

Morgan (Edward Harrington)

When Morgan crossed the Murray to Peechelba and doom
Fab.Bal 230; Make I 115

Rafferty Rides Again (T. V. Tierney)

There's a road outback that becomes a track
Act I 70

The Wild Colonial Boy (Anon)

There was a wild colonial boy, Jack Doolan (Donahue) by name
All 8; B.B 100; Bird II 7; Fab.Bal 229; Read II 58; Song IV 93; Them III 11

BUTCHERS

A Butcher (Thomas Hood)

Whoe'er has gone thro' London street
S.D 34

I can't abear (Walter de la Mare)

I can't abear a Butcher
De la M.Col 39; De la M.P.P 15; De la M.S 40; Key I 101

BUTTERFLIES

Blue Butterfly (Edmund Blunden)

Here Lucy paused for the Blue Butterfly
Blu.Mi 34

Blue-Butterfly Day (Robert Frost)

It is blue-butterfly day here in spring
Fro.You 47

Butterflies (Chinese—trans Henry Hart)

The blossoms fall like snowflakes
Flock 14

Butterfly (S. Thomas Ansell)

Down the air
F.Feet 71

A Butterfly (Shinkichi Takahashi)

Even on this cloudy day, a butterfly is flying
Shep 181

Cabbage White (Christopher Hassall)

One afternoon/And again it was hot
J.Mod 140

Flying Crooked (Robert Graves)

The butterfly, a cabbage white
Ark 18; Choice 256; Com 175; Dan 100; Day 43; Flock 208; Key IV 159; P.F.P I 125; Shep 131; Sphe 81; Start 11

The King of Yellow Butterflies (Vachel Lindsay)

The King of yellow butterflies
Mer 288

This Loafer (C. Day Lewis)

In a sun-crazed orchard
A.S.L.A 79

The Saffron Butterfly (Teresa Hooley)

Out of its dark cocoon
F.Feet 170

Was Worm (May Swenson)

Was worm swaddled in white
G.Tr.P 73

BUTTER-MAKING

Churning Day (Seamus Heaney)

A thick crust, coarse-grained as
limestone rough-cast
Cent 77; Yim I 84

CABOTE, JOHN

North-West Passage A.D. 1497
(F. B. Young)

On the second day of the month of May
T.C.N 29

CADIZ

The Winning of Cales (Anon)

Long the proud Spaniards had vaunted
to conquer us
D.P III 100; P.Tong I 80; Wheel I 39

CAGES

'Bird and Cage' (Geoffrey Chaucer)

Take any bird and put it in a cage
Ark 17; B.B.F 26; Key I 72

Cage (Bernard Spencer)

That canary measures out its prison
Sev 79; Them III 58

The Caged Bird in Springtime
(James Kirkup)

What can it be/This curious anxiety
*Drag 30; Exp III 42; J.Mod 132; Quest
IV 49; Song III 70; Way 53*

The Caged Goldfinch (Thomas
Hardy)

Within a churchyard, on a recent grave
Riv II 20

Calyptorhynchus Funereus (Zoe
Bailey)

One wan bird walks close to the mesh of
the aviary
Exp III 19

Death of a Bird (Jon Silkin)

After those first days
*A.S.L.A 65; Dawn 70; D.P.R II 13; Voi
I 98*

The Red Cockatoo (Po Chu I—trans
Arthur Waley)

Sent as a present from Annam—
*Ark 37; Bird III 20; Cher 98; Hap 16;
Iron II 45; Voi III 149*

CALLIOPES

The Kallyope Yell (Vachel Lindsay)

Proud men/Eternally
Ver II 68

CAMBRIDGE

The Backs in February (John Press)

Winter's keen blade has stripped
Peg IV 48

*Inside of King's College Chapel,
Cambridge* (William Wordsworth)

Tax not the royal Saint with vain expense
Sphe 270; Wor.So 49

King's College Chapel (Charles
Causley)

When to the music of Byrd or Tallis
Isle 86; Sphe 271

Sunday Morning King's Cambridge
(John Betjeman)

File into yellow candlelight, fair
choristers of King's
Pat 145

CAMELS

See also Dromedaries

Camel (Alan Brownjohn)

I am a camel in all the sand
Bro.B 38

The Camel (Carmen Bernos de
Gasztold—trans Rumer Godden)

Lord, do not be displeased
Ark 161

Camel (William Jay Smith)

The camel is a long-legged humpbacked beast
Puf.Y 109

Exile (Verna Sheard)

Ben-Arabie was the Camel
Kal 10; Look 189; Make I 36; P.Life III 76

The Plaint of the Camel (Charles Edward Carryl)

Canary-birds feed on sugar and sand
B.P II 56; D.P I 24; Ex.Tro 51; Fab.N.V 80; Fun II 58; G.Tr.P 37; Key I 25; Min IV 32; Mood II 58; P.Life III 84; Quest III 84; Rhyme IV 29; Six VI 12; T.P.W 77

CANADA

See Ver III 366–377 Canadian Verse

CANDLES

The Dreamer (Christian Morgenstern—trans Max Knight)

Palmstroem lights a bunch of candles
J.Vo IV 47

CANNIBALISM

The Yarn of the 'Nancy Bell' (W. S. Gilbert)

'Twas on the shores that round our coast
D.P.R II 34; Fab.C.V 179; Peg II 26; P.F.P II 62

CANOES

Canoe Story (Geoffrey Summerfield)

We went in a long canoe, two of us
Them V 30

CAPITAL PUNISHMENT

See Hanging

CARPENTERS

The Carpenter (Clifford Dyment)

With a jack plane in his hands
D.P.R II 2; Prel II 48; Read II 11; Sev 54; Yim I 23

CARS

See Motor Cars, Motoring

CARTERS

The Carter and his Team (Anon)

I was once a bold fellow and went with a team
Fun II 75; Mood III 62; P.Bk 32; Tree III 21

Jim the Carter-lad (Anon)

My name is Jim the carter, a jolly lad am I
Broad 45

The Jolly Waggoner (Anon)

When first I went a-waggoning
Broad 44

The Waggoner (Edmund Blunden)

The old waggon drudges through the miry lane
D.P.R IV 78

CATERPILLARS

The Caterpillar (Christina Rossetti)

Brown and furry
F.Feet 130; Fuji 48; Go.Jo 90; G.Tr.P 73; Key I 112; Mer 92; Puf.Y 93

The Caterpillar (Ogden Nash)

I find among the poems of Schiller
Key I 112

The Tickling Rhyme (Ian Serraillier)

'Who's that tickling my back?' said the wall
Bits p; Fab.N.V 57; Key I 113; P.Life III 87; Puf.Q 174

CATS (LYRIC & DESCRIPTIVE)

See also G.Tr.P 44–54

See also Death of Cats, Kittens

Apartment Cats (Thom Gunn)

The Girls wake, stretch and pad up to the door
Bird II 2; Sphe 114

The Bird Fancier (James Kirkup)

Up to his shoulders
Them I 21

Calling in the Cat (Elizabeth Coatsworth)

Now from the dark, a deeper dark
Ark 16

Cat! (Eleanor Farjeon)

Cat!/Scat!
All 37; A.S.L.A 72; Hap 65; Mood II 54; Ox.P.C 104; P.Life III 82; Puf.Q 38; Six VI 44; Speak I 78; Tree III 90

The Cat (Richard Church)

Hark! She is calling to her cat
Mood III 58; Prel I 52

A Cat (Edward Thomas)

She had a name among the children
Bird I 16; Hap 57; Iron II 45; Make II 122; Ox.P.C 109; Riv II 28; Six VI 42; Them I 16; Tho.Gr 41

Cat (Alan Brownjohn)

Sometimes I am unseen
Bro.B 21

Cat (J. R. R. Tolkien)

The fat cat on the mat
Cor 178

The Cat (Edward Braithwaite)

To plan plan to create to have
Drag 32

Cat (Michael Hamburger)

Unfussy lodger, she knows what she wants
Drag 32

Catalogue (Rosalie Moore)

Cats sleep fat and walk thin
Act III 31; Chal I 26; Cor 164; G.Tr.P 50; Look 181

The Cat and the Moon (W. B. Yeats)

The cat went here and there
A.D.L 178; B.B.F 104; Fab.C.V 69; Flock 57; Go.Jo 245; Iron II 54; J.Vo II 28; Kal 7; Ox.V.J IV 80; Pers 125; Read II 83; Shad 105; This W.D 23; Weal I 2; Yea.Run 71

Cat and the Weather (May Swenson)

Cat takes a look at the weather
Chal II 15; J.Vo II 50

Cat-Goddesses (Robert Graves)

A perverse habit of cat-goddesses
Voi III 84

Cats (A. S. J. Tessimond)

Cats, no less liquid than their shadows
A.D.L 179; M.Ver 83; Peg IV 14; Song III 59

The Cats (Jan Struther)

In Sycamore Square
Peg I 36

Cats Sleep Anywhere (Eleanor Farjeon)

Cats sleep/Anywhere
B.L.J I 13; Ex.Tra 40; First III 34; Min II 96; P.Life II 23; Puf.Y 104; Rhyme I 33; Tree I 32

Diamond Cut Diamond (Ewart Milne)

Two cats/One up a tree
Fab.C.V 76; J.Mod 105; Key IV 62; Prem 191; Start 10

Esther's Tomcat (Ted Hughes)

Daylong this tomcat lies stretched flat
Drag 33; Make IV 28; Peng.An 59

Five Eyes (Walter de la Mare)

In Hans' old mill his three black cats
Bird I 16; De la M.Ch 30; De la M.Col 84; De la M.P.P 82; De la M.S 51; D.P.I 13; D.P.R I 2; Ex.Ch 11; Fab.N.V 28; Key I 40; Mer 108; Min III 77; Mood I 37; Ox.V.J IV 39

Fourteen Ways of touching the Peter (George Macbeth)

You can push
Flock 59

French Persian Cats having a Ball
(Edwin Morgan)

Chat/Shah Shah/Chat
A.S.L.A 73; J.Vo III 15; Mod.P 207

The Fur Coat (James Stephens)

I walked out in my Coat of Pride
Ox.V.J. III 30

Garden-Lion (Evelyn Hayes)

O Michael, you are at once the enemy
Cher 122

London Tom-Cat (Michael
Hamburger)

Look at the gentle savage, monstrous
gentleman
Sphe 113

The Lost Cat (E. V. Rieu)

She took a last and simple meal when
there were none to see her steal
Puf.Q 102; Sto II 111

Mad Cat (R. J. Pickles)

See the mad cat dance
Man I 37

The Manciple's Tale (part)
(Geoffrey Chaucer)

Let take a cat and foster him well with
milk
*Act I 48; Ark 17; B.B.F 26; Cher 117;
Key I 109;*

Milk for the Cat (Harold Munro)

When the tea is brought at five o'clock
*Bird I 17; By 238; D.P III 14; G.Tr.P
47; My 130; Ox.P.C 109; P.F.P I 40;
Plea IV 43; Sphe 111; Spo I 134; Them I
8; This W.D. 21; Ver II 221*

Moon (William Jay Smith)

I have a white cat whose name is Moon
V.F 154

My Cat Jeoffry (Christopher Smart)

For I will consider my cat Jeoffry
*B.B.F 61; Cher 120; Com 47; Fab.C.V
72; G.Tr.P 46; M.M.A 9; Ox.P.C 107;
Peng.An 55; P.W.R 145; Song I 67;
Speak I 82; Sto II 109; Voi I 88*

My Old Cat (Hal Summers)

My old cat is dead
J.Mod 107; Quest IV 45

The Mysterious Cat (Vachel
Lindsay)

I saw a proud mysterious cat
*B.P II 62; Cher 119; Fab.N.V 174;
Go.Jo 88; Mood III 59; Quest I 62*

Nodding (Stevie Smith)

Tizdal my beautiful cat
Them I 5

On a Cat Ageing (Alexander Gray)

He blinks upon the hearth-rug
*Bird II 5; Ex.Ch 10; F.Feet 97; Make II
26; Song II 57; Tree IV 60*

On a Night of Snow (Elizabeth J.
Coatsworth)

Cat, if you go outdoors you must walk in
the snow
*F.Feet 187; G.Tr.P 48; Ox.V.J III 56;
Patch 18; P.Life IV 17; Quest II 58; Say
50; Shad 105; Song I 71*

Pangur Ban (Gaelic—trans Robin
Flower)

I and Pangur Ban, my cat
Ark 110; B.L.J IV 9; Fab.C.V 70;

Poem (William Carlos Williams)

As the cat/climbed over
D.P.R I 2

That Cat (Ben King)

The cat that comes to my window sill
Act III 32

The Tom Cat (Don Marquis)

At midnight in the alley
*J.Vo IV 46; Peg I 37; P.Life IV 16; Song
I 69; Spir 43; Spir.R 36; Way 66*

To Mrs Reynold's Cat (John Keats)

Cat! who hast pass'd thy grand
climacteric
*B.B.F 61; Fab.C.V 74; Key IV 162;
Peng.An 59*

The Tortoiseshell Cat (Patrick
Chalmers)

The tortoiseshell cat
Mood I 38; Spo I 104

Two Songs of a Fool (W. B. Yeats)

A speckled cat and a tame hare
Act III 96; A.D.L 176; Ark 14; Bat 95; Cor 175; F.Feet 127; Key III 138; Man III 18; Ox.VJ IV 36; Voi I 83; Wheel III 138

I slept on my three-legged stool by the fire
Act III 97; Ark 15; Bat 95; F.Feet 128; Voi I 84

CATS (NARRATIVE)

The Captain's Cats (Watson Kirkconnell)

The captain of our sooty craft
Tell I 34

The Cat (Mervyn Griffiths—aged 14)

His black feline shape picks itself
Them I 17

Cat meets Hedgehog (Christopher de Cruz)

Cat sees round prickly ball
A.S.L.A 76

The Cats have come to Tea (Kate Greenaway)

What did she see—oh, what did she see?
Fuji 101

Death of the Cat (Ian Serraillier)

Alas! Mowler, the children's pride
Tree II 66

The Matron-Cat's Song (Ruth Pitter)

So once again the trouble's o'er
By 281

Mehitabel tries Marriage (Don Marquis)

boss i have seen mehitabel the cat
Weal II 118

On a Favourite Cat, Drowned in a Tub of Goldfishes (Thomas Gray)

'Twas on a lofty vase's side
Shep 94

The Owl and the Pussy-Cat (Edward Lear)

The owl and the pussy-cat went to sea
All 39; B.P I 16; By 174; Ch.Gar 149; Ex.H 60; Fab.C.V 87; Fab.N.V 250; Fuji 34; Go.Jo 14; G.Tr.P 224; Mer 214; Min III 72; Mood II 49; My 163; Ox.P.C 117; Ox.V.J I 64; P.F.P I 13; Plea III 9; P.Life I 52; P.Rem 37; Puf.V 167; Puf.Y 150; Rhyme II 43; Riv I 75; Sphe 226; Tree II 42; Weal I 94

The Rescue (Hal Summers)

The Boy climbed up into the tree
Bird I 18; Chal I 32; Cor 104; Dawn 58; D.P.R I 42; J.Mod 26; Make I 102; Prel I 16; Quest V 75; Six VI 62; Song I 64; Sto I 11; Tell I 10; T.P.R 64

The Singing Cat (Stevie Smith)

It was a little captive cat
Act I 47; Dawn 21; Hap 69; Pat 67; Say 38; Song I 70

CATS (ELIOT)

See El.O.P throughout

The Ad-dressing of Cats (T. S. Eliot)

You've read of several kinds of cat
D.P I 9; El.O.P 61; G.Tr.P 54; Key II 86; Mood IV 75

Growltiger's Last Stand (T. S. Eliot)

Growltiger was a bravo cat, who lived upon a barge
B.P III 41; D.P.R I 3; El.O.P 17; Fab.C.V 182; Hap 19; Make I 59; M.M.A 4; Plea IV 45; Read I 152

Gus the Theatre Cat (T. S. Eliot)

Gus is the Cat at the Theatre Door
D.P IV 28; El.O.P 49; Nar 30; Speak II 133; Sphe 235

Macavity the Mystery Cat (T. S. Eliot)

Macavity's a Mystery Cat; he's called the Hidden Paw
A.D.L 179; B.P IV 25; By 264; Choice 225; El.O.P 45; Look 605; M.Ver 84; My 132; Peg I 38; Plea VI 87; Rain 49;

Song II 60; Sphe 232; Spir 10; Spir.R 8; Ver II 229; V.F 57; Wheel II 142

Mungojerrie and Rumpelteazer (T. S. Eliot)

Mungojerrie and Rumpelteazer were a very notorious couple of cats
El.O.P 29

The Naming of Cats (T. S. Eliot)

The naming of cats is a difficult matter
Ch.Gar 54; El.O.P 9

Of the Awefull Battle of the Pekes and the Pollicles (T. S. Eliot)

The Pekes and the Pollicles, everyone knows
El.O.P 37; T.P.R 46

The Old Gumbie Cat (T. S. Eliot)

I have a Gumbie Cat in mind, her name is Jennyanydots
B.P.II 64; El.O.P 13; Fab.N.V 168; G.Tr.P 44; Quest II 81; Wheel III 160

The Rum Tum Tugger (T. S. Eliot)

The Rum Tum Tugger is a Curious Cat
El.O.P 21; Ex.Ch 12; F.Feet 117

Skimbleshanks: The Railway Cat (T. S. Eliot)

There's a whisper down the line at 11.39
Ch.Gar 52; D.P II 30; D.P.R II 21; El.O.P 57; Ex.Ch 156; Fab.C.V 285; J.Mod 107; Mood II 51; Plea V 74; Read I 152; Song I 31; T.P.W 36; V.F 58; Wheel I 149

The Song of the Jellicles (T. S. Eliot)

Jellicle Cats come out to-night
Ch.Gar 52; El.O.P 25; Ex.Tro 10; Fab.C.V 75; Fab.N.V 175; Ox.P.C 105; Plea III 10; Quest III 79; Speak I 65

CATTLE

See also Bulls, Oxen

Bags of Meat (Thomas Hardy)

'Here's a fine bag of meat'
Iron IV 17; Voi II 62; Yim I 20

The Best Beast of the Fat Stock Show at Earl's Court (Stevie Smith)

The Best Beast of the Show
Peng.An 47

Cattle in Winter (Jonathan Swift)

The Scottish hinds, too poor to house
Key II 40

The Cow (Robert Louis Stevenson)

The friendly cow all red and white
F.Feet 30; Fuji 50; Min I 49; My 124; Ox.P.C 116; P.Life I 46; Puf.V 46; Ste.C.G 41

The Cow in Apple-time (Robert Frost)

Something inspires the only cow of late
Act II 22; Ark 72; Fro.You 53; Mood III 64

Cows (James Reeves)

Half the time they munched the grass and all the time they lay
All 64; Ox.P.C 118; Puf.Q 64; Tree IV 50

Fetching Cows (Norman MacCaig)

The black one, last as usual, swings her head
Flock 227

The Gracious and the Gentle Thing (Robert P. T. Coffin)

The three young heifers were at Summer supper
Ark 84

Lament for a Dead Cow (Francis Carey Slater)

(Chant by Xhosa family on the death of Wetu, their only cow)

Siyalila, siyalila, inkomo yetu ifile!
Act II 19; Ver III 246

Man and Cows (Andrew Young)

I stood aside to let the cows
Dawn 63

CELANDINES

To the Small Celandine (William Wordsworth)

Pansies, lilies, kingcups, daisies
Puf.V 21

CELERY

Celery (Ogden Nash)

Celery, raw
V.F 104

CENTIPEDES

A Centipede was happy quite (Anon)

A centipede was happy quite
Fuji 40; G.Tr.P 77; Ox.P.C 123; V.F 171

CHAMELEONS

Chameleon (Alan Brownjohn)

I can think sharply
Bro.B 15

CHARCOAL BURNERS

The Pigs and the Charcoal Burner (Walter de la Mare)

The old pig said to the little pigs
De la M.Col 92; De la M.P.P 81; F.Feet 86; Iron II 60

CHARLES I

By the Statue of King Charles at Charing Cross (Lionel Johnson)

Sombre and rich, the skies
Trea 299

Hide and Seek (Hugh Chesterman)

King Charles the First to Parliament came
Mood III 37

Horatian Ode (part) (Andrew Marvell)

He nothing common did or mean
Cher 378

King Charles (Anon)

As I was going by Charing Cross
Fab.C.V 139; Fab.N.V 261; Mer 45; Ox.Dic 114; Ox.N.R 81; Ox.P.C 146; P.Tong I 7; Puf.N.R 53

CHARLES II

On the Lord Mayor 1674 (Andrew Marvell)

The Londoners Gent to the King do present
Fab.Bal 177

When the King enjoys his own again (Martin Parker)

What Booker can prognosticate
Fab.C.V 140

CHARLIE, BONNIE PRINCE

See also Culloden, Jacobites

Charlie he's my darling (Anon)

An' Charlie he's my darling
Plea V 12

O'er the Water to Charlie (Robert Burns)

We'll o'er the water and o'er the sea
Peg I 87; Plea VI 50

Sing me a Song (Robert Louis Stevenson)

Sing me a song of a lad that is gone
A.D.L 213; By 199; Com 188; D.P III 84; Puf.V 181; Song IV 190; Spir 100; Spir.R 75; Ste.Ho 42

Will ye no come back again? (Anon)

Royal Charlie's now awa
By 99

CHARMS & SPELS (LYRIC & DESCRIPTIVE)

See also Isle 53–69, J.Vo II 64–65, Shad throughout

See also Enchantment, Magic, Witches

For Charms to Cure Fevers, Hiccups, Burns, Warts, *see J.Vo I 47–49, Ox.N.R 74–75*

Apple-tree Rhyme (Anon)

Here stands a good apple-tree
B.P I 13; Tree II 44

Here's to thee, old Apple-tree!
Fuji 100; M.G 191; Ox.P.C 139; Ox.V.J I 21; Puf.N.R 29

Celanta at the Well of Life (George Peele)

Gently dip, but not too deep
Cher 174; Fab.C.V 227; Ox.P.C 158; This W.D 66

Chanson Innocente II (e. e. cummings)

hist whist/little ghost things/tip toe
A.S.L.A 41; Fab.N.V 204; Mer 113; M.G.B 145; Scrap 92

A Charm (Robert Herrick)

If ye fear to be affrighted
Cher 167; Mood II 10; Scrap 52

A Charm against the Stitch (Anon)

Loud were they, loud, when they rode in a cloud
Flock 233

A Charm against the Toothache (John Heath-Stubbs)

Venerable Mother Toothache
Dawn 53; Flock 231; My 159

Charmes (Robert Herrick)

Bring the holy crust of Bread
Voi I 68

A Charm for Milkmaids (Anon)

Cush-a-cow bonny, come let down your milk
M.G.B 49; M.G.E 127; Ox.V.J I 19

A Charm for Travellers (Anon)

Here I am and forth I must
Ox.V.J III 52

A Charm to make Butter come (Anon)

Come butter come
M.G.B 85; Ox.Dic 107; Ox.V.J I 19

Charms and Knots (George Herbert)

Who reade a chapter when they rise
Iron I 61

Gipsy Song (Ben Jonson)

The faery beam upon you
A.D.L 20; Fab.C.V 226; Ver III 6

Good Wish (Gaelic—trans Alexander Carmichael)

Power of raven be thine
Fab.C.V 229

Grey Goose and Gander (Anon)

Grey goose and gander
B.B.F 195; Cher 174; Mer 113; Mer.Puf 84

Her eyes the Glow-worm lend thee (Robert Herrick)

Her eyes the glow-worm lend thee
Tree IV 102

Here we come a-piping (Anon)

Here we come a-piping
Fuji 76; Mer 31; Mer.Puf 28; Ox.P.C 102; Plea II 9

Hinx, Minx, the old Witch winks (Anon)

Hinx, minx, the old witch winks
Ones 74; Plea II 29; Shad 97

The Key of the Kingdom (Anon)

This is the key of the kingdom
Ex.H 52; Fab.C.V 227; Mer 287; Mer.Puf 214; M.G.B 133; Mood II 9; Ox.P.C 158; Ox.N.R 125; Ox.V.J II 52; P.Life III 63; P.Tong I 165; Rhyme II 59; Sto I 140; This.W.D 43; Tree II 20

Luriana, Lurilee (Charles Elton)

Come out and climb the garden path
Plea VI 67

Mary, Mary Magdalene (Charles Causley)

Mary, Mary Magdalene,/Lying on the wall
Cau.Fig 87

A Masque of Queens (part) (Ben Jonson)

I have been out all day looking after
Com 117; Shad 96; Speak I 114

The Nativity Chant (Sir Walter Scott)

Canny moment, lucky fit;
Fab.C.V 221

Now the hungry lion roars (William Shakespeare)

Now the hungry lion roars
Midsummer Night's Dream V ii 1; Cher 154; Flock 125; Isle 55; My 34; P.Bk 94; Peg I 100; P.F.P I 109; Riv I 47; S.D 98; Spo I 149; This W.D 40; Tree IV 66; Ver II 10

The River God's Song (F. Beaumont and J. Fletcher)

Do not fear to put thy feet
P.Bk 62

Sabrina (John Milton)

Sabrina fair/Listen where thou art sitting
Ch.Gar 32; Fab.C.V 217

Song (Anon)

And can the physician make sick men well?
Ox.P.C 157; Rhyme IV 19; This.W.D 63

A Spell for Sleeping (Alastair Reid)

Sweet William, silverweed, sally-my-handsome
Scrap 106; Shad 21

A Spell of Invisibility (Christopher Marlowe)

Whilst on thy head I lay my hand
Cher 154

Spells (James Reeves)

I dance and sing without any feet
A.D.L 224; B.P II 63; Ex.Tro 83; Key I 90; My 43; Song I 99

Spread Table Spread (George Peele)

Spread, Table, spread
Mer 144; Mer.Puf 107

A Spriting go We (John Jeffere)

Like bugbears, with vizards, to make old sots dizzards
Song II 90

Three Charms (Robert Herrick)

In the morning when ye rise
Mood II 10

Thrice toss these Oaken Ashes (Thomas Campion)

Thrice toss these oaken ashes
Fab.C.V 226; Iron III 64

Round about the Cauldron go (William Shakespeare)

Round about the cauldron go
Macbeth IV i 4; All 78; M.M.A 34; Tree IV 89

Witches' Charms (Ben Jonson)

Dame, dame! the watch is set
Mer 360; Mer.Puf 272; Shad 94; Speak I 112; This W.D 35

The owl is abroad, the bat and the toad
B.B.F 105; Cher 360; Fab.C.V 224; F.Feet 158; Iron I 48; Mer 360; Mer.Puf 272; Ox.P.C 88; Plea I 16; P.F.P I 19; Scrap 110; Shad 94; Speak I 113; Start 102; This.W.D 35

The weather is fair, the wind is good
Mer 360; Mer.Puf 272; Shad 94; This W.D 35; Speak I 112

CHARMS AND SPELLS (NARRATIVE)

C is for Charms (Eleanor Farjeon)

I met a strange woman
Look 288

The Evil Eye (John Ciardi)

Nona poured oil on the water and saw the eye
Ris 19

Goody Blake and Harry Gill (William Wordsworth)

Oh! What's the matter? What's the matter?
Riv II 73

Night of the Scorpion (Nissim Ezekiel)

I remember the night my mother
Exp VIII 42; Make IV 166; Sev 29

CHAUCER, GEOFFREY

Sir Geoffrey Chaucer (Robert Greene)

His stature was not very tall
Fab.C.V 116; Speak II 23; Weal II 123

CHEETAHS

Cheetah (Charles Eglington)

Indolent and kitten-eyed
Peng.An 63

CHERRIES

Bread and Cherries (Walter de la Mare)

'Cherries, ripe Cherries!'
De la M.Col 39; De la M.P.P 19; Ex.Tra 76; First II 11; Ox.V.J I 13

CHERRY TREES

The Cherry Trees (Walter de la Mare)

Under pure skies of April blue I stood
P.Life I 55

Loveliest of Trees (A. E. Housman)

Loveliest of trees, the cherry now
A.D.L 82; B.P III 16; Cher 47; D.P IV 52; D.P.R IV 28; Flock 13; Fun II 123; Mood IV 38; My 142; Plea VIII 52; Puf.V 23; Song IV 36; Sphe 80; Ver II 198

Oh, Fair to See (Christina Rossetti)

Oh, fair to see
Fuji 107

CHEVY CHASE

Chevy Chase (Anon)

God prosper long our noble king
Bal 454 B; B.B 121; Bun 97; Fab.Bal 96; Iron II 60

CHICAGO

Chicago (Carl Sandburg)

Hog Butcher for the World
Peg III 52

CHILDREN

See also Adolescence, Babies, Boys, Girls, Growing Up, Imagination (Children's), Japan, Mothers, School, Tales (Cautionary), Tales (Cautionary)(Belloc)

Allie (Robert Graves)

Allie, call the birds in
B.P II 30; Dawn 46; Go.Jo 81; Mer 252; Mer.Puf 185; Ox.V.J I 50; Pat 64; T.P.W 62; Tree IV 26

Bunches of Grapes (Walter de la Mare)

'Bunches of grapes,' says Timothy
De la M.Col 25; De la M.S 41; Fab.N.V 123; Go.Jo 23; Min I 23

The Child is Father to the Man (Ogden Nash)

Once there were some children and they were uninterested in chores
Hap 71

Child on Top of a Greenhouse (Theodore Roethke)

The wind billowing out the seat of my britches
A.S.L.A 21; Bird II 38; Hap 22; J.Vo III 90; Ox.V.J IV 100; Say 26; Them III 3; Them V 64; Voi I 132; Weal I 110

Children's Games (William Carlos Williams)

This is a schoolyard
Yim I 124

Discord in Childhood (D. H. Lawrence)

Outside the house an ash-tree hung its terrible whips
Camb 69; D.P.R III 14; Law.S 58; Pers 32

Foreign Children (Robert Louis Stevenson)

Little Indian, Sioux or Crow,
Go.Jo 105

A Free Man (Anselm Hollo)

he will punish the wind
Man III 49

Good and Bad Children (Robert Louis Stevenson)

Children, you are very little
B.B.G.G 98; Fab.C.V 94; Ox.P.C 31; Puf.V 145; Ste.C.G 46

Hard Cheese (Justin St. John)

The grown-ups are all safe
J.Vo III 68

My Parents kept me from Children who were Rough (Stephen Spender)

My parents kept me from children who were rough
A.S.L.A 23; Chal I 75; Com 38; Dawn 79; D.P.R III 4; Exp.IV 16; Flock 62; Kal 25; Man II 13; Peg III 88; Rhyme IV 71; Sphe 409; Them III 28; Yim I 98

The Place's Fault (Philip Hobsbaum)

Once, after a rotten day at school
D.P.R I 41; Mod.P 126

Six Year Darling (Vernon Scannell)

The poets are to blame, or partly so
Them IV 4

CHILDREN (ILL-TREATED)

The Fisherman's Apprentice (Peter Grimes) (George Crabbe)

Now lived the youth in freedom, but debarred
Weal II 65

Peter had heard there were in London then
D.P.R I 38; Tell II 60

Fourpence a Day (Anon)

The ores are waiting in the tubs, and snow's upon the fell
Broad 41; D.P.R I 37; Song IV 99

The Orphan (Chinese—trans Arthur Waley)

To be an orphan
Iron III 64; Start 38

CHIMNEY SWEEPS

The Chimney Sweeper (William Blake)

A little black thing among the snow
Bla.Gr 55; D.P.R I 36

The Chimney Sweeper (William Blake)

When my mother died I was very young
Bla.Gr 54; Ox.V.J II 30; P.Bk 10; Prel II 44; Puf.V 211; Rhyme III 48; This W.D 142; Tree II 34

Sooeep (Walter de la Mare)

Black as a chimney is his face
De la M.P.P 60; Ex.Tro 56; Mer 227; Mer.Puf 168

CHINA

Sampan (Tao Lang Pee)

Waves lap lap/Fish fins clap clap
Kal 61; Speak I 103; Weal I 1

CHOICE

The Railway Junction (Walter de la Mare)

From here through tunnelled gloom the track
Cent 14; De la M.Ch 46; P.Rem 198; Song III 2

The Road not Taken (Robert Frost)

Two roads diverged in a yellow wood
Act III 120; Bird III 4; Cher 314; Fab.C.V 292; Fro.You 91; Look 49; Man III 23; Pat 116; P.Rem 197; P.W.R 285; Quest V 19; Song III 1; Sphe 388; Way 39

Traveller's Choice (Jon Stallworthy)

Counsel yourself that traveller
J.Vo IV 89

CHOUGHS

Chough (Rex Warner)

Desolate that cry as though world were unworthy
Kal 4; Sphe 156; Under 68

CHRIST

See also Christmas, Crucifixion, Easter, Epiphany, Palm Sunday

All in the Morning (Anon)

It was on Christmas Day
Mer 161; Mer.Puf 121

Ballad of the Bread Man (Charles Causley)

Mary stood in the kitchen/Baking a loaf of bread
Chal III 70; D.P.R I 72; Mod.P 198; Tell II 51

The Birds (Hilaire Belloc)

When Jesus Christ was four years old
Rhyme III 68

The Bitter Withy (Anon)

As it befell on a bright holiday
Tell I 7

A Christmas Hymn (Richard Wilbur)

A stable-lamp is lighted
Mod.P 100

For unto us a Child is Born (The Bible—Isaiah 9)

The people that walked in darkness
Song I 153

The Holy Well (Anon)

As it fell out one May morning
Fab.C.V 360

In the Wilderness (Robert Graves)

Christ of his gentleness
B.B.F 212; Ev.M 105; Pat 164; R.R 166; Song III 167; Ver III 61

Jesus and His Mother (Thom Gunn)

My only son, more God's than mine
Liv 90; Mod.P 70; Pat 122; Voi III 60

Lord of the Dance (Sydney Carter)

I danced in the morning
Dan 76

My dancing Day (Anon)

Tomorrow shall be my dancing day
Mer 296; Mer.Puf 220; Song III 172

On the Swag (R. A. K. Mason)

His body doubled/under the pack
Chal III 78

Sometime During Eternity (Lawrence Ferlinghetti)

Sometime during eternity
Chal III 73

Yet if His Majesty (Anon)

Yet if His Majesty, our sovereign Lord
Bird III 13; D.P IV 182; D.P.R IV 152; Fab.C.V 364; Kal 135; Peg V 102; Plea VIII 95; R.R 156; S.D 156; Song III 162; Spo II 57; Trea 180; Weal I 137; Wheel I 44

CHRISTMAS

See also G.Tr.P 287–295

CHRISTMAS (RELIGIOUS)

See also Christ

See also Cher 412–426

African Christmas (John Press)

Here are no signs of festival
Dawn 109

The Baboushka (a legend of Russia) (Anon)

Low wailed the wind round her house long ago
T.P.W 119

Before the Paling of the Stars (Christina Rossetti)

Before the paling of the stars
Mer 165; Mer.Puf 124

The Burning Babe (Robert Southwell)

As I in hoary winter's night stood shivering in the snow
Bat 27; Fab.C.V 358; Flock 288; Pat 62; S.D 160

Carol (John Short)

There was a boy bedded in bracken
Fab.C.V 358; Liv 138; Mod.P 13; S.D 159

Children's Song of the Nativity
(Frances Chesterton)

How far is it to Bethlehem
*A.D.L 260; B.P I 58; Ch.Gar 137; Ex.H
46; Quest I 82; Rhyme I 46; Scrap 55*

Christmas (Anon)

An azure sky
Rhyme I 46

Christmas (John Betjeman)

The bells of waiting Advent ring
*Act IV 195; Song III 163; Weal I 134;
Wheel III 177*

A Christmas Caroll (Robert
Herrick)

What sweeter musick can we bring
Go.Jo 256

Christmas Day (Andrew Young)

Last night in the open shippen
*A.D.L 60; Dawn 108; Ex.Tro 36;
Ox.V.J IV 106; Pat 60; You.Qu 32*

Christmas Star (Boris Pasternak)

It was winter/The wind blew from the
Steppe
Flock 282

The Cultivation of Christmas Trees
(T. S. Eliot)

There are several attitudes towards
Christmas
Bird III 16

Eddi's Service (Rudyard Kipling)

Eddi, priest of St Wilfrid
*Key III 148; Mood III 100; Plea IV 55;
Speak I 132*

The Huron Carol (J. Edgar
Middleton)

'Twas in the moon of winter-time
Rhyme III 68

Joly Joly Wat (part) (Anon)

The shepherd upon a hill he sat
By 14; Wheel I 16

Moonless Darkness Stands Between
(Gerard Manley Hopkins)

Moonless darkness stands between
Song III 167

New Prince, New Pomp (Robert
Southwell)

Behold a silly tender babe
*Flock 281; G.Tr.P 287; Ox.V.J III 83;
Rhyme IV 120; This W.D 94*

The Old Sheperds (Eleanor Farjeon)

Do ye remember? ... Surelye I
remember ...
A.D.L 261

On the Morning of Christ's Nativity
(part) (John Milton)

But peaceful was the night
Fab.C.V 355

This is the month, and this the happy
morn
Song IV 202; Ver III 108

The Oxen (Thomas Hardy)

Christmas Eve, and twelve of the clock
*B.B.F 228; Cent 15; D.P.R I 68; F.Feet
173; Har.Ch 21; Key III 150; Look 368;
Ox.V.J III 82; R.R 165; Song II 142;
Sphe 97; Spo II 96; T.P.W 76; Wheel I
122*

The Shepherd's Play (Anon)

Oh, I've been walking on wolds full wild
Voi I 137

The Shepherd's Tale (Raoul
Ponchon—trans James Kirkup)

Woman you'll never credit what
Act II 65; J.Mod 30; S.D 154

Standing at the Door (Christopher
Logue)

Where in the world has Jesus gone?
Act IV 198

The Story of Christmas
(Bible—*Luke* II 7)

And she brought forth her first-born son
Ch.Gar 118

CHRISTMAS (SECULAR)

Autumn Journal (part) (Louis
MacNiece)

A week to Christmas, cards of snow and
holly
Day 32; Song IV 207; Wheel III 179

Ceremonies for Christmas (Robert Herrick)

Come, bring with a noise
Wheel I 50

Christmas Landscape (Laurie Lee)

To-night the wind gnaws
Pat 58

Christmas Mummers' Play (part) (Anon)

Here come I, old Father Christmas
Voi II 167

Christmas Shopping (Louis MacNiece)

Spending beyond their income on gifts for Christmas
Day 25; Ev.M 45

The Computer's First Christmas Card (Edwin Morgan)

jolly merry/holly berry
A.S.L.A 57; Drag 86; J.Vo III 101; Mod.P 208

I remember Yule (Ogden Nash)

I guess I am just an old fogey
Song IV 208

Keepen up o' Chris'mas (William Barnes)

An'zoo you didden come athirt
Voi I 133

The Mummers' Play (part) (Anon)

Presenter: I open the door, I enter in
P.Tong I 187

Now Thrice Welcome Christmas (Anon)

Now thrice welcome Christmas
Puf.V 253

The Revesby Play (part) (Anon)

You gentle lords of honour
P.Tong I 190

The Shepherd's Calendar: December (part) (John Clare)

The shepherd now, no more afraid
Voi II 165

The Twelve Days of Christmas (Anon)

The first day of Christmas
B.P II 11; Ex.H 53; F.S.N.A 245; Key III 47; Mer 238; M.G.B 51; M.G.E 136; Min I 67; Mood II 104; Ones 121; Ox.Dic 119; Ox.N.R 198; Plea III 40; P.Life III 56; P.Tong I 125; Puf.N.R 184; Rhyme III 76; Sto II 139

A Visit from St Nicholas (Clement Moore)

'Twas the night before Christmas, when all through the house
G.Tr.P 292; P.Life I 73

Well, so That is That (W. H. Auden)

Well, so that is that. Now we must dismantle the tree
Song IV 209

The Yule Days (Anon)

The king sent his lady on the first Yule day
Cher 415; Ones 121

CHRISTMAS TREES

The Christmas Tree (C. Day Lewis)

Put out the lights now!
Speak I 143; Wheel II 149

Little Tree (e. e. cummings)

little tree/little silent Christmas tree
Flock 286; T.P.R 116

CHURCHGOING

Christmas Church (Shirley Toulson)

Because I am not used to such a place
Under 104

Church Going (Philip Larkin)

Once I'm sure there's nothing going on
M.Ver 164

Diary of a Church Mouse (John Betjeman)

Here among the long-discarded cassocks
Key IV 78; Wheel II 151

In Church (William Barnes)

The church do seem a touching sight
Song II 138; Weal I 140

In Westminster Abbey (John Betjeman)

Let me take this other glove off
Liv 70

The Return (L. A. G. Strong)

The village church, so small it has hardly shrunk
M.Ver 166

CHURCHILL, SIR WINSTON

Letters to Malaya iv (part) (Martyn Skinner)

Then came Dunkirk to mitigate the news
A.D.L 252

CINEMA

Autobiographical Note (Vernon Scannell)

Beeston, the place, near Nottingham
Bird III 22; Chal II 66; Make IV 128; Man III 21; Mod.P 123; Way 76

The Projectionist's Nightmare (Brian Patten)

This is the projectionist's nightmare
Drag 59

CIRCUSES

See also Acrobats, Elephants

Circus (part) (Louis MacNiece)

Tonnage of instinctive/wisdom in tinsel
Exp III 25

The Circus Band (Charles E. Ives)

All summer long, the boys
J.Vo IV 75

Circus Lion (C. Day Lewis)

Lumbering haunches, pussyfoot tread
Exp III 27; Mod.P 110; Speak II 137; Under 42

Clowns (Louis MacNiece)

Clowns, Clowns and/Clowns
Dawn 82

Hazardous Occupations (Carl Sandburg)

Jugglers keep six bottles in the air
Exp II 22; Voi III 162

Horses (Louis MacNiece)

The long whip lingers
Dawn 61; Ev.M 56; Way 62

Knife-Thrower's Girl (Peter Levi)

Then I was steel
Exp II 29

Nino the Wonder Dog (Roy Fuller)

Act III 130; Dawn 60; Sev 80; Them I 68

The Tale of the Lion Sertonius (Ian Serraillier)

Do you know the mighty king of the circus
P.P 51

Two Performing Elephants (D. H. Lawrence)

He stands with his forefeet on the drum
Drag 27; Exp III 26; Peg IV 17; Riv IV 33; Quest V 18; Voi I 92

CITIES & TOWNS

See also Them VII 3–21

See also Skyscrapers, Town and Country, Villages

See also Birmingham, Cambridge, Chicago, Edinburgh, Hiroshima, Jerusalem, London, Troy, York

Cologne (S. T. Coleridge)

In Köln, a town of monks and bones
Wheel III 110

Hot Night on Water Street (Louis Simpson)

A hot midsummer night on Water Street
D.P.R IV 47; Them VII 8

In the Cities (D. H. Lawrence)

In the cities
Song IV 106; Them VII 47; Weal II 161

Late Night Walk down Terry Street (Douglas Dunn)

A policeman on a lowpowered motorcycle stops
Drag 55

The Londoner in the Country (Richard Church)

Exiled to bowers of beauty
M.Ver 47; Song I 22

Lo-Yang (Emperor Ch'ien-Wen-Ti—trans Arthur Waley)

A beautiful place is the town of Lo-yang
Act I 103; Riv II 21

On Roofs of Terry Street (Douglas Dunn)

Television aerials, Chinese characters
Drag 44

Prelude No 1 (Thomas Stearns Eliot)

The winter evening settles down
Cent 39; Choice 217; Com 73; Dawn 105; D.P IV 66; D.P.R III 29; Fla 61; Key IV 47; Liv 136; Look 174; Man I 11; Peg I 107; Pers 100; P.F.P II 111; P.W 259; P.W.R 306; Riv IV 30; Song I 23; Way 34; Weal II 162; Wheel IV 157

To See the Rabbit (Alan Brownjohn)

We are going to see the rabbit
Chal I 94; D.P.R I 12; Hap 36; Mod.P 106; Peng.An 261; Sev 125; Six II 10; Them VII 60; Yim I 139

CITIZENS, UNKNOWN

See Unknown Citizens

CIVIL SERVANTS

A Civil Servant (Robert Graves)

While in this cavernous place employed
Voi II 123

CLARE, JOHN

At the Grave of John Clare (Charles Causley)

Walking in the scythed churchyard, around the locked church
Com 197

Clare's Ghost (Edmund Blunden)

Pitch-dark night shuts in, and the rising gale
Blu.Mi 78

CLAVERHOUSE

Bonny Dundee (Sir Walter Scott)

To the Lords of Convention 'twas Claverhouse spoke
Fab.C.V 252; Spo I 38

CLERGYMEN

The Canterbury Tales (part) (Geoffrey Chaucer)

A good man was ther of religioun
Flock 29

A holy-minded man of good renown (trans N. Coghill)
Flock 28; Ver III 198

The Country Clergy (R. S. Thomas)

I see them working in the old rectories
Cent 111; Exp II 26; Pers 59; Song III 160; Them VI 18

The Deserted Village (part) (Oliver Goldsmith)

A man he was to all the country dear
R.R 164; Weal II 125

Near yonder copse where once the garden smiled
Them VI 17; Trea 19; Ver III 205; Wheel III 84

The Vicar of Bray (Anon)

In good King Charles's golden days
Plea VII 91; Sphe 246

CLOUDS

Cloud (Hideyuki Tsuno—trans Naoshi Koriyama)

A cloud that moves like something alive
Shep 48

The Cloud-Mobile (May Swenson)

Above my face is a map
G.Tr.P 255; J.Vo II 10

Clouds (Christina Rossetti)

White sheep, white sheep
Fuji 107

Over the Dark Highway (Lou Lipsitz)

Over the dark highway
J.Vo II 25

COBBLERS

The Cobbler (Anon)

Wandering up and down one day
B.P I 38; Min III 10

Snobs (Richard Church)

I like a snob. I mean a mender of shoes
Mood IV 27

COCKATOOS

The Red Cockatoo (Po Chü I—trans Arthur Waley)

Sent as a present from Annam
Ark 37; Bird III 20; Cher 98; Hap 16; Iron II 45; Voi III 149

COCKNEYS

The Hob-Nailed Boots what Farver wore (Anon)

My farver's feet filled up arf a street
J.Vo IV 27

Rabbit and Pork, Rhyming Talk (Anon)

Abraham's willing shilling
J.Vo IV 95

Tottie (Anon)

As she walked along the street
J.Vo IV 94

COCKS

See also Hens, Weathercocks

The Cock and the Fox (Geoffrey Chaucer—trans F. E. Hill)

Once, long ago, set close beside a wood
D.P II 22; D.P.R II 15

A yard she had enclosed al aboute
(simplified A. Burrell)
P.Bk 324

Cock-Crow (Edward Thomas)

Out of the wood of thoughts that grows by night
Camb 57; Choice 174; F.Feet 159; Fla 40; Iron III 46; Key IV 150; P.W.R 292; Read II 74; Shep 115; Them II 44; Tho.Gr 23; Voi I 110

He leaves the Nest (trans John Brough)

He leaves the nest
J.Vo I 68

I have a gentil Cock (Anon)

I have a gentil cock
B.B.F 55; Ox.V.J I 10

O my pretty Cock (Anon)

O my pretty cock, my pretty crowing cock
Mer 128; Mer.Puf 97

To be or not to be (Anon)

I sometimes think I'd rather crow
Act I 40; A.D.L 228; B.P IV 60; G.Tr.P 228; Key II 62; Song III 51; Start 16; Weal II 12

COCOA

Lament for Cocoa (John Updike)

The scum has come
Hap 79; Six II 14

COLOURS

Blue (Susan Goss—aged 9)

The light blue of the sky
Man I 15

The Colour (Thomas Hardy)

What shall I bring you?
Song II 133

Colours (Christina Rossetti)

What is pink? A rose is pink
Fuji 78; Go.Jo 3; Min II 17; Ox.V.J I 46; Puf.Y 68; Rhyme II 48; T.P.R 80; Tree II 81

The Flint (Christina Rossetti)

An emerald is as green as grass
A.D.L 206; G.Tr.P 306; Mer 268; Mer.Puf 199; Rain 111; Riv I 16; Tree IV 63

Grey (James Reeves)

Grey is the sky and grey the woodman's cot
Riv II 13

Hear the Voice of the Critic (Adrian Mitchell)

There are too many colours
Exp IV 10

Symphony in Yellow (Oscar Wilde)

An omnibus across the bridge
Cor 124; Key III 139; Pat 153

Uncle Edward's Affliction (Vernon Scannell)

Uncle Edward was colour-blind
Prel IV 10

Water has no Colour (Ilo Orleans)

Water has no colour
V.F 109

What is White? (Mary O'Neill)

White is a dove
Patch 26

COLUMBUS

Columbus Returns (Louis MacNiece)

Your Catholic Majesties . . . it is hard for me
D.P.R II 65

How in all Wonder (A. H. Clough)

How in all wonder Columbus got over
P.Rem 67

There was an Indian (Sir John Squire)

There was an Indian who had known no change
Kal 37; Look 71; P.F.P I 181; P.Life IV 50; Sphe 203; Ver III 102

COMMUNICATIONS

See Newspapers, Radio, Television

COMPARISONS

As (Anon)

As wet as a fish—as dry as a bone
All 50; B.L.J II 36; Fab.N.V 133; G.T P 24; Rhyme III 3

The Flint (Christina Rossetti)

An emerald is as green as grass
A.D.L 206; G.Tr.P 306; Mer 268; Mer.Puf 199; Rain 111; Riv I 16; Tree IV 63

COMPUTER'S POEMS

The Computer's First Christmas Card (Edwin Morgan)

jollymerry/hollyberry
A.S.L.A 57; Drag 86; J.Vo III 101; Mod.P 208

The Computer's Spring Greeting (Gary Lewis—aged 9)

Spring gling
J.Vo II 25

CONDORS

Condors (Padraic Colum)

We watched the Condors winging towards the Moon
Go.Jo.75; Look 244

CONJURORS

The Conjuror (John Gay)

The cards, obedient to his words
Tree III 82

CONSTRUCTION

The Excavation (Max Endicoff)

Clusters of electric bulbs
R.R 72

CONTENTMENT

Tell me now (Wang Chi—trans Arthur Waley)

Tell me now, what should a man want
Fab.C.V 374

CORAL

Coral (Christina Rossetti)

O sailor come ashore
B.L.J IV 26; First II 14; Ox.V.J I 49; Scrap 33

The Coral Grove (James G. Percival)

Deep in the wave in a coral grove
G.Tr.P 262; Ox.V.J IV 88; Sto II 61

CORBIES

See Ravens

CORMORANTS

The Common Cormorant (Anon)

The common cormorant or shag
*Act I 41; A.D.L 227; Cher 21; Fab.C.V
88; Fab.N.V 82; G.Tr.P 223; Min IV 32;
My 158; Plea VIII 41; P.Tong I 123;
Sphe 251; Spir 1; Spir.R 1; Sto II 80*

Cormorants (John Blight)

The sea has it this way: if you see
Flock 94

CORNWALL

Cornish Cliffs (John Betjeman)

Those moments, tasted once and never
done
Mod.P 171

CORTEZ

Cortez (William Kean Seymour)

Cortez one night trod
My 50

CORUNNA

*The Burial of Sir John Moore after
Corunna* (Charles Wolfe)

Not a drum was heard, not a funeral note
*By 151; Cher 342; Com 148; Look 91;
Mood III 35; P.Bk 278; P.F.P II 77;
Plea VI 69; Riv III 109; Spir 84; Spir.R
65; Trea 30; Ver II 111*

COUNTIES

See Cornwall, Essex, Wiltshire

COUNTING RHYMES

See also Puf.Y 169–181

See also Chinese-Counting, *Ox.N.R
111–112*

COUNTING RHYMES (DOWN)

Ten Little Injuns (Anon)

Ten little Injuns/Standing in a line
Puf.N.R 68

Ten Little Nigger Boys (Anon)

Ten little nigger boys went out to dine
*Fab.N.V 108; M.G.E 92; Ox.Dic 327;
Ox.N.R 193*

Twelve Huntsmen (Anon)

Twelve Huntsmen with horns and
hounds
*Fab.N.V 141; Iron II 78; Mer 240;
Mer.Puf 174; Ox.V.J I 23; Say 34; Tree
I 50*

COUNTING RHYMES (UP)

As I went down Zig-Zag (Charles
Causley)

As I went down Zig-Zag/The clock
striking one
Cau.Fig 24

Cottage (Eleanor Farjeon)

When I live in a cottage
Patch 30; Puf.Q 45; Tree I 13

*A Gaping Wide-Mouthed Waddling
Frog* (Anon)

(*Twelve Huntsmen* reversed)

A gaping wide-mouthed waddling frog
*Act II 52; All 58; J.Vo I 73; Ox.Dic 181;
P. Life III 60*

Green grow the Rushes-O (Anon)

I'll sing you one-o!
*Key III 48; Peg II 102; P.Life IV 80; Riv
III 46*

The Holy Baby (Anon)

Children, go and I will send thee
F.S.N.A 482

Nick-Nock Padlock (Anon)

There was an old woman and she went
one
Puf.N.R 131

Old Joe Braddle-Um (Anon)

Number one, number one
Mer 304; Mer.Puf 227

One Old Ox (Anon)

One old ox opening oysters
Cher 31

One, Two (Anon)

One, Two/Buckle my shoe
*Fab.N.V 34; G.Tr.P 23; Mer 62; M.G.B
40; M.G.E 51; M.G.R 31; Ox.Dic 333;
Ox.N.R 112; Puf.N.R 165; Tree I 38*

Over in the Meadow (Anon)

Over in the meadow in the sand in the
sun
Fab.N.V 24; Rhyme II 39

Ten Little Indian Boys
(M. M. Hutchinson)

One little Indian boy making a canoe
Ex.Tra 10

This Old Man (Anon)

This old man, he played one
*Fab.N.V 125; Mer 74; Mer.Puf 52;
P.Life II 62; Rhyme II 27*

The Twelve Apostles (Anon)

Stay and I'll sing
Song I 143

The Twelve Days of Christmas
(Anon)

The first day of Christmas
*B.P II 11; Ex.H 53; F.S.N.A 245; Key
III 47; Mer 238; M.G.B 50; M.G.E 136;
Min I 66; Mood II 104; Ones 21; Ox.Dic
119; Ox.N.R 198; Plea III 40; P.Life III
56; P.Tong I 125; Puf.N.R 184; Rhyme
III 76; Sto II 139*

COUNTING-OUT RHYMES

*See Fab.N.V 19; Fuji 64; J.Vo I 76,
80–81; M.G.R 123; Ox.Dic 156–7,
208, 211, 223, 224, 334–6; Ox.N.R
111–2; P.Tong I 49*

COUNTRIES

See Australia, Canada, China,
England, France, Holland, Ireland,
Jamaica, Japan, Netherlands, New
Zealand, Scotland, Sicily, South
Africa, Wales

44

COUNTRY LIFE

See also Cla.Wo throughout

See also Farming, Town and
Country

Forefathers (Edmund Blunden)

Here they went with smock and crook
Blu.Mi 18

The Forester (part) (Robert
Bloomfield)

I marked the owl that silent flies
B.B.F 80

His Grange, or *Private Wealth*
(Robert Herrick)

Though clock
*B.B.F 55; Go.Jo 21; Her.Mu 32; Key IV
83; Ox.V.J III 47; P.Bk 13; Puf.V 237*

The Looker-On (Frank Kendon)

And ladders leaning against damson
trees
Peg V 39

The Passionate Shepherd (part)
(Nicholas Breton)

Who can live in heart so glad
Ark 39; B.B.F 81

The Pasture (Robert Frost)

I'm going out to clean the pasture spring
*Bird I 20; Bits p; Bl.J III 40; By 230;
Choice 277; Eye 4; F.Feet 26; Fro.You
20; Go.Jo 44; J.Vo I 56; Make I 26;
Mood I 66; Ox.V.J II 45; Rhyme II 20;
Weal I 31*

A Saxon Song (Victoria Sackville-
West)

Tools with the comely names
P.Bk 122; Peg V 37

Summer Farm (Norman MacCaig)

Straws like tame lightnings lie about the
grass
Shep 25; Them VII 31; Voi III 28

Unwilling Country Life (Alexander
Pope)

She went, to plain-work, and to purling
brooks
R.R 79

Village Sketch (Edmund Blunden)

Horses, their heads together under a tree
Com 163

COURAGE

Indomitable (Mark Van Doren)

The chickadee the cat clawed
J.Vo III 19

Mother to Son (Langston Hughes)

Well, son, I'll tell you
Cor 101

Still Here (Langston Hughes)

I've been scarred and battered
J.Vo III 33

COURTSHIP (LYRIC & DESCRIPTIVE)

Billy Boy (Anon)

O where have you been, Billy Boy, Billy Boy?
Key I 21; Ox.Dic 78; Ox.N.R 189; Song III 47

If you'll give me a Kiss (Leo Aylen)

If you'll give me a kiss and be my girl
Act IV 24; Exp I 42; Them V 63

The Keys of Canterbury/my Heart/Heaven (Anon)

O madam I will give to you the keys of Canterbury
Cor 112; Key III 104; Rhyme II 22

I will give you a new lace cap
Puf.N.R 82

I will give you the keys of heaven
Rhyme III 60

My Man John (Anon)

My man John, what can the matter be?
Key III 101

O No, John (Anon)

On yonder hill there stands a creature
G.Tr.P 169; Rhyme III 4

Paper of Pins (Anon)

Madam, I present you with six rows of pins
Bird I 28; Broad 76; Ones 104; Song I 60

The Saucy Sailor (Anon)

Come, my own one, come, my fond one
Key III 24

A Subaltern's Love Song (Sir John Betjeman)

Miss J. Hunter Dunn, Miss J. Hunter Dunn
Make IV 156

COURTSHIP (NARRATIVE)

Bessie Stokoe (Wilfrid Gibson)

He stood with the other young herds
Tell II 137

The Comedy of Billy and Betty (Anon)

When shall we be married?
Ox.N.R 194

The Courtship of Billy Grimes (Anon)

Tomorrow, Pa, I'm sweet sixteen, and Billy Grimes the drover
Bird IV 27; Tell I 126

Flowers in the Valley (Anon)

O there was a woman and she was a widow
Bird I 26; Cor 109; Key I 94; Ox.P.C 40; Riv II 41

The Laird o' Cockpen (Carolina Nairne)

The laird o' Cockpen, he's proud an' he's great
Mood III 46

Soldier, Soldier (Anon)

Soldier, soldier, won't you marry me
Chor 9; D.P I 98; D.P.R I 77; Ex.Tro 74; Mer 142; Mer.Puf 92; M.G.B 186; Ox.P.C 35; P.Life II 60; Puf.N.R 176; Puf.Y 142; Puf.S.B 78; Rain 31; Rhyme III 20; R.R 143

Spanish Gold (Norman Lindsay)

When I was young I used to hold
Key III 22

When Pat came over the Hill (Anon)

And when Pat came over the hill his colleen fair to see
Riv IV 12

COWBOYS

See also B.L.A.F 192–221, F.S.N.A 353–388, Y.I.M I 49–72

Andy Adams (Carl Sandburg)

There have been thousands of Andy Adams
Y.I.M 53

The Buffalo Skinners (Anon)

'Twas in the town of Jacksboro in the year of '73
Bal 773; Bird IV 25; B.L.A.F 174; Make II 62; Song IV 126; Tell II 81

Bury me not on the Lone Prairie (Anon)

Oh, bury me not on the lone prairie
B.L.A.F 208

Cowboy Song (Charles Causley)

I come from Salem County
Peg III 76; Spir.R 33

Cowboys (Jon Stallworthy)

Panther-footed saunter in the street
Voi II 120

The Dying Cowboy or *The Streets of Laredo* (Anon)

As I rode out by Tom Sherman's bar-room
Fab.Bal 242; F.S.N.A 384; Read II 62
As I walked out in the streets of Laredo
B.B 110; B.L.A.F 206; Cher 137; Chor 36; Iron III 12; Make II 139; Peg II 70; Rhyme IV 63; Riv III 41; Say 81; Song IV 130; Tree III 89; Wheel IV 126

Git along little Dogies (Anon)

As I was walking one morning for pleasure
B.L.A.F 204; F.S.N.A 372 & 373; Wheel I 106

Home on the Range (Anon)
O give me a home where the buffalo roam
B.L.A.F 212

Lament for the Cowboy Life (Julian Mitchell)

Where the trails met, our herds met too
Start 130; Them VI 36

Old Blue (R. P. Tristram Coffin)

Old Blue was tough/As steers can be
Ark 79

The old Chisholm Trail (Anon)

Well, come along boys and listen to my tale
B.L.A.F 200 & 202; F.S.N.A 370; Make I 101

Rodeo (Edward Lueders)

Leathery, wry and rough
Chal III 66

The Wild Rippling Water (Anon)

As I was out walkin' an' a-ramblin' one day
Fab.Bal 237; F.S.N.A 382

COWS

See Cattle

COYOTES

Coyote (Bret Harte)

Blown out of the prairie in twilight and dew
Key III 54; P.Bk 55; Spir 44; Spir.R 37; Sto I 111

CRABS

The Dead Crab (Andrew Young)

A rosy shield upon its back
Ark 157; Kal 18; R.R 53; Ten 164

The Giant Crab (John Walsh)

Along the steep wall at the old pier's side
Them V 32

CRAFTSMANSHIP

The Penknife Glides (Ian Griffiths)

The penknife glides through the polystyrene
J.Vo IV 86

CRANES

The Cranes (Anne Ridler)

We thought they were gulls at first, while they were distant
D.P IV 25; D.P.R IV 14

Du Bartas, His Divine Weeks (part) (Joshua Sylvester)

I hear the crane (if I mistake not) cry
Ark 152; Peng.An 70

Walking on Stilts (John Smith)

Walking on stilts with the high bright windy sky
Pat 39

CRANES (MACHINES)

The Crane (part) (John Redwood Anderson)

On the atlas shoulders of its strength
Exp II 38

It stuns/The rapt attention, and it lifts
D.P IV 118; D.P.R IV 90

Cranes (J. R. S. Davies)

Across a sky suddenly mid-February blue
Drag 41

CREATION

See also Eve

The Creation (James Weldon Johnson)

And God stepped out on space
Rhyme IV 1; Six II 48; Weal I 141

Genesis (Palestine 5th Century B.C.—trans E. A. Speiser)

When God set about to create heaven and earth
Flock 1

In the Beginning (Bible—*Genesis* I 1)

In the beginning God created the heaven and the earth
Ch.Gar 105; Riv III 127

Paradise Lost (parts) (John Milton)

And God said, let the Waters generate
Peng.An 71

When God said/Let the earth bring forth foul living in her kind
B.B.F 16; Peg IV 16

The Spell of Creation (Kathleen Raine)

Within the flower there was a seed
Fab.C.V 228; Liv 161

CRICKET

At Lord's (Francis Thompson)

It is little I repair to the matches of the southron folk
By 206

Cricket at Swansea (John Arlott)

From the top of the hill-top pavilion
Sto III 68

Cricket at Worcester 1938 (John Arlott)

Dozing in a deck-chair's gentle curve
Them V 8

A Cricket Triolet (C. Kernahan)

I ran for a catch
Six V 42; Weal I 11

The Joys of the Game (A. E. Chadwick)

Now the joys of the game are chiefly these
Sto III 69

Ninth Wicket (A. P. Herbert)

The bowling looks exceptionally sound
Sto III 70

Rabbit (Geoffrey Johnson)

This is a grim to-do
J.Mod 120

Test Match at Lord's (Alan Ross)

Bailey bowling, McLean cuts him late for one
Key IV 130

Village Cricket (Gerald Bullett)

Flowing together by devious channels
Them V 7

CRICKETS

The Cricket (William Blake)

Little inmate, full of mirth
Peng.An 77

CROCODILES

A Crocodile (Thomas Lovell
Beddoes)

Hard by the lilied Nile I saw
B.B.F 179; Peng.An 80

How doth the Little Crocodile
(Lewis Carroll)

How doth the little crocodile
*Car.J 28; Fab.C.V 89; F.Feet 115; Fuji
83; G.Tr.P 70; Ox.P.C 116; Rain 57*

If you should meet a Crocodile
(Anon)

If you should meet a crocodile
F.Feet 106

On the Crocodile (Thomas Heyrick)

I am the Terrour of the Sea
Peng.An 78

CROMWELL, OLIVER

To the Lord General Cromwell
(John Milton)

Cromwell, our chief of men who through
a cloud
Trea 185

CROWS

Crow (Mark van Doren)

A hundred autumns he has wheeled
Ark 60

The Crow (William Canton)

With rakish eye and plenished crop
Trea 283

The Frog and the Crow (Anon)

A jolly fat frog did in the river swim-o
Mer 182; Mer.Puf 140

Scaring Crows (Anon)

O, all you little blacky tops
Mer 68; Mer.Puf 49

To Be or not to Be (Anon)

I sometimes think I'd rather crow
*Act I 40; A.D.L 228; B.P IV 60; G.Tr.P
228; Key II 62; Song III 51; Start 16;
Weal II 12*

CRUCIFIXION

The Carpenter's Son
(A. E. Housman)

Here the hangman stops his cart
Riv IV 74

Friday Morning (Sidney Carter)

It was on a Friday morning that they
took me from the cell
Song IV 212

The Office of the Holy Cross (part)
(Richard Crashaw)

The third hour's deafen'd with the cry
Bat 55

'When he had scourged Jesus'
(W. R. Rodgers)

They took him out to die
Six II 54; Weal I 25

CUCKOOS

See also Puf.N.R 34

Cuckoo (Andrew Young)

Cuckoo, cuckoo/Is it your double note I
hear
Cher 49; You.Qu 16

The Cuckoo (Anon)

Cuckoo, cuckoo,/What do you do?
*Ex.Tra 22; Fab.N.V 76; M.G.B 20; Min
I 55; Ox.V.J I 29; P.Life II 51; Puf.V 16;
Rhyme I 21; Scrap 14*

The Cuckoo (Anon)

The cuckoo's a bonny bird
*B.B.F 51; Cher 49; Fun I 29; Ox.V.J I
29; Plea V 83; Tree I 39*

The cuckoo, she's a pretty bird
F.S.N.A 217

The Cuckoo (Anon)

In April/Come he will
B.B.F 50

In April/He shows his bill
Fun I 28

Cuckoo (Andrew Young)

When coltsfoot withers and begins to wear
Cher 50; Com 205; Key III 112; Mood II 62; Peng.An 81; Read I 144; Shep 116; Sphe 137; You.Qu 15

The Exeter Book (part—riddle)
(Anon—trans K. Crossley-Holland)

In former days my mother and father
Drag 39; Peng.An 81; Rid 48

One in these days as dead abandoned
B.B.F 193

Spring (E. Lucia Turnbull)

'My dear' said Mrs Wren, 'if Mrs Cuckoo comes to call
F.Feet 41

Summer is icumen in (Anon)

Summer is icumen in
By 13; Cher 48; Com 57; Flock 34; Kal 137; Key I 51; P.Bk 11; Song IV 39

The Woods and Banks
(W. H. Davies)

The woods and banks of England now
Mer 361; Mer.Puf 274

CULLODEN

Culloden: the Last Battle (George Mackay Brown)

The black cloud crumbled
Make IV 193

CUMULATIVE RHYMES

Betty and her Ducks (Anon)

Oh Betty Betty have you seen my ducks today?
Mer 166; Mer.Puf 125

The House that Jack built (Anon)

This is the house that Jack built
Fun I 85; Mer 32; M.G.B 30; M.G.E 94; M.G.R 37; Ox.Dic 229; Ox.N.R 47; P.Life I 22; Puf.N.R 23

I Bought me a Cat (Anon)

I bought me (had a) cat, my (and the) cat pleased me
J.Vo I 52; Ox.N.R 182

John Ball (Anon)

John Ball shot them all
All 60; Fab.N.V 189; P.Life III 54

The Old Woman and her Pig (Anon)

An old woman was coming home from market
Tree II 82

An old woman was sweeping her house
M.G.E 194; M.G.R 68

An old woman went to market and bought a pig
M.G.B 68; Ox.N.R 207

There was an old woman (Anon)

There was an old woman who swallowed a fly
All 56; B.L.J III 10; G.Tr.P 231; J.Vo I 24; Key I 13; Peg I 24; Scrap 72

The Train to Glasgow (Wilma Horsburgh)

Here is the train to Glasgow
B.P I 9; Fab.N.V 251

The Tree on the Hill
The Tree in the Wood (Anon)

There was a tree upon a hill

There was a tree grew in a wood
All 54; Key II 79; Mer 235; Mer.Puf 172; Scrap 16

CURSES

The Curse (J. M. Synge)

Lord confound this surly sister
Cher 472; Song II 92

A Glass of Beer (James Stephens)

The lanky hank of a she in the inn over there
Comp 48; Liv 129; Song IV 119

The Jackdaw of Rheims (part)
(R. H. Barham)

The Cardinal rose with a dignified look
*M.M.A 64; Peng.An 163; P.F.P I 81;
Spo I 22; Sto II 35; Trea 34; Ver II 191*

Mean Song (Eve Merriam)

Snickles and podes
J.Vo II 43

Nell Flaherty's Drake (Anon)

My name is Nell, right candid I tell
Ark 86

On a Cock at Rochester (Sir Charles
Sedley)

Thou cursed Cock, with thy perpetual
Noise
Peng.An 64

Philip Sparrow (part) (John Skelton)

God send cats sorrow and shame!
Tree IV 18

O cat of churlish kind
B.B.F 135; Kal 3; P.Bk 19; R.R 170

That vengeance I ask and cry
Ark 105; Cher 118

Soliloquy of the Spanish Cloister
(Robert Browning)

Grrr there go my heart's abhorrence
Vic 77

Spleen at a Country Inn (Alfred
Lord Tennyson)

Black Bull of Aldgate, may thy horns rot
from the sockets
Ten.Fa 38

Traveller's Curse after Misdirection
(Robert Graves)

May they stumble, stage by stage
*Act III 143; Day 43; Song II 91; Voi II
87*

CUTTY SARK, THE

The Cutty Sark (George Barker)

I think of her where she lies there on her
stone couch by the Thames
Flock 51

CYCLOPS

The Song of Cyclops (Thomas
Dekker)

Brave iron, brave hammer, from your
sound
D.P IV 112; Ver II 49

DAFFODILS

To Daffodils (Robert Herrick)

Fair daffodils, we weep to see
*B.P III 28; Ch.Gar 89; Fab.C.V 51;
Go.Jo 70; Her.Mu 49; P.Bk 31; P.F.P II
230; P.Rem 147; Puf.V 22; Shep 76;
Song IV 157; Spo I 120; Ver III 16;
Weal I 115*

DAISIES

Daisies (Andrew Young)

The stars are everywhere tonight
Say 47; You.Qu 18

DAHLIAS

Dahlias (Padraic Colum)

When we behold
Go.Jo 81

DANCING (LYRIC & DESCRIPTIVE)

Buffalo Gals (Anon)

Buffalo gals, woncha come out to-night
B.L.A.F 104

Come, Lasses and Lads (Anon)

Come, lasses and lads, get leave of your
dads
D.P I 94; P.F.P I 5; Weal I 38

The Dance (William Carlos
Williams)

In Breughel's great picture, The Kermess
Go.Jo 137; Liv 57

The Dance (Thomas Campion ?)

Robin is a lovely lad
Fab.C.V 42

The Dancers of Huai-Nan (Chang Heng—trans Arthur Waley)

The instruments of music are made ready
Act II 92; Them V 58

The Dancing Cabman (J. B. Morton)

Alone on the lawn
A.D.L 220; Ex.Tro 62; Fab.N.V 213; Peg II 98; P.F.P I 11; Speak I 16

Elves Dance (John Lyly)

By the moon we sport and play
Mer 97; Mer.Puf 73

Facade (part) (Edith Sitwell)

Tra la la la—/See me dance the polka
P.F.P II 20

Fancy's Knell (A. E. Housman)

When lads were home from labour
D.P IV 30; Fab.C.V 43; Plea VIII 87; P.Tong II 187

A Lobster Quadrille (Lewis Carroll)

'Will you walk a little faster?' said a whiting to a snail
All 79; B.B.F 197; Car.J 9; Cher 29; D.P II 45; D.P.R II 37; Ex.Tro 53; Fun II 21; Make I 45; Mer 353; Mer.Puf 268; Min IV 31; Plea III 18; P.Life II 26; P.Rem 27; P.Tong I 185; Riv II 83; Sto I 96; V.F 30

My Dancing Day (Anon)

Tomorrow shall be my dancing day
Mer 296; Mer.Puf 220; Song III 172

On the Coast of Coromandel (Osbert Sitwell)

On the coast of Coromandel
P.F.P II 18

Orchestra (part) (Sir John Davies)

For lo! the sea that fleets about the land
Cher 191

Skip to my Lou (Anon)

Choose your partner, skip to my Lou
J.Vo I 56

Lost my partner, what'll I do?
B.L.A.F 98

Song for a Dance (Francis Beaumont)

Shake off your heavy trance
Fab.C.V 42

Tarantella (Hilaire Belloc)

Do you remember an inn, Miranda
All 35; Bird II 30; Fab.C.V 45; Fun II 18; Look 42; Make III 92; Nar 5; P.F.P II 19; P.Tong I 22; Six II 60; Song II 40; Sphe 259; Weal II 2; Wheel II 134

DANCING (NARRATIVE)

Lord of the Dance (Sidney Carter)

I danced in the morning
Dan 76

The Lost Shoe (Walter de la Mare)

Poor little Lucy
De la M.Col 67; De la M.P.P 42; De la M.S 94; Ex.H 66; Fab.N.V 95; Tree III 78

Off the Ground (Walter de la Mare)

Three jolly farmers
Chor 11; De la M.Col 21; De la M.S 116; De la M.P.P 50; Down 47; Ex.Ch 56; Fab.N.V 60; Min III 78; Ox.V.J II 66; P.F.P I 8; Plea III 22; P.Life III 32

DANCING (POEMS FOR MOVEMENT)

See Dan throughout

The Cataract of Lodore (Robert Southey)

How does the water/Come down at Lodore?
All 27; D.P I 43; D.P.R I 27; Key III 28; Ver II 50

The cataract strong/Then plunges along
Dan 40

DANDELIONS

A Yellow Circle (May Swenson)

A green/string
J.Vo IV 18

DANGER

Alarm at first entering the Yang-Tze Gorges (Po Chu-I—trans Arthur Waley)

Above, a mountain ten thousand feet high
Riv IV 69

Good Taste (Christopher Logue)

Travelling, a man met a tiger, so . . .
Cor 118; Dawn 69; Ev.M 83; Hap 63; Prel IV 25; Say 30

DANIEL

Daniel (Vachel Lindsay)

Darius the Mede was a king and a wonder
Cher 143; Chor 39; Dan 84; Key IV 28; My 59; P.F.P I 25; P.W 249; P.W.R 293; Read I 115; Riv IV 18; Six III 12; Song I 147; Voi I 39; Weal I 80

DAUGHTERS

See Fathers and Daughters

DAVID & GOLIATH

David and Goliath (Bible—I Samuel 17.4)

And there went out a champion out of the camp of the Philistines
Ch.Gar 111; M.M.A 39

David and Goliath (Herbert Palmer)

Let Goliath have his say
J.Mod 29

The David Jazz (Edwin Meade Robinson)

David was a Young Blood, David was a striplin'
Chal I 97; Peg II 72; Spir.R 9

Goliath (Walter de la Mare)

Still as a mountain with dark pines and sun
Peg IV 90; Sphe 344; T.C.N 20

DAWN (COUNTRY)

Aubade (Edith Sitwell)

Jane, Jane/Tall as a crane
Weal II 6

Break of Day (John Clare)

The lark he rises early
Peg III 11; Sto I 76; Tree IV 100

The Cock (Christina Rossetti)

Kookoorookoo! kookoorookoo!
Ox.V.J I 28

Cock-Crow (Edward Thomas)

Out of the wood of thoughts that grows by night
Camb 57; Choice 174; F.Feet 159; Fla 40; Iron III 46; Key IV 150; P.W.R 292; Read II 74; Shep 115; Them II 44; Tho.Gr 23; Voi I 110

Cock-crow Song (trans Arthur Waley)

In the eastern quarter dawn breaks, the stars flicker pale
Key IV 149

Dawn (John Masefield)

The dawn comes cold: the haystack smokes
Man I 53

Daybreak (Henry Wadsworth Longfellow)

A wind came up out of the sea
Pat 178; Sto I 77

Hark, Hark! the Lark (William Shakespeare)

Hark, hark! the lark at heaven's gate sings
Cymbeline II iii 21; B.B.F 44; Cher 264; Ch.Gar 23; Fab.C.V 47; Mer 272; Mer.Puf 203; My 16; Ox.P.C 94; Ox.V.J II 18; P.Bk 98; P.F.P II 126; Riv I 55; Tree II 59; Ver II 5

Hassan (part) (James Elroy Flecker)

Thy dawn, O Master of the world, thy dawn
Act III 37

L'Allegro (part) (John Milton)

To hear the lark begin his flight
Key III 59; Shep 158

Matin Song (Thomas Heywood)

Pack, clouds, away! and welcome, day!
B.B.F 169; By 29; Ox.P.C 42; Peg IV 112; P.F.P II 125; P.Rem 49; Spo I 122; Trea 12

Pippa Passes (part) (Robert Browning)

Day!/Faster and more fast
A.D.L 28; Peg III 10

Venus and Adonis (part) (William Shakespeare)

Lo! here the gentle lark, weary of rest
Venus & Adonis 853; B.B.F 44

The Wayside Station (Edwin Muir)

Here at the wayside station, as many a morning
Shep 21

DAWN (CITY)

Dawn (Walter de la Mare)

Near, far, unearthly, break the birds
Act I 32

A Description of the Morning (Jonathan Swift)

Now hardly here and there an Hackney-Coach
Key IV 46; Shep 159; Wheel III 81

DAY DREAMS

The Bedpost (Robert Graves)

Sleepy Betsy from her pillow
Isle 67; Ox.V.J III 79

The Ice Cart (Wilfrid Wilson Gibson)

Perched on my city office stool
D.P IV 77; D.P.R IV 45; Look 164; Mood IV 112; Peg II 2; P.F.P II 41; Spir 42; Spir.R 35; Spo I 115; Ver II 45; Wheel II 139

The Shell (James Stephens)

And then I pressed the shell
A.D.L 77; Bits 6; B.P IV 52; Chor 22; D.P IV 76; Flock 43; Kal 57; P.F.P I 113; Rhyme IV 38; Six V 34; Them II 55; Yim I 77

DEATH

See also Mortality

As He lay Dying (Randolph Stow)

As he lay dying, two fat crows
Flock 257

The Bed says to the Carpenter (Indian—trans Verrier Elwin)

The bed says to the carpenter, do not make me
J.Vo IV 84

Daisies (Andrew Young)

The stars are everywhere tonight
Say 47; You.Qu 18

Death (African, Kuba)

There is no needle without piercing point
D.P.R III 120

Death, be not Proud (John Donne)

Death, be not proud, though some have called thee
Cher 381; D.P.R IV 144; Pat 139; P.W 89; P.W.R 88; R.R 104; Say 127; Sphe 449; Wheel IV 59

First Death (D. J. Enright)

It is terrible and wonderful; we wake in the strange night
Chal II 48; Liv 62

The Glories of our Blood and State (James Shirley)

The glories of our blood and state
By 70; Cher 350; Pat 138; P.Bk 110; Plea VIII 53; P.W 99; Riv IV 132; R.R 103; Spo II 135; Trea 173

It's Coming (Emily Dickinson)

It's coming—the postponeless creature
Voi III 103

Lights Out (Edward Thomas)

I have come to the border of sleep
Camb 56; Flock 177; Rain 123; P.Rem 249; R.R 112; Tho.Gr 86; Ten 138

Mid-Term Break (Seamus Heaney)

I sat all morning in the college sick-bay
D.P.R III 4; Liv 51; Spir.R 78
5294 taps

A Memento for Mortality (William Basse ?)

Mortality behold and fear!
Fab.C.V 380

My Busconductor (Roger McGough)

My busconductor tells me
Chal I 78; D.P.R III 117

Never Weather-Beaten Sail (Thomas Campion)

Never weather-beaten sail more willing bent to shore
Cher 226

The Pardoner's Tale (Geoffrey Chaucer—trans Neville Coghill)

It's of three rioters I have to tell
Tell I 52

Proud Maisie (Sir Walter Scott)

Proud Maisie is in the wood
B.B.F 167; Cher 364; Comp 24; Fab.C.V 267; Ox.P.C 154; P.F.P II 239; Plea VI 75; Puf.V 192; R.R 110; Ver III 32

Squire Hooper (Thomas Hardy)

Hooper was ninety. One September dawn
Make III 106; Tell II 151

Travelling through the Dark (William Stafford)

Travelling through the dark I found a deer
Cent 103; Flock 225; Song IV 161; Them I 48; Voi II 65; Yim II 77

The Twin of Sleep (Robert Graves)

Death is the twin of sleep, they say
Voi III 138

Upon His Departure (Robert Herrick)

Thus I/Pass by
Her.Mu 79

DEATH (OF CATS)

Cat's Funeral (E. V. Rieu)

Bury her deep, down deep
Puf.Q 147; Scrap 111; T.P.R 68

Death of a Cat (Brian Jones)

Always fastidious, it removed its dying
Read III 117

Death of a Cat (Anthony Thompson)

I rose early/On the fourth day
A.S.L.A 74

The Early Purges (Seamus Heaney)

I was six when I first saw kittens drown
Chal II 20

My Old Cat (Hal Summers)

My old cat is dead
Chal II 21; Quest IV 45

DECEMBER

A Spirit haunts the Year's last Hours (Alfred Lord Tennyson)

A spirit haunts the year's last hours
Peg V 41

DEER

See also Fawns, Stags

The Fallow Deer at the Lonely House (Thomas Hardy)

One without looks in tonight
B.B.F 113; F.Feet 148; J.Mod 99; Ox.P.C 125; Ox.V.J III 62; Rhyme III 43; Tree IV 82

DENTISTS

See also Toothache

Dentist at Work (Keith Harrison)

Mister, if I could illustrate this moment
Them VI 14

This is going to Hurt just a little bit (Ogden Nash)

One thing I like less than most things is sitting in a dentist chair with my mouth wide open
Cent 52; Day 124; Song II 33; Them VI 54

DESERTERS

Running Commentary (Anthony Rye)

Here's a commotion at a railway terminus
Tell II 36

DEW

No Jewel (Walter de la Mare)

No jewel from the rock
Mer 300; Mer.Puf 224; P.Life III 89

DIGGING

Digging (Seamus Heaney)

Between my finger and my thumb
Liv 31; Mod.P 146; Nev 80; Sev 57

Digging (Edward Thomas)

Today I think
Choice 174; Iron I 53; Prel IV 44; Quest IV 17; Tho.Gr 28; Voi I 112; Yim III 93

DIRGES & LAMENTS

Anthem for Doomed Youth (Wilfred Owen)

What passing bells for those who die as cattle?
Camb 122; Cher 349; Choice 158; Flock 250; Make IV 220; P.W.R 319; Song IV 78; Sphe 359; Ver III 103; Voi III 125; Under 73

The Bonny Earl of Moray (Murray) (Anon)

Ye highlands and ye lowlands
Bal 492; Bun 36; Fab.Bal 144; Fab.C.V 270; Mood IV 28; Ox.P.C 152; Peg II

65; Plea VI 48; P.Rem 99; Puf.V 97; Riv III 97; Song II 123; Spo I 37; Wheel II 38

Burial Song I (Arthur Waley)

How swiftly it dries
P.W. 262; P.W.R 315

Burial Song II (Arthur Waley)

What man's land is the graveyard?
P.W 262; P.W.R 315

Cock Robin (Anon)

Who killed Cock Robin?
All 52; Fab.N.V 114; F.S.N.A 181; Fun II 5; G.Tr.P 62; Mer 9; M.G.B 60; M.G.E 84; M.G.R 143; Ox.Dic 130; Ox.N.R 166; Plea I 41; P.Life I 28; Puf.N.R 76; Puf.S.B 94; Puf.V 38; Tree I 40

Who killed Cocky Robin?
Iron I 60

Come Away Death (William Shakespeare)

Come away, come away death
Twelfth Night II iv 51; Com 93; Plea VIII 25; S.D 82; Ver II 5

David's Lament over Saul and Jonathan (Bible—Samuel ii 18)

And David lamented with this lamentation over Saul and Jonathan his son
Cher 343; Plea VII 22; P.W 85; P.W.R 84

The beauty of Israel is slain upon thy high places
Pers 18; P.Tong II 141; Riv IV 51; Song II 141; Spo II 42

Deadman's Dirge (George Darley)

Prayer unsaid, and Mass unsung
Bat 70

A Dirge (John Webster)

Call for the robin redbreast and the wren
B.B.F 167; Cher 363; D.P.R II 97; Fab.C.V 265; Ox.P.C 153; P.Bk 34; P.F.P I 111; Plea VIII 53; P.W 91; P.W.R 93; This W.D 30

Elegy for Jane (Theodore Roethke)

I remember the neck curls, limp and damp as tendrils
Exp I 54

Elegy for Tom Roding (John Pudney)

After the death spelt out in headlines, after the grains
Mod.P 32

Fear no More (William Shakespeare)

Fear no more the heat o' the sun
Cymbeline IV ii 258; Act II 89; Bat 93; By 41; Cher 332; Com 92; D.P IV 175; D.P.R IV 137; Fab.C.V 265; Man III 54; Peg III 102; P.F.P II 247; Plea VIII 59; P.Rem 204; Puf.V 244; P.W 66; P.W.R 61; Rain 113; Song IV 199; Sphe 447; Spir 101; Spir.R 76; Spo I 150; Trea 165; Weal II 19

The Flowers of the Forest (Jean Elliot)

I've heard them lilting at our yowe-milking
Fab.C.V 269; Plea VII 25; Song IV 66

Full Fathom Five (William Shakespeare)

Full fathom five thy father lies
Tempest I ii 394; B.P II 53; Cher 231; Com 187; D.P II 119; D.P.R II 167; Fab.C.V 268; Flock 42; Go.Jo 141; Key III 118; Mer 270; Mer.Puf 200; My 29; Ox.P.C 52; Ox.V.J IV 89; P.F.P I 111; Plea VI 47; P.Rem 202; P.W 65; P.W.R 60; Rhyme IV 56; Riv I 53; S.D 129; Speak I 88; This W.D 83; Ver II 10

How sleep the Brave (William Collins)

How sleep the Brave who sink to rest
D.P.R IV 65

In Plague Time (Thomas Nashe)

Adieu, farewell earth's bliss
Bat 89; By 27; Cher 358; Fab.C.V 274; Plea VIII 119; P.W 78; P.W.R 75; Riv IV 54; R.R 98; Song IV 196; Wheel III 69

Rich men trust not in wealth
Kal 133

Let the day perish (Bible —Job iii 3)

Let the day perish wherein I was born
P.Tong II 79

Loss of the Royal George (William Cowper)

Toll for the brave!
Chor 26; Fun I 145; Plea VI 20; P.W 137; P.W.R 148; Riv III 107; Spo I 106

Lost in France (Ernest Rhys)

He had the ploughman's strength
Chal I 35; Peg IV 87; Song III 105

A Lyke-Wake Dirge (Anon)

This ae night, this ae night
Bun 236; Cher 366; D.P.R 190; Fab.C.V 264; Flock 258; Iron II 74; Kal 132; Make IV 171; Peg V 104; Plea VII 47; Puf.V 204; P.W 1; P.W.R 1; Song IV 197; Voi II 156; Wheel III 34

On Salathiel Pavy (Ben Jonson)

Weep with me, all you that read
P.Bk 7

The Raven's Tomb (Walter de la Mare)

'Build me my tomb' the Raven said
Plea VI 87

Requiem (Robert Louis Stevenson)

Under the wide and starry sky
D.P IV 88

Shepeardes Calendar: November (part) (Edmund Spenser)

Up then Melpomene, thou mournfulest Muse of nine
Cher 181

The Soldier's Death (Anne Finch, Countess of Winchilsea)

Trail all your pikes, dispirit every drum
By 95; D.P.R IV 59; R.R 46

Stop all the Clocks (W. H. Auden)

Stop all the clocks, cut off the telephone
Chal II 58; Chor 42; Mood IV 24; Peg V 53; Weal II 29

DISASTERS

See Accidents, Earthquakes, Fire, Floods

DIVERS

Frogman (Seamus Heaney)

Unsettling silt/in the holds of liners

DIVES & LAZARUS

Dives and Lazarus (Anon)

As it fell out upon a day
Bal 177; Fab.Bal 153; Read II 61; Tell I 45

DIVING

The Diver (Ian Serraillier)

I put on my aqua-lung and plunge
Chal I 15; Cor 15; Sto II 62; Them V 37

The Diver (W. W. E. Ross)

I would like to dive/Down
Chal III 66

The Diver (Theobald Purcell-Buret)

Poised for the leap, clear in the morning light
Start 137; Sto III 51

DOGS

See also G.Tr.P 38–43

See also Beagles, Greyhounds, Sheepdogs

An Addition to the Family: for M. L. (Edwin Morgan)

A musical poet, collector of basset-horns
Mod.P 181

Argus and Ulysses (Eleanor Farjeon)

Argus was a puppy
P.Life II 22

The Bandog (Walter de la Mare)

Has anybody seen my Mopser?
De la M.Col 83; De la M.P.P 14; De la M.S 68; F.Feet 92

A Boy is a Boy (Ogden Nash)

There once was a dog, he was really just a pup
B.P II 24

Dog (Harold Munro)

O little friend your nose is ready; you sniff
Bird II 4

A Dog in Snow (Margaret Stanley-Wrench)

Overnight the world has become delft china
Shep 97

A Dog in the Quarry (Miroslav Holub—trans George Thiener)

The day was so bright
J.Vo IV 16

Elegy on the Death of a Mad Dog (Oliver Goldsmith)

Good people all, of every sort
Fab.C.V 82; P.F.P II 99

Fidelity (William Wordsworth)

A barking sound the shepherd hears
Key II 53; P.Bk 217; P.F.P II 97; Song III 82; Spo I 71; Sto I 31; Tell I 37; Wor.So 59

An Introduction to Dogs (Ogden Nash)

The dog is man's best friend
Cor 180; G.Tr.P 38

Lament of a Poor Blind (Thomas Hood)

Oh what shall I do for a dog?
Peng.An 85

The Little Dog's Day (Rupert Brooke)

All in the town were still asleep
Sto I 33; T.P.W 112

Lone Dog (Irene MacLeod)

I'm a lean dog, a keen dog, a wild dog and lone
A.D.L 177; B.P IV 22; Cor 176; Ex.Ch 19; Hap 93; Mood I 40; Peg I 42; Puf.V 42; Spo I 134; Sto I 110; T.P.W 101

Mick (James Reeves)

Mick my mongrel-O
Puf.Q 80; Tree II 51

Night Song (Frances Cornford)

On moony nights the dogs bark shrill
Bird I 1

Nino the Wonder Dog (Roy Fuller)

A dog emerges from the flies
Act III 130; Dawn 60; Sev 80; Them I 68

Of the Awefull Battle of the Pekes and the Pollicles (T. S. Eliot)

The Pekes and the Pollicles, everyone knows
El.O.P 37; T.P.R 46

Old Blue (Anon)

I had a dog, and his name was Blue
Song I 38; Voi II 61; Wheel III 130

The Old Coon-Dog Dreams (Kenneth Porter)

The moon . . . the moon . . . the moon . . . the moon—
G.Tr.P 40

The Song of Quoodle (G. K. Chesterton)

They haven't got no noses
Act I 108; Go.Jo 107; P.F.P I 19; Them I 11; Weal I 10

The Task (part) (William Cowper)

Forth goes the woodman, leaving unconcerned
D.P.R III 23

Shaggy, and lean, and shrewd, with pointed ears
A.D.L 176; D.P III 19; Kal 5; Speak I 19

The Turkish Trench Dog (Geoffrey Dearmer)

Night held me as I crawled and scrambled near
Peg III 46; Trea 334; Ver II 210

DOLPHINS

Dolphins in Blue Water (Amy Lowell)

Hey! Cracker-jack—jump!
Man I 48

DONKEYS

The Donkey (G. K. Chesterton)

When fishes flew and forests walked
By 221; Look 372; Make II 35; Mood III 81; P.Bk 41; Plea VII 50; Rain 53; Rhyme IV 118; Six VI 18; Song II 146; Ver II 226

Nicholas Nye (Walter de la Mare)

Thistle and darnel and dock grew there
Ark 73; De la M.Col 82; De la M.Ch 45; De la M.P.P 79; De la M.S 72; Fun II 78; Mer 205; Ox.P.C 120; Peg I 40; P.F.P I 48; Plea VI 22; Rhyme IV 102; Riv I 12; Six VI 15

A Prayer to go to Paradise with the Donkeys (Francis Jammes—trans Wilbur)

When I must come to you, O my God, I pray
Ark 20

DOVES

The Old Sweet Dove of Wiveton (Stevie Smith)

'Twas the voice of the sweet dove
Ark 4; Bat 19

DRAGON-FLIES

A Dragon-Fly (Eleanor Farjeon)

When the heat of the summer
Bits b; Look 187; Min III 11; P.Life III 71

The Two Voices (part) (Alfred Lord Tennyson)

Today I saw the dragon-fly
Act II 104; Ark 70; B.B.F 124; B.L.J IV 43; P.Life III 71; Scrap 81

DRAGONS

Beowulf the Warrior (part) (Anon)

After Hygelac was dead and Heardred had been slain
Ser.B 42

58

The Dragon of Wantley (Anon)

Old stories tell how Hercules
Voi II 29

The Faerie Queene (part) (Edmund Spenser)

By this dreadful beast drew nigh to hand
Key IV 112; Riv III 65

So dreadfully he towards him did pass
Riv III 67

Fafnir and the Knights (Stevie Smith)

In the quiet waters
A.S.L.A 81; Peng.An 94

Sir Eglamore (Samuel Rowlands)

Sir Eglamore, that worthy knight
Fab.C.V 170; Mer 324; Mer.Puf 244; Mood I 77; Ox.P.C 25; P.Rem 22; P.Tong I 114; Riv II 96

A Small Dragon (Brian Patten)

I've found a small dragon in the woodshed
Drag 28

St George and the Dragon (part) (Anon)

Here stand I St George; from
Com 160

St Martha and the Dragon (Charles Causley)

In far Provence, where runs the brawny river
Cau.Nar 65

The Tale of Custard the Dragon (Ogden Nash)

Belinda lived in a little white house
Fab.N.V 170; G.Tr.P 166; Make I 12; Rhyme III 25; Six II 16; T.P.R 37; Weal I 100

DRAKE, SIR FRANCIS

See also Armada

Drake's Drum (Sir Henry Newbolt)

Drake he's in his hammock an' a thousand mile away

By 208; Fab.C.V 246; Spir 67; Spir.R 53; Spo I 137; Trea 142; Ver II 155; Weal I 68

Epitaph on Drake (Thomas Beedome)

Drake, who the world hast conquered like a scroll
By 31

Of the Great and Famous Sir Francis Drake (Robert Hayman)

The Dragon that our Seas did raise his Crest
Fab.C.V 145; P.Tong 123

Upon Sir Francis Drake's Return (Anon)

Sir Francis, Sir Francis, Sir Francis is come
Fab.C.V 144

DREAMS

See also Daydreams, Nightmares

The Bedpost (Robert Graves)

Sleepy Betsy from her pillow
Isle 67; Ox.V.J III 79

I had a Boat (M. E. Coleridge)

I had a boat, the boat had wings
P.Tong I 43

What did I Dream? (Robert Graves)

What did I dream? I do not know
Quest III 6; Them II 37; T.W.P 23

DRESSES

Cotton (Eleanor Farjeon)

My wedding-gown's cotton
Puf.Q 30

DRESSMAKERS

A Dressmaker (Jean Kenward)

Mrs Binns
My 83

DRINKING

See also Ale, Wine

A Catch (Henry Aldrich)

If all be true that I do think
P.W 120

Drinking (Abraham Cowley)

The thirsty earth soaks up the rain
Tree IV 102; Weal II 141; Wheel III 77

Drinking Song (James Kirkup)

Sip a little, sup a little
Make I 11

Three Men of Gotham (Thomas Love Peacock)

Seamen three! What men be ye?
Fab.C.V 188

DRINKS

See Ale, Cocoa, Tea, Wine

DROMEDARIES

See also Camels

The Dromedary (A. Y. Campbell)

In dreams I see the dromedary still
Exp III 17; Kal 9; P.F.P I 94; Way 23

DROUGHT

Drought (Denys Lefebvre)

Heat, all pervading, crinkles up the soil
Read III 118

Drought (Australia) (Flexmore Hudson)

Midsummer noon, and the timbered walls
Ver III 304

Drought (South Africa) (David John Darlow)

The burning skies are steel
Ver III 253

Drought (part) (South Africa) (Francis Carey Slater)

The sky is a blue, coiled serpent
Ver III 248

DROVERS

Ballad of the Drover (Henry Lawson)

Across the stony ridges
All 99; Make I 51

The Drove-Road (Wilfrid Gibson)

'Twas going to snow—'twas snowing! Curse his luck!
Tell I 62

In the Droving Days (A. B. Paterson)

'Only a pound,' said the auctioneer
Spir 52; Spir.R 43

The New-Chum's First Trip (Anon)

Now if you will listen I'll tell you a story
Fab.Bal 232; Read II 153

Saltbush Bill (A. B. Paterson)

Now this is the law of the Overland that all in the West obey
Sto II 18

DROWNING

Caught by the Tide (George Crabbe)

Sometimes a party, rowed from town, will land
Tell II 78

Clarence's Dream (William Shakespeare)

Lord, Lord! methought, what pain it was to drown
Richard III I iv 21; Act I 39; Cher 229; P.W 70; P.W.R 65; Riv III 19; Song I 121; Sto II 62

On a Friend's Escape from Drowning (George Barker)

Came up that cold sea at Cromer like a running grave
D.P.R III 17; Mod.P 61; Say 127; Tell II 157

The Sands of Dee (Charles Kingsley)

O Mary go and call the cattle home
B.P IV 41; Look 63; Ox.P.C 153; P.Bk 270; P.F.P II 49

DRUMS

Darby Kelly (Anon)

My grandsire beat a drum so neat
P.W 22; Riv III 29

The Drum (John Scott)

I hate that drum's discordant sound
Key III 71; Read III 72; Riv III 6; Song III 102; Them III 61; Voi II 73

The Toy Band (Sir Henry Newbolt)

Dreary lay the long road, dreary lay the town
Bird I 62

DUCKS

Dilly Dilly (Anon)

O what have you got for dinner, Mrs Bond?
Mer 16; Mer.Puf 18; Ox.Dic 91; Ox.N.R 171; Puf.S.B 42

Ducks (Clifford Dyment)

The ducks are clacking by the brook
J.Mod 104

Ducks (F. W. Harvey)

From troubles of the world
Ch.Gar 64; D.P III 9; P.F.P I 41; Rain 66; Sto II 107; Ver II 216

Ducks (Phoebe Hesketh)

A small procession waddles single file
J.Mod 103

Duck's Ditty (Kenneth Grahame)

All along the backwater
Ex.H 23; Fab.N.V 78; Go.Jo 50; Mood I 42; P.Bk 116; P.Rem 17; Quest I 13; Scrap 27; Six I 56; T.P.R 72

Feeding Ducks (Norman MacCaig)

One duck stood on my toes
Drag 12; Sphe 129

Flo, the White Duck (Gwen Dunn)

All white and smooth is Flo
F.Feet 67

Quack (Walter de la Mare)

The duck is whiter than whey is
De la M.Col 229; Ex.H 21; Mer 218; Mer.Puf 160

DUNWICH

At Dunwich (Anthony Thwaite)

Fifteen churches lie here
Cor 83; Mod.P 176; Ris 89; Sev 97

DWARFS

The Dwarf (Walter de la Mare)

Now Jinnie, my dear, to the dwarf be off
D.P.R I 83

EAGLES

The Eagle (Alfred Lord Tennyson)

He clasps the crag with crooked hands
B.B.F 218; Bird I 25; B.L.J IV 50; By 164; Chal I 23; Dan 99; D.P.R II 9; Ex.Ch 18; Fab.C.V 89; Fuji 90; Fun II 74; Go.Jo 74; G.Tr.P 58; Iron I 12; Key IV 70; Make II 107; Ox.P.C 66; Peng.An 99; P.F.P I 36; Plea V 19; P.Life IV 18; Rhyme IV 105; Riv II 4; Shep 106; Six VI 29; Song I 48; Sphe 157; Sto III 92; Ten.Fa 33; Them I 25; This W.D 120; Weal I 27

The Eagle (Andrew Young)

He hangs between his wings outspread
P.F.P I 36; P.Life IV 18; Six VI 30; Song I 48; Weal I 33; You.Bu 22

The Dalliance of the Eagles (Walt Whitman)

Skirting the river road (my forenoon walk, my rest)
Sto III 92

EARTHQUAKES

Earthquake (James Kirkup)

An old man's flamingo-coloured kite
Dan 62; Make IV 96; Under 47

EARWIGS

Earwig or
The Horny Golloch (Scotland Anon)

The horny golloch is an awesome beast
Fab.C.V 92; J.Vo II 57

EASTER

Easter (George Herbert)

I got me flowers to strew thy way
Fab.C.V 362; Shep 57

Easter (Edmund Spenser)

Most Glorious Lord of Life! that, on this day
Com 203; Song IV 212

Easter Wings (George Herbert)

Lord, who createst man in wealth and store
Key IV 63; Song IV 211

Hail thee, Festival Day! (Bishop Venantius Fortunatus)

Hail thee, Festival Day! blest day that are hallowed for ever
P.Tong 34

The World itself keeps Easter Day (J. M. Neale)

The World itself keeps Easter Day
Com 205

EDEN

See also Creation, Eve

Des Bones Gwine to Rise Again (Anon)

De Lord He thought He'd made a man—

Paradise Lost (part) (John Milton)

About them frisking played
B.B.F 24

So spake our mother Eve, and Adam heard
P.Rem 124

EDINBURGH

Edinburgh Courtyard in July (Norman MacCaig)

Hot light is smeared as thick as paint
Liv 44

EDITORS

Editor Whedo (Edgar Lee Masters)

To be able to see every side of every question
Tell II 17

EDUCATION

See also Scholars, School, Schoolmasters, Schoolmistresses

Against Education (Charles Churchill)

Accursed the man, whom Fate ordains, in spite
Peg V 73

EGOISTS

Satire (Gilbert Islands—trans Sir Arthur Grimble)

That man came shouting, 'I am a chief'
J.Vo IV 83

The Song of Mr Toad (Kenneth Grahame)

The world has held great heroes
Go.Jo 108

ELDORADO

Eldorado (Edgar Allen Poe)

Gaily bedight
Bl.J III 9; Fab.C.V 187; Peg II 25; P.Life IV 96; Puf.V 86

ELEPHANTS

The Blind Men and the Elephant (John G. Saxe)

It was six men of Hindostan (Indostan)
Bird I 54; Cor 59; D.P I 26; D.P.R I 21; Ex.Tro 49; Fun II 60; G.Tr.P 200; Key III 40; Min IV 55; Ox.V.J II 63; Speak I 50; Sto I 108

Circus (part) (Louis MacNiece)

Tonnage of instinctive/Wisdom in tinsel
Exp III 25

Elephant (Alan Brownjohn)

It is quite unfair to be
Bro.B 44

The Elephant (Hilaire Belloc)

When people call this beast to mind
Mer 176

The Elephant is slow to hate
(D. H. Lawrence)

The elephant, the huge old beast
Law.S 22

Elephants are Different to Different People (Carl Sandburg)

Wilson and Pilcer and Snack stood before the zoo elephant
J.Vo III 18

Elephants in the Circus
(D. H. Lawrence)

Elephants in the Circus
Them I 69; Voi I 93

Erin (Elephant) (Yoruba—trans Ulli Beier)

Elephant who brings death
Ark 121

Hunting Song (Sir Maurice Bowra)

On the weeping forest, under the wing of the evening
Chal II 72

Two Performing Elephants
(D. H. Lawrence)

He stands with his forefeet on the drum
Drag 27; Exp III 26; Peg IV 17; Riv IV 33; Quest V 18; Voi I 92

ELIZABETH I

A Ditty (Edmund Spenser)

See where she sits upon the grassy green
Fab.C.V 137

The Looking Glass (Rudyard Kipling)

Queen Bess was Harry's daughter
Shad 24

ELVES

Puk-Wudjies (Patrick R. Chalmers)

They live 'neath the curtain
P.Bk 24

EMOTIONS

See Moods

ENCHANTMENT

See also Charms & Spells

Kemp Owyne (Anon)

Her mother died when she was young
Isle 64

The Sleeping Beauty (Alfred Lord Tennyson)

Year after year unto her feet
Isle 60

Song of Enchantment (Walter de la Mare)

A song of Enchantment I sang me there
Isle 59

ENGINE DRIVERS & FIREMEN

Casey Jones (Anon)

Come all you rounders, listen here
All 9; B.B 93; Bird I 33; B.L.A.F 266; Chor 32; D.P II 34; D.P.R II 75; Ex.Ch 164; F.S.N.A 564; Iron IV 6; Key I 84; Make I 122; M.M.A 23; Mood II 20; Ox.P.C 76; Ox.V.J IV 25; Peg II 78; P.F.P I 156; Plea VIII 68; P.Tong I 17; Riv III 39; Sphe 181; Spir 58; Spir.R 47

Coal for Mike (Bertolt Brecht)

I have heard how in Ohio
D.P.R II 77

Fireman's Calypso (Ewan MacColl)

You give her water
Key II 26; Song I 29

ENGINEERS

See also Machines

Engineers (Jimmy Garthwaite)

Pistons, valves and wheels and gears
Fab.N.V 41

ENGLAND

The Island (Charles Dibdin)

Daddy Neptune one day to Freedom did say
Riv II 59

Jerusalem (William Blake)

And did those feet in ancient time
*Act I 54; Bla.Gr 83; B.P IV 39; By 111;
Ch.Gar 75; D.P IV 187; D.P.R IV 155;
Ex.Ch 25; Fab.C.V 126; P.F.P I 180;
P.Life IV 74; P.Tong I 6; Puf.V 247;
P.W 142; Song IV 98; Sphe 380; Ver III
24*

This Royal Throne of Kings
(William Shakespeare)

This royal throne of kings, this sceptr'd
isle
*Richard II II i 40; D.P IV 177; Mood IV
5; Song IV 97; Ver II 241*

ENGLAND: HISTORY

See also Kings & Queens, War,
Wars

The Land (Rudyard Kipling)

When Julius Fabricius, Sub-Prefect of
the Weald
Song III 19

Puck's Song (Rudyard Kipling)

See you the dimpled track that runs
*B.L.J IV 28; Com 111; D.P I 104; D.P.R
I 81; Fab.C.V 129; Plea VI 93; P.Life IV
72; Riv III 13*

See you the ferny ride that steals
P.Bk 346

The Vicar of Bray (Anon)

In good King Charles's golden days
Plea VII 91; Sphe 246

ENGLAND: HISTORY
(PREHISTORIC)

The River's Tale (Rudyard Kipling)

I walk my beat before London town
Key III 78

ENGLAND: HISTORY
(ROMAN)

A Pict Song (Rudyard Kipling)

Rome never looks where she treads
J.Vo IV 35

The Roman Wall (Andrew Young)

Though moss and lichen crawl
Ten 171

Roman Wall Blues (W. H. Auden)

Over the heather the wet wind blows
*Choice 242; Dawn 43; Eye 25; J.Mod
34; J.Vo IV 37; Kal 36; My 79; Peg V
95; Say 83; Them VI 37; Ver III 67;
Weal I 122*

ENGLAND: HISTORY
(SAXONS AND NORMANS)

The Battle of Maldon (Anglo-
Saxon)

. . . go broken/He made each warrior
lash free his horse
P.W 32

The Battle of Stamford Bridge
(Laurence Binyon)

Haste thee, Harold, haste thee North!
D.P III 98; D.P.R III 70

The Pirates in England (Rudyard
Kipling)

When Rome was rotten ripe to her fall
Key III 20; Wheel I 128

ENGLAND: HISTORY
(HENRY I)

The White Ship (D. G. Rossetti)

By none but me can the tale be told
D.P III 33; Fun II 158

Swifter and swifter the white ship sped
P.Bk 258

ENGLAND: HISTORY (HENRY V)
See Agincourt, Harfleur

ENGLAND: HISTORY (RICHARD
Young Edgcumbe (Charles
Causley)

Young Edgcumbe spoke by river
Cau.Nar 23

ENGLAND: HISTORY (HENRY VII)

See Cabote, John

ENGLAND: HISTORY (HENRY VIII)

O Death, Rock me on Sleep (attrib. Anne Boleyn)

O Death, rock me on sleep
Cher 357

ENGLAND: HISTORY (ELIZABETH I)

See also Armada, Cadiz, Drake, Elizabeth I, Gilbert, Grenville, Revenge

Brave Lord Willoughby (Anon)

The fifteenth day of July
Broad 24

His was the Word (Queen Elizabeth Tudor—as a girl)

His was the Word that spake it
Bat 54

In Plague Time (Thomas Nashe)

Adieu, farewell earth's bliss
Bat 89; By 27; Cher 358; Fab.C.V 274; Plea VIII 119; P.W 78; P.W.R 75; Riv IV 54; R.R 98; Song IV 196; Wheel III 69

Rich men trust not in wealth
Kal 133

To the Virginian Voyage (Michael Drayton)

You brave heroic minds
Trea 3

ENGLAND: HISTORY (JAMES I)

Farewell, Rewards and Fairies (Richard Corbet)

Farewell, rewards and fairies
Fab.Bal 175; Fab.C.V 205; Mer 265; Mer.Puf 195; Plea V 94 (part)

The Gunpowder Plot (Sir Edward Phillips)

(From his great speech, January 27th, 1606)
They, the conspirators
Flock 268

ENGLAND: HISTORY (CHARLES I)

See Charles I

ENGLAND: HISTORY (CIVIL WAR & COMMONWEALTH)

See also Cromwell, Naseby

Edgehill Fight (Rudyard Kipling)

Naked and grey the Cotswolds stand
Plea VII 15

A Garden (Andrew Marvell)

See how the flowers as at parade
R.R 45

Marching Along (Robert Browning)

Kentish Sir Byng stood for his King
Mood III 34; P.Bk 74

ENGLAND: HISTORY (CHARLES II)

See also Buckingham, Charles II, London (Great Fire of)

London Sad London (Anon—1662)

What wants thee, that thou art in this sad taking? A king
P.Rem 137

ENGLAND: HISTORY (JAMES II)

See also Sedgemoor

The Duchess of Monmouth's Lamentation (Anon)

Loyal hearts of London City, Come I pray and sing my Ditty
Fab.Bal 180

Song of the Western Men (Robert Stephen Hawker)

A good sword and a trusty hand
Mer 225; Mer.Puf 167; Mood II 11; Plea III 39; Riv I 70; Sto III 135

ENGLAND: HISTORY (QUEEN ANNE)

See Blenheim

ENGLAND: HISTORY (THE GEORGES)

See also Corunna, Napoleon, Nelson, Trafalgar, Wellington, Waterloo

The Georges (Walter Savage Landor)

George the First was always reckoned
Cher 473

The Press-Gang (Anon)

Here's the tender coming
Rhyme IV 52

A Smuggler's Song (Rudyard Kipling)

If you wake at midnight and hear a horse's feet
All 43; B.P IV 47; Chor 16; D.P I 72; D.P.R I 60; Ex.Ch 117; Fun I 120; Key II 94; Look 68; Make I 55; Mood II 18; Ox.P.C 52; Ox.V.J II 10; Peg I 62; Plea IV 20; P.Life III 92; Rhyme IV 54; Spir 22; Spir.R 18

We be the King's Men (Thomas Hardy)

We be the King's men, hale and hearty
B.P IV 24; Chor 8; Ex.Ch 105; Mer 346; Mer.Puf 263; Min I 67; Mood I 27; Riv II 45

ENGLAND: HISTORY (VICTORIA)

Alphabetical Song on the Corn Law Bill (Anon)

Good people draw near as you pass along
P.Tong II 30

The Cry of the Children (Elizabeth Barrett Browning)

Do ye hear the children weeping, O my brothers
Vic 102

A New Song (Anon)

There's a pretty fuss and bother both in country and in town
Fab.Bal 187; Iron IV 125; S.D 130

Ode on the Death of the Duke of Wellington (Lord Tennyson)

Bury the Great Duke
Trea 265; Vic 56

All is over
Spo I 157

The Song of the Shirt (Thomas Hood)

With fingers weary and worn
P.Bk 52; S.D 111; Six III 20; Them VI 41; Trea 36

ENGLISH, THE

The True-Born Englishman (Daniel Defoe)

The Romans first with Julius Caesar came
Wheel II 65

These are the heroes who despise the Dutch
Kal 40

EPIPHANY

Journey of the Magi (T. S. Eliot)

A cold coming we had of it
Bird IV 6; Cent 40; Choice 219; Ev.M 103; Fab.C.V 359; Iron III 9; Make IV 134; Man III 9; Nar 29; P.Tong II 1; P.W 260; P.W.R 308; Song IV 203; Sphe 109; T.C.N 132; Ten 64; Ver III 197; Weal II 174; Wheel III 158

EPITAPHS

See also: Act I 66–67; Act II 18, 29, 76–77, 82, 83, 90–91; Act III

14–15, 38–39, 74–76, 144, 153; By 31, 146; G.Tr.P 237–239; M.M.A 15, 52; Ox.P.C 154; Peg I 3; Plea VI 21, 75; Plea VII 24, 95; Plea VIII 62, 70, 117; P.Tong I 39; P.Tong II 12, 40, 99; Riv II 14; Riv III 51; R.R 97; Spir 3; Weal II 12, 14, 18, 146

Epitaph on a Child (Thomas Gray)

Here, freed from pain, secure from misery, lies
Mood II 42

Epitaph on a Dead Statesman (Rudyard Kipling)

I could not dig; I dared not rob;
R.R 168

Fighting South of the Castle (Arthur Waley)

They fought south of the castle
P.W 261

A Housewife's Epitaph (Anon)

Here lies a poor woman who was always tired
Key III 58; My 91; Sto III 62; Them VI 11; Weal I 9; Wheel I 147

A Jacobite's Epitaph (Thomas B. Macaulay)

To my true king I offered free from stain
Plea VII 19

On the University Carrier (John Milton)

Here lies old Hobson, Death hath broke his girt
Fab.C.V 272

ESKIMOS

Eskimo Hunting Song (Anon—trans Sir Maurice Bowra)

I wanted to use my weapon
J.Vo II 54

The Father's Song (Eskimo—trans Peter Freuchen)

Great snowslide/Stay away from my igloo
Chal I 45; Prel III 45; Voi I 129

Glorious it is (Eskimo—trans Dr Edward Carpenter)

Glorious it is to see
Rhyme III 44; Yim II 16

The Mother's Song (Eskimo—trans Peter Freuchen)

It is so still in the house
Chal I 46; Voi III 12

A Salmon Trout to her Children (trans William Thalbitzer & Willard R. Trask)

There by the promontory the kayak is coming out
J.Vo I 69

Two Paddlers' Songs (Eskimo—trans William Thalbitzer)

When I'm out of the house in the open I feel joy
J.Vo II 59

ESSEX

Essex (Sir John Betjeman)

'The vagrant visitor erstwhile'
Ten 37

EUROPA

Europa (William Plomer)

A woman one wonderful morning
Ris 32

Europa and the Bull (Anon)

Now lows the milk-white bull on Afric's strand
B.B.F 180

EVE

See also Eden

Eve (Ralph Hodgson)

Eve with her basket was
My 46; Weal II 95

Eve (Christina Rossetti)

While I sit at the door
P.Tong II 200; Vic 174

Thus sat she weeping
B.B.F 147

67

EVENING

Evening (Ralph Hodgson)

I climbed a hill as light fell short
Fun I 69

Evening (Walter de la Mare)

When twilight darkens, and one by one
D.P.R IV 40; Ver II 208

The Evening Comes (Matthew Arnold)

The evening comes, the fields are still
Man I 70; Sphe 68

The Midges dance aboon the Burn (Robert Tannahill)

The midges dance aboon the burn
B.B.F 85

Nod (Walter de la Mare)

Softly along the road of evening
Ch.Gar 59; G.Tr.P 303; P.F.P II 26; Rhyme III 63; This W.D 144

Paradise Lost (part) (John Milton)

Now came still evening on, and twilight gray
Bat 87; Peg III 10

Prelude (T. S. Eliot)

The winter evening settles down
Cent 39; Com 73; Dawn 105; D.P IV 66; D.P.R III 29; Fla 61; Key IV 47; Liv 136; Look 174; Man I 11; Peg I 107; Pers 100; P.F.P II 111; P.W 259; Riv IV 30; Song I 23; Way 34; Weal II 162; Wheel IV 157

Recollections after an Evening Walk (John Clare)

Just as the even-bell rang, we set out
Cla.Wo 45

Summer Evening (part) (John Clare)

Crows crowd croaking overhead
B.B.F 98; Cla.Wo 44; Make II 118; Sto I 87

The frog, half fearful, jumps across the path
B.B.F 98; P.Rem 184

Summer Evening (Walter de la Mare)

The sandy cat by the farmer's chair
Bits b; B.B.F 100; De la M.Ch 50; De la M.P.P 86; De la M.S 22; Ex.Ch 14; F.Feet 147; Fun II 95; Ox.V.J II 92; Scrap 29; Tree II 15

Time to go Home (James Reeves)

Time to go home!
All 26; Puf.Q 94

EVENING PRIMROSES

Evening Primrose (John Clare)

When once the sun sinks in the west
Cla.Wo 48; Sphe 90

EVEREST

Everest Climbed (parts) (Ian Serraillier)

It was April when they came to the ice-fall—Hilary
Puf.Q 183; Song II 98; Them V 52

Near Katmandu was the meeting-place
Ser.B 122

See them crawl from the tunnelled tent
Chal I 20

They toiled to the foot of the Southern Peak
Peg II 11

A Prayer for Everest (Wilfrid Noyce)

That I may endure
Pat 135

EXPLORERS

See also Cabote, Columbus, Cortez, Gilbert, Nansen

The Ballad of Kon-Tiki (parts) (Ian Serraillier)

All day the plane had searched for them, the wild
Look 108; Puf.Q 177; Ser.B 91

Now nothing could stop them. Drawn
Tell I 69

They were not lonely. They found the sea
Puf.Q 180; Song I 112

The Discoverer of the North Cape
(H. W. Longfellow)

Othere, the old sea-captain
Ver II 25

Henry Hudson's Voyage (Dorothy
Wellesley)

The Queen of Westminster declared
J.Mod 40

FABLES

Aesop Revised by Archy (Don
Marquis)

A wolf met a spring
Act IV 61

The Ant and the Cricket (Anon)

A silly young cricket, accustomed to sing
Fun I 95; Rain 44

The Ass in the Lion's Skin
(Aesop—versified William E.
Leonard)

An ass put on a lion's skin and went
Ark 167

The Caterpillar and the Ant (Alan
Ramsey)

A pensy ant, right trig and clean
B.B.F 200

Crow and Fox (Krylov—trans Bernard Pares)

How often have they told us, please
Rhyme IV 109

Departmental (Robert Frost)

An ant on the tablecloth
Fro.You 48

The Donkey's Fancy (John
Hookham Frere)

A dingy donkey, formal and unchanged
Key III 37

A Drumlin Woodchuck (Robert
Frost)

My own strategic retreat
Fro.You 50

*The Fable of the Old Man, the Boy
and the Donkey* (Ian Serraillier)

Hobbled to market an old man and his
boy
Cor 90

*The Fable of the Trained White
Horses* (Jiri Filip)

The trained white horses
Them III 59

The Fagot (Jonathan Swift)

Observe the dying father speak
Key IV 64

Fishes' Heaven or
Heaven (Rupert Brooke)

Fish fly-replete in depth of June
*A.D.L 167; By 259; D.P IV 30; Pat 43;
Plea VI 65; Quest IV 50; Wheel I 147*

The Fox and the Grapes (Joseph
Lauren)

One summer's day a fox was passing
through
G.Tr.P 170

The Frogs who wanted a King
(Joseph Lauren)

The frogs were living happy as could be
G.Tr.P 169

The Gardener and the Hog (John
Gay)

A Gardener of peculiar taste
B.B.F 201

Haec Fabula Docet (Robert Frost)

A Blindman by the name of La Fontaine
Key IV 127

Mending Wall (Robert Frost)

Something there is that doesn't love a
wall
*Fro.You 70; Iron III 52; Song IV 58;
Ten 76*

The Mountain and the Squirrel
(Ralph Waldo Emerson)

The Mountain and the Squirrel had a
quarrel
*Ark 91; Fuji 27; Go.Jo 26; G.Tr.P 57;
Plea III 69*

The Mouse that gnawed the Oak-Tree down (Vachel Lindsay)

The mouse that gnawed the oak-tree down
J.Vo II 6; Mood III 63

A Pretty Tale of a Pidgeon and an Ant (Nicholas Breton)

A dove some time did sit upon a tree
B.B.F 150

The Shape God wears (Sara Henderson Hay)

So questioning, I was bold to dare
G.Tr.P 82

The Shepherd's Dog and the Wolf (John Gay)

A Wolf, with hunger fierce and bold
Ark 132

A Spider and a Fly (Don Marquis)

I heard a spider
Act IV 64

The Theology of Bongavi the Baboon (Roy Campbell)

This is the wisdom of the Ape
Ver III 263; Wheel I 155

The Town Mouse and the Country Mouse (Alexander Pope)

Once on a time (so runs the fable)
Key III 38; Speak I 72

The Turkey and the Ant (John Gay)

A Turkey, tired of common food
Key IV 64

Warty Bliggens the Toad (Don Marquis)

I met a toad
Act IV 119; Ev.M 112; Peg V 112

FACES

Phizzog (Carl Sandburg)

This face you got
V.F 131; Voi II 94; Yim III 189

FACTORIES

Factory Windows (Vachel Lindsay)

Factory windows are always broken
P.F.P II 110; R.R 68

70

FAIRIES (LYRIC & DESCRIPTIVE)

See also Dwarfs, Elves, Goblins, Robin Goodfellow

The Fairies (Robert Herrick)

If ye will with Mab find grace
Her.Mu 37; Mer 176; Mer.Puf 135; Ox.P.C 90; Riv I 24

Farewell, Rewards and Fairies (Bishop Richard Corbet)

Farewell, rewards and fairies
Fab.Bal 175; Fab.C.V 205; Mer 265; Mer.Puf 195; Plea V 94 (part)

The Fairy Queen (Anon)

Come follow, follow me
Mer 104; Mer.Puf 78; My 32; Plea III 31; Scrap 84

Fairy Things (John Clare)

Grey lichens, mid thy hills of creeping thyme
Mer 267; Mer.Puf 197

The Mocking Fairy (Walter de la Mare)

'Won't you look out of your window, Mrs Gill'
De la M.Ch 81; De la M.Col 123; De la M.P.P 94; De la M.S 111; Plea V 93; Weal I 24

Oberon's Feast (Robert Herrick)

A little mushroom table spread
Her.Mu 25

On Fairies (W. B. Yeats)

And then an answering whisper flew
Scrap 33
Under the golden evening light
Scrap 86

Queen Mab (William Shakespeare)

O! then I see Queen Mab hath been with you
Romeo & Juliet I iv 53; Flock 186; Six II 56; Tree II 71

She is the fairies' midwife and she comes
G.Tr.P 108

Queen Mab (Ben Jonson)

This is Mab, the Mistress Fairy
D.P.R III 101

FAIRIES (NARRATIVE)

Berries (Walter de la Mare)

There was an old woman
*De la M.Col 116; De la M.P.P 47;
Ex.Tro 80; Mood II 76; Ox.V.J II 38*

The Changeling (Charlotte Mew)

Toll no bell for me, dear Father, dear
Mother
Ox.V.J II 89

The Fairies (William Allingham)

Up the airy mountain
*B.P II 41; Cher 157; Ch.Gar 39; Com
198; Ex.H 76; Fab.C.V 209; Mer 97;
Min III 61; P.Bk 87; Plea V 10 (part);
Puf.V 190; Ox.P.C 92; Fuji 38; Fun I 91*

The Fairies of the Caldon Low
(Mary Howitt)

And where have you been, my Mary?
Mer 100; Mer.Puf 74

The Host of the Air (W. B. Yeats)

O'Driscoll drove with a song
*Act I 68; D.P IV 164; D.P.R IV 128; Isle
28; Make IV 130; Plea VII 56; T.C.N
104; Yea.Run 38*

The Stolen Child (W. B. Yeats)

Where dips the rocky highland
*Isle 57; Ox.V.J III 63; S.D 102; Spo I
167; Trea 318; Yea.Run 28*

Thomas the Rhymer (Anon)

True Thomas lay on the Huntlie bank
*Bal 133; Bun 5; Cher 175; Fab.Bal 127;
Fab.C.V 5; Flock 181; G.Tr.P 124; Isle
38; Puf.V 94; Riv II 70; Song III 92;
Wheel IV 19*

The Wee Wee Man (Anon)

As I was walking all (mine) alane
*Bal 135; Bun 12; Ex.Ch 64; Fab.C.V
212; Wheel I 30*

The Wicked Fairy (Edith Sitwell)

The wicked fay descended, mopping,
mowing
Ox.V.J III 65

FAIRIES SONGS

Come unto these yellow sands
(William Shakespeare)

Come unto these yellow sands
*Tempest I ii 375; Ch.Gar 21; Ex.Tro 66;
Fab.C.V 216; Go.Jo 138; Mer 259;
Mer.Puf 191; Ox.P.C 90; Ox.V.J I 9;
P.Bk 98; P.F.P I 101; Plea V 51; Riv I
53; S.D 129; This W.D 74; Tree I 77;
Ver II 9*

The Elfin Pedlar (George Darley)

Ladies and Gentlemen fays, come buy!
B.P II 18

Full Fathom Five (William
Shakespeare)

Full fathom five thy father lies
*Tempest I ii 394; B.P II 53; Cher 231;
Com 187; D.P II 119; D.P.R II 67;
Fab.C.V 268; Flock 42; Go.Jo 141; Key
III 118; Mer 270; Mer.Puf 200; My 29;
Ox.P.C 52; Ox.V.J IV 89; P.F.P I 111;
Plea VI 47; P.Rem 202; P.W 65; P.W.R
60; Rhyme IV 56; Riv I 53; S.D 129;
Speak I 88; This W.D 83; Ver II 10*

Over hill, over dale (William
Shakespeare)

Over hill, over dale
*Midsummer Night's Dream II i 2;
Ch.Gar 16; Ox.P.C 90; Ox.V.J I 62;
P.Bk 93; P.F.P I 101; P.Life III 70; Riv I
52; Six V 8; Song I 102; This W.D 75;
Tree IV 103; Ver II 8*

Where the Bee sucks (William
Shakespeare)

Where the bee sucks there suck I
*Tempest V i 88; Ch.Gar 20; Com 177;
Ex.Tro 75; G.Tr.P 297; Isle 15; Mer
348; Mer.Puf 264; Mood III 7; My 26;
Ox.P.C 91; Ox.V.J I 56; P.Bk 98; P.F.P
I 102; Plea V 50; P.Life III 70; P.W 65;
P.W.R 59; Rhyme III 53; Riv I 52;
This.W.D 76; Tree I 19; Ver II 12*

You Spotted Snakes (William
Shakespeare)

You spotted snakes with double tongues
*Midsummer Night's Dream II ii 9; B.B.F
165; B.P IV 94; By 40; Ch.Gar 18; D.P I
103; D.P.R I 80; Ex.Ch 28; F.Feet 157;*

G.Tr.P 297; Isle 53; Mer 367; Mer.Puf 279; My 27; Ox.P.C 160; Ox.V.J II 75; P.Bk 94; P.F.P I 102; P.Life II 78; P.Rem 40; Rhyme II 52; Song II 90; This W.D 37; Tree II 32; Ver II 7

FAIRS

See also Roller Coasters, Roundabouts

At a Country Fair (Thomas Hardy)

At a bygone Western country fair
Voi II 20

Back to the Fair (John Arlott)

Tonight, a cloud-rimmed flowering of the air
A.S.L.A 35; Bird II 29; Look 77

The Big Wheel (Carol Fitchett—aged 11)

Waiting to go on the big wheel
Prel II 29

The Dance (William Carlos Williams)

In Breughel's great picture, The Kermess
Go.Jo 137; Liv 57

The Prelude (part) (William Wordsworth)

What say you then
P.Rem 144

Scarborough Fair (Anon)

Are you going to Scarborough Fair?
S.D 128; Song II 16; Voi II 107

Strawberry Fair (Anon)

As I was going to Strawberry Fair
Mer 334; Mer.Puf 254; P.Life IV 76

Widdecombe Fair (Anon)

Tom Pearse, Tom Pearse, lend me your gray mare
Down 7; D.P I 100; Key I 96; Mer 350; Mer.Puf 265; P.Bk 340; P.F.P I 6; Plea IV 16; P.Life IV 75; Puf.S.B 109; Riv II 87

FALLING ASLEEP

Falling Asleep (Siegfried Sassoon)

Voices moving about in the quiet house
Ox.V.J III 56; Sphe 433; T.P.W 24

72

FAMILIES

See Brothers, Fathers, Fathers and Daughters, Fathers and Sons, Mothers, Mothers and Daughters, Mothers and Sons, Sisters, Sons, Twins, Uncles

FAMOUS PEOPLE

See also Admirals, Explorers, Generals, Outlaws, Sailors, Soldiers

Soup (Carl Sandburg)

I saw a famous man eating soup
Chal I 51

Their name liveth
(Apocrypha—*Ecclesiasticus* xliv)

Let us now praise famous men
D.P IV 186; D.P.R IV 154; Peg IV 65

FANTASY

See also Isle *throughout*

See also Mystery, Tales Tall

The Big Nasturtiums (Robert Beverley Hale)

All of a sudden the big nasturtiums
J.Vo III 65

The Crystal Cabinet (William Blake)

The Maiden caught me in the Wild
Fab.C.V 200

I Saw a Fishpond all on Fire (Anon)

I saw a fishpond all on fire
Act I 37; B.L.J III 56; Cher 153; Fab.N.V 143; Key I 29; M.G.B 92; Ox.Dic 171; Ox.N.R 136; Puf.N.R 106

I saw a Pack of Cards (Anon)

I saw a pack of cards gnawing a bone
M.G.B 123; Puf.N.R 107

I Saw a Peacock (Anon)

I saw a peacock with a fiery tail
Act I 36; B.P IV 15; Cher 154; Com 117; Fab.C.V 276; G.Tr.P 228; Man I 26; Mer 282; M.G.B 195; My 22; Ox.Dic 342; Ox.N.R 141; Ox.P.C 26; Plea III 20; P.Tong I 43; Puf.N.R 106; Riv I 93

If all the Seas (Anon)

If all the seas were one sea
*B.L.J I 53; B.P I 42; Fab.N.V 132; Mer
38; M.G.B 175; M.G.E 48; M.G.R 76;
Ox.Dic 379; Ox.N.R 137; P.Life I 15;
Puf.N.R 150; Puf.Y 196; Tree I 49*

If all the World were Paper (Anon)

If all the world were paper
*A.D.L 223; Ex.Tro 48; Iron I 16; Mer
116; Mer.Puf 87; Ox.Dic 436; Ox.N.R
135; Ox.P.C 20; Plea III 80; P.Life II
76; Puf.N.R 150; Riv I 88*

I'll sail upon the dog-star (Thomas Durfey)

I'll sail upon the dog-star
Com 175; Fab.C.V 188

Kubla Khan (Samuel Taylor Coleridge)

In Xanadu, did Kubla Khan
Fab.C.V 201; This.W.D 173

Legend (Judith Wright)

The blacksmith's boy went out with a rifle
Rain 91

The Mewlips (J. R. R. Tolkien)

The shadows where the Mewlips dwell
Shad 72

Moon Hops (Ted Hughes)

Hops are a menace on the moon, a nuisance crop
J.Vo III 65

My Hat (Stevie Smith)

Mother said if I wore this hat
Look 332

The Pumpkin (Robert Graves)

You may not believe it for hardly could I
Mer 135; Mer.Puf 102

The Rolling English Road (Gilbert K. Chesterton)

Before the Roman came to Rye or out to Severn strode
*D.P IV 79; D.P.R IV 48; Fab.C.V 292;
Plea VIII 9; Six V 58; Song III 54*

Romance (W. J. Turner)

When I was but thirteen or so
*A.D.L 140; B.P IV 42; By 270; D.P III
89; Go.Jo 220; Look 48; Min III 76; Pat
193; Peg II 106; P.F.P II 5; Puf.V 209;
Song I 106; This W.D 135; Weal I 7*

The Song of Finis (Walter de la Mare)

At the edge of All the Ages
De la M.Ch 125; De la M.Col 205

The Song of the Mad Prince (Walter de la Mare)

Who said 'Peacock Pie'?
*Camb 65; De la M.Ch 127; De la M.Col
260; De la M.P.P 113; De la M.S 63;
D.P.R III 119; Fab.C.V 282; Go.Jo 136;
Iron IV 68; My 32; P.F.P II 240; Plea V
62; P.Tong I 184; Puf.V 203; R.R 115*

The Song of Wandering Aengus (W. B. Yeats)

I went out to the hazel wood
Go.Jo 38; Say 114

Strange Story (Anon)

I saw a pigeon making bread
Puf.Y 195

Tartary (Walter de la Mare)

If I were Lord of Tartary
*De la M.Col 204; Ex.Tro 85; G.Tr.P
105; Pers 113; P.F.P II 6; P.Life IV 92;
Tree IV 93*

Tom O'Bedlam's Song (part) (Anon)

The moon's my constant mistress
*Cher 172; D.P IV 69; D.P.R IV 41;
Fab.C.V 186; Ox.V.J IV 42; Plea VIII
85; P.Tong I 134*

From the hag and hungry goblin
By 15

Travel (Robert Louis Stevenson)

I should like to rise and go
*Cor 131; D.P I 48; D.P.R I 46; Fab.C.V
100; G.Tr.P 263; Mood III 21; Peg I 52;
Riv I 38; Sphe 163; Start 78; Ste.C.G
27; T.P.W 49*

The Tuba (Morton Marcus)

a flaming tuba
J.Vo IV 65

Warning to Children (Robert Graves)

Children, if you dare to think
Choice 257; Day 40; Fab.C.V 98; Flock 195; Look 338; Man III 12; Ox.P.C 32; S.D 26; Song II 8

FARMERS

The Hill Farmer Speaks (R. S. Thomas)

I am the farmer, stripped of love
Mod.P 53

FARMING

See also Apple-Picking, Barley, Beanfields, Cattle, Country Life, Farmers, Farmworkers, Harvest, Haystacks, Milking, Mowing, Ploughing, Scarecrows, Scything, Sheep

A Farmer's Boy (Anon)

The sun went down behind yon hill, across yon dreary moor
Fun I 104

Scaring Crows (Anon)

O all you little blacky tops
Mer 68; Mer.Puf 49

FARMWORKERS (LYRIC & DESCRIPTIVE)

See also Carters, Farmers, Molecatchers, Ploughmen

The Brave Ploughing Boy (Anon)

Come all you jolly ploughboys
Sto I 135

Countrywork in March (John Clare)

Muffled in baffles, leathern coat and gloves
D.P.R IV 73

Cynddylan on a Tractor
(R. S. Thomas)

Ah, you should see Cynddylan on a tractor

Bird III 22; Chal I 84; Choice 307; Dawn 78; D.P.R IV 79; Hap 26; Liv 18; Make IV 37; Mod.P 54; Six IV 28; Song III 17; Speak II 110; Sto III 59; Them VII 53; Wheel IV 188

The Foddering Boy (John Clare)

The foddering boy along the crumping snows
Prel II 47

Milkmaid (Laurie Lee)

The girl's far treble, muted to the heat
Mod.P 47

Soil (R. S. Thomas)

A field with tall hedges and a young
Drag 65; Eye 44

Term Time (Anon)

There's some that sing of the hiring fair
Voi II 23

We Field Women (Thomas Hardy)

How it rained
Peg IV 38; Speak II 109

FARMWORKERS (NARRATIVE)

The Code (Robert Frost)

There were three in the meadow by the brook
Nar 34; Tell I 154

FARRIERS

See Blacksmiths

FATHERS

Our Father (Ray Mathew)

She said my father had whiskers and looked like God
Voi II 92

When Father papered the Parlour
(Weston & Barnes)

Our parlour wanted papering and pa said it was waste
Prel I 18

FATHERS & DAUGHTERS

The Chinese Poet laments the Birth of a Daughter, Golden Bells (Po Chu-I—trans Arthur Waley)

When I was almost forty
Iron IV 136

Father and Child (W. B. Yeats)

She hears me strike the board and say
Bird IV 9; Pers 36; Voi III 70

If I should ever by chance (Edward Thomas)

If I should ever by chance grow rich
Fab.C.V 107

A Prayer for my Daughter
(W. B. Yeats)

Once more the storm is howling, and half-hid
Ten 152

Remembering Golden Bells (Po Chu-I—trans Arthur Waley)

Ruined and ill—a man of two score
Iron IV 137

A Sense of Property (Anthony Thwaite)

After the usual rounds at night
Mod.P 134

Song to be Sung by the Father of Infant Female Children (Ogden Nash)

My heart leaps up when I behold
Cent 50; Spir 12; Spir.R 12; Wheel IV 168

FATHERS & SONS

Blaming Sons (T'ao Ch'ien—trans Arthur Waley)

White hairs cover my temples
Voi II 96

Digging (Seamus Heaney)

Between my finger and my thumb
Liv 31; Sev 57

Follower (Seamus Heaney)

My father worked with a horse plough
A.S.L.A 25; D.P.R II 4; Sev 53; Six III 18; Them IV 63; Voi III 14

The Man who finds his Son has become a Thief (Raymond Souster)

Coming into the Store at first angry
Bird III 26; Them III 3

A Parental Ode to my Son (Thomas Hood)

Thou happy, happy elf!
Prel I 2; V.F 87; Wheel I 84

To his Son, Vincent Corbet (Bishop Richard Corbet)

What I shall leave thee, none can tell
Fab.C.V 106

FAUNS

The Faun (Ezra Pound)

Ha! sir, I have seen you sniffing and snoozling
Fab.C.V 68

FAWNS

The Fawn in the Show (William Rose Benet)

The brown-dappled fawn
Ark 183; Ox.V.J IV 31

FEAR

Before the Anaesthetic or A Real Fright (Sir John Betjeman)

Intolerably sad, profound
Ten 40

The Bridge of Dread (Edwin Muir)

But when you reach the Bridge of Dread
Liv 34

Fear (Rudyard Kipling)

Ere Mor the Peacock flutters, ere the Monkey People cry
Spo I 124

The Fear (Robert Frost)

A lantern light from deeper in the barn
Ev.M 27

The Rescue (Hal Summers)

The boy climbed up into the tree
*Bird I 18; Chal I 32; Cor 104; Dawn 58;
D.P.R I 42; J.Mod 26; Make I 102; Prel
I 16; Quest V 15; Six VI 62; Song I 64;
Sto I 11; Tell I 10; T.P.R 64*

FEBRUARY

February (James Berry Bensel)

Around, above the world of snow
G.Tr.P 269

February (John Clare)

The milkmaid singing leaves her bed
Wheel I 74

February: a thaw (John Clare)

The snow is gone from cottage tops
D.P.R I 15

FEET

A Portrait of the Foot (John Logan)

At the top of crossed foot branches
Voi I 17

FERNS

The Ferns (Gene Baro)

High, high in the branches
My 119

FERRYMEN

The Ferryman (Christina Rossetti)

Ferry me across the water
*B.P I 15; Cher 9; Ex.Tra 45; Fab.N.V
240; Fuji 77; Go.Jo 11; Mer 107;
Mer.Puf 80; Min III 63; Mood I 24;
Ox.V.J I 16; P.Life I 58; Tree II 52*

The Jolly Young Waterman
(Charles Dibdin)

And did you not hear of a jolly young
waterman
Plea VII 26

FESTIVALS

See Christmas, Easter, Epiphany,
Guy Fawkes Night, Hallowe'en,
Harvest, Lent, May Day, New Year,
Palm Sunday

FIDDLES

See Violins

FIDDLERS

The Fiddler of Dooney (W. B. Yeats)

When I play on my fiddle in Dooney
*A.D.L 127; Ex.Ch 154; Fab.C.V 41;
Fun II 25; Mood IV 10; Ox.V.J II 26;
P.F.P I 86; P.Life III 42; Riv II 33; R.R
167; Sphe 258; Spo I 166; Sto I 59;
Them VI 18; Yea.Run 47*

FIFES

See Drums

FIGHTING

The Combat (Edwin Muir)

It was not meant for human eyes
Sev 44; T.C.N 136; Ten 113

David and Goliath (Bible—I
Samuel xvii)

And it came to pass when the Philistine
arose
Ch.Gar 111; M.M.A 39

Emperors of the Island (Dannie
Abse)

There is a story of a deserted island
Dawn 87; Day 99; Shad 70

*The Fox-coloured Pheasant enjoyed
his Peace* (Peter Levi S. J.)

The fox-coloured pheasant enjoyed his
peace
Dawn 36; Make IV 201

Johnny Wayne and Randy Scott
(Robert Service)

Johnny Wayne and Randy Scott
Mood II 44

FINANCIERS

Thrushes (Humbert Wolfe)

The City Financier
B.P II 49; Drag 39; Man II 24; Ox.V.J III 29; P.Life III 72; Six III 34; Song I 5

FINGERS

An Exchange between the Fingers and the Toes (John Fuller)

Fingers: Cramped, you are hardly anything but fidgets
Quest V 8; Sev 74

FIRE

See also London, Great Fire of

FIRE (LYRIC & DESCRIPTIVE)

Fire Down Below (Anon)

Fire in the galley, fire down below
Mer 179; Mer.Puf 138; P.Life III 65; Puf.S.B 123; Rain 19; Rhyme II 6; Tree I 22

Fire (Riddle) (Anglo-Saxon—trans K. Crossley-Holland)

On earth there's a warrior of curious origin
Rid 21

Incendiary (Vernon Scannell)

That one small boy with a face like pallid cheese
Chal III 43; Prel II 36

FIRE (NARRATIVE)

A Fire in London, 1715 (John Gay)

But hark! distress with screaming voice draws nigh'r
Iron II 4; R.R 64; Say 84

The Progress of the Fire (Michael ? Baldwin ? Jesse)

John struck a match or two, then tossed them away
Quest V 73; Tell I 75

The Smithfield Market Fire (Fred Dallas)

The coldest day in all the year
Weal I 84

The Streets of Laredo (Louis MacNiece)

O early one morning I walked out like Agag
Cher 309; Fla 111; Mod.P 36; Ris 112

FIREFLIES

Fireflies in the Garden (Robert Frost)

Here come real stars to fill the upper skies
A.D.L 267; Ark 62; F.Feet 149; Fro.You 46

The Firefly (part) (Samuel Rogers)

There is an Insect that, when Evening comes
Say 60

FIREMEN

See Enginedrivers

FIREMEN (FIRE FIGHTING)

The Firemen's Ball (part) (Vachel Lindsay)

Give the engines room
Mood II 5; Riv II 99

A Fire-Truck (Richard Wilbur)

Right down the shocked street with a siren-blast
Voi II 17

Homage to Wren (Louis MacNiece)

At sea in the dome of St Paul's
Under 73

FIREWOOD

Buying Fuel (Richard Church)

Now I come to the farmer about some logs
Six V 56

The Wood Fire (Anon)

Beechwood fires are bright and clear
Scrap 38

FIREWORKS

See also Guy Fawkes Night

Fireworks (James Reeves)

They rise like sudden fiery flowers
B.L.J III 6; Dan 27; P.Life II 56; Puf.Q
59; Quest II 47; Six I 18; Sto II 77;
T.P.W 102

Fireworks at the Redentore (Rob
Lyle)

The clouds have sprouted orange leaves
Act I 29

Fourth of July Night (Carl
Sandburg)

The little boat at anchor
Dan 28

FIRS

Fir Wood (John Clare)

The fir-trees taper into twigs and wear
Cla.Wo 32

FISHERMEN

See also Fishing, Smugglers

The Cleggan Disaster (Richard
Murphy)

Five boats were shooting their nets in the
bay
Make IV 29; Nar 95

Fishermen (Elizabeth Jennings)

This is to be peace, they think beside the
river
Sev 15

The Fisher's Life (Anon)

What joy attends the fisher's life
Cher 219

I Sit up Here (Robert Louis
Stevenson)

I sit up here at midnight
Ste.Ho 30

Morning Herring (Naomi
Mitchison)

It will be morning soon
Ox.V.J IV 86

The Night Fishing (part)
(W. S. Graham)

We are at the hauling then hoping for it
Fla 143; Flock 48

Nile Fishermen (Rex Warner)

Naked men, fishing in Nile without a
licence
Ev.M 23; Under 112

Off Brighton Pier (Alan Ross)

I saw him, a squat man with red hair
Sto III 78

The Stone Fisherman (Bertolt
Brecht—trans H. R. Hays)

The big fisherman has appeared again.
He sits in his rotted
D.P.R II 53

Three Fishers (Charles Kingsley)

Three fishers went sailing out into the
West
Song I 113; Spir 71

Uncle Roderick (Norman MacCaig)

His drifter swung in the night
Mod.P 180

FISHES & SEA CREATURES

See also Aquaria

See also Anemones (Sea), Crabs,
Dolphins, Flying Fish, Goldfish,
Jellyfish, Kraken, Lobsters, Min-
nows, Octopi, Oysters, Pike,
Salmon, Sea Monsters, Sharks,
Skates, Trout, Turtles, Whales

Alas, Alack! (Walter de la Mare)

Ann, Ann!/Come! quick as you can!
De la M.Col 227; De la M.P.P 10; De la
M.S 87; Fab.N.V 64; First III 32; Fun I
75; Mer 88; Peg I 99; Tree I 59

Allie (Robert Graves)

Allie, call the birds in
B.P II 30; Dawn 46; Go.Jo 81; Mer 252;

Mer.Puf 185; Ox.V.J I 50; Pat 64; T.P.W 62; Tree IV 26

The Ballad of Kon-Tiki (part) (Ian Serraillier)

Then did ocean
P.Life IV 58

They were not lonely. They found the sea
Ser.B 99

The Best of Fishes in my Flood (William Browne)

The best of fishes in my flood
Shep 128

The Fish (parts) (Rupert Brooke)

In a cool curving world he lies
Ark 148

Those silent waters weave for him
Peg III 39

Fish (John Donne)

Is any kind subject to rape like fish?
R.R 173

The Fish (Marianne Moore)

wade/through black jade
Pers 132

Fishes' Heaven or
Heaven (Rupert Brooke)

Fish fly-replete in depth of June
A.D.L 167; By 259; D.P IV 30; Pat 43; Plea VI 65; Quest IV 50; Wheel I 147

The Flattered Flying Fish (E. V. Rieu)

Said the Shark to the Flying Fish over the phone
B.P III 31; Chal I 66; Make I 121; Min III 38; Puf.Q 122; Quest II 73; Six VI 56; Sto I 35; T.P.W 74

The Great Sea Cucumber (Gene Baro)

What is the power/of the Great Sea Cucumber
Peng.An 130

The Hideaway Fish (E. Jennings)

A fish I knew who was so shy
Say 20

Leaves of Grass (part) (Walt Whitman)

Sea-water and all living below it
Act I 96

The Rime of the Ancient Mariner (part) (S. T. Coleridge)
The Water Snakes

Beyond the shadow of the ship
Act II 86; D.P III 67; D.P.R III 51; Fab.C.V 310; P.Bk 168; P.F.P II 172; P.Life IV 56; P.W 166; P.W.R 188; Riv IV 160; Weal II 77

St Brendan and the Fishes (Ian Serraillier)

St Brendan chanted Mass in voyage
Ser.B 60; Tell I 32

FISHING

See also Herring, Lobsters, Shrimping, Whaling

Ballade to a Fish of the Brooke (John Wolcot)

Why flyest thou away with fear?
R.R 174; Voi II 41

The Boy Fishing (E. J. Scovell)

I am cold and alone
Bird I 3; Bits grey; B.L.J III 3; Cor 10; Drag 11; F.Feet 146; Key III 46; Make II 20; M.Ver 119; My 150; Ox.V.J III 37; Prel II 22; Quest III 10; Sto I 79; Them V 31; This W.D 14; Way 80

Catching a Fish (D. H. Lawrence)

I have waited long with a rod
Them V 32; Yim I 49

The Fish (Elizabeth Bishop)

I caught a tremendous fish
Cor 96; Day 129; Go.Jo 67; G.Tr.P 128; Peg III 40; Peng.An 114; Shep 120; Voi II 45

The Fisher (William Renton)

The fisher is holding his handle-net
Weal II 126

Fisherman's Lore (Anon)

When the wind is in the east
Ex.Tra 58; Fab.N.V 230; Fun II 111;

79

G.Tr.P 23; M.G.B 152; M.G.E 14; M.G.R 91; Ox.N.R 117; P.Life II 52; Puf.V 166

When the wind is in the north
Tree I 27

The Giant Crab (John Walsh)

Along the steep wall at the old pier's side
Them V 32

How to catch Tiddlers (Brian Jones)

Watch that net drift. Grey tides
Flock 55

The Lady and the Bear (Theodore Roethke)

A Lady came to a Bear by a Stream
Go.Jo 151; J.Mod 52; Quest II 75; V.F 129; Voi I 95

Rural Sports (part) (John Gay)

If an enormous salmon chance to spy
Peng.An 269

FISHMONGERS

Cockles and Mussels (Anon)

In Dublin's fair city, where the girls are so pretty
P.Life III 68; Puf.S.B 67

Miss Thompson goes shopping (Martin Armstrong)

A little further down the way
P.F.P I 45

FITTERS

The Fitters Song (Ewan MacColl)

I am a roving rambler, a fitter to me trade
Song II 26

FLEAS

The —— (A. P. Herbert)

I never know why it should be
V.F 74

FLIES

The Blue-Tailed Fly (American Anon)

When I was young I used to wait
F.S.N.A 505; R.R 176

The Fly (Walter de la Mare)

How large unto the tiny fly
B.B.F 118; By 228; De la M.Ch 37; De la M.Col 74; De la M.S 59; D.P.R I 6; Ex.H 19; F.Feet 186; First III 44; Ox.V.J I 56; Peng.An 119; Plea II 41; Quest II 4; Shep I 38; Start 9; Tree I 61; Way 30

The Fly (William Blake)

Little Fly/The summer's play
B.B.F 122; G.Tr.P 81; Ox.P.C 130; Peng.An 118

The Fly (Miroslav Holub—trans I. Milner & G. Theiner)

She sat on a willow-trunk/watching
Comp 56

The Fly (Gerry Gilbert)

The small green fly with long wings settled
Comp 57

The Spider and the Fly (Anon)

'Will you walk into my parlour?'
Ex.Tra 26; M.G.E 151; Tree II 68

FLODDEN

The Battle of Flodden (part) (Sir Walter Scott)

By this, though deep the evening fell
Kal 93

The Flowers of the Forest (Jean Elliot)

I've heard them lilting at our yowe-milking
Fab.C.V 269; Plea VII 25; Song IV 66

Marmion (part) (Sir Walter Scott)

But as they left the dark'ning heath
Spo II 130; Trea 208

FLOOD, THE

See Noah

FLOODS

February Floods 1953 (Jenny Joseph)

Those who saw where far inland
Sev 42

The Flood (John Dryden—after Ovid)

Th'expanded waters gather on the plain
Cher 203

The High Tide on the Coast of Lincolnshire, 1571

The old mayor climbed the belfry tower
P.Bk 210; P.Tong I 135; P.W 201; Rhyme IV 30; Riv III 99; Spir 150; Spir.R 112

Twentieth Century Flood (Alison Bielski)

When the rain started to fall it was Wednesday
Prel II 17

FLOWERS

See also Anemones, Celandines, Daffodils, Dahlias, Daisies, Dandelions, Evening Primroses, Gentians, Lad's Love, Lupins, Nettles, Primroses, Ragwort, Snowdrops, Sweet Peas, Thistles

The Flower Market (Po Chu-I—trans Arthur Waley)

In the Royal City spring is almost over
Act II 32

Flowers by the Sea (William Carlos Williams)

When over the flowery sharp pastures
Go.Jo 86

Lycidas (part) (John Milton)

And call the vales, and bid them hither cast
Weal II 20

Planting Flowers on the Eastern Embankment (Po Chu-I)

I took money and bought flowering trees
Act I 103

The Question (Percy Bysshe Shelley)

I dreamed that, as I wandered by the way
By 128; Shep 58

The Wild-Flower Nosegay (part) (John Clare)

From the sweet time that spring's young thrills are born
Com 52

Flowers (William Shakespeare)

Here's flowers for you
Winter's Tale IV iii 103; Bat 72

Now, my fair'st friend
Winter's Tale IV iii 111; Cher 249

FLYCATCHERS

The Flycatcher (Sylvia Lynd)

That is the flycatcher's wing beneath the eaves
Key IV 69

FLYING

The Old Pilot's Death (Donald Hall)

He discovers himself on an old airfield
D.P.R II 50; Mod.P 142

On the Wings of the Morning (Jeffery Day)

A sudden roar, a mighty rushing sound
Sto III 53

Take-off (Geoffrey Parsons)

Throttle is open, nose in wind, stick just back from central
Sto III 52

FLYING FISH

The Flying Fish (John Gay)

Of the birds that fly in the farthest sea
Cher 213

FOG

See also Mist

Fog (Frances Horner)

Curling and writhing, slowly
Dan 32

Fog (Carl Sandburg)

The fog comes/on little cat feet
A.S.L.A 55; Bits grey; Dan 32; D.P.R I 18; Drag 34; Ev.M 43; Flock 266; G.Tr.P 255; Mood IV 43; Read I 132; Voi I 124; Way 75

Fog (Crosbie Garstin)

Over the oily swell it heaved, it rolled
Peg III 31; R.R 38; Song III 125

Fog (Tony Jardine)

The swirling fog
Ev.M 43

The Fog (W. H. Davies)

I saw the fog grow thick
B.L.J III 5; D.P III 93; D.P.R I 17; J.Vo III 98; Key IV 128; Make I 58; Man I 61; Peg I 103; P.Life IV 28; Song III 126; Ver II 199

The Fog (F. R. McCreary)

Slowly the fog/hunch shouldered with a gray face
Drag 34

November (parts) (John Clare)

The landscape sleeps in mist from morn till noon
Com 65; Flock 266

The shepards almost wonder where they dwell
Bat 14; Cla.Wo 35; G.Tr.P 282; Prel III 34; R.R 88; Sphe 36

The timid hare seems half its fears to lose
B.B.F 71

The Prelude (part) (William Wordsworth)
A Dripping Fog

It was a close, warm, breezeless summer night
Act I 34

Ship in Fog (James Kirkup)

A suffocating room
Shep 37

FOOD

See also Apple Pies, Baking, Bread, Breakfast, Drinking, Drinks, Fruits, Honey, Ice Cream, Meals, Nuts, Soup

Don't ask for Bread or *One Fishball* (Anon)

A wretched man walked up and down
Tell I 121

Eating Bamboo Shoots (Po Chu-I—trans Arthur Waley)

My new province is a land of bamboo-groves
Act I 78

Figgie Hobbin (Charles Causley)

Nightingales' tongues, your majesty?
Cau.Fig 26

Fish and Chips (A. Elliott-Cannon)

Fish and chips today for tea
Man I 60

Food and Drink (Louis Untermeyer)

Why has our poetry eschewed
Peg V 29

Food, Glorious Food (Lionel Bart)

Is it worth the waiting for?
Prel IV 17

Homely Meats (John Davies)

If there were, oh! an Hellespont of cream
Fab.C.V 109

Hot Cake (Shu Hsi)

Winter is come; fierce is the cold
Act I 76; A.D.L 101; Flock 280; Iron III 82; Prel IV 24

Miss T (Walter de la Mare)

It's a very odd thing
De la M.Ch 63; De la M.Col 234; De la M.P.P 30; De la M.S 42; Go.Jo 22; Iron I 19; J.Vo I 22; Riv I 81; Tree II 23; V.F 52

The National English Meal (Linda Hughes—aged 14)

The taste of fresh-fried filleted fish
Man I 68; Song II 32

The Pancake (Christina Rossetti)

Mix a pancake/Stir a pancake
First I 18; Ox.V J I 11

Robbin the Bobbin (variants) (Anon)

Robin the Bobbin, the big-bellied Ben
*B.L.J I 9; Fab.N.V 59; M.G.B 101;
Ox.Dic 372; Ox.N.R 84; Tree II 12*

Robin and Bobbin, two big-bellied men,
Puf.N.R 133

FOOTBALL

The Game (Dannie Abse)

Follow the crowds to where the turnstiles click
J.Mod 121; Sto III 73; Them V 4

Men on the Terraces (Gordon Jeffery)

Rain fell sadly throughout the match
Sto III 74

Rhythm (Iain Crichton Smith)

They dunno how it is. I smack a ball
Mod.P 169; Prel II 6; Sev 16

Stanley Matthews (Alan Ross)

Not often *con brio*, but *andante, andante*
Day 89; Them V 5

FOOTPATHS

See Paths

FORESTS

See Trees, Woods

FOWLERS

The Fowler (John Clare)

With boots of monstrous leg and massy strength
Them VII 29

The Wicked Fowler (Patric Dickinson)

The wicked fowler took his gun
T.C.N 106

FOXES

The Cock and the Fox
(G. Chaucer—trans F. E. Hill)

Once, long ago, set close beside a wood
D.P II 22; D.P.R II 15

A yard she had enclosed al aboute
(simplified A. Burrell)
P.Bk 324

The False Fox (Anon)
The false fox came unto our croft
Cher 113

A Fellow Mortal (John Masefield)
I found a fox caught by the leg
Tell I 26

The Fox (C. Day Lewis)
'Look, it's a fox!'—their two hearts spoke
Drag 27

The Fox (John Clare)
The shepherd on his journey heard when nigh
Make I 105; Read I 142; Tell I 22; Voi I 107

The Fox and the Goose (Anon)

It fell again the next night
B.B.F 57

A Fox came into my Garden
(Charles Causley)

A fox came into my garden
Cau.Fig 17

A Fox jumped up (variants) (Anon)

A fox jumped up on a moon light night
*Bal 749; B.B 174; B.L.J II 13; Down 15;
D.P.I 17; Ex.H 50; Fun I 100; G.Tr.P
32; J.Vo I 62; Key II 117; Mer 109;
M.G.B 206; M.G.R 146; Min III 44;
Mood I 86; My 57; Ox.Dic 173; Ox.N.R
190; Ox.P.C 114; P.F.P I 52; P.Life III
88; Puf.V 50; Rain 26; Tree III 18*

Reynard the Fox (John Masefield)

The fox raced on, up the Barton Balks
Read II 84

For a minute he ran and heard no sound
T.C.N 99

The Fox knew well as he ran in the dark
Ver III 225

The fox was strong he was full of running
Kal 11; Peng.An 119; Rhyme IV 111; Them I 63

From the Gallows Hill to Tineton Copse
P.Tong II 26

And here as he ran to the huntsman's yelling
M.M.A 50

On Ghost Heath turf was a steady drumming
Rain 62

On old Cold Crendon's windy tops
Ark 51

The pure clean air came sweet to his lungs
D.P IV 41; D.P.R IV 21; Spo I 44

The Three Foxes (A. A. Milne)

Once upon a time there were three little foxes
B.P I 47; Fab.N.V 90; Go.Jo 12; Mil.V.Y 38; Min I 70

The Vixen (John Clare)

Among the taller wood with ivy hung
B.B.F 94; B.L.J IV 52; Cla.Wo 80; Eye 6; Kal 12; Make I 126; Tree III 37

FRANCE

See Napoleon

FREEDOM

Robert the Bruce to his Army (John Barbour)

Ah! Freedom is a noble thing!
Fab.C.V 142

Warning (Jenny Joseph)

When I am an old woman I shall wear purple
Mod.P 144

FREEDOM SONGS

Battle-Hymn of the Republic (Julia Ward Howe)

Mine eyes have seen the glory of the coming of the Lord
G.Tr.P 311

Go Down, Moses
(American—Anon)

Go down Moses
B.L.A.F 372; J.Vo IV 35; Riv II 49

If I had a Hammer (Lee Hays & Pete Seeger)

If I had a hammer
Man I 67; Song I 3

Many Thousands Gone (Anon)

No more auction block for me
F.S.N.A 455

Midway (Naomi Long Madgett)

I've come this far to freedom and I won't turn back
Chal III 32

We Shall Overcome (Anon)

We shall overcome, we shall overcome
Dan 118; Song III 109

FROGS

See also Bullfrogs

Death of a Naturalist (Seamus Heaney)

All the year the flax-dam festered in the heart
D.P.R IV 36; Yim II 70

The Frog (Hilaire Belloc)

Be kind and tender to the frog
Bel.C.V 108; Fab.N.V 77; F.Feet 113; Go.Jo 10; Mood II 58; Rhyme IV 28; Sphe 220

The Frog (Anon)

What a wonderful bird the frog are
B.B.F 191; Drag 22; J.Vo III 14; Sphe 220

The Frog and the Crow (Anon)

A jolly fat frog did in the river swim, O
Mer 182; Mer.Puf 140

The Frog and the Mouse or *A Frog he would a wooing go* or *The Marriage of the Frog and the Mouse* (and variants) (Anon)

A frog he would a-wooing go

Ark 64; Ex.Tra 30; Fab.N.V 114; Fun I 97; G.Tr.P 19; Mer 24; Mer.Puf 23; M.G.B 112; M.G.R 93; Min I 86; Ox.Dic 177; Ox.N.R 172; Plea II 42; P.Life I 37; Puf.S.B 104; Rhyme I 25; Tree III 60

Frogs (Norman MacCaig)

Frogs sit more solid
Voi III 11

FRONTIERS

At the Great Wall of China (Edmund Blunden)

Perched in a tower of this ancestral wall
M.Ver 133

Under the Frontier Post (Wang Chang-Ling—trans Rewi Alley)

We cross a stream and my horse
Cher 340

War (Li Po—trans Rewi Alley)

Last year the war was in the northeast
Cher 341

FROST & ICE

See also Skating, Winter

A Frosty Day (John Leicester Warren, Lord de Tabley)

Grass afield wears silver thatch
Shep 43

A Frosty Night (Philip Callow)

All night the constellations sang
Act III 49

The Frozen Thames (John Gay)

Then hoary Thames, with frosted oziers crowned
Key IV 71

Hard Frost (Andrew Young)

Frost called to water 'Halt!'
Drag 11; Key IV 73; Look 15; Pat 18; Prel III 39; Six I 28; Ten 168; Voi I 124; You.Qu 5

Ice (Walter de la Mare)

The North Wind sighed
De La M.Ch 53; De La M.Col 167;

Ex.Ch 32; Min IV 17; P.Life IV 30; Under 91

The Ice-Cart (Wilfrid Wilson Gibson)

Perched on my city office stool
D.P IV 77; D.P.R IV 45; Look 164; Mood IV 112; Peg II 2; P.F.P II 41; Spir 42; Spir.R 35; Spo I 115; Ver II 45; Wheel II 139

Ice-Storm in Cincinnati (John Press)

The ice-storm littered roads with red-hot wires
Quest II 52

Snow (Apocrypha—Ecclesiasticus xliii 18)

The eye marvels at the beauty of its whiteness
Prel III 40

FRUITS

See also Apples, Bananas, Blackberries, Blueberries, Lychees, Peaches, Pears

Goblin Market (parts) (Christina Rossetti)

Morning and evening
Min IV 37; P.Bk 185; P.F.P II 198; Plea V 82; Rhyme III 56

Come and buy our orchard fruits
Weal I 3

In the Street of the Fruit Stalls (John Stalworthy)

Wicks balance flame, a dark dew falls
Cent 105; Prel IV 21

FRUSTRATION

You and Me and P. B. Shelley (Ogden Nash)

What is life? Life is stepping down a step or sitting in a chair
Song IV 129

FUNERALS

Aunt Abigail (Ada Jackson)

Aunt Abigail was practical
D.P.R IV 139

The Choirmaster's Burial (Thomas Hardy)

He often would ask us
Look 124; T.C.N 56; Ten 99; Them II 10; Voi II 154

There's been a Death (Emily Dickinson)

There's been a Death in the Opposite House
Voi III 104

FUSCHIAS

Fuschias (John Pudney)

Unspellable, unsmellable,
Peg V 24

GAMEKEEPERS

The Gallows (Edward Thomas)

There was a weasel lived in the sun
Bird IV 52; Cor 144; D.P.R III 25; Drag 14; Iron IV 53; Key III 144; Liv 138; Make IV 198; Mood IV 80; M.Ver 70; Pat 176; Plea VII 37; Read II 100; Tho.Gr 44; Voi I 74; Wheel III 143

The Keeper (Anon)

The keeper did a-shooting go
Mer 118; Mer.Puf 88; P.Life III 50

Malefactors (Edmund Blunden)

Nailed to these green laths long ago
Them I 28

GAMES

See also Basketball, Blind Man's Buff, Bouncing Balls, Cricket, Football (Soccer), Golf, Hide and Seek, Marbles, Rugby

Confessions of a Born Spectator (Ogden Nash)

One infant grows up and becomes a jockey
Them V 69

Lines and Squares (A. A. Milne)

Whenever I walk in a London street
Fab.N.V 18; Mil.V.Y 12

The Old Man's Toes (Eleanor Farjeon)

Up the street/down the street
Fab.N.V 20

Those were the Games! (R. N. Currey)

Now that our fertile acres yield
Them V 60

GARDENERS

The Broken-Hearted Gardener (Anon)

I'm a broken-hearted Gardener and don't know what to do
Cher 271

GARDENING

See also Digging, Sowing, Transplanting

The Garden Hose (Beatrice Janosco)

In the grey evening
J.Vo III 22

GARDENS

Appleton House (part) (Andrew Marvell)

See how the flowers as at parade
Pat 42; Wheel III 78

The Garden (parts) (Andrew Marvell)

How vainly men themselves amaze
By 79; P.W 108

What wond'rous life is this I lead
Cher 268

Oh thou, that dear and happy isle
P.Tong II 93

Kitchen Garden (Christopher Hassall)

There is no moving water in this garden
Com 61

Old Shellover (Walter de la Mare)

'Come!' said old Shellover
B.B.F 106; Com 46; De la M.Ch 125; De la M.Col 211; De la M.P.P 20; De la M.S 74; Key I 33; Mer 209; Plea II 63; Riv I 15; Song II 56

GEESE

The Farmer's Goose (Jonathan Swift)

The farmer's goose, who in the stubble
Key III 51

The Goose (Alfred Lord Tennyson)

I knew an old wife lean and poor
Key II 118; Ox.V.J. III 44; Sto I 127

Something told the Wild Geese (Rachel Field)

Something told the wild geese
Chal I 28; Cor 148; My 114; Rhyme IV 13; T.P.W 87

The Wild Geese (Lu Kuei Meng)

From South to North, how long is the way
T.P.R 71

GENERALS

See Hannibal, Napoleon, Wellington

GENTIANS

Bavarian Gentians
(D. H. Lawrence)

Not every man has gentians in his house
Camb 82; Choice 198; Fab.C.V 54; Go.Jo 84; Law.S 101; Liv 94; Man I 25; Peg V 25; Pers 115

GETTING UP

What You should do each Morning (Brian Patten)

At last it cannot matter
A.S.L.A 33

GHOSTS (LYRIC & DESCRIPTIVE)

See also Isle *79–91*, Shad *throughout*

See also Mystery

The Call (Charlotte Mew)

From our low seat beside the fire
Act III 45; Man III 27; Ox.V.J IV 92

The Garden Seat (Thomas Hardy)

Its former green is blue and thin
Go.Jo 237; Har.Ch 85; Shad 31; Wheel I 124

The Ghost's Lament or
Wae's Me (Anon)

Wae's me, wae's me! *or* Woe's me, woe's me!
B.P III 70; Bun 84; Cher 155; Com 140; Fab.C.V 228; Mer 346; Mer.Puf 263; M.M.A 44; Ox.P.C 156; Peg II 69; Plea V 48; Puf.V 186; Riv I 33; Shad 53; Start 102; Tree III 55

hist whist (e. e. cummings)

hist whist
Dan 104; Fab.N.V 204; Mer 113; Mer.Puf 84; M.G.B 145

The House of Ghosts (Humbert Wolfe)

First to describe the house
Kal 63; Them II 3

No Room for Ghosts (Laurence Lerner)

This house has no room for ghosts
Them II 5

Something Tapped (Thomas Hardy)

Something tapped on the pane of my room
Them II 17

Song (from *Ruddigore*)
(W. S. Gilbert)

When the nightwind howls in the chimney cowls
Yim II 4

The Strange House (Thomas Hardy)

I hear the piano playing
Under 126

Tom (Osbert Sitwell)

The farmhand Tom, with his apple and turnip face
Cor 34; Dawn 49

For clanking and lank
Ox.V.J III 78

The Unseen Housemate (Wilfrid Gibson)

A shuffling step across the upper floor
Them II 5

Which? (Walter de la Mare)

'What did you say?'
J.Vo II 29

The Wicked Hawthorn Tree (W. B. Yeats)

First Attendant: O, but I saw a solemn sight
Shad 51

GHOSTS (NARRATIVE)

The Alice Jean (Robert Graves)

One moonlight night a ship drove in
Drag 56; J.Vo I 31; Shad 40; Them II 7

A Chilly Night (Christina Rossetti)

I rose at the dead of night
Vic 168

Colonel Fazackerley (Charles Causley)

Colonel Fazackerley Butterworth-Toast
Cau.Fig 50

Daniel Webster's Horses (Elizabeth Coatsworth)

If when the wind blows
Shad 56

Dicky (Robert Graves)

Mother: O what a heavy sigh
Exp VIII 4; Make II 50; Shad 29; Them II 8

The Fakenham Ghost (Robert Bloomfield)

The lawns were dry in Euston Park
Com 140; Rain 39

The False Knight and the Wee Boy or

The False Knight upon the Road or *Meet-on-the-Road* (Anon)

O whare are ye gaun?
B.P I 70; Bun 84; Fab.C.V 105; Kal 44; Key IV 92; M.M.A 30; Ox.V.J II 33; P.Tong I 99

Now pray where are you going, child? said Meet-on-the-Road
Bird I 10; Ex.H 29; Mer 122; Mer.Puf 92; Ox.P.C 84; P.F.P I 56; Puf.V 205; Shad 18; Tree IV 116

The knight met a child in the road
Bird I 9

The Ghost's Walk (John Kendall)

They came with lorries, they came with vans
M.M.A 32

A Lincolnshire Tale (Sir John Betjeman)

Kirkby with Muckby-cum-Sparrowby-cum-Spinx
Cent 67; Nar 7; T.C.N 125

Miller's End (Charles Causley)

When we moved to Miller's End
Cau.Fig 81

Miss Bailey's Ghost (Anon)

A captain bold, in Halifax, who dwelt in country quarters
B.B 34; Fab.Bal 194

The Morning Apparition (Jabez Hughes)

(written at Wallington House, 1719)
All things were hush'd, as noise itself were dead
Comp 82

The Parklands (Stevie Smith)

Through the Parklands, through the Parklands
Ris 94

The Old Wife and the Ghost (James Reeves)

There was an old wife and she lived all alone
B.L.J III 66; Make I 18; Ox.V.J II 35; P.Life II 37; Puf.Q 76; Quest I 78; Shad 80; Tree IV 74

Rafferty Rides Again (T. V. Tierney)

There's a road outback that becomes a track
Act I 70

Still She Sat (Scots—Anon)

A wife was sitting at her reel at night
Cher 132; Cor 48; Fab.C.V 195; J.Vo III 63; Key IV 89; Ox.P.C 86; P.Life IV 45; P.Tong I 3

Sweet William's Ghost (Anon)

There came a ghost to Margret's door
B.B 31

The Two Old Women of Mumbling Hall (James Reeves)

The two old trees on Mumbling Hill
Mood IV 109

The Wife of Usher's Well (Anon)

There lived a wife at Usher's Well
Act I 4; Bal 263; B.B 29; Bird III 14; Bun 37; Cher 134; Fab.Bal 58; Isle 88; Make IV 119; M.M.A 87; Mood IV 107; Ox.V.J IV 93; P.Bk 130; Peg I 92; P.F.P I 145; P.Life IV 48; P.Tong II 166; P.W 2; P.W.R 2; Riv III 63; Shad 36; Song IV 170; Them II 18; Yim I 25

Winter Cockcrow (Wilfrid Gibson)

Slicing swedes/To feed the sheep
Fun II 139

GIANTS

The Faerie Queene (part) (Edmund Spenser)

Therewith the Giant buckled him to fight
D.P III 144; D.P.R III 102

Giant Thunder (James Reeves)

Giant Thunder, striding home
My 120; Pat 182; Quest II 28

Grim (Walter de la Mare)

Beside the blaze, as of forty fires
De la M.Ch 94; De la M.Col 233; De la M.P.P 85; Tree III 51

Gulliver in Lilliput (Alexander Pope)

From his nose/Clouds he blows
Say 18; Tree III 85

In amaze/Lost I gaze
Wheel II 68

Hard Lewis Rock (Isles of Scilly) (Crosbie Garstin)

In ages forgotten/The isles of the west
Tell I 87

In the Orchard (James Stephens)

There was a giant by the orchard wall
J.Vo IV 44

GILBERT, SIR HUMPHREY

Sir Humphrey Gilbert (H. W. Longfellow)

Southward with fleet of ice
P.Bk 246; Spir 65; Spir.R 52

GIPSIES

See Gypsies

GIRAFFES

The Giraffe (Geoffrey Dearmer)

Hide of a leopard and hide of a deer
A.D.L 168; Rain 60; Song I 40; V.F 48; Weal I 12

GIRLS

See also Tales, Cautionary (Belloc)

Adventures of Isabel (Ogden Nash)

Isabel met an enormous bear
A.D.L 24i; All 62; Ex.Ch 78; Fab.N.V 105; Make I 77; Ox.V.J IV 73; P.Life II 10; Quest III 81; Sphe 218; Spir.R 10; T.P.W 96; Yim I 5

An English Girl (W. S. Gilbert)

A wonderful joy our eyes to bless
Sto III 75

Griselda (Eleanor Farjeon)

Griselda is greedy, I'm sorry to say
G.Tr.P 100

Pooh! (Walter de la Mare)

Pretty Miss Apathy
S.D. 141

The Ruined Maid (Thomas Hardy)

O 'Melia, my dear, this does everything crown!
Bat 82

Sally in our Alley (Henry Carey)

Of all the girls that are so smart
By 101; Com 39; Iron III 37; Pat 100; Plea VI 16

GLIDING

In a Sailplane (James Kirkup)

Still as a bird
J.Vo II 13; S.D 116; Sev 123

GNATS

The Gnat (Joseph Beaumont)

One Night all tired with the weary Day
Shep 136

Gnat (Rosalie Moore)

People simper and drawl
G.Tr.P 80

The Gnats (Odette Tchernine)

The gnats are dancing in the sun
My 147

GOATS

The Goat Paths (James Stephens)

The crooked paths/Go every way
Act III 71; A.D.L 53; Ark 55; Bird I 59; D.P IV 31; Ox.V.J II 46

GOBLINS

Goblin Market (Christina Rossetti)

Morning and evening/Maids heard the goblins cry
Min IV 37; P.Bk 185; P.F.P II 198; Plea V 82; Rhyme III 56

Overheard on a Saltmarsh (Harold Munro)

Nymph, nymph, what are your beads?
Go.Jo 227; J.Vo I 16; Look 290; Patch 17; Peg I 94; P.F.P I 110; Quest I 81; This W.D 33; T.P.W 64

GOD

See also Religious Themes

The Indian upon God (W. B. Yeats)

I passed along the water's edge below the humid trees
Yea.Run 27

What Tomas said in a Pub (James Stephens)

I saw God! Do you doubt it?
By 243

GOLDFINCHES

A Goldfinch (Walter de la Mare)

This feather-soft creature
B.B.F 6; B.L.J II 44; De la M.Ch 42; De la M.Col 102; De la M.S 152; Scrap 26

Goldfinches (John Keats)

Sometimes goldfinches one by one will drop
Sto II 101; Tree IV 72

The Hollow Wood (Edward Thomas)

Out in the sun the goldfinch flies
P.F.P I 123

GOLDFISH

Goldfish (Russell Howell)

Orange Shapes
J.Vo I 68

GOLF

Seaside Golf (Sir John Betjeman)

How straight it flew, how long it flew
Make IV 18; Sto III 79; Them V 9

GOLIATH

See David & Goliath

GOODNESS

The Character of a Happy Life (Sir Henry Wotton)

How happy is he born and taught
P.Bk 62; P.F.P II 229; Trea 172

Integer Vitae (Thomas Campion)

The man of life upright
P.F.P II 229; P.W 77; Sphe 376; Trea 172; Wheel II 60

GRACES

Blessing to God (Charles Wesley)

Blessing to God, for ever blest
Rhyme I 52

Grace for a Child (Robert Herrick)

Here a little child I stand
Bat 96; Ch.Gar 147; Fab.C.V 109; Go.Jo 29; Her.Mu 30; My 176; Plea III 54; This W.D 98

Grace (Robert Herrick)

What God gives and what we take
Her.Mu 30; Plea III 55

Two Graces (Anon)

Some hae meat that canna eat
Hurly, hurly, roun the table
Fab.C.V 115

GRANTCHESTER

The Old Vicarage, Grantchester (Rupert Brooke)

Just now the lilac is in bloom
Cent 7; Sto III 44; Weal II 129

Watercolour of Grantchester Meadows (Sylvia Plath)

There, spring lambs jam the sheepfold. In air
Act V 71; Cent 91

GRASSHOPPERS

A Grasshopper (Richard Wilbur)

But for a brief/Moment, a poised minute
Voi I 77

Grasshoppers (John Clare)

Grasshoppers go in many a thrumming spring
B.B.F 119; Iron II 15

GRENVILLE, SIR RICHARD

See Revenge, The

GREYHOUNDS

A Ballad of Master McGrath (Anon)

Eighteen sixty-nine being the date of the year
Fab.Bal 215

The Properties of a Good Greyhound (Dame Juliana Berners)

A greyhound should be headed like a snake
Peng.An 132

To a Black Greyhound (Julian Grenfell)

Singing black in the shining light
A.D.L 177; P.F.P I 93; Rain 59; Sto II 111

GRIEF

The Sick Wife (Chinese—trans Arthur Waley)

She had been ill for years and years
D.P.R III 8

GROWING UP

See also Adolescence

Norfolk (Sir John Betjeman)

How did the devil come? when first attack
Ten 36

The Picnic (John Logan)

It is the picnic with Ruth in the spring
Exp I 40

Nursery Rhyme of Innocence and Experience (Charles Causley)

I had a silver penny
Dawn 30; Go.Jo 170; Hap 32; Read III 143; Weal I 82; Wheel III 197

GULLS

See Sea-Gulls

GUY FAWKES NIGHT

See also Fireworks

After the Fireworks (Vernon Scannell)

Back into the light and warmth
D.P.R IV 110

Anagram for Guy Fawkes Night (Frances Cornford)

Give me crowding children. A front lawn damp
Bird II 1; Key III 44

Gunpowder Plot (Vernon Scannell)

For days these curious cardboard buds have lain
Fla 172; Flock 267; Make IV 173; Mod.P 64; Read II 63; Sto II 78; Them II 58; Voi II 17

Guy Fawkes Day (Charles Causley)

I am the caught, the cooked, the candled man
Voi II 19

Guy Fawkes Day (Anon)

Please remember/The fifth of November
Key II 107

Please to Remember (Walter de la Mare)

Here am I/A poor old Guy
Bird II 2; B.L.J I 11; De la M.Ch 69; De la M.Col 44; De la M.S 132; Ex.Tra 55; Mer 19; Mer.Puf 20; Min III 91; Ox.V.J II 77; P.Life II 55; T.P.W 103; Tree III 26

GYPSIES

All your Fortunes we can tell Ye (Ben Jonson)

Be not frighted with our fashion
Cher 162

Gipsies (John Clare)

The gipsies seek wide sheltering woods again
Cher 164; Cor 145; Man I 52; Rain 97; Rhyme IV 17; S.D 40

The snow falls deep; the forest lies alone
Bird II 14; Cher 165; Key II 102; Speak I 19; Them III 37; Way 29; Wheel II 86

The Gipsy Laddie or
Black Jack Davy or
The Wraggle-Taggle Gypsies (Anon)

Three gipsies stood at the castle gate
All 75; B.P III 83; Key II 100; Mer 246; Mer.Puf 180; Min IV 47; Mood II 69; P.F.P I 51; P.Life IV 22; Riv II 43; This W.D 157

The gypsies they came to my lord Cassiles' yett
Bal 539, 540; Bun 106; Cher 162; D.P II 54; Fab.Bal 72

There were three gypsies a-come to my door
D.P.R II 79; P.Bk 345; Yim I 30

It was late in the night when the Squire came home
Bird II 13; Cor 116; Fab.C.V 173; G.Tr.P 96; Ox.P.C 70; Plea V 37; P.Tong I 72

Black Jack Davy came a-riding through the woods
Bal 543; Song I 15

The Gypsy's Camp (John Clare)

How oft on Sundays, when I'd time to tramp
P.Bk 44

The Gypsy (Ezra Pound)

That was the top of the walk, when he said
This W.D 139

Gypsy Crone (Dorothy Una Ratcliffe)

A gypsy crone banged on our back door
J.Mod 62

The Idlers (Edmund Blunden)

The gypsies lit their fires by the chalk-pit gate anew
Bird II 12; Blu.Mi 24; Hap 34; Key II 104; Ox.V.J IV 41; Them VI 23

Meg Merrilies (John Keats)

Old Meg she was a gipsy
A.D.L 133; Ex.Ch 152; Fab.C.V 117; Fun I 109; Look 64; Mer 293; Min IV 14; Mood II 42; My 88; Ox.P.C 149;

93

This Malefactor (John Pudney)

This malefactor dies how many times a day
Them III 21

To Hang a Man (Ralph Hodgson)

To hang a man
S.D 85; Them III 22

HANNIBAL

Hannibal (Eleanor Farjeon)

Hannibal crossed the Alps!
Ex.H 9; P.Life II 43; Scrap 70

HAPPINESS

Happiness (Carl Sandburg)

I asked the professors who teach the meaning of life to tell me what is happiness
Chal I 76

Pippa's Song (Robert Browning)

The year's at the spring
Chal I 76; Ch.Gar 84; Fuji 98; G.Tr.P 273; Make II 158; P.Bk 58; Plea IV 53; Spo I 99; Sto I 76

Saul (part) (Robert Browning)

Oh the wild joys of living! The leaping from rock to rock
Peg V 20

Song (Abraham Cowley)

The merry waves dance up and down, and play
A.D.L 220

HARDY, THOMAS

Afterwards (Thomas Hardy)

When the Present has latched its postern behind my tremulous stay
Cent 16; Cher 353; Choice 144; Har.Ch 91; Peg V 88; P.Tong II 190; P.W 225; P.W.R 261; Song IV 193; Sphe 450; Ten 98

Birthday Poem for Thomas Hardy (Cecil Day Lewis)

Is it birthday weather for you, dear soul?
Com 154

Thomas Hardy (Walter de la Mare)

Mingled the moonlight with daylight
De la M.Ch 72

Thoughts of Thomas Hardy (Edmund Blunden)

Are you looking for someone, you who come pattering
Blu.Mi 81

HARES

Epitaph on a Hare (William Cowper)

Here lies whom hound did ne'er pursue
Bat 62; B.B.F 143; Ox.P.C 121; Peng.An 138; Puf.V 55; R.R 108; Shep 86

The Hare (Walter de la Mare)

In the black furrow of a field
De la M.Col 214; First III 43; Ox.V.J III 66

Hares at Play (John Clare)

The birds are gone to bed, the cows are still
Ark 44; Cla.Wo 81; Riv II 5

The Hunted Hare (Anon)

By forest as I 'gan fare
B.B.F 78

March Hares (Andrew Young)

I made myself as a tree
Fla 51; M.Ver 73; Prel IV 8; Ten 163; Them I 39

Two Songs of a Fool (W. B. Yeats)

A speckled cat and a tame hare
Act III 96; A.D.L 176; Ark 14; Bat 95; Cor 175; F.Feet 176; Key III 138; Man III 18; Ox.V.J IV 36; Voi I 83; Wheel III 138

I slept on my three-legged stool by the fire
Act III 97; Ark 15; Bat 95; F.Feet 128; Voi I 84

Venus and Adonis (part) (William Shakespeare)

But if thou needs wilt hunt, be ruled by me
R.R 171

And when thou hast on foot the purblind hare
Act I 22; Wheel II 57

Yolp, Yolp, Yolp, Yolp (Anon)

Hark! They cry! I hear by that
Ark 50

HARFLEUR

Henry V before Harfleur (William Shakespeare)

Once more into the breach, dear friends, once more
Henry V III i 1; D.P IV 86; D.P.R IV 64; Song II 111; Sphe 351; Trea 169; Wheel III 60

HARVEST

Exmoor Harvest Song (R. D. Blackmore)

The corn, oh the corn, 'tis the ripening of the corn!
Sto III 133

Harvest Home (Anon)

Harvest home! Harvest home!
Ox.V.J II 55

Watching the Reapers (Po Chu-I—trans Arthur Waley)

Tillers of the earth have few idle months
Act III 140

HARVEST FESTIVALS

Harvest Festival (Peter Mullineaux—aged 13)

Bread, golden, crispy, curled and
Man I 62

HAWKS

The Hawk (George Mackay Brown)

On Sunday the hawk fell on Bigging
Liv 102

The Hawk (Richard Church)

The hawk! He stands on air
Them I 24

The Hawk in the Rain (Ted Hughes)

I drown in the drumming ploughland, I drag up
Pat 56

Hawk Roosting (Ted Hughes)

I sit on top of the wood, my eyes closed
Ark 145; Cent 82; Ev.M 18; Mod.P 81; Peng.An 140; Pers 130; Sev 103; Them I 24; Wheel IV 198

Hurt Hawks (Robinson Jeffers)

The broken pillar of the wing jags from the clotted shoulder
Voi III 143

Tamer and Hawk (Thom Gunn)

I thought I was so tough
Exp III 37

HAYSTACKS

The Haystack (Andrew Young)

Too dense to have a door
Bits b; Cor 144; Dawn 99; Tree III 94; You.Qu 25

HEDGEHOGS

Cat meets Hedgehog (Christopher De Crutz)

Cat sees round prickly ball
A.S.L.A 76

The Hedgehog (John Clare)

The hedgehog hides beneath the rotten hedge
Cla.Wo 76; Read I 142; Voi I 105

Hedgehog (Anthony Thwaite)

Twitching the leaves just where the drainpipe clogs
A.S.L.A 76; Bird II 36; Cor 170; Dawn 64; D.P.R I 7; Drag 52; Hap 17; Make II 81; Sphe 107; Them VII 59; Under 87

The Shepherd's Calendar (part) (John Clare)

The hedgehog, from his hollow root
Ark 78

HENS

See also Cocks

The Clucking Hen (A. Hawkshawe)

'Pray will you take a walk with me
Ex.Tra 24; Fab.N.V 28; Fuji 45; Puf.V 35

The Complete Hen (Elizabeth Coatsworth)

Now and again I like to see
G.Tr.P 66

Hen and Ducklings (Christopher Smart)

The witless hen, disturb'd by causeless fright
B.B.F 56

The Hen and the Carp (Ian Serraillier)

Once in a roostery
A.D.L 222; J.Mod 53; Ox.V.J III 32; P.Life IV 11; Puf.Q 157; Tree IV 24

The Hens (Elizabeth Madox Roberts)

The night was coming very fast
Go.Jo 51; G.Tr.P 66; Say 46

Hen's Nest (John Clare)

Among the orchard weeds from every search
Ark 71

The Poultries (Ogden Nash)

Let's think of eggs
V.F 104

Song of the Battery Hen (Edwin Brock)

We can't grumble about accommodation
D.P.R IV 15; Mod.P 112; Sev 108; Them I 58

HERMITS

The Hermit (Hsü Pên—trans H. H. Hart)

I dwell apart
Flock 85

The Three Hermits (W. B. Yeats)

Three old hermits took the air
Flock 86

HEROD

Innocents' Song (Charles Causley)

Who's that knocking on the window
Dawn 110; D.P.R I 75; Mod.P 102; Sev 50; Shad 19

King Herod and the Cock (Anon)

There was a star in David's land
P.Tong I 152

HERONS

Boy into Heron (Celia Randall)

High on a stilt-raised bed above the reeds
Exp VI 23; J.Mod 138; My 152; Them V 44

The Heron (Vernon Watkins)

The cloud-backed heron will not move
Sphe 210

The Heron (Roger Lindley—aged 11)

He stands in rippling water, alone. The water
Song II 50

The Heron (Theodore Roethke)

The heron stands in water where the swamp
Bird II 45; Chal II 14

HERRING

Morning Herring (Naomi Mitchison)

It will be morning soon
Quest II 34

Net-Hauling Song (Ewan MacColl)

It's busk ye, my lads, get you up on the deck
Song IV 151

Shoals of Herring (Ewan MacColl)

O it was a fine and a pleasant day
Song II 1

HIAWATHA

Hiawatha (parts) (Henry Wadsworth Longfellow)

At the stern sat Hiawatha
Bat 94

By the shores of Gitchee-Gumee
Spo I 126; Wheel I 86

Forth upon the Gitchee-Gumee
Wheel I 96

Give me of your bark, O Birch-Tree!
Spir 106; Spir.R 82; Trea 98; Wheel I 92

Oh the long and dreary winter
Speak II 37

Out of childhood into manhood
D.P I 74; Song I 83

Slowly upward, wavering, gleaming
Spo I 127

This is the dance of Pau-Puk-Keewis
Speak II 98

Then the little Hiawatha
B.P III 52; Look 86; Min IV 64; Puf.V 57

Two good friends had Hiawatha
Mood II 33

When he heard the owls at midnight
B.L.J IV 25

You shall hear how Pau-Puk-Keewis
Wheel II 94

HIDE & SEEK

Hidden (Eleanor Farjeon)

In the green woods the doves all coo
Patch 21

Hide and Seek (Vernon Scannell)

Call out. Yoo-hoo! I'm ready! Come and find me!
A.S.L.A 19; Cor 3; D.P.R III 13; Hap 29; J.Vo IV 70; Prel II 32; Quest III 13; Six II 8; Them V 59; Way 77

HIGHWAYMEN

See also Turpin, Dick

Brennan on the Moor (Anon)

It's of a fearless highwayman a story now I'll tell
B.B 138; Fab.Bal 204; Riv I 20; Song I 82; Sto I 124

'Tis of a fearless Irishman
Bal 745

The Quaker's Meeting (Samuel Lover)

A traveller wended the wilds among
D.P III 136

HIPPOPOTAMI

The Hippopotamus (Hilaire Belloc)

I shoot the hippopotamus
Mer 191; Peg III 45; Plea V 65; Riv I 97; Spir I; Spir.R 1

I had a Hippopotamus (Patrick Barrington)

I had a hippopotamus, I kept him in a shed
Chal II 81; Fab.N.V 181; Key II 60; Rhyme IV 90; Sphe 230; Way 17

HIROSHIMA

Hiroshima (A Schoolchild)

Noon, and a hazy heat
Chal I 37; Dan 118; Ev.M 77; Wheel IV 210

The Monuments of Hiroshima (D. J. Enright)

The roughly estimated ones, who do not sort well with our common phrases
Day 88

No More Hiroshimas (James Kirkup)

At the station exit, my bundle in my hand
Fla 167; Them III 70

HOBOES

See also Tramps

The Big Rock Candy Mountains
(Anon)

One evenin' as the sun went down
*Act II 47; B.L.A.F 278; Cher 280; Iron I
38; Key III 56; Peg II 74; P.W 28;
P.W.R 24; Riv III 121; Weal I 96*

The Dying Hobo

Beside a western tank
Act II 46; Tell I 120

Hard Travellin' (Anon)

I been havin' some hard travellin'
F.S.N.A 435

HOHENLINDEN

Hohenlinden (Thomas Campbell)

On Linden when the sun was low
*Cher 339; Fab.C.V 256; P.Bk 295;
P.F.P II 74; Plea VI 10; Spir 83; Spir.R
64; Trea 26; Weal I 58*

HOLIDAYS

See Seaside

HOLLAND

See Netherlands

HOMES

See Stately Homes

HOMESICKNESS

The Alien (Charles Murray)

In Afric's fabled mountains I have pan-
ned the golden sand
Ver III 242

Homesick Blues (Langston Hughes)

De railroad bridge's
Kal 66

Lament of Hsi-Chun
(Chinese—trans Arthur Waley)

My people have married me
Iron I 28; Riv IV 53

The old Vicarage, Grantchester
(Rupert Brooke)

Just now the lilac is in bloom
Cent 7; Sto III 44; Weal II 129

Psalm 137

By the rivers of Babylon
Kal 66

Sailing Homeward (Chang Fang-
Sheng—trans Arthur Waley)

Cliffs that rise a thousand feet
Fab.C.V 290

The Song of Wawina (James
Devaney)

I did not cry at all
Chal I 81

To S. R. Crockett (Robert Louis
Stevenson)

Blows the wind today, and the sun and
the rain are flying
Peg II 14; Plea VII 66; Puf.V 201

HONEY

Sing a song of Honey (Barbara
Euphan Todd)

Honey from the white rose, honey from
the red
Puf.V 143; Quest I 67

HOPPING

Hoppity (A. A. Milne)

Christopher Robin goes hoppity,
hoppity
Mil.V.Y 60

HORATIUS

Horatius (Lord Macaulay)

Lars Porsena of Clusium
*Fab.C.V 150; P.Bk 281; Plea VII 75;
Riv II 102; Spir 126; Spir.R 96*

HORNS

The Song of Roland (part) (John Masefield)

Roland gripped his horn with might and main
P.W 242

HORSES

See also Ponies, Racehorses, Racing, Riding

HORSES (LYRIC & DESCRIPTIVE)

The Army Horse and the Army Jeep (John Ciardi)

Where do you go when you go to sleep
Quest II 70

At Amberley Wild Brooks (Andrew Young)

Watching the horses stand
Ark 193

At Grass (Philip Larkin)

The eye can hardly pick them out
Dawn 62; Day 96; M.Ver 79; Pat 200; Sphe 105

The Dead Horse (Anon)

They say, old man, your horse will die
Bird I 39

A Gigantic Beauty of a Stallion (part) (Walt Whitman)

A gigantic beauty of a stallion, fresh and responsive to my caresses
B.B.F 22; B.P IV 102; Ox.V.J IV 39; Peg V 18; Them I 7

The Horse (Bible—*Job* xxxix 19)

Hast thou given the horse strength? has thou clothed his neck with thunder?
B.B.F 22; Cher 124; Ch.Gar 50; D.P II 126; D.P.R II 97; G.Tr.P 28; Iron II 15; Peg III 47; Pers 128; P.W 84; P.W.R 83; Riv III 129; Rhyme III 54; Tree IV 19

The Horse (William Shakespeare)

I will not change my horse with any that treads

Henry V III vii 11*; G.Tr.P 28*

The Horse (William Carlos Williams)

The horse moves/Independently
Ark 19

Horses (Ted Hughes)

I climbed through woods in the hour-before-dawn dark
Cent 79; Com 49; Drag 15; Shep 92

Horses (Edwin Muir)

Those lumbering horses in the steady plough
A.D.L 186; Fab.C.V 78; Fla 56; Liv 143; Ten 115

The Horses of Cuchullin (Anon)

What do we see in that Chariot?
B.B.F 19

The Horses of the Sea (Christina Rossetti)

The horses of the sea
B.L.J I 55; First II 20; Go.Jo 42; Ox.V.J II 79; Rain 48; Rhyme II 42; Tree II 27

Horses on the Camargue (Roy Campbell)

In the grey wastes of dread
Ark 153; Dawn 88; Day 134; Liv 58; P.F.P I 129; Plea I 129; Spo II 67; Ver III 260; Wheel III 169

Poor Old Horse (Anon)

My clothing was once of the linsey woolsey fine
All 17; Bird I 40; Iron I 21; Mer 216; Mer.Puf 158; Mood III 60; Riv I 25

Oh! once I lay in a stable, a hunter well and warm
Fun II 76

Once I was clothed in linsey woolsey fine
Ex.Tro 13; P.Tong I 90

Venus and Adonis (part) (William Shakespeare)

Round-hoofed, short-jointed, fetlocks shag and long
B.B.F 23

Imperiously, he leaps, he neighs, he bounds
Peng.An 144; Wheel I 46

HORSES (NARRATIVE)

The Horses (Edwin Muir)

Barely a twelvemonth after
Cent 90; M.Ver 158; Pers 128; Read III 86; R.R 185; Ten 120

How the Sailor Rode the Brumby (Anon)

Act III 104

How they brought the Good News from Ghent to Aix (Robert Browning)

I sprang to the stirrup, and Joris and he
By 169; Down 35; D.P II 83; G.Tr.P 149; Look 95; Make II 126; Min IV 65; Mood II 14; P.Bk 254; Peg II 53; P.Rem 89; Sphe 171; Spir 29; Spir.R 24; Sto I 70; Trea 117; Ver II 23; Weal I 66

HOUSES

Animals' Houses (James Reeves)

Of animals' houses
Puf.Q 75

House Coming Down (Eleanor Farjeon)

They're pulling down the house
Puf.Y 16

Portrait of a House (E. V. Rieu)

The house that we live in was built in a place
Cor 77

HOUSES, LONELY

The Deserted House (Mary Coleridge)

There's no smoke in the chimney
Bat 48; Cor 140; Ex.Tro 93; Fun II 107; Mer 175; Mer.Puf 133; Riv I 4; Song I 138; This W.D 110; Tree III 36

The Haunted House (Thomas Hood)

Unhinged the iron gates half open hung
Them II 3

Home no more home to me (Robert Louis Stevenson)

Home no more home to me, whither must I wander?
Man II 13

House Fear (Robert Frost)

Always—I tell you this they learned—
Look 335

The House of Ghosts (Humbert Wolfe)

First to describe the house. Who has not seen it
Exp.VI 10; Kal 69; Them II 3

The House on the Hill (Edward Arlington Robinson)

They are all gone away
Shep 14

I know some lonely houses (Emily Dickinson)

I know some lonely houses off the road
Iron II 22; J.Mod 44; J.Vo III 73; Key IV 34; Make II 45; Pers 64; P.W.R 246; Shep 142; Them III 5

Lone (Walter de la Mare)

Shrill rang the squeak in the empty house
De la M.S 62

The Old Stone House (Walter de la Mare)

Nothing on the grey roof, nothing on the brown
De la M.Ch 102; De la M.Col 141; De la M.P.P 88; Mood I 64; Riv I 5; Scrap 37; Sphe 424

The Shepherd's Hut (Andrew Young)

The smear of blue peat smoke
Act I 85; B.L.J IV 27; Dawn 48; Wheel II 142; You.Qu 12

The Vacant Farmhouse (Walter de la Mare)

Three gables; clustered chimney stacks; a wall
De la M.Ch 44; M.Ver 38

HOUSEWIVES

Domestic Thoughts in a Bathroom (Bronwen Evans)

After a tired day the cold clean paint
Man II 27

The Housewife's Lament (Anon)

One day I was walking, I heard a complaining
Cor 111; F.S.N.A 133; Read II 10; Them VI 10; Voi I 45

On a Tired Housewife (Anon)

Here lies a poor woman who was always tired
Key III 58; My 91; Sto III 62; Them VI 11; Weal I 9; Wheel I 147

Robin-a-Thrush (Anon)

Oh, Robin-a-Thrush he married a wife
Mer 223; Mer.Puf 165; Rhyme II 34; Tree III 27

Sall Scratch (Charles Causley)

Sall Scratch/Wore her husband's cap
Cau.Fig 22

HOUSEWORK

See also Baking, Butter-Making, Washing Clothes

Sink Song

Scouring out the porridge pot
All 33; A.S.L.A 33; J.Vo III 36; Key II 97; Rhyme III 31

HUMAN RIGHTS

Cage (Bernard Spencer)

The canary measures out its prison
Sev 79; Them III 58

For a'that (Robert Burns)

Is there, for honest poverty
D.P IV 96

The People of Tao-Chou (Po Chu-I—trans Arthur Waley)

In the land of Tao-Chou
Cher 374; Tell II 73

Prayer before Birth (Louis MacNiece)

I am not yet born: O hear me
Com 91; Dan 58; Day 23; D.P.R III

111; Kal 127; Mod.P 43; Peg V 100; Pers 3; S.D 15; Sev 72; Sphe 404; Wheel IV 174

HUMMING BIRDS

Humming-bird (D. H. Lawrence)

I can imagine, in some other world
A.D.L 173; Bird IV 1; Camb 76; Dan 44; Law.S 17; Look 195; Pat 174; Peng.An 150

On an Indian Tomineios, the Least of Birds (Thomas Heyrick)

I'm made in sport by Nature, when
Peng.An 149

HUMP, THE

The Hump (Rudyard Kipling)

The camel's hump is an ugly lump
Ch.Gar 153; Fab.N.V 104; Six VI 10

HUNGER

Lazy Morning (Jacques Prevert—trans Lawrence Ferlinghetti)

Its terrible/the faint sound of a hard-boiled egg cracked on a tin counter
Prel IV 25

HUNTING

See also Beagles, Boar Hunting, Fowlers, Foxes, Gamekeepers, Hares, Shooting, Stags

Drink, Puppy, Drink (G. J. Whyte-Melville)

Here's to the fox in his earth below the rocks
Ch.Gar 60

Eskimo Hunting Song (Eskimo—trans Sir Maurice Bowra)

I wanted to use my weapon
J.Vo II 54

Friar's Hunting Song (Thomas Love Peacock)

Though I be now a gray, gray friar
G.Tr.P 89

The Hunt (Walter de la Mare)

Tally-ho! Tally-ho!—/Echo faints far astray
De la M.Ch 33; De la M.Col 21

The Hunt is up (? William Gray ? Henry VIII)

The hunt is up! The hunt is up!
B.P III 99; Fun II 38; P.Bk 77

Hunting Song (Sir Maurice Bowra)

On the weeping forest, under the wing of the evening
Chal II 72

Hunting Song (Henry Fielding)

The dusky night rides down the sky
Chor 63; Mer 277; Mer.Puf 207; Mood II 65; P.Rem 194; Riv I 48; Trea 17

Hunting Song (Donald Finkel)

The fox he came lolloping, lolloping
Chal I 63; Read II 99

I Saw a Jolly Hunter (Charles Causley)

I saw a jolly hunter
Cau.Fig 14

John Peel (John Woodcock Graves)

D'ye ken John Peel with his coat so gray?
Bat 74; D.P I 102

The Keeper (Anon)

The keeper did a-shooting go
Mer 118; Mer.Puf 88; P.Life III 50

A Moon Man-Hunt (Ted Hughes)

A man-hunt on the moon is full of horrible sights and sounds
Them I 64

Three Jovial Welshmen (Anon)
There were three jovial Welshmen
B.P II 44; D.P I 28; Ex.H 47; Fab.N.V 140; Mer 337; Mer.Puf 256; Min III 93; Mood II 72; Ox.Dic 421; Ox.N.R 161; Ox.P.C 24; Plea III 14; P.Life III 48; P.Rem 31; P.Tong I 155; Puf.V 162; Puf.Y 156; Riv I 22; Tree III 62

There were three jovial huntsmen
G.Tr.P 216; M.G.B 198; My 17; Ox.V.J I 61

Vice Versa (C. Morgenstern—trans R. F. C. Hill)

The rabbit sits upon the green
Ark 36

Waken, Lords and Ladies gay (Sir Walter Scott)

Waken, lords and ladies gay
Fun II 37

ICARUS

Icarus (R. Bottrall)

In his father's face flying
Exp VII 12

ICE

See Frost & Ice, Winter

ICEBERGS

Iceberg (Riddle) (Anglo-Saxon—trans K. Crossley-Holland)

A curious, fair creature, came floating on the waves
Rid 39

ICE-CREAM

Tableau at Twilight (Ogden Nash)

I sit in the dusk, I am all alone
Look 75

ILLNESS

Being Visited by a Friend during Illness (Po Chu-I—trans Arthur Waley)

I have been ill so long that I do not count the days
Act III 82

The Sniffle (Ogden Nash)

In spite of her sniffle
Chal II 84; Ox.V.J II 97; Six III 29; Weal II 15

The Sniffle (Christian Morgenstern—trans Max Knight)

A sniffle crouches on the terrace
J.Vo II 79

The Watch (Frances Cornford)

I wakened on my hot, hard bed
S.D 83

IMAGINATION, CHILDREN'S

Boy into Heron (Celia Randall)

High on a stilt-raised bed above the reeds
Exp VI 23; J.Mod 138; My 152; Them V 44

Busy (A. A. Milne)

I think I am a muffin man. I haven't got a bell
Mil.N.S 7

The Centaur (May Swenson)

The summer that I was ten—
Peng.An 60

A Child's Garden (George Macbeth)

Who was here. Before his cat
Them IV 3

Digging for China (Richard Wilbur)

'Far enough down is China,' somebody said
Go.Jo 224; Look 324; Them II 54; T.P.W 10; Voi I 56

The Door (Miroslav Holub—trans Ian Milner)

Go and open the door
J.Vo IV 2; Nev 36

Down the Glimmering Staircase (Siegfried Sassoon)

Down the glimmering staircase, past the pensive clock
J.Mod 72

The Hero (Gordon Gridley)

Young Jimmy Stone lived a life of his own
Start 86

The Land of Story-Books (Robert Louis Stevenson)

At evening when the lamp is lit
Ste.C.G 83

My Kingdom (Robert Louis Stevenson)

Down by a shining water well
Ste.C.G 76

The Secret Brother (Elizabeth Jennings)

Jack lived in the green-house
Prel I 14

The Toaster (William Jay Smith)

A silver-scaled dragon, with jaws flaming red
Chal I 88; Fab.N.V 173; J.Vo III 7

INDIANS, RED

See also Buffaloes, Hiawatha

Chief Standing Water or *My Night on the Reservation* (Charles Tomlinson)

Chief Standing Water
Comp 106

The Flower-fed Buffaloes (Vachel Lindsay)

The flower-fed buffaloes of the spring
Cher 124; Go.Jo 203; Liv 125; Look 194; Peg V 19; P.F.P II 232; Six VI 58; Them VII 62; This W.D 123; T.P.R 44

The Forsaken (Duncan Campbell Scott)

Once in the winter/Out on a lake
Tell II 11

Lovewell's Fight (Anon)

Of worthy Captain Lovewell, I purpose now to sing
Bal 714

Rattlesnake Ceremony Song (trans A. L. Kroeber)

The king snake said to the rattlesnake
J.Vo III 9

The Sioux Indians (Anon)

I'll sing you a song and it'll be a sad one
B.B 88; Read I 60; Voi I 51

The Siouxs (Charles Adams)

A wandering tribe called the Siouxs
Act I 102

The Squaw Dance (Lew Sarett)

Beat, beat, beat, beat, beat upon the tom-tom
Speak II 102

INJUSTICE

Beauty always gets the best of it (Don Marquis)

(a) *unjust*
poets are always asking
Act IV 177

(b) *the hen and the oriole*
well boss did it/ever strike you that a
Act IV 179

INSECTS & RELATED CREATURES

See also Ants, Bees, Beetles, Butterflies, Caterpillars, Centipedes, Crickets, Dragon-flies, Earwigs, Fireflies, Fleas, Flies, Gnats, Grasshoppers, Ladybirds, Locusts, Mosquitoes, Moths, Spiders, Wasps

A Considerable Speck (Robert Frost)

A speck that would have been beneath my sight
Song III 65

John Deth (part) (Conrad Aiken)

With myriad voices grass was filled
Ark 43

INSIDE

See Outside & Inside

INSOMNIA

Insomniac (Sylvia Plath)

The night sky is only a sort of carbon paper
Them II 35

The Shadow of Night (Coventry Patmore)

How strange it is to wake
Them II 41

IRELAND

The Closing Album (part) (Louis MacNiece)

In Sligo the country was soft; there were turkeys
Act III 16; Com 194; Wheel II 155

The Croppy Boy (Anon)

It was early, early in the spring
D.P.R II 82; Fab.Bal 203

Dunlavin Green (Anon)

In the year of one thousand seven hundred and ninety-eight
Fab.Bal 202

Easter 1916 (W. B. Yeats)

I have met them at close of day
Camb 31; Fla 32; Liv 48; P.Tong II 45; Ten 148

Galway Races (Anon)

It's there you'll see confectioners with sugar sticks and dainties
Mood IV 17

Red Hanrahan's Song about Ireland (W. B. Yeats)

The old brown thorn-trees break in two high over Cummen Strand
Fab.C.V 135; Yea.Run 51

The Rose Tree (W. B. Yeats)

'O words are lightly spoken
Wheel IV 142

The Wearing of the Green (Anon)

Oh Paddy dear, and did you hear the news that's going round?
Kal 67; Song IV 96

JACKDAWS

The Jackdaw (William Cowper)

There is a bird who, by his coat
Peng.An 159; Shep 112

The Jackdaw of Rheims (R. H. Barham)

The Jackdaw sat on the Cardinal's chair
M.M.A 66; Peng.An 160; P.F.P I 79; Spo I 20; Sto II 35; Trea 32; Ver II 189

JACKSON, ANDREW

Andrew Jackson (Martha Keller)

He was a man as hot as whiskey
G.Tr.P 92

JACOB

The fox-coloured pheasant enjoyed his peace (Peter Levi)

The fox-coloured pheasant enjoyed his peace
Dawn 36; Make IV 201

JACOBITES

See also Charlie, Bonnie Prince, Killecrankie

Hieland Laddie (Anon)

Where have you been all the day
Puf.S.B 164

Moy Castle (Anon)

There are seven men in Moy Castle
Song II 80

O'er the Water to Charlie (Robert Burns)

We'll o'er the water and o'er the sea
Fab.C.V 141

Sing me a Song (Robert Louis Stevenson)

Sing me a song of a lad that is gone
A.D.L 213; By 199; Com 188; D.P III 84; Puf.V 181; Song IV 190; Spir 100; Spir.R 75; Ste.Ho 42

There'll never be peace (Robert Burns)

By yon castle wa' at the close of the day
Riv IV 5

JAEL & SISERA

The Song of Deborah (The Bible)

The kings came and fought
Judges V 19; Tell II 93

JAGUARS

The Jaguar (Ted Hughes)

The apes yawn and adore their fleas in the sun
Bird III 28; Exp III 15; Them I 71; Ver III 79

JAMAICA

Song of the Banana Man (Evan Jones)

Touris' white man, wipin' his face
Mod.P 162

JAMES, JESSE

Jesse James (Anon)

It was on a Wednesday night, the moon was shining bright
Bird II 8; Song I 75

Jesse James was a lad that killed many a man
B.L.A.F 296

Jesse James was one of his names
B.B 119

Yes, I went down to the depot
Bal 753; Iron II 88

Jesse James (William Rose Benet)

Jesse James was a two-gun man
Kal 45; Peg I 74; Spir 167; Spir.R 124

JANUARY

Odes of the Months (part)
(Aneirin—trans W. Probert)

Month of January—smoky is the vale
Flock 4

JAPAN

Japanese Children (James Kirkup)

The round, calm faces rosy with the cold
Flock 68

JAZZ

See also Blues

And now— (J. B. Boothroyd)

It's a *rum-*/Ba band another *rum-*
Peg IV 64

Jazz Fantasia (Carl Sandburg)

Drum on your drums, batter on your banjoes
Kal 37; S.D 124; Voi III 79; Weal II 151

Jazz for Five (parts) (John Smith)

Colin Barnes, Drums: Listen, listen/There's walking in the world
Mod.P 186

Shake Keane, Trumpet: Have you ever heard the sun in the sky
Mod.P 188

J is for Jazz-Man (Eleanor Farjeon)

Crash and/CLANG!
J.Vo I 14; T.P.R 112

JEALOUSY

Last Night (Christina Rossetti)

Where were you last night? I watched at the gate
Vic 172

JELLYFISH

The Borough (George Crabbe)

Now it is pleasant in the summer eve
Com 186; Peng.An 165; Shep 33

JERICHO

See Joshua

JERUSALEM

Jerusalem (William Blake)

And did those feet, in ancient times
Act I 54; Bla.Gr 83; B.P IV 39; By 111; Ch.Gar 75; D.P IV 187; D.P.R IV 155; Ex.Ch 25; Fab.C.V 126; P.F.P I 180;

P.Life IV 74; P.Tong I 6; Puf.V 247; P.W 142; P.W.R 156; Song IV 98; Sphe 380; Ver III 24

Jerusalem (Anon)

Jerusalem my happy home
Fab.C.V 370; Riv III 58; Voi II 149

JERVIS BAY, THE

The Jervis Bay (part) (Michael Thwaites)

But the days and the weeks and the months ran on
Spir 171; Spir.R 127

The fifth day of November, fifty North and forty West
Nar 162

The Jervis Bay was a liner in the proper days of peace
Hap 74; R.R 35

Now the convoy are nosing
Sto III 23

JESUS

See Christ

JEWELS

The Flint (Christina Rossetti)

An emerald is as green as grass
A.D.L 206; G.Tr.P 306; Mer 268; Mer.Puf 199; Rain 111; Riv I 16; Tree IV 63

The Jew of Malta (part)
(Christopher Marlowe)

Give me the merchants of the Indian mines
Act I 95; Cher 219

Precious Stones (Walter de la Mare)

Ruby, amethyst, emerald, diamond
A.D.L 206; De la M.Col 79; De la M.S 18; P.Life III 89; Riv II 16

106

JOHN, KING

King John and the Abbot or *Bishop* (Anon)

An ancient story I'll tell you anon
Bal 154; B.B 176; Bird I 44; B.P III 9; D.P II 71; G.Tr.P 120; Min IV 81; Tell I 96; Tree III 44; Wheel I 31

JOHN THE BAPTIST

St John Baptist (Sidney Keyes)

I, John, not reed but root
Song IV 200

JONAH

Jonah (Aldous Huxley)

A cream of phosphorescent light
Cher 211

Jonah (Thomas Blackburn)

He stands in rags upon the heaving prow
Dawn 38; Ev.M 38

The Whale and Jonah (Viola Meynell)

He sported round the watery world
By 254; Peng.An 327

JOSEPH

Joseph fell a-dreaming (Eleanor Farjeon)

Joseph fell a-dreaming
Puf.Q 20

JOSHUA

Joshua fit de Battle of Jericho (Anon)

Joshua fit de battle of Jericho
B.L.A.F 374; J.Vo III 96; Riv II 48

JUDAS

Judas (Anon)

It was upon a Maundy Thursday that our Lord arose
P.Tong II 75

Judas (Anon—modernised Brian Stone)

Upon a Holy Thursday, up rose our Lord
Tell I 92

JUDGEMENT, DAY OF

The Day of Judgement (Isaac Watts)

When the fierce North-wind with his airy forces
P.Tong II 190

End of the World (Basil Dowling)

I was but nine years old
Spir 103

Holy Sonnet VII (John Donne)

At the round earth's imagined corners, blow
Flock 175; P.F.P II 128; P.W 90; Riv IV 57

Wake All the Dead! (Sir William Davenant)

Wake all the dead! What ho! What ho!
Fab.C.V 275

JUDGES

Judge Selah Lively (Edgar Lee Masters)

Suppose you stood just five feet two
Bird III 8; Them VI 16

JULY

July (John Clare)

Loud is the summer's busy song
G.Tr.P 276; Wheel I 76

JUNE

June Thunder (Louis MacNiece)

The Junes were free and full, driving through tiny
Mod.P 20

KALLYOPES

See Calliopes

KANGAROOS

Kangaroo (D. H. Lawrence)

In the northern hemisphere
Ark 139; Camb 77; Flock 214; Law.S 47; Peng.An 171; Pers 133; Shep 100; Song IV 91; Sphe 115; Sto II 177; Voi I 81

The Kangaroo (Australian Singing Game)

Old Jumpety-Bumpety-Hop-and-Go-One
Fab.N.V 74; F.Feet 80; Min II 81; Rain 54; Rhyme I 30; Tree I 25

KEATS, JOHN

At Lulworth Cove a Century Back (Thomas Hardy)

Had I but lived a hundred years ago
Fla 24; Pat 128

KELLY, NED

The Death of Ned Kelly (John Manifold)

Ned Kelly fought the rich men in country and in town
J.Vo IV 32

Stringybark Creek (Bushranger's Song)

A sergeant and three constables set out from Mansfield town
Tell I 113

KIDD, CAPTAIN

Captain Kidd (Anon)

My name is Captain Kidd, as I sailed
Broad 20

My name was Robert Kidd
F.S.N.A 15

Captain Kidd 1650?–1701 (Rosemary & Stephen Benet)

This person in the gaudy clothes
Fab.N.V 40; P.Life III 11

KIDNAPPING

John Polrudden (Charles Causley)

John Polrudden/All of a sudden
Cau.Nar 9

KILLIECRANKIE

The Battle of Killiecrankie (W. E. Aytoun)

On the heights of Killiecrankie
Nar 2; Ver II 152

KINGFISHERS

The Kingfisher (part) (Andrew Marvell)

The viscous air, wheres'e'r she fly
B.B.F 174

Kingfishers (John Clare)

Look where two splendid feathered things
B.B.F 175; Cla.Wo 67

KINGS & QUEENS

See also Fab.N.V 258–272

See also Charles I, Charles II, Elizabeth I, Henry V, John, King, Nefertiti

Henry and Mary (Robert Graves)

Henry was a young king
Mer 168; Mer.Puf 145

KITTENS

See also Cats

Choosing their Names (Thomas Hood)

Our old cat has kittens three
B.L.J II 22; First III 20; Puf.Y 105; Rain 38; Rhyme II 41; Tree III 56

The Colubriad (William Cowper)

Close by the threshold of a door nailed fast
Key IV 134; P.F.P II 103; Sto II 33

The Kitten and the Falling Leaves (William Wordsworth)

See the kitten on the wall
B.B.F 64; Fuji 23; G.Tr.P 52; Ox.P.C 106; Pat 198; Puf.V 48; Tree IV 48

Miss Tibbles (Ian Serraillier)

Miss Tibbles is my kitten; white
Puf.Q 155; T.P.R 67

Two Little Kittens (Jane Taylor)

Two little kittens, one stormy night
B.L.J I 26; Ex.Tra 36; Fab.N.V 166; F.Feet 111; Fuji 73; Rhyme I 31

KIWIS

The Apteryx (Robert Sward)

The infected apteryx (or kiwi) would appear
Peng.An 174

KNIFE GRINDERS

The Knife Grinder (Walt Whitman)

Where the city's ceaseless crowd moves on the livelong day
Peg V 15

The Man with the Treadle (Geoffrey Johnson)

Sir, I can set your shears as fine
J.Mod 63; Sto I 133

KNIGHTS & LADIES

See also Arthur, King

KNIGHTS & LADIES (LYRIC & DESCRIPTIVE)

All in green went my love riding (e. e. cummings)

All in green went my love riding
Flock 203; Go.Jo 121; This W.D 149

Eldorado (Edgar Allen Poe)

Gaily bedight/A gallant knight
B.L.J III 9; Ch.Gar 177; Ex.Tro 86; Fab.C.V 187; Peg II 25; P.F.P II 7; Plea III 78; P.Life IV 96; Puf.V 86

The Faerie Queene (part) (Edmund Spenser)

A gentle knight was pricking on the plain
Com 159; Trea 158; Ver III 229

So dreadfully he toward him did pass
Riv III 67

Fafnir and the Knights (Stevie Smith)

In the quiet waters
A.S.L.A 80; Peng.An 94

The Knight in Prison (William Morris)

Wearily, drearily
J.Vo III 83; P.Rem 96; P.W 219; P.W.R 255; Sphe 348

Middle Ages (Siegfried Sassoon)

I heard a crash and a cry
J.Vo III 78; Ox.V.J IV 96; Rhyme IV 21

KNIGHTS & LADIES (NARRATIVE)

Advice to a Knight (T. H. Jones)

Wear modest armour; and walk quietly
Flock 245

The Holy Grail (part) (Alfred Lord Tennyson)

Then there remains but Lancelot, for the rest
Vic 68

The Knight's Leap (Charles Kingsley)

So the foemen have fired the gate, men of mine
D.P.R II 43

The Lady of Shalott (Alfred Lord Tennyson)

On either side the river lie
B.P IV 76; D.P IV 166; D.P.R IV 130; Isle 69; Look 311; Make IV 106; P.Bk

205; *Peg II 110; P.F.P II 184; Plea VII 29; Puf.V 197; Rhyme III 6; Spir 138; Ten.Fa 19; Weal I 59*

A bowshot from her bower-eaves
P.Life IV 36

The Marriage of Sir Gawain (Anon)

King Arthur lives in merry Carlisle and seemely is to see
Bal 119

Sir Eglamour (Samuel Rowlands)

Sir Eglamour that worthy knight
Fab.C.V 170; Mer 324; Mer.Puf 244; Mood I 77; Ox.P.C 25; P.Rem 22; P.Tong I 114; Riv II 96

Sir Gawain and the Green Knight (part) (trans Ian Serraillier)

King Arthur was at Camelot one Christmas-tide
Start 115

The Slain Knight (Anon)

My love he built me a bonny bower
Mer 328; Mer.Puf 249

KRAKEN

The Kraken (Alfred Lord Tennyson)

Below the thunders of the upper deep
Bat 26; B.B.F 186; Key III 118; Peg II 31; Peng.An 176; P.Life IV 59; Shep 36; Six VI 48; Start 134; This W.D 119

LADIES

See Knights & Ladies

LAD'S-LOVE

Old Man (Edward Thomas)

Old Man, or Lad's-Love—in the name there's nothing
Camb 54; Cent 21; Ten 135

LADYBIRDS

Clock-a-Clay (John Clare)

In the cowslip pips I lie
B.B.F 127; Cla.Wo 73; D.P.R I 6; Mer

258; *Mer.Puf 190; Ox.P.C 119; Ox.V.J II 57; P.F.P I 103; Rain 47; Riv I 2; Say 34; This W.D 118; Tree IV 58*

LAMBS

A Child's Voice (Andrew Young)

On winter nights shepherd and I
Quest III 24; You.Qu 1

First Sight (Philip Larkin)
Lambs that learn to walk in snow
Act IV 109; Ark 186; By 303; Chal II 18

The Lambs of Grasmere 1860 (Christina Rossetti)

The upland flocks grew starved and thinned
F.Feet 33; Key II 56; Ox.V.J IV 44

Spring Song (Christina Rossetti)

On the grassy banks
F.Feet 32; Tree I 25

LAMENTS

See Dirges

LANDRAILS

The Landrail (John Clare)

How sweet and pleasant grows the way
P.Rem 57

LANGUAGE

See also Words

Their Lonely Betters (W. H. Auden)

As I listened from a beach-chair in the shade
A.S.L.A 64; Drag 27

LAPWINGS

Lapwing (Rex Warner)

Leaves, summer's coinage spent, golden are all together whirled
P.F.P I 124; Sphe 134

LARKS

The Ecstatic (C. Day Lewis)

Lark, skylark, spilling your rubbed and round
A.D.L. 172; D.P IV 17; Song II 52; Sphe 154; Ver II 237

A Green Cornfield or *The Skylark* (Christina Rossetti)

The earth was green, the sky was blue
Bat 60; B.L.J III 47; Ex.Tro 8; F.Feet 55; G.Tr.P 61; Rain 48; Sto I 114; Trea 121

Hark, Hark! The Lark (William Shakespeare)

Hark, hark! The lark at Heaven's gate sings
Cymbeline II iii 20; B.B.F 44; Cher 264; Ch.Gar 23; Fab.C.V 47; Mer 272; Mer.Puf 203; My 16; Ox.P.C 94; Ox.V.J II 18; P.F.P II 146; Riv I 55; Tree II 59; Ver II 5

The Lark Ascending (part) (George Meredith)

He rises and begins to round
Ark 53; Prel.IV 31; Shep 108; Sto II 99

Lark Descending (Edmund Blunden)

A singing firework; the sun's darling
J.Mod 134

The Lark in the Morn (Anon)

As I was a-walking one morning in the Spring
Cher 41; Com 25; F.Feet 70; Mer 290; Song I 6

The Lark's Nest (John Clare)

From yon black clump of wheat that grows
B.L.J III 55; Key III 111; Wheel I 77

The Sea and the Skylark (Gerard Manley Hopkins)

On ear and ear two noises too old to end
P.W 228; P.W.R 264; Song IV 153; Voi I 116

The Skylark (Frederick Tennyson)

How blithe the lark runs up the golden stair
B.B.F 48

The Skylark (Edmund Waller)

The lark, that shuns on lofty boughs to build
P.F.P I 121

The Skylark (John Clare)

The rolls and harrows lie at rest beside
Cla.Wo 57

LAUGHING

A Laughing Song (William Blake)

When the green woods laugh with the voice of joy
B.P III 88; Ch.Gar 183; D.P I 22; Fun I 34; Go.Jo 41; G.Tr.P 11; Min III 31; Ox.V.J I 35; P.Bk 40; P.F.P I 103; P.Tong I 180; P.W 139; This W.D 91

Laughing Time (William Jay Smith)

It was laughing time, and the small Giraffe
Fab.N.V 12

Mrs Reece laughs (Martin Armstrong)

Laughter, with us, is no great undertaking
Look 100; Peg II 96; Prel IV 43; Sphe 215; V.F 17

LAZARUS

See also Dives

Lazarus (Elizabeth Jennings)

It was the amazing white, it was the way he simply
Them II 22

LAZINESS

I is for Idle in Yorkshire (Eleanor Farjeon)

In Idle/in Yorks
Tree II 56

Lazy Man's Song (Po Chu-I—trans Arthur Waley)

I could have a job, but I am too lazy to choose it
Chal I 51; Cor 156; Hap 72; Iron IV 90; Them VI 22

Pooh! (Walter de la Mare)

Dainty Miss Apathy
B.P II 17; De la M.Ch 62; De la M.Col 35; V.F 50

The Sluggard (Isaac Watts)

'Tis the voice of the sluggard, I hear him complain
Ex.Ch 146; Fun II 110; Key II 43; Puf.V 147; Riv III 4; S.D 43; Spo I 62; Them VI 20

LEAR, EDWARD

See also Nonsense (Lear)

Edward Lear (Edward Lear)

How pleasant to know Mr Lear!
Cher 463; Cor 52; Fab.C.V 124; G.Tr.P 212; Plea V 23; P.Life III 30; Riv IV 6; Sphe 221; V.F 100

Edward Lear (W. H. Auden)

Left by his friend to breakfast alone on the white
Camb 132; Peg IV 74; Pers 50

LEGS

The Legs (Robert Graves)

There was this road
J.Vo III 61; M.Ver 41

LENT

To keep a true Lent (Robert Herrick)

Is this a Fast, to keep
Her.Mu 71

LEOPARDS

Yellow Eyes (Kingsley Fairbridge)

Blended by fading moonlight with the grass
Exp III 2

LEPANTO

Lepanto (G. K. Chesterton)

White founts falling in the Courts of the sun
A.D.L 245; P.F.P II 12; Spo II 16; T.C.N 22; Ver II 60

LETTERS

Country Letter (John Clare)

Dear brother robin this comes from us all
P.W.R 209; Riv II 26

A Letter (Matthew Prior)

My noble, lovely, little Peggy
Ch.Gar 190

Night Mail (W. H. Auden)

This is the night mail crossing the border
A.D.L 147; All 24; Bird I 34; B.P IV 92; Cher 407; Cor 124; D.P III 90; D.P.R II 71; Ex.Ch 160; Kal 64; Key IV 120; Mood II 22; Ox.V.J III 23; Peg II 86; P.F.P II 154; P.Life IV 40; P.Rem 52; S.D 50; Six IV 14; Song I 26; Sphe 177; Spir 60; Spir.R 48; Sto II 56; T.P.W 42; Ver II 47; Weal I 132; Wheel II 157; Yim II 5

LEVIATHAN

Leviathan (Bible)

Can'st thou draw out leviathan with an hook?
Job xli 1; Bat 78; B.B.F 187; Key IV 115; Riv IV 23; Spo I 81

Leviathan (Louis Untermeyer)

God's deathless plaything rolls an eye
G.Tr.P 36

Visions of the World's Vanity (part) (Edmund Spenser)

Toward the sea, turning my troubled eye
Cher 207

LIARS

What kind of a liar are you? (Carl Sandburg)

What kind of a liar are you?
J.Vo III 53

LIGHTHOUSES

The Sea Lights (Crosbie Garstin)

Flashed light to Lizard
Speak I 99

Spurn Light (J. Redwood Anderson)

Punctually/moment by moment, hour on
hour, all night
J.Mod 129; Peg III 35; Song I 114

LIGHTHOUSE KEEPERS

The Light-keeper (Robert Louis
Stevenson)

The brilliant kernel of the night
Ox.V.J IV 87; Ste.Ho 33

LIMERICKS

*Act I 15–16, 40, 91, 102, 110; Act II 11,
12, 71–72, 96–97; Act III 9–10, 47–48,
100, 112–13, 121, 122, 128–29; Act IV
163; Act V 127; B.B.F 194; B.B.G.G 29,
109; Bird IV 57–58; B.L.J II 56; B.P I
25; Chal I 67, 68, 69; Chal II 78, 80;
Cher 14, 27, 28, 31, 154; Cor 58, 59;
Ex.Tra 9, 12; Fab.N.V 27, 95, 151, 214,
218–224; Fuji 48, 49, 65, 105; Fun I 82,
84, 85; Fun II 59; Go.Jo 9; G.Tr.P
240–243; Iron III 11; J.Vo III 44; Key I
100; Key IV 75; Mer 131, 150, 208–9,
264, 306; Mer.Puf 99, 111, 156–157,
195, 229; Mil.S.V 43; M.M.A 31, 44, 73,
78, 80, 98, 102, 103; Mood II 39; My 91,
164, 165; Ox.Dic 91, 267, 359, 400, 407;
Ox.V.J II 96; Peg I 15, 17, 23, 25; Peg II
91, 101; Peg III 31; Plea V 56; P.Life III
31, 47; P.P 45, 47, 50; P.Tong II 56,
168; Puf.V 36, 168; Puf.Y 192; Rhyme
III 31, 32; Riv I 97, 101; Riv II 93–95;
Scrap 62; S.D 150; Song I 89; Sphe
244–245; Sto I 90–91; Sto II 82–83;
Sto III 111–112; Tree I 21, 52; Tree II
15, 57; Tree III 42; V.F 99–100, 102,
131, 156, 175–176; Weal I 100*

LINCOLN, ABRAHAM

Abraham Lincoln walks at Midnight
(Vachell Lindsay)

It is portentous and a thing of state
Spir 96; Spir.R 72

Nancy Hanks (Rosemary Benet)

If Nancy Hanks
P.Life IV 43; Spir 33; Spir.R 27

O Captain! My Captain! (Walt
Whitman)

O Captain! My Captain! our fearful trip
is done
Fab.C.V 149; Trea 92

LINES

Lines (Deborah Bestwick)

Straight lines, long lines
Dan 48

LINNETS

A Linnet in Hell (James Elroy
Flecker)

A linnet who had lost her way
Mer 290; Mer.Puf 215

The Linnet (Walter de la Mare)

Upon this leafy bush
*B.B.F 2; P.F.P I 122; Sphe 131; Ver III
49*

Linnet's Nest (Robert Burns)

Within the bush, her covert nest
B.B.F 36

LIONS

Circus Lion (C. Day Lewis)

Lumbering haunches, pussyfoot tread, a
pride of lions
*Exp III 27; Mod.P 110; Speak II 137;
Under 42*

The Lion (Vachell Lindsay)

The lion is a kingly beast
Key II 60

Riverdale Lion (John Robert
Colombo)

Bound lion, almost blind from meeting
their gaze and popcorn
Exp III 12

The Tale of the Lion Sertorius (Ian Serraillier)

Do you know the mighty King of the Circus
P.P 51

LITTER

Traces (Gavin A. Maclaren)

Here beneath the hazel boughs
Look 198

LLAMAS

The Llama (Hilaire Belloc)

The llama is a woolly sort of fleecy hairy goat
Bel.C.V 126; Fab.C.V 90

The one-l lama (Ogden Nash)

The one-l lama
Chal I 66; Fab.C.V 90; Spir 1

LOBSTERS

The Lobster Pot (John Arden)

Who can tell how the lobster got
A.S.L.A 83

A Lobster Quadrille (Lewis Carroll)

'Will you walk a little faster?' said a whiting to a snail
All 79; B.B.F 197; Car.J 9; Cher 29; D.P II 45; D.P.R II 37; Ex.Tro 53; Fun II 21; Make I 45; Mer 353; Mer.Puf 268; Min IV 31; Plea III 18; P.Life II 26; P.Rem 27; P.Tong I 185; Riv II 83; Sto I 96; V.F 30

LOCUSTS

The Locust (Madagascar—trans A. Marre, W. R. Trask)

What is a locust
J.Vo III 13

LOGGERS

The Frozen Logger (Anon)

As I sat down one evening
F.S.N.A 120

The Jam on Gerry's Rock (Anon)

Come all of you bold shanty boys and list while I relate
Bal 771; B.L.A.F 170; Fab.Bal 240; Iron III 17; Make II 67; Tell II 143

James Whaland (Anon)

Come all you brave young shanty boys
Song II 100

LONDON

See also Cockneys, London (Great Fire of), Street Cries

The Bells of London (Anon)

The bells of London all fell wrangling
Mood I 62

The Caledonian Market (William Plomer)

A work basket made of an old armadillo
M.Ver 51; Speak II 76

A description of a City Shower (parts) (Jonathan Swift)

Careful observers may foretell the hour
P.W.R 131

Now in contiguous drops the the flood comes down
D.P.R III 31

Hay's Wharf (Richard Church)

Who hasn't heard of London Bridge?
M.Ver 53

London (William Blake)

I wander thro' each chartered street
Bla.Gr 51; Cher 304; Choice 47; Make IV 206

London (William Wordsworth)

Rise up, thou monstrous ant-hill on the plain
R.R 65

The New London (John Dryden)

Methinks already, from this Chymick flame
Fab.C.V 126

Oranges and Lemons or
The Bells of London (Anon)

Gay go up and gay go down
*B.P I 74; Cher 296; Ex.Tra 14; Fab.N.V
116; Fun I 4; Mer 60; M.G.B 138;
M.G.E 16; M.G.R 84; Min II 80; Ox.Dic
337; Ox.N.R 68; P.Tong I 35; Puf.N.R
46; Puf.V 178; S.D 132; Tree I 46*

Regent's Park Terrace (Bernard
Spencer)

The noises round my house. On cobbles
bounding
R.R 71

Smelling the end of Green July
(Peter Yates)

Smelling the end of green July
Man I 57

South Side (Alexander Franklin)

Overalls and dirty faces
Chor 28

The Streets of Laredo (Louis
MacNiece)

O early one morning I walked out like
Agag
Cher 309; Fla 111; Mod.P 36; Ris 112

Sweet Thames flow softly (Ewan
MacColl)

I met my girl at Woolwich pier, beneath a
big crane standing
Song IV 1

To the City of London (William
Dunbar)

London, thou art of townes, A *per se*
Cher 288

Upon Westminster Bridge (William
Wordsworth)

Earth has not anything to show more fair
*A.D.L 59; Bat 59; By 124; Cher 290;
Ch.Gar 171; Choice 28; Com 193; D.P
IV 126; D.P.R IV 88; Fab.C.V 128; Iron
IV 10; Kal 52; Key IV 47; Peg III 57;
P.F.P I 174; Plea VIII 96; Prel IV 8;
Puf.V 249; Rain 114; Riv IV 42; S.D 49;
Song I 1; Sphe 267; Trea 229; Ver III
94; Weal II 126; Wor.So 43*

LONELINESS

The Boarder (Louis Simpson)

The time is after dinner. Cigarettes
Them III 40

The Clock-Winder (Thomas Hardy)

It is dark as a cave
Yim III 31

Eleanor Rigby (John Lennon & Paul
McCartney)

Eleanor Rigby picks up the rice in the
church
Read III 27

The Hill Wife (part) (Robert Frost)

She had no saying dark enough
Comp 66

Human Condition (Thom Gunn)

Now it is fog. I walk
Nev 89

The Lonely Farmer (R. S. Thomas)

Poor hill farmer astray in the grass
Make III 144; Song III 29

Nobody Comes (Thomas Hardy)

Tree-leaves labour up and down
Sphe 425

Not Waving but Drowning (Stevie
Smith)

Nobody heard him, the dead man
Them III 46

The River-Merchant's Wife
(Rihaku—trans Ezra Pound)

While my hair was still cut straight
across my forehead
*Camb 90; Cent 53; Comp 65; Liv 158;
Pers 19; S.D 38; Tell II 117*

Sunday Afternoons (Antony
Thwaite)

On Sunday afternoons
Drag 88

LORRIES

Long-distance Lorry (Philip Callow)

Red truck slumbering in the alley
Make III 11; Quest V 35

LORRY DRIVERS

I'm Champion at Keeping 'em Rolling (Ewan MacColl)

I am an old timer, I travel the road
Song III 16

Song of the Wagondriver
(B. S. Johnson)

My first love was the ten-ton truck
Them VI 5

LOVE

The Anniversary (John Donne)

All Kings, and all their favourites
P.W.R 89

An Arundel Tomb (Philip Larkin)

Side by side, their faces blurred
Fla 163; Mod.P 74; Pers 26; Sev 94; Them IV 33

Brown Penny (W. B. Yeats)

I whispered, 'I am too young'
Nev 3

The Clod and the Pebble (William Blake)

Love seeketh not itself to please
Choice 44; R.R 146; Voi III 97

The Confirmation (Edwin Muir)

Yes, yours, my love, is the right human face
Ten 115; Weal II 60

Hawthorn white, hawthorn red (Charles Causley)

Hawthorn white, hawthorn red
Hap 64

Love (George Herbert)

Love bade me welcome; yet my soul drew back
By 68; Cher 433; Iron IV 101; Pat 75; S.D 70

Love will find out the way (Anon)

Over the mountains/And over the waves
Fab.C.V 332; P.Bk 17; Voi III 74

Part of Plenty (Bernard Spencer)

When she carries food to the table and stoops down
D.P.R IV 105

Sonnet 116 (William Shakespeare)

Let me not to the marriage of true minds
By 37; Iron IV 29; Peg V 56; P.W 69; P.W.R 65; Riv IV 65; Sphe 285; Them IV 20; Ver III 89; Weal II 52

Spoils (Robert Graves)

When all is over and you march for home
Liv 156

Symptoms of Love (Robert Graves)

Love is a universal migraine
Sev 61; Them IV 19

The Telephone (Robert Frost)

When I was just as far as I could walk
Fro.You 43; Voi III 95

Walsinghame or
As you came from the Holy Land (Sir Walter Ralegh)

As you came from the holy land
Cher 55; Fab.C.V 336; Iron I 4; Plea VIII 26; Song IV 22

LOVE SONGS

Electric Love (Denis Glover)

My love is like a dynamo
Man II 61

The First Time ever I saw your Face (Ewan MacColl)

The first time ever I saw your face
Wheel IV 191

If you'll give me a kiss (Leo Aylen)

If you'll give me a kiss and be my girl
Act IV 24; Exp.I 42; Them V 63

I know where I'm going (Anon)

I know where I'm going
Com 18; Make IV 99; Peg IV 113

Jig (C. Day Lewis)

That winter love spoke spoke and we raised no objection
Weal II 110

Love in a Space Suit (James Kirkup)

Dear, when on some distant planet
Mod.P 116

O Mistress Mine (William Shakespeare)

O mistress mine, where are you roaming?
Twelfth Night II iii 39; *By 39; D.P IV 148; Go.Jo 140; Iron IV 43; Pat 79; P.Bk 91; Peg III 68; Plea VII 14; P.W.R 60; Song IV 11; Sphe 300; Weal II 53*

O my luve is like a red red rose (Robert Burns)

O my luve is like a red red rose
By 114; Cher 64; Com 16; D.P IV 154; D.P.R IV 104; Fab.C.V 335; Make IV 155; Peg IV 110; Plea VIII 16; P.Rem 148; P.W 143; P.W.R 160; R.R 146; Weal I 40

A Pavane for the Nursery (William Jay Smith)

Now touch the air softly
Go.Jo 124

Remembrance (Emily Bronte)

Cold in the earth and the deep snow piled above thee
Vic 149

Song (John Clare)

O wert thou in the storm
B.P II 35; Cla.Wo 89; Ex.Tro 33; Ox.V.J I 37; Voi II 108

Tonight at Noon (Adrian Henri)

Tonight at noon
Mod.P 184

Twentieth Century Love Song (Richard Church)

In these latter days/Few poets have the habit
M.Ver 124

When Molly smiles (Anon)

When Molly smiles beneath her cow
Voi III 73

White Clouds are in the Sky (Chinese—B.C. 1121)

White clouds are in the sky
Weal II 63

Will you come? (Edward Thomas)

Will you come?
Go.Jo 120

Yes is a pleasant country (e. e. cummings)

yes is a pleasant country
Eye 47

LOVE SONGS (HAPPY)

An Immortality (Ezra Pound)

Sing we for love and idleness
Go.Jo 119

It was a Lover and his Lass (William Shakespeare)

It was a lover and his lass
As You Like It V iii 15; *Mer 194; Mer.Puf 150; P.Bk 92; Song IV 35; Ver II 2*

My True-Love hath my Heart (Sir Philip Sidney)

My true-love hath my heart, and I have his
By 17; D.P IV 157; Peg IV 110; Plea VIII 52; S.D 73; Song IV 10; Sphe 286; Weal II 51

LOVE SONGS (UNHAPPY)

Adrian Henri's Talking after-Christmas Blues (Adrian Henri)

Well I woke up this mornin' it was Christmas Day
Mod.P 201

Blow away the Morning Dew (Anon)

Upon the sweetest summer time
P.Life III 52

Down in the Valley (Anon)

Down in the valley/The valley so low
B.L.A.F 62; F.S.N.A 289; Wheel III 131

A New Courtly Sonnet of the Lady Greensleeves (Anon)

Alas! my love you do me wrong
D.P II 121; D.P.R I 79; Fab.C.V 338; Puf.S.B 28; Riv III 44; Song IV 24; Ver III 179

117

O do not Love too Long
(W. B. Yeats)

Sweetheart, do not love too long
Peg V 59

Old Smokey (Anon)

On top of Old Smokey all covered in snow
Bal 739; B.L.A.F 60; Iron IV 44

On top of old Smokey/On the mountain so high
F.S.N.A 221

O, Open the Door to Me, O! (Robert Burns)

O, open the door some pity to show
Fab.C.V 347

O Waly, Waly (Anon)

Down in the meadows the other day
P.W.R 164

O Waly, waly up the bank
Fab.Bal 143; Plea VIII 50

The water is wide; I cannot get o'er
Bal 550; Iron IV 129

Queen of Hearts (Anon)

To the Queen of Hearts is the Ace of Sorrow
Nev 105

Sea Love (Charlotte Mew)

Tide be runnin' the great world over
Bird III 3

The Seeds of Love (Anon)

I sowed the seeds of love
Fab.C.V 334; Iron IV 92; P.W.R 165; Sphe 325

She's like the swallow (Anon)

She's like the swallow that flies so high
B.B 162; Voi III 87

Song for the Saracen Lady (John Heath-Stubbs)

Oh I am come far over the sea
J.Mod 39; Quest IV 44

Sweet Thames flow softly (Ewan MacColl)

I met my girl at Woolwich pier beneath a big crane standing
Song IV 1

Then my love and I'll be married
(Anon)

When roses grow on thistle tops
Voi III 68

The Turtle-Dove (Anon)

O don't you see the turtle-dove
Sphe 295

Ye Banks and Braes or
Ye Flowery Banks of Bonnie Doon
(Robert Burns)

Ye banks and braes o' bonnie Doon
D.P IV 155; Make IV 27

LOVERS

See also Courtship

The Foggy Foggy Dew (Anon)

Oh I am a bachelor I live all alone
Bat 51; F.S.N.A 89, 90

Maud (part) (Alfred Lord Tennyson)

Come into the garden, Maud
Plea VIII 65; Ten.Fa 27; Ver III 35

Birds in the high Hall garden
Ten.Fa 29

Under the Olives (Robert Graves)

We never would have loved had love not struck
Ev.M 100

LOVERS (FAITHLESS)

Ballad (Anon)

A faithless shepherd courted me
Voi III 80

Dolly's Mistake or *The Ways of the Wake* (John Clare)

Ere the sun o'er the hills, round and red 'gan a-peeping
Iron IV 81

Johnny Todd (Anon)

Johnny Todd he took a notion
Bird II 20

The K'e still ripples to its Banks
(Chinese—B.C. 718)

The K'e still ripples to its banks
Weal II 105

Mariana (Alfred Lord Tennyson)

With blackest moss the flower plots
*Choice 84; Pat 88; Plea VII 69; P.Rem
152; Ten.Fa 13*

O the Valley in the Summer
(W. H. Auden)

O the valley in the summer where I and
my John
Pers 22; Them IV 22; Wheel IV 179

Ou Phrontis (Charles Causley)

The bells assault the maiden air
Voi III 90

Polly Perkins (Anon)

I'm a broken-hearted milkman, in grief
I'm arrayed
M.M.A 66

LOVERS (HAPPY)
(LYRIC & DESCRIPTIVE)

In a Bath Tea-shop (Sir John
Betjeman)

'Let us not speak, for the love we bear
one another
Man II 57; Pers 23

Moon Rondeau (Carl Sandburg)

Love is a door we shall open together
Them IV 19

Plucking the Rushes
(Chinese—trans Arthur Waley)

Green rushes with red shoots
*Act IV 19; Iron IV 87; P.W 263; P.W.R
317; Voi III 73*

Sally in our Alley (Henry Carey)

Of all the girls that are so smart
*By 101; Com 39; Iron III 37; Pat 100
Plea VI 16*

She tells her love while half asleep
(Robert Graves)

She tells her love while half asleep
Cent 73; Eye 61; Weal II 110

Strawberries (Edwin Morgan)

There were never strawberries
Voi III 70

LOVERS (REUNITED)
(NARRATIVE)

The Bailiff's Daughter of Islington
(Anon)

There was a youth, and a well-beloved
youth
*Bal 313; B.B 71; Fab.Bal 67; G.Tr.P
114; Mood II 74*

Cawsand Bay (Anon)

In Cawsand Bay lying, with the Blue
Peter flying
Cor 95

The Gay Goshawk (Anon)

O well is me, my gay goshawk
B.B 54; P.F.P I 136

Hynd Horn (Anon)

Hynd Horn's bound, love, and Hynd
Horn's free
*Bal 98; B.B 59; Bun 229; Mer 278; Riv I
64*

Lochinvar (Sir Walter Scott)

Oh young Lochinvar is come out of the
West
*By 119; G.Tr.P 134; Min IV 86; Mood
II 98; P.Bk 215; Peg I 88; P.F.P I 158;
Plea V 84; P.Life IV 68; P.Rem 91; Spir
27; Spir.R 22; Spo I 3; Trea 79; Ver II
21*

The Simple Ploughboy (Anon)

O the ploughboy was a ploughing
Fab.C.V 349

Waiting (Y. Yevtushenko—trans
P. Levi & R. Milner-Gulland)

My love will come
Eye 62

Young Beichan or *Bekie* or *Bicham*
(Anon)

In London city was Bicham born
B.B 50; Fab.Bal 41; Flock 146

Young Bekie was as brave a knight
Bal 169; Bun 13; Fab.C.V 340

119

LOVERS (UNHAPPY) (LYRIC & DESCRIPTIVE)

Bredon Hill (A. E. Housman)

In summertime on Bredon
Man II 60; Song IV 18; Sphe 439

Careless Love (Anon)

Love, O love, O careless love
B.L.A.F 64; F.S.N.A 585

The Despairing Lover (William Walsh)

Distracted with care
Fab.C.V 345; Weal II 113

Down by the Salley Gardens (W. B. Yeats)

Down by the salley gardens my love and I did meet
Cher 72; Com 145; Iron I 10; Make IV 168; Sphe 319

Hard Road Blues (Anon)

Keep on walkin' and walkin', talkin' to myself
Eye 54

The Knight in the Bower (Anon)

The heron flew east, the heron flew west
Cher 186

Lost Love (Robert Graves)

His eyes are quickened so with grief
Fab.C.V 346; Liv 43; Plea VII 92; Them II 48

Love without Hope (Robert Graves)

Love without hope, as when the young bird-catcher
Cent 73; Cher 71; Iron II 37

The Man on the Flying Trapeze (Anon)

O the girl that I loved she was handsome
M.M.A 92

Maud (part) (Alfred Lord Tennyson)

O that 'twere possible
Vic 64

No one so much as you (Edward Thomas)

No one so much as you
Pers 20

Parting Speech (The Caucasian Chalk Circle) (Bertolt Brecht)

Simon Shashava, I shall wait for you
D.P.R IV 101

Symptoms of Love (Robert Graves)

Love is a universal migraine
Sev 61; Them IV 19

Western Wind (Anon)

O Western Wind, when wilt thou blow
Fab.C.V 351; Peg V 49

What once I was (Sir Thomas Wyatt)

Ons in your grace I knowe I was
Comp 21

Winter Night (Chinese)

My bed is so empty that I keep waking up
Weal II 145

LOVERS (UNHAPPY) (NARRATIVE)

Barbara Allen (Anon)

Down in London where I was raised
Fab.Bal 235

In Scarlet Town, where I was born
B.B 65; Eye 56; Plea VII 39; Spo II 8

It was in and about the Martinmas time
Bal 277; Riv IV 98; Six III 38; Song III 86

Was in the merry month of May
F.S.N.A 183

Beyond the Last Lamp (Thomas Hardy)

While rain, with eve in partnership
Ten 103

Fair Margaret and Sweet William (Anon)

Sweet William he rose one morning in May
Iron III 54

Lord Lovel (Anon)

Lord Lovel he stood at his castle gate
B.B 74; F.S.N.A 401; Tell I 127

Miss Bailey's Ghost (Anon)

A captain bold in Halifax who dwelt in country quarters
B.B 34; Fab.Bal 194

Richard of Taunton Dene (Anon)

Last New Year's Day, as I've heard say
Puf.S.B 85

She moved through the Fair (Anon)

My young love said to me, "My mother won't mind
Make III 122

The Unquiet Grave (Anon)

Cold blows the wind tonight, true love!
Act I 82; Tell II 124; Yim III 11

The wind doth blow today, my love,
Act I 81; Bal 262; Bird IV 65; Fab.Bal 146; Iron IV 133; Isle 91; Pers 27; Plea VIII 45; Voi III 76; Weal II 17; Wheel IV 22

Villikens and his Dinah (Anon)

It is of a rich merchant I am going for to tell
Bal 768; B.B 63; Iron IV 59

LULLABIES

See also Ox.N.R 18–20

All the Pretty Little Horses (Anon)

Hush-you-bye/Don't you cry
B.L.A.F 14; Scrap 48

All through the Night (Anon)

Sleep my babe, lie still and slumber
Fuji 117; G.Tr.P 301

Can ye sew cushions? (Anon)

O can ye sew cushions?
Fab.C.V 93

A Cradle Song (Padraic Colum)

O men from the fields!
Mood II 103

Golden Slumbers (Thomas Dekker)

Golden slumbers kiss your eyes
B.L.J III 4; B.P II 55; Fuji 29; Fun II 96; Mer 271; Mer.Puf 202; My 177; Ox.P.C 161; Ox.V.J II 16; This W.D 89; Tree IV 15; Ver III 5

Hush a Ba Birdie (Anon)

Hush a ba, birdie, croon, croon
B.B.F 166; Mer 34; Mer.Puf 29

Hush, Little Baby (Anon)

Hush, little baby, don't say a word
Fab.N.V 126; M.G.B 89; Ox.N.R 18

Japanese Cradle Song (James Kirkup)

Grass for my pillow
S.D 131

Lullaby (Christina Rossetti)

Love me—I love you
Plea II 62

Lullaby of a Woman of the Mountains (Padraic H. Pearse)

House, be still, and ye little grey mice
F.Feet 156

Now through Night's caressing Grip (W. H. Auden)

Now through night's caressing grip
Com 133

Nurse's Song (German)

Sleep, baby, sleep
G.Tr.P 301; Mood III 9; My 186; This W.D 88

Still the Dark Forest (W. H. Auden)

Still the dark forest, quiet the deep
Cor 129; Ex.Tro 188; Ox.V.J I 71

Sweet and Low (Alfred Lord Tennyson)

Sweet and low, sweet and low
First II 24; Fuji 47; Fun I 71; G.Tr.P 300; Mood IV 49; My 185; Ox.P.C 160; Ox.V.J I 40; Plea II 61; P.Life II 77; This W.D 87; Tree II 49; Ver II 93

Three Fishers went sailing (Charles Kingsley)

Three fishers went sailing out into the west
Mood III 10

Wynken, Blynken and Nod (Eugene Field)

Wynken, Blynken and Nod one night
Fab.N.V 244; Fuji 18; G.Tr.P 302; Mer 80; Mer.Puf 57; Min II 94

121

You Spotted Snakes (William Shakespeare)

You spotted snakes with double tongue
Midsummer Night's Dream II ii 9; *B.B.F 165; B.P IV 94; By 40; Ch.Gar 18; D.P I 103; D.P.R I 80; Ex.Ch 28; F.Feet 157; G.Tr.P 297; Isle 53; Mer 367; Mer.Puf 279; My 27; Ox.P.C 160; Ox.V.J II 75; P.Bk 94; P.F.P I 102; P.Life II 78; P.Rem 40; Rhyme II 52; Song II 90; This W.D 37; Tree II 32; Ver II 7*

LUPINS

Lupin (Humbert Wolfe)

Said the deaf old gardener
Bits y

LYCHEES

The Lychee (Wang I—trans Arthur Waley)

Fruit white and lustrous as a pearl
Fab.C.V 110; Peg V 31

MACHINES

See also Chal III 88–96

See also Bulldozers, Cranes, Factories, Lorries, Motor Cars, Motor Cycles, Motor Launches, Steam Shovels, Tractors, Trains, U.S.A. Railroads, Washing (Clothes)

The Army Horse and the Army Jeep (John Ciardi)

Where do you go when you go to sleep?
Quest II 70

The Excavation (Max Endicoff)

Clusters of electric bulbs
D.P.R IV 95; Them VI 70

The Guillotine (Wilfrid Gibson)

Obedient to the will of men
Bird III 23; B.P IV 46; Key III 108; Ox.V.J IV 22

The Machine (Carl Sandburg)

The machine yes the machine
Chal III 88

La Marche des Machines (A. S. J. Tessimond)

This piston's infinite recurrence is
Mod.P 6

Night Shift (Sylvia Plath)

It was not a heart, beating
Nev 62; Them VI 68

The Pigeon or
The Seal (Richard Church)

Throb, throb from the mixer
A.S.L.A 60; Exp II 37; Mood IV 58; P.F.P II 108; Six IV 34; Song IV 115; Them VI 69; Weal II 166

Portrait of a Machine (Louis Untermeyer)

What nudity as beautiful as this
Day 125; D.P IV 117; D.P.R IV 94; Exp II 35; Mood IV 63; Peg III 50; P.F.P II 106; R.R 73; Song IV 114; Ver III 105

The Release (Wilfrid Gibson)

All day he shoved the pasteboard in
Ver III 53

The Secret of the Machines (Rudyard Kipling)

We were taken from the ore-bed and the mine
Dan 49; Mood IV 60; P.F.P II 107; R.R 74; Song III 14

The Toaster (William Jay Smith)

A silver-scaled dragon with jaws flaming red
Chal I 88; Fab.N.V 173; J.Vo III 7

A Trial Run (Robert Frost)

I said to myself almost in prayer
Six IV 10; Weal II 152

MADNESS

Counting the Mad (Donald Justice)

This one was put in a jacket
Them III 31

MAGI, THE

See Epiphany

MAGIC

See also Charms & Spells, Conjurors, Transformations

The Image (Sylvia Townsend Warner)

Why do you look so pale, my son William?
Exp VIII 23; Ver III 185

Kiph (Walter de la Mare)

My Uncle Ben, who's been
A.D.L 136; B.P II 75

On a Night of Snow (Elizabeth J. Coatsworth)

Cat, if you will go out of doors you must walk in the snow
F.Feet 187; G.Tr.P 48; Ox.V.J III 56; Patch 18; P.Life IV 17; Quest II 58; Say 50; Shad 105; Song I 71

Parsley, Sage, Rosemary and Thyme (Anon)

Can you make me a cambric shirt
Fab.N.V 120; Ox.Dic 108; Ox.N.R 196

Tillie (Walter de la Mare)

Old Tillie Turvey combe
De la M.Col 183; De la M.P.P 27; De la M.S 161; Fab.N.V 153; Iron I 37; Mer 339; Quest I 77

MAGICIANS

See also Isle 15–31

Errantry (J. R. R. Tolkien)

There was a merry passenger
Isle 16

Kubla Khan (part) (Samuel Taylor Coleridge)

Beware! beware!
Isle 13

Oh! My name is John Wellington Wells (W. S. Gilbert)

Oh! my name is John Wellington Wells
Song I 96

La Tour du Sorcier (Osbert Sitwell)

Whence comes the crooked wind
Dawn 52

The Two Magicians (Anon)

The Lady stands in her bower door
Bal 152

O, she looked out of the window
Cher 68; Min III 84; Mer 341; Mer.Puf 260; Pat 169; P.Tong I 98; Speak I 124

MAGPIES

A shot Magpie (Andrew Young)

Though on your long-tailed flight
You.Qu 25

MALDON

The Battle of Maldon (Anglo-Saxon)

... got broken/He made each warrior lash free his horse
P.W 32

MALLARD

Mallard (Rex Warner)

Squawking they rise from reeds into the sun
Drag 24; P.F.P I 124; R.R 183

MAN

An Essay on Man (part) Alexander Pope)

Know then thyself, presume not God to scan
Ten 201

Man (Sir John Davies)

I know my soul hath power to know all things
Trea 165

MARBLES

Marbles (R. N. Currey)

Now that our fertile acres yield
Prel II 24

MARCH

March (A. E. Housman)

The sun at noon to higher air
Fab.C.V 51

Written in March (William Wordsworth)

The cock is crowing
A.D.L 89; Bat 13; B.L.J III 32; B.P IV 71; Cor 22; Ex.Tro 24; Fun I 35; Go.Jo 95; G.Tr.P 270; Key II 90; Mer 362; Mer.Puf 274; Min IV 26; Mood I 46; Pat 28; P.Bk 11; P.Life II 46; Rain 81; Rhyme II 49; Riv I 3; Say 29; This W.D 103

MARCHING

Boots (Rudyard Kipling)

We're foot slog-slog-slog-sloggin' over Africa—
Six VI 46; Read II 47

March for Drum, Trumpet and Twenty-One Giants (C. S. Lewis)

With stomping stride in pomp and pride
Voi I 65

March for Strings, Kettledrums and Sixty-Three Dwarfs (C. S. Lewis)

With plucking pizzicato and the prattle of the kettledrum
Voi I 65; Yim I 8

Marching Along (Robert Browning)

Kentish Sir Byng stood for his King
Mood III 34; P.Bk 74

The Song of Soldiers (Walter de la Mare)

As I sat musing by the frozen dyke
De La M.Col 50; De La M.P.P 108

MARRIAGE

See also Weddings

An Arundel Tomb (Philip Larkin)

Side by side, their faces blurred
Fla 163; Mod.P 74; Pers 26; Sev 94; Them IV 33

Get up and Bar the Door (Anon)

It fell about the Martinmas time
Bal 657; B.B 167; Cor 67; Fab.Bal 77; G.Tr.P 123; Min III 20; Ox.P.C 19; Peg I 90; P.F.P I 154; Plea VI 24; Spo I 8; Sto II 122; Tell I 49

The Home-Coming (A. E. Wylde)

Maureen! Maureen! Why are you waiting
Them IV 27

Mag (Carl Sandburg)

I wish to God I never saw you, Mag
Them IV 26

On Thomas Bond and his Wife (Anon)

Here lie the bodies
Voi III 91

Robin-a-Thrush (Anon)

Oh, Robin-a-Thrush he married a wife
Mer 223; Mer.Puf 165; Puf.N.R 88; Tree IV 27

Scaffolding (Seamus Heaney)

Masons when they start upon a building
Them IV 30

The Single Girl (Anon)

Single girl, single girl
Nev 110

When I was single, went dressed all so fine
Say 86

A Slice of Wedding Cake (Robert Graves)

Why have such scores of lovely gifted girls
Nev 143; Sphe 324

Les Sylphides (Louis MacNiece)

Life in a day: he took his girl to the ballet
Kal 123; Them IV 29

To his Wife (General Su Wu)

Since our hair was plaited and we became man and wife
Nev 147

To my Dear and Loving Husband
(Anne Bradstreet)

If ever two were one, then surely we
Voi III 87

They did not expect this
(Vernon Scannell)

They did not expect this. Being neither
wise nor brave
J.Mod 60

The Whitsun Weddings (Philip
Larkin)

That Whitsun, I was late getting away
Mod.P 72

MARTENS

The Marten (John Clare)

The martin cat long shaged of courage
good
B.B.F 94; Iron IV 49; Voi II 49

MARTHA

Martha of Bethany (Clive Sansom)

It's all very well
Chal II 40; Spo II 129; Them VI 31

MARTINS

The House Martin (M. Hamburger)

Pines I remember, the air crisp
Drag 38

MAY

Home Pictures in May (John
Clare)

The sunshine bathes in clouds of many
hues
Cla.Wo 22; Key III 80; Wheel III 111

The May Day Garland (Edmund
Blunden)

Though folks no more go maying
Blu.Mi 32

The May Magnificat (Gerard
Manley Hopkins)

May is Mary's month, and I
Key III 81; Iron III 33; Ox.V.J IV 65

The Month of May (John Fletcher
& Francis Beaumont)

London, to thee I do present the merry
Month of May
Cher 44

MAY DAY

Come Lasses and Lads (1671)
(Anon)

Come lasses and lads
D.P I 94; P.F.P I 5; Weal I 38

Corinna's going a-Maying
(Robert Herrick)

Get up, get up for shame, the Blooming
Morn
*A.D.L 35; Her.Mu 45; Plea VII 83; P.W
96; P.W.R 98*

Furry Day Carol (Anon)

Remember us poor Mayers all!
P.Tong I 113

May Day Song (Anon)

The moon shines bright; the stars give a
light
G.Tr.P 274

May Song (Thomas Nashe)

Trip and go! Heave and ho!
Mer 124; Mer.Puf 93

Obby Oss (Charles Causley)

Early one morning/Second of May
Cau.Nar 45

Old May Song (Anon)

All in this pleasant evening, together
come are we
Com 155

All on this May Day morning, together
come are we
Sto I 134

Song of the Mayers (Anon)

Oh, we've been rambling all the night
Fun II 121

MEALS

See Breakfast

MEDICINE

Our Fathers of Old (Rudyard Kipling)

Excellent herbs had our fathers of old
Plea VI 27

Poor Henry (Walter de la Mare)

Thick in its glass
De la M.S 99

MERMAIDS AND MERMEN (LYRIC AND DESCRIPTIVE)

Deadman's Dirge (George Darley)

Prayer unsaid and mass unsung
Bat 70

The Mermaid (Alfred Lord Tennyson)

Who would be/A mermaid fair
Tree IV 36

Song of the Mermaids (George Darley)

Troop home to silent grots and caves
Cher 202

MERMAIDS & MERMEN (NARRATIVE)

The Forsaken Merman (Matthew Arnold)

Come, dear children, let us away
Ch.Gar 34; Ex.Ch 174; Fab.C.V 325; Fun I 152; My 68; Ox.P.C 59; Ox.V.J III 57; P.Bk 201; P.F.P II 214; Plea VI 51; P.W 210; P.W.R 239; Rhyme IV 44; Riv III 70; Spir 121; Spir.R 92; Spo I 32; Tell II 53; Trea 83; Ver II 96; Vic 114

Little Fan (James Reeves)

I don't like the look of little Fan, mother
J.Mod 54; Make II 19; Puf.Q 87; Quest II 71; Rhyme IV 50; Scrap 32; Shad 82; Sto II 12; V.F 112

The Mermaid (Anon)

As I walked out one evening fair
Song I 120

The Mermaid (Anon)

On a Friday morn, as we set sail
All 91; Bal 673; B.P III 72; Ex.Ch 26; Fun II 173; Min IV 40; P.Bk 75; P.F.P I 57; Sto I 137

Mermaiden (Thomas Hennell)

Chilled with salt dew, tossed on dark waters deep
Them II 15

The Mermaids (Walter de la Mare)

Sand, sand, hills of sand
De la M.Ch 86

The Neckan (Matthew Arnold)

In summer, on the headlands
Ex.Ch 61; Speak I 58

MICE

Anne and the Field-Mouse (Ian Serraillier)

We found a mouse in the chalk quarry today
Hap 15; Look 72; Prel I 20; Quest II 40; Say 51

Little Fable (Roy Fuller)

The mouse like halting clockwork, in the light
Drag 72

Madame Mouse Trots (Edith Sitwell)

Madame Mouse trots
Dawn 23; Fab.C.V 78; Song I 64; Start 9

The Meadow Mouse (Theodore Roethke)

In a shoe box stuffed in an old nylon stocking
Act III 98; Ark 33; Chal II 12; Exp III 4; J.Vo IV 15; Make I 131; Tell I 19; Yim I 34

Mouse (e. e. cummings)

here's a little mouse/and
Cent 34; Ver III 81; Weal II 7; Yim I 108

The Mouse (Elizabeth Coatsworth)

I hear a mouse
Puf.V 45

The Mouse in the Wainscot (Ian Serraillier)

Hush Suzanne!
Key I 111; Patch 16; Puf.Q 154; Rhyme IV 28; Scrap 28

The Mouse that gnawed the Oak-tree down (Vachel Lindsay)

The mouse that gnawed the oak-tree down
J.Vo II 6; Mood III 63

Mouse's Nest (John Clare)

I found a ball of grass among the hay
Cher 123; Cla.Wo 78; Shep 84

Supper (Walter de la Mare)

Her pinched grey body
De la M.Ch 129; De la M.Col 85

MILKING

Milking Time (Elizabeth Madox Roberts)

When supper time is almost come
Go.Jo 45

Milkmaid (Laurie Lee)

The girl's far treble, muted to the heat
Mod.P 47

MILLERS

See also Windmills

The Canterbury Tales (part) (Geoffrey Chaucer)

The miller was a stout carles for the nones
Flock 31; Iron III 58; M.M.A 53; P.Tong I 133

(trans N. Coghill)

The miller was a chap of sixteen stone
Flock 30; M.M.A 54; Ver III 199; Weal I 105

(trans L. Untermeyer)

The Miller, stout and sturdy as the stones
G.Tr.P 81

The Jolly Miller (Isaac Bickerstaffe)

There was a jolly miller once
G.Tr.P 94; Mer 194; Mer.Puf 151; M.G.E 118; Ox.Dic 308; P.Bk 33

The Miller (Sir John Clerk)

Merry may the mard be
Cher 84

The Unfortunate Miller (A. E. Coppard)

On windy days the mill
Kal 130

MILTON

Milton! Thou should'st be Living (William Wordsworth)

Milton! thou should'st be living at this hour
Peg V 78

MINERS

See also Accidents (Mines), Ponies (Pit), Strikes

Caliban in the Coal Mines (Louis Untermeyer)

God, we don't like to complain
Chal I 86; Man II 24; Mood III 47; Peg III 64; Quest IV 38; Six IV 38

Cleator Moor (Norman Nicholson)

From one shaft at Cleator Moor
Mod.P 35

The Coal-Filler's Song (Johnny Handle)

O the collier lad, he's a canny lad
Wheel III 194

The Collier (Vernon Watkins)

When I was born on Amman Hill
*Dawn 80; D.P.R III 6; Exp I 29; Flock
197; J.Vo IV 90; Make IV 126; Mod.P
9; S.D 36*

The Collier's Wife (William
Henry Davies)

The collier's wife had four tall sons
R.R 114

The Collier's Wife
(D. H. Lawrence)

Somebody's knockin' at th'door
*Bird III 5; D.P.R III 9; Fla 42; Law.S
65; M.Ver 94; Read I 83; Six III 30;
Tell I 66; Them VI 60*

The Durham Lockout (Thomas
Armstrong)

In our Durham country I am sorry for to
say
Broad 39; D.P.R IV 82

The First Snow (Wilfrid Gibson)

From the pit's mouth men pour, a stream
of black
Bird II 16

Fourpence a Day (Anon)

The ore is waiting in the tubs, the snow's
upon the fell
Broad 41; D.P.R I 37; Song IV 99

Get Up (Joseph Skipsey)

'Get up!' the caller calls, 'Get up!'
Song IV 100

The Greeting (Wilfrid Gibson)

What fettle, mate? to me he said
Wheel III 143

Low Seam Miners (Robert Morgan)

And he returns, day after day
S.D 35

Miners (Wilfred Owen)

There was a whispering in my hearth
*Bird IV 33; Camb 125; D.P IV 108;
D.P.R IV 79; Iron IV 126; Riv IV 125;
Song III 108; Wheel IV 160*

Miners above Ground (George
Barker)

Dead men and miners go underground
Peg IV 96; R.R 128

Mother Wept (Joseph Skipsey)

Mother wept, and father sigh'd
Prel II 50

The Mountain over Aberdare
(Alun Lewis)

From this high quarried ledge I see
Day 71

Names of Trades (part of *The Big
Hewer*) (Ewan MacColl)

You're at the pit-bank
Song III 140

Out of the dirt and darkness I was born
Speak II 113

The Plodder Seam (Anon)

The Plodder seam is a wicked seam
Make III 72

Schooldays End (Ewan MacColl)

Schooldays over—come on then, John
Bird II 42

The Silver Mine (Tachibana
Akemi—trans D. Keene)

Stark naked, the men
S.D 48

Statue of a Miner (Ernest Rhys)

Let it be marble, but as black
Man I 51

MINNOWS

I Stood tiptoe upon a little hill
(part) (John Keats)

How silent comes the water round that
bend!
Sto I 80

Swarms of minnows show their little
heads
F.Feet 69; G.Tr.P 72

MISERY

Breakfast (Jacques Prevert)

He put the coffee
Chal II 33

Song of the Mackerel Pike (Harvo Sato—trans Shozo Tokunaga)

O! Autumn winds
Shep 126

The Woodspurge (Dante Gabriel Rossetti)

The wind flapped loose, the wind was still
By 184; Shep 73; Vic 188

MISFITS

Adjust your Dress before leaving (A. Edkins)

The man who is sidling towards me has a worried look on his face
Bird III 19

4 C Boy (Robert Morgan)

He was passive, one of seven
Act V 42

The Misfit (C. Day Lewis)

At the train depot that first morning
Day 20

Nobody loses all the time (E. E. Cummings)

I had an uncle named
Flock 132; Peg V 110; Wheel III 164

Not Waving but Drowning (Stevie Smith)

Nobody heard him, the dead man
Them III 46

Timothy Winters (Charles Causley)

Timothy Winters comes to school
A.S.L.A 11; Chal I 73; Com 171; Mod.P 67; My 100; Read II 66; Sev 17; Them IV 43; Under 59; Voi II 90; Wheel II 167

MISSEL THRUSHES

The Missel-Thrush (Andrew Young)

That missel thrush
You.Bu 27

Missel Thrush (Walter de la Mare)

When from the brittle ice, the fields
B.B.F 116; De la M.Col 104; Iron II 80

MIST

See also Fog

Mist (Andrew Young)

Rain do not fall
Flock 119; You.Bu 21

November (parts) (John Clare)

The landscape sleeps in mist from morn till noon
Com 65; Flock 266

The shepherds almost wonder where they dwell
Bat 14; Cla.Wo 35; G.Tr.P 282; Prel III 34; R.R 88; Sphe 36

The timid hare seems half its fears to lose
B.B.F 71

Ploughing in Mist (Andrew Young)

Pulling the shoulder-sack
You.Qu 27

MITHRAS

A Song to Mithras (Rudyard Kipling)

Mithras, God of the Morning, our trumpets waken the Wall!
Plea V 92

MOLECATCHERS

The Mole-Catcher (Anon)

A mole-catcher am I, and that is my trade
Riv III 113

The Mole-Catcher (John Clare)

When melted snow leaves bare the black-green rings
Iron III 78

Mole Catcher (Edmund Blunden)

With coat like any mole's, as soft and black
Bird III 17; Blu.Mi 26; J.Mod 67; R.R 127; Wheel II 144

MOLES

A Dead Mole (Andrew Young)

Strong-shouldered mole
Drag 72; Peng.An 203; Say 20; You.Qu 26

Mole (Alan Brownjohn)

To have to be a mole?
Bro.B 16

MOLLUSCS

See Crabs, Lobsters, Oysters, Slugs, Snails

MONEY

As I sat at the Cafe (Arthur Hugh Clough)

As I sat at the café, I said to myself
Comp 49

Ballade of the Good Life (Bertolt Brecht)

Those who from duty's path are never shaken
Nev 58

The Hardship of Accounting (Robert Frost)

Never ask of money spent
Eye 33; J.Mod 23

Money-Madness (D. H. Lawrence)

Money is our madness, our vast collective madness
Cent 47; Under 78

Wages (D. H. Lawrence)

The wages of work is cash
Ev.M 111

MONKEYS

See Apes & Monkeys

MONSOON

Monsoon (David Wevill)

A snake emptied itself into the grass
A.S.L.A 52; Under 52; Yim III 3

MONTHS

See also April, August, December, February, January, July, June, March, May, November, October

The Months (Anon)

Januar/By thys fyre I warme my handys
Cher 425

The Months (Christina Rossetti)

January (cold) desolate
Cor 23; Puf.Y 55

The Months of the Year or
The Garden Year (Sara Coleridge)

January brings the snow
B.P II 59; Fab.N.V 227; Fuji 30; Fun I 51; G.Tr.P 268; M.G.E 144; Min III 32; P.Bk 12; P.Life I 54; Puf.V 15; Rain 78; Tree III 20

Winter (John Clare)

Old January clad in crispy rime
Voi I 131

MOODS

See Anger, Contentment, Frustration, Happiness, the Hump, Laughing, Laziness, Loneliness, Misery, Pessimism, Pride, Sympathy

MOON

See also Exp VII 43–56

Above the Dock (Thomas E. Hulme)

Above the quiet dock in midnight
Bits g; B.L.J II 50; Fla 40; P.W 252; P.W.R 297; Weal II 152

Autumn (Thomas E. Hulme)

A touch of cold in the autumn night
Act II 39; Fla 40; My 10; P.W 252; P.W.R 297

The Cat and the Moon
(W. B. Yeats)

The cat went here and there
B.B.F 104; Fab.C.V 69; Flock 57; Go.Jo 245; Iron II 54; J.Vo II 28; Kal 7; Ox.V.J IV 80; Pers 125; Read II 83; Shad 104; This W.D 23; Weal I 2; Yea.Run 71

Full Moon (Walter de la Mare)

One night as Dick lay half-asleep
De la M.Col 224; De la M.P.P 38; Riv II 24; Scrap 42

Full Moon Rhyme (Judith Wright)

There's a hare in the moon tonight
Shad 52

Is the Moon tired? (Christina Rossetti)

Is the moon tired? She looks so pale
Mer 193; Mer.Puf 150; Mood II 64

The Moon (P. B. Shelley)

And like a dying lady, lean and pale
Bat 75; Fab.C.V 49; Look 243

Moon (William Jay Smith)

I have a white cat whose name is Moon
V.F 154

The Moon (Robert Louis Stevenson)

The moon has a face like the clock in the hall
B.P I 13; Fun I 57; Min I 31; P.Life I 68; Puf.V 225; Ste.C.G 54; Tree II 30

The Moon and the Sun (Anglo-Saxon Riddle—trans Gavin Bone)

I saw a creature sally with booty
P.W 31; P.W.R 27; Riv IV 24

(trans Burton Raffel)

I saw a silvery creature scurrying
Go.Jo 244

(trans K. Crossley-Holland)

I saw a strange creature
Rid 17

The Moon's the North Wind's Cooky (Vachel Lindsay)

The moon's the North wind's cooky
G.Tr.P 258

Night (William Blake)

The sun descending in the west
Mer 207

Silver (Walter de la Mare)

Slowly, silently, now the moon
De la M.Col 222; De la M.P.P 100; First

III 26; Fun II 91; G.Tr.P 262; Key III 138; Mer 323; Mer.Puf 244; Ox.V.J III 71; P.F.P I 37; Plea III 52; P.Life III 90; Rhyme IV 10; Riv I 14; Sphe 90; Ver II 207

Who knows if the moon's (e. e. cummings)

Who knows if the moon's
Cor 130; Sto II 43

The Wind and the Moon (George Macdonald)

Said the Wind to the Moon
Fun I 18; Go.Jo 35; G.Tr.P 258

MORTALITY

See also Time

To Daffodils (Robert Herrick)

Fair Daffodils, we weep to see
B.P III 28; Ch.Gar 89; Fab.C.V 51; Go.Jo 70; Her.Mu 49; P.Bk 31; P.F.P II 230; P.Rem 147; Puf.V 22; Shep 76; Song IV 157; Spo I 120; Ver III 16; Weal I 115

Fare Well (Walter de la Mare)

When I lie where shades of darkness
Ten 51

The hat given to the Poet by Li Chien (Arthur Waley)

Long ago to a white-haired gentleman
P.W 263

His Poetrie his Pillar (Robert Herrick)

Onely a little more
Comp 25

The Life of Man (Barnabe Barnes)

A blast of wind, a momentary breath
S.D 156

The Life of this World (Anon 13th Century—trans B. Stone)

The life of this world/Is governed by wind
D.P.R IV 121

Like as the Damask Rose (Anon)

Like as the damask rose you see
A.D.L 195; Fab.C.V 381; Song IV 158

Like to the falling of a Star
(Henry King)

Like to the falling of a star
Key IV 32; Peg IV 106; S.D 175;
Song III 156

Like to the grass (Anon)

Like to the grass that's newly sprung
Sphe 437

Lines before Execution
(Chidiock Tychborn)

My prime of youth is but a frost of cares
Cher 324; Voi II 148

O Death, rock me on sleep
(attributed Anne Boleyn)

O Death, rock me on sleep
Cher 357

On the Vanity of Earthly Greatness
(A. Guiterman)

The tusks that clashed in mighty brawls
Plea VI 13

To Virgins, to make much of Time
(Robert Herrick)

Gather ye rosebuds while ye may
By 65; Cher 51; D.P IV 143; Her.Mu
22; Make IV 44; Plea VI 32; R.R 141;
Weal II 140

MOSES

Go Down, Moses (Anon)

Go down, Moses
B.L.A.F 372; J.Vo IV 35; Riv II 49

MOSQUITOES

Mosquito (John Updike)

On the fine wire of her whine she walked
Flock 206

The Mosquito (D. H. Lawrence)

When did you start your tricks
Camb 74; Choice 191; Law.S 34;
Peng.An 210; Voi II 42

MOTHERS

The Forsaken (Duncan Campbell
Scott)

Once in the winter/Out on a lake
Tel II 11

The Song of the Old Mother
(W. B. Yeats)

I rise in the dawn and I kneel and blow
Ex.Ch 149; Iron I 17; Ox.V.J II 30; Peg
II 101; Them IV 58; Tree IV 33;
Yea.Run 42

To my Mother (George Barker)

Most near, most dear, most loved and
most far
By 296; Flock 63; Kal 25; Pat 117; Prel
I 26

MOTHERS & DAUGHTERS

A Frosty Night (Robert Graves)

Alice, dear, what ails you
Ris 15; Them IV 25

Getting Ready for School (Caryl
Brahms)

Kate, Kate,/I know you'll be late!
Fun I 72; Min III 16

The Row (Linda Whitehead—aged
14)

I've explained it all to her
Them III 53

MOTHERS & SONS

Mother and Son (R. S. Thomas)

At nine o'clock in the morning
Chal II 37; Exp.I 7; Liv 25; Them IV 40

MOTHS

Book-Moth (Old English—trans
Charles W. Kennedy)

A moth ate a word. To me it seemed
Ark 29

Lunar Moth (Robert Hillyer)

From the forest of the night
Ark 9

The Moth (Walter de la Mare)

Isled in the midnight air
B.B.F 122; De la M.Ch 56; Ver III 50

The Moths (Julian Bell)

The narrow paths beside the flower beds run
Pat 52

MOTOR CARS

The Car under the Steam-Hammer (David Holbrook)

There's a hammer up at Harwich and it's worked by steam
Key IV 160

Highway: Michigan (Theodore Roethke)

Here from the field's edge we survey
Chal III 94

Limousine (Christopher Hassall)

Limousine, superb, imposing
Key IV 161

Man on Wheels (Karl Shapiro)

Cars are wicked, poets think
Chal III 96

She being Brand
(e. e. cummings)

she being Brand/-new
S.D 52

MOTOR CYCLES

Fifteen (William Stafford)

South of the bridge on Seventeenth
Chal II 39; Voi II 89

Poems of my Lambretta 1 & 2 (Paul Goodman)

This pennant new
Chal III 58

MOTOR LAUNCHES

Motor Launch (G. Rostrevor Hamilton)

See how her leaping bows divide
Key IV 159

MOTORING

See also Accidents (Road)

Ambition (Morris Bishop)

I got pocketed behind 7X-3824
Six IV 8; Wheel IV 162

Southbound on the Freeway (May Swenson)

A tourist came in from Orbitville
Chal I 93; J.Vo IV 54

The Wiper (Louis MacNiece)

Through purblind night the wiper
Under 123

MOTORWAYS

Merrit Parkway (Denise Levertov)

As if it were/forever that they move that we
Bird IV 11; Voi III 28

MOUNTAIN LIONS

Mountain Lion (D. H. Lawrence)

Climbing through the January snow into the Lobo Canyon
Camb 79; Day 54; Drag 10; Iron III 15; Law.S 39; M.Ver 86; Nar 73; P.Bk 351; R.R 180; Them I 43; Wheel IV 152

MOUNTAINEERING

See also Everest

Breathless (Wilfrid Noyce)
Heart aches/Lungs pant
Ev.M 31; R.R 41

Climbing Suilven (Norman MacCaig)

I nod and nod to my own shadow and thrust
Them V 51

The Cragsman (Geoffrey Winthrop Young)

In this short span
Peg V 20; Ver III 60

Every Man to his Taste (St John Hankin)

I am an unadventurous man
Them V 70

John Muir on the Ritter
(Gary Snyder)

After scanning its face again and again
Flock 140

The Snowslide (Wilfrid Noyce)

It came so slow
Make III 38

MOWING

Man with Scythe (A. W. Russell)

Shambling Frank the labourer
Make III 61

Mowing (Robert Frost)

There was never a sound beside the wood
but one
Choice 277; P.F.P II 132; Ten 78

The Scythe (Stanley Snaith)

This morning as the scythe swung in my
grasp
Act III 10; Peg V 36

The Scythe Song (Andrew Lang)

Mowers, weary and brown and blithe
Min III 36

MURDER

See also F.S.N.A 261–275

The Ballad of Charlotte Dymond
(Charles Causley)

Charlotte Dymond, a domestic servant
aged eighteen, was
Voi II 112

Burke's Confession (Anon)

All ye that stand around me, I pray to me
attend
Broad 23

By the Exeter River (Donald
Hall)

What is it you're mumbling, old Father,
my Dad?
Act II 26; Mod.P 141

Coroner's Jury (L. A. G. Strong)

He was the doctor up to Combe
Tell I 51

The Croodin' Doo (Anon)

Where hae ye been a' the day?
Ox.Dic 77; Ox.N.R 203

The Dorking Thigh (William
Plomer)

About to marry and invest
Make IV 49; Weal II 116

Edward, Edward (Anon)

Why does your brand so drop wi' blood,
Edward, Edward?
*Bal 86; B.B 142, 189; Bun 39; Com 108;
Fab.Bal 119; Iron II 20; Key I 19; Make
III 133; Peg III 89; P.F.P I 149; Plea IV
72; P.W 4; P.W.R 4; Riv IV 92; Spo II 9;
Ver III 178; Wheel III 25*

How came that blood on your shirt
sleeve?
F.S.N.A 25

*Farewell to Barn and Stack and
Tree* (A. E. Housman)

Farewell to barn and stack and tree
Read III 141

Five Ways to Kill a Man (Edwin
Brock)

There are many cumbersome ways to kill
a man
Chal III 20

The Irish Ballad (Tom Lehrer)

About a maid I'll sing a song
Dan 81

Johnny Sands (Anon)

A man whose name was Johnny Sands
B.B 151; Chal I 43

Life of the Mannings (Anon)

See the scaffold it is mounted
Fab.Bal 188

Lord Randall (Anon)

Where have you been, Lord Randall my
son?
*Bal 81; Bat 84; B.B 164; Fab.Bal 34;
Fun I 136; Kal 108; Make II 100;
M.M.A 65; Mood III 72; Ox.Dic 76;
Ox.V.J IV 24; P.Bk 135; P.F.P I 147;
Plea IV 74; P.Tong I 101; P.W 16;*

P.W.R 14; Read III 23; Riv III 130; R.R 26; Say 73; Song III 146; Voi II 133; Yim II 8

No Man Takes the Farm (John Masefield)

No man takes the farm
Speak II 59

Nora Criona (James Stephens)

I have looked him round and looked him through
Eye 17

Notting Hill Polka
(W. Bridge-Adams)

We've—had—
Song II 70

The Other Time (Peter Appleton)

He killed a man/In a drunken brawl
D.P.R II 51; Key IV 18

Porphyria's Lover (Robert Browning)

The rain set in early tonight
Act V 29; Vic 76

The Rich Old Lady (Anon)

A rich old lady in ouer town
Key I 38

Shooting of his Dear (Anon)

Come all you young people who handle the gun
M.M.A 29

Come all you young fellows that carry a gun
P.W.R 19

A Small Tragedy (Sally Roberts)

They came up in the evening
Them III 10

The Sorrowful Lamentation . . . of John Lomas (Anon)

May fate be a warning to sinful men, whereby they may
Voi II 118

A Trampwoman's Tragedy (Thomas Hardy)

From Wynyard's Gap the livelong day
Song III 24

MUSHROOMS

The Forest (Miroslav Holub—trans George Theiner)

Among the primary rocks
J.Vo IV 72

Mushrooms (Sylvia Plath)

Overnight, very/whitely, discreetly
A.S.L.A 42; Bird III 42; Cent 94; Drag 68; My 150; Read III 113; Sphe 87; Them II 66; Voi II 52; Yim III 132

MUSIC

See also Bagpipes, Bands, Banjos, Bells, Blues, Bugles, Calliopes, Drums, Horns, Jazz, Orpheus, Pipers, Singing, Violins

Alexander's Feast or *The Power of Music* (John Dryden)

'Twas at the royal feast for Persia won
Ver III 120

At a Solemn Music (John Milton)

Blest pair of Sirens, pledges of Heaven's joy
Pat 150

Concert Interpretation
(Siegfried Sassoon)

The Audience pricks an intellectual ear
Pat 148

How sweet the moonlight (William Shakespeare)

How sweet the moonlight sleeps upon this bank
Merchant of Venice V i 54; Bat 32; By 44; Ch.Gar 24; P.W.R 69; P.W 74; Riv IV 140

The Lotus Eaters: Choric Song (Alfred Lord Tennyson)

There is sweet music here that softer falls
Man I 35; Ox.V.J IV 48; P.F.P II 13; Spo II 145; Trea 260; Vic 42

Old King Cole (Anon)

Old King Cole was a merry old soul
B.P III 100; Ex.Tra 16; Fab.N.V 265; M.G.B 147; M.G.R 137; Min I 82;

135

Ox.Dic 134; Puf.N.R 120; Puf.S.B 132;
Rhyme II 2

Orpheus with his Lute (William
Shakespeare)

Orpheus with his lute made trees
*Henry VIII III i 3; Cher 82; Fab.C.V 36;
Fun II 26; P.F.P II 130; Riv IV 2; Sphe
263; Spo I 150; Trea 1*

Song for St Cecilia's Day
(John Dryden)

From harmony, from heavenly harmony
*P.F.P II 128; P.Tong I 33; P.W 116;
P.W.R 123; Spo II 82; (part) D.P IV
129*

The trumpet's loud clangour
Peg IV 61

MYSTERY

See also Fantasy, Ghosts

MYSTERY
(LYRIC & DESCRIPTIVE)

At the Keyhole (Walter de la
Mare)

'Grill me some bones' said the cobbler
*De la M.Ch 121; De la M.Col 134; De la
M.P.P 87; De la M.S 50; Ox.P.C 88;
Shad 23*

The Call (Charlotte Mew)

From our low seat beside the fire
Act III 45; Man III 27; Ox.V.J IV 92

The Door (Miroslav Holub—trans
Ian Milner)

Go and open the door
J.Vo IV 2; Nev 36

The Way through the Woods
(Rudyard Kipling)

They shut the road through the woods
*Act III 67; Bird I 25; D.P IV 64; D.P.R
IV 38; Fab.C.V 377; Isle 81; Look 294;
Ox.V.J IV 63; P.F.P II 223; Plea VII 53;
P.Life IV 26; Rain 80; Rhyme IV 16;
Song I 139; Sphe 86; Start 126; Them II
6; This W.D 163; Weal I 107; Way 52*

What has happened to Lulu?
(Charles Causley)

What has happened to Lulu, mother?
Cau.Fig 16

MYSTERY (NARRATIVE)

The Ballad of Minepit Shaw
(Rudyard Kipling)

About the times that taverns shut
Plea VI 80

Flannan Isle (Wilfrid Gibson)

Though three men dwell on Flannan Isle
*Chal II 60; Make III 114; M.M.A 11;
Mood II 89; Ox.P.C 78; P.F.P II 219;
R.R 29; Six II 26; Song I 116; Speak II
55; T.C.N 116; T.P.W 54; Way 41;
Weal I 76; Yim I 93*

Lady, Weeping at the Crossroads
(W. H. Auden)

Lady, weeping at the crossroads
Cent 29

The Landing at Night (Sir John
Squire)

As twilight fell the wind blew strong
J.Mod 42

The Listeners (Walter de la Mare)

'Is there anybody there?' said the
Traveller
*B.P IV 67; By 228; Cent 12; De la M.Ch
99; De la M.S 121; D.P IV 70; D.P.R IV
32; Drag 52; Isle 83; Look 292; Make II
64; P.F.P II 218; Plea VII 12; P.Life IV
42; Prel IV 35; Read I 67; Riv IV 99;
Shad 38; Six II 24; Song II 94; Sphe
422; T.C.N 20; Ten 46; This W.D 147;
Trea 316; Way 31; Wheel III 141; Yim I
92*

Lollocks (Robert Graves)

By sloth on sorrow fathered
*Cher 155; Choice 262; Day 38; Flock
196; Key IV 60; Them II 14*

The Strange Visitor (Anon)

A wife was sitting at her reel ae night
*Cher 132; Cor 48; Fab.C.V 195; J.Vo
III 63; Key IV 89; Ox.P.C 86; P.Life IV
45; P.Tong I 3*

Welsh Incident (Robert Graves)

But that was nothing to what things came out
Com 121; Ev.M 22; J.Mod 48; Nar 51; Peg IV 22; Pers 66; P.F.P II 222; R.R 178; Six II 33; Song III 133; Them II 50; Voi II 11; Weal II 114

MYTHOLOGY

See also Arthur, Baucis and Philemon, Cyclops, Europa, Icarus, Mithras, Orpheus, Pan, Sirens, Sisyphus

Outlaws (Robert Graves)

Owls: they whinney down the night
P.F.P II 224

NABARA, THE

The Nabara (part) (C. Day Lewis)

Freedom is more than a word, more than the base coinage
M.Ver 143

The year, Nineteen-thirty-seven; month March; the men descendants
Kal 83

NAMES

See also Song III 135–141

American Names (Stephen Vincent Benet)

I have fallen in love with American names
Peg V 66; S.D 24

Boys' and Girls' Names (Eleanor Farjeon)

What splendid names for boys there are!
P.Life II 9

Choosing their Names (Thomas Hood)

Our old cat has kittens three
B.L.J II 22; First III 20; Puf.Y 105; Rain 38; Rhyme II 41; Tree III 56

Dorset (Sir John Betjeman)

Rime Intrinsica, Fontmell Magna, Sturminster
Mod.P 2

Jargon (James Reeves)

Jerusalem, Joppa, Jericho
Hap 51; Rhyme III 1; V.F 116

Maple (Robert Frost)

Her teacher's certainty it must be Mabel
Quest III 7

My Name and I (Robert Graves)

The impartial Law enrolled a name
Pers 8

Names for Twins (Alastair Reed)

Each pair of twins
Tree III 58

The Naming of Cats (T. S. Eliot)

The naming of cats is a difficult matter
Ch.Gar 54; El.O.P 9

Stormy (William Carlos Williams)

What name could
Peng.An 275

NANSEN

Nansen (Eleanor & Herbert Farjeon)

This is the saga of Nansen, pioneer of the North
Peg II 20

NAPOLEON

See also Waterloo, Wellington

Boney was a Warrior (Anon)

Boney wes a warrior
P.Tong I 13; P.W 25; P.W.R 21; Riv III 34

Napoleon (Walter de la Mare)

What is the world, O soldiers?
De la M.Ch 139; Fab.C.V 147; P.Rem 117

137

A St Helena Lullaby (Rudyard Kipling)

How far is St Helena from a little child at play?
Fab.C.V 147; Plea VI 71

We be the King's Men (Thomas Hardy)

We be the King's men, hale and hearty
B.P IV 24; Chor 8; Ex.Ch 105; Mer 346; Mer.Puf 263; Min I 67; Mood I 27; Riv II 45

NASEBY

The Battle of Naseby (Lord Macauley)

Oh! Wherefore come ye forth, in triumph from the North
Trea 46; Ver II 139

NATIONALITY

Nationality (Mary Gilmore)

I have grown past hate and bitterness
Voi III 113

NAVVIES

Come, my little son (Ewan MacColl)

Come, my little son, and I'll tell you what we'll do
Exp II 47

Florida Road Workers (Langston Hughes)

I'm makin' a road
Chal II 76

Muckers (Carl Sandburg)

Twenty men stand watching the muckers
J.Vo IV 90

NEFERTITI

Queen Nefertiti (Anon)

Spin a coin, spin a coin
My 22; Scrap 115; Shad 99

NEGROES

See also F.S.N.A 448–595

See also Race Relations, Refugees

Award (Ray Durem)

Well old spy/looks like I
Chal III 47

Incident (Countee Cullen)

Once riding in old Baltimore
Chal I 40

I, too, Sing America (Langston Hughes)

I, too, sing America
Chal III 34

The Little Black Boy (William Blake)

My mother bore me in the southern wild
Bird I 37; Bla.Gr 63; Ch.Gar 172; Com 40; Iron I 22; Mer 291; Mer.Puf 216; Pers 29; Prel I 42; P.Rem 34; P.W 139; P.W.R 153; Riv I 36; Sphe 378; Wheel II 71

Me and the Mule (Langston Hughes)

My old mule
Chal II 22

The Negro (Langston Hughes)

I am a Negro
Bird I 36; Chal II 57; Exp IV 39

Prayer of a Black Boy (Guy Tirolien)

Lord, I am so tired
Chal II 56; Exp IV 18

NEIGHBOURS

'Bus to School (John Walsh)

Rounding the corner
Cor 82; Key II 18; Mood I 24; Prel II 2

The Good Samaritan (The Bible)

A certain man went down from Jerusalem to Jericho
Luke X 30–36; B.L.J III 44

Mending Wall (Robert Frost)

Something there is that doesn't love a wall

Choice 278; Fro.You 70; Iron III 52;
Song IV 58; Sphe 59; Ten 76

Parable (William Soutar)

Two neighbours, who were rather dense
M.Ver 111

The People Upstairs (Ogden Nash)

The people upstairs all practise ballet
Cor 87; Prel IV 30; Rhyme IV 82

The Unexploded Bomb (C. Day
Lewis)

Two householders (semi-detached) once
found
Under 108

NELSON

See also Trafalgar

The Death of Nelson (Anon)

Come all gallant seamen that unite a
meeting
P.Tong I 15

1805 (Robert Graves)

At Viscount Nelson's lavish funeral
*Day 35; Fab.C.V 146; M.Ver 136; Pers
57; P.F.P II 73; P.W 264; P.W.R 320;
Riv IV 119; R.R 51; Them VI 73*

NETHERLANDS, THE

The Character of Holland
(Andrew Marvell)

Holland, that scarce deserves the name
of land
Cher 204

Such is Holland! (Petrus
Augustus de Genestet)

O, land of mud and mist where man is
wet and shivers
Flock 42

NETTLES

Tall Nettles (Edward Thomas)

Tall nettles cover up, as they have done
*Bird III 41; Cent 23; Cher 237; Choice
169; Iron I 43; Pat 167; P.F.P I 43;
Read II 73; Say 52; Sphe 66; Ten 128;
Tho.Gr 30; Tree IV 95; Voi I 113*

NEWSBOYS

Fleet Street (Shane Leslie)

I never see the newsboys run
Man II 26

NEWSPAPERS

See also Editors, Reporters

*The Great Newspaper Editor to his
Subordinate* (D. H. Lawrence)

Mr Smith, Mr Smith
D.P.R III 34; Iron IV 30; Law.S 83

Gutter Press (Paul Dehn)

News Editor./Peer Confesses,/Bishop
Undresses
Act IV 79

NEW YEAR

New Year (Alfred Lord Tennyson)

Ring out, wild bells, to the wild sky
D.P.R I 20

NEW ZEALAND

See Ver III 308–364, New Zealand
Verse

See Kiwis

NIGHT

See also Moon

Check (James Stephens)

The night was creeping on the ground
*Ex.Ch 182; Ox.V.J I 41; P.Life III 95;
Spo I 152*

Christabel (part)
(S. T. Coleridge)

'Tis the middle of the night by the castle
clock
Mer 295; Mer.Puf 219

*The Complaint of Henrie, Duke of
Buckinghame* (part) (Thomas
Sackville)

Midnight was come, and every vital thing
Ark 205; B.B.F 103; Tree IV 47

The Country Bedroom (Frances Cornford)

My room's a square and candle-lighted boat
B.P IV 72; By 254; J.Mod 72; Ox.V.J III 55; Quest III 28; Shep 147; Them VII 36

Night (William Blake)

The sun descending in the west
B.B.F 228; B.L.J II 9; B.P I 72; Ex.Ch 183; Fuji 13; Fun I 56; G.Tr.P 263; Mer 207; Ox.V.J II 15; Plea II 63; Say 54; Song III 32; Trea 199

Night Song (Frances Cornford)

On moony nights the dogs bark shrill
Bird I 1

The Night Song of the Bards (Anon)

The distant dog is howling from the hut of the hill
B.B.F 101

Old Shellover (Walter de la Mare)

'Come!' said Old Shellover
B.B.F 106; Com 46; De la M.Ch 125; De la M.Col 211; De la M.P.P 20; De la M.S 74; Key I 33; Mer 209; Plea II 63; Riv I 15; Song II 56

Out in the Dark (Edward Thomas)

Out in the dark over the snow
F.Feet 154; Iron IV 111; Plea VII 108; Ten 143; Tho.Gr 74

Shadow March (Robert Louis Stevenson)

All round the house is the jet-black night
Ox.V.J II 16; P.Life III 94; Scrap 23; Ste.C.G 66

Silver (Walter de la Mare)

Slowly, silently, now the moon
De la M.Col 222; De la M.P.P 100; First III 26; Fun II 91; G.Tr.P 262; Key III 138; Mer 323; Mer.Puf 244; Ox.V.J III 71; P.F.P I 37; Plea III 52; P.Life III 90; Rhyme IV 10; Riv I 14; Sphe 90; Ver II 207

A Winter Night (William Barnes)

It was a chilly winter's night
Bat 16

NIGHTINGALES

The New-Come Nightingale (John Clare)

When we first hear the shy-come nightingale
Song II 52

Ode to a Nightingale (John Keats)

My heart aches, and a drowsy numbness pains
Cher 102; Puf.V 222

Philomena (part) (Richard Barnfield)

As it fell upon a day
B.B.F 49

NIGHTMARES

Drugged (Walter de la Mare)

Inert in his chair
De la M.Ch 113; Them II 37

The Nightmare (Elizabeth Jennings)

The dream was that old falling one
Them II 38

The Nightmare (Wang Yen-Shou— trans Arthur Waley)

One night, about the time I came of age, I dreamt that
Read I 65; Voi II 13

Nightmare (from *Iolanthe*) (W. S. Gilbert)

When you're lying awake with a dismal headache
Bird IV 29; Ch.Gar 155; Chor 45; M.M.A. 70; Peg IV 24; Plea VIII 54; P.Tong II 192; Sphe 240; Spo II 87; Sto III 119; Them II 39

NOAH

The Ballad of Mrs Noah (Robert Duncan)

Mrs Noah in the Ark
Mod.P 103

Ballad of the Flood (Edwin Muir)

Last night I dreamed a ghastly dream
Ris 34

The Chester Play of the Deluge
(part) (Anon)

Noe: Have done! you men and women
all
Cher 93; Key IV 104

Sem: Sir! heare are lions, leopardes, in
Peng.An 17

Dem Bones Gonna Rise Again
(Anon)

In come de animals two by two
Chor 37

Didn't it Rain (Anon)

Now, didn't it rain, chillun
J.Vo II 20

Every Living Creature (Michael
Drayton)

And now the Beasts are walking from the
wood
Peng.An 19; P.Bk 149

The Flaming Terrapin (part)
(Roy Campbell)

Out of the Ark's grim hold
*A.D.L 161; Ark 134; Key IV 106; Mood
IV 74; Spir 45; Spir.R 38*

When Noah thundered with his
monstrous axe
Wheel II 147

The History of the Flood (John
Heath-Stubbs)

Bang, Bang, Bang/Said the nails in the
Ark
*A.S.L.A 84; Down 55; Flock 38; Peg II
29; Peng.An 21; Ris 40; Sev 46*

Lady Zouch (Eleanor Farjeon)

Lady Zouch could not keep deer
F.Feet 211

The Late Passenger (C. S. Lewis)

The sky was low, the sounding rain was
falling dense and dark
Tell I 23

Noah (Roy Daniels)

They gathered round and told him not to
do it
Them III 57

Noah (Siegfried Sassoon)

When old Noah stared across the floods
Key IV 107; Ox.V.J III 20; Prel III 19

Noah's Ark (Anon)

Then, as the lifted land lay upwards
Peng.An 265

One More River (Anon)

The animals came in two by two
*P.Life IV 78; P.Tong I 121; Puf.V 158;
Rhyme III 65*

Old Noah once he built the ark
*All 11; Key IV 102; Mood III 12; Rain
28*

NOISES

See also Bells, Sounds

A Big Noise (William Brighty
Rands)

Twenty whales
P.Life II 17

Noise (Jessie Pope)

I like noise/The whoop of a boy the thud
of a hoof
*B.L.J III 65; Cor 78; Man I 21; Mood I
7; Quest III 51; Speak I 23; T.P.W 17*

The People Upstairs (Ogden Nash)

The people upstairs all practise ballet
Cor 87; Prel IV 30; Rhyme IV 82

Regent's Park Terrace (Bernard
Spencer)

The noises round my house. On cobbles
bounding
R.R 71

NONSENSE

Adventures of Isabel (Ogden Nash)

Isabel met an enormous bear
A.D.L 241; All 62; Ex.Ch 78; Fab.N.V

105; Make I 77; Ox.V.J IV 73; P.Life II 10; Quest III 80; Sphe 218; Spir.R 10; T.P.W 96; Yim I 5

Anyone lived in a pretty how town (e. e. cummings)

Anyone lived in a pretty how town
Cent 33; S.D 146; Wheel IV 163

The Dancing Cabman (J. B. Morton)

Alone on the lawn
A.D.L 220; Ex.Tro 62; Fab.N.V 213; Speak I 16

Eletelephony (Laura Richards)

Once there was an elephant
Fab.N.V 56; Go.Jo 7; P.Life III 87

The Hole in the Bucket (Anon)

There's a hole in my bucket, dear Liza, dear Liza
All 48

The Man in the Moon stayed up too Late (J. R. R. Tolkien)

There is an inn, a merry old inn
Hap 60; Key II 45; Quest III 71

Poor Old Woman (Anon)

There was an old woman who swallowed a fly
All 56; B.L.J III 10; J.Vo I 24; Key I 13; Peg I 24; Scrap 72

'Quack!' said the Billy-Goat (Charles Causley)

'Quack!' said the billy-goat
Cau.Fig 20

Queer Things (James Reeves)

Very, very queer things have been happening to me
Puf.Q 68

The Ship of Rio (Walter de la Mare)

There was a ship of Rio
De la M.Col 94; De la M.P.P 26; Ex.Ch 76; Fab.N.V 242; Min IV 49; Ox.V.J I 66; Plea III 70; P.Life III 19

So she went into the garden (Samuel Foote)

So she went into the garden to cut a cabbage
Mer 330; Mer.Puf 250; Yim I 10

Soldier Freddy (Spike Milligan)

Soldier Freddy/Was never ready
Ev.M 66

Three Jovial Welshmen or Huntsmen (Anon)

There were three jovial Welshmen
Bird I 11; B.P II 44; D.P I 28; Ex.H 47; Fab.N.V 140; Mer 337; Mer.Puf 256; M.G.B 198; Min III 93; Mood II 72; Ox.Dic 421; Ox.N.R 161; Ox.P.C 24; Plea III 14; P.Life III 48; P.Rem 31; P.Tong I 155; Puf.V 162; Puf.Y 156; Riv I 22; Tree III 62

There were three jovial huntsmen
G.Tr.P 217; My 17; Ox.V.J I 61

Tonight at Noon (Adrian Henri)

Tonight at Noon
Mod.P 184

NONSENSE (CARROLL)

See Car.J throughout

Beautiful Soup (Lewis Carroll)

Beautiful soup so rich and green
All 34; Ex.Tro 41; Man I 27; Mer 340; Mer.Puf 259; Min III 9; My 160; Ox.P.C 12; Plea VIII 24; P.Life II 28; P.Tong I 12; Riv I 90; V.F 30

Brother and Sister (Lewis Carroll)

'Sister, sister, go to bed!'
Act II 58; Cher 26; Key I 64

How doth the little Crocodile (Lewis Carroll)

How doth the little crocodile
Car.J 28; Fab.C.V 89; F.Feet 115; G.Tr.P 70; Ox.P.C 116; Rain 57

Humpty Dumpty's Song (Lewis Carroll)

In winter when the fields are white
B.L.J III 12; Cher 29; Ex.Tro 45; Fab.N.V 130; G.Tr.P 209; Look 298; Ox.P.C 14; Plea VI 138; P.Rem 189; P.Tong I 49; Puf.V 75; Read I 78; Riv II 81; Scrap 60; Wheel I 118

The Hunting of the Snark (part) (Lewis Carroll)

There was one who was famed for the number of things
Fab.N.V 209; Min II 86; Mood II 41; Tree III 31

'Just the place for a snark!' the Bellman cried
M.M.A 107

Jabberwocky (Lewis Carroll)

'Twas brillig and the slithy toves
A.D.L 221; B.P IV 70; Car.J 29; Chor 43; Dan 69; Go.Jo 148; G.Tr.P 208; Key II 98; Mer 283; Mer.Puf 212; M.M.A 91; Peg I 34; Plea IV 10; P.Life IV 10; P.Tong I 169; P.W 216; P.W.R 252; Rhyme IV 87; Riv I 91; Song II 36; Spir 4; Spir.R 4; Spo I 103; Voi I 19; Wheel II 122

Lobster Quadrille (Lewis Carroll)

'Will you walk a little faster?' said a whiting to a snail
All 79; B.B.F 197; Car.J 9; Cher 29; D.P II 45; D.P.R II 37; Ex.Tro 53; Fun II 21; Make I 45; Mer 353; Mer.Puf 268; Min IV 31; Plea III 18; P.Life II 26; P.Rem 27; P.Tong I 185; Riv II 83; Sto I 96; V.F 30

A Sea Dirge (Lewis Carroll)

There are certain things—a spider, a ghost
Key III 97; V.F 32

Speak roughly to your little boy (Lewis Carroll)

Speak roughly to your little boy
Car.J 20; Fab.C.V 97; Mood I 11; V.F 31

Sylvie and Bruno (parts) (Lewis Carroll)

He thought he saw an elephant
B.P IV 91; By 190; Car.J 11; D.P II 39; D.P.R II 32; Ex.Ch 82; Fab.N.V 144; Fun II 54; Kal 138; M.M.A 75; P.Bk 118; Peg I 14; Plea IV 34; P.Life IV 85; Puf.V 169; Rain 42; Song I 90; Spir 5; Spo I 25; Sto II 83; Tree IV 14; Wheel I 116

They told me you had been to her (Lewis Carroll)

They told me you had been to her
Dan 68; Say 119

The Three Badgers and the Herrings' Song (Lewis Carroll)

There be three badgers on a mossy stone
P.Bk 119

'Tis the voice of the Lobster (Lewis Carroll)

'Tis the voice of the lobster; I heard him declare
Car.J 21; Fab.N.V 146; Key II 44; Plea VIII 48; P.Tong I 167

Tweedledum and Tweedledee (Lewis Carroll)

Tweedledum and Tweedledee
Car.J 14; Mood IV 51

The Walrus and the Carpenter (Lewis Carroll)

The Sun was shining on the sea
Car.J 1; Down 39; Fab.N.V 245; Fun II 56; Min III 85; Ox.P.C 125; Plea IV 66; P.Rem 108; Sto I 97; Tree IV 52

The White Knight's Song (Lewis Carroll)

I'll tell thee everything I can;
B.P III 91; Car.J 23; Fab.C.V 277; Fab.N.V 142; G.Tr.P 210; M.M.A 95; Plea V 16; Spo II 69

And now if e'er by chance I put
P.Rem 106; P.Tong II 4

You are Old, Father William (Lewis Carroll)

'You are old, Father William' the young man said
Car.J 7; Cor 159; Ex.Tro 43; Go.Jo 154; G.Tr.P 206; Iron I 62; Mer 366; Mer.Puf 278; Min IV 30; Peg I 16; Plea VI 79; P.Life IV 84; Rhyme IV 77; Riv I 99; Sphe 238; Tree III 86; V.F 28

NONSENSE (HUGHES)

The Adaptable Mountain Dugong (Ted Hughes)

The Mountain Dugong is a simply fantastic animal
Start 141

Folks (Ted Hughes)

I've heard so much
Bits y; Tree IV 21

Grandma (Ted Hughes)

My grandmother's a peaceful person,
and she loves to sit
Quest IV 40

My Aunt (Ted Hughes)

You've heard how a green thumb
Bird I 41; Shad 87

My Brother Bert (Ted Hughes)

Pets are the hobby of my brother Bert
*B.B.G.G 27; Cor 61; Rhyme III 23;
Them I 3; Wheel I 165; Yim I 11*

My Father (Ted Hughes)

Some fathers work at the office, others
work at the store
Quest III 22; Read I 109; Voi I 58

My Grandpa (Ted Hughes)

The truth of the matter, the truth of the
matter
B.P IV 20; Yim I 12

My Sister Jane (Ted Hughes)

And I say nothing—no, not a word
*Cent 84; Cor 157; D.P.R I 32; Flock 95;
Hap 16; Prel I 11; Rhyme IV 98; Start
49; Yim I 13*

My Uncle Dan (Ted Hughes)

My Uncle Dan's an inventor, you may
think that's very fine
Tree IV 98

NONSENSE (LEAR)

The Akond of Swat (Edward Lear)

Who, or why, or which, or what, is the
Akond of Swat?
*All 45; B.P III 74; Fab.C.V 121; G.Tr.P
226; M.M.A 41; My 80; Peg I 26; P.F.P
I 23; Plea IV 62; P.Life III 27; P.Tong I
181*

Calico Pie (Edward Lear)

Calico Pie/The little birds fly
*B.P I 62; Fab.C.V 85; Fab.N.V 88;
G.Tr.P 225; Mood I 15; Ox.P.C 12;
Scrap 76; Tree I 62*

**The Courtship of the Yonghy-
Bonghy-Bo** (Edward Lear)

On the coast of Coromandel
*G.Tr.P 213; Plea VI 60; P.Life III 22;
Wheel II 118*

The Daddy Long-Legs and the Fly
(Edward Lear)

Once Mr Daddy Long-Legs
Plea V 20

The Dong with a Luminous Nose
(Edward Lear)

When awful darkness and silence reign
*Cher 24; D.P II 47; D.P.R II 38; Ex.Ch
84; M.M.A 36; P.Bk 342; Peg I 29;
P.F.P I 20; P.Life II 29; P.Tong I 175;
Riv III 117; Spo I 55; Sto I 101; Wheel I
107*

The Duck and the Kangaroo
(Edward Lear)

Said the Duck to the Kangaroo
Puf.Y 122; Wheel I 111

Edward Lear (Edward Lear)

How pleasant to know Mr Lear!
*Cher 463; Cor 52; Fab.C.V 124; G.Tr.P
212; Plea V 23; P.Life III 30; Riv IV 6;
Sphe 221; V.F 110*

**Incidents in the Life of my Uncle
Arly** (Edward Lear)

O my aged Uncle Arly
*A.D.L 242; Comp 92; Min II 69; Pers
50; Plea V 44; P.Life II 33; Prel I 39;
V.F 94*

The Jumblies (Edward Lear)

They went to sea in a sieve, they did
*All 96; Cher 6; Ch.Gar 150; Dan 71;
Fab.N.V 248; Go.Jo 145; Mer 195; Min
II 39; Mood IV 11; My 104; Ox.P.C 54;
P.F.P I 16; Plea IV 49; P.Life III 16;
P.Rem 28; P.Tong I 162; Puf.V 77; Rain
34; Riv I 56; Spo I 52*

Mr and Mrs Spikky Sparrow
(Edward Lear)

On a little piece of wood
B.P III 33; Cor 69

The New Vestments (Edward Lear)

There lived an old man in the kingdom of Tess
Plea III 37

The Nut-crackers and the Sugar-tongs (Edward Lear)

The Nut-crackers sat by a plate on the table
My 48; Plea III 49; Wheel I 112

The Owl and the Pussy-cat (Edward Lear)

The Owl and the Pussy-cat went to sea
All 39; B.P I 16; By 174; Ch.Gar 149; Ex.H 60; Fab.C.V 87; Fab.N.V 250; Fuji 34; Go.Jo 14; G.Tr.P 224; Mer 214; Min III 72; Mood II 49; My 163; Ox.P.C 117; Ox.V.J I 64; P.F.P I 13; Plea III 9; P.Life I 52; P.Rem 37; Puf.V 167; Puf.Y 150; Rhyme II 43; Riv I 75; Sphe 226; Tree II 42; Weal I 94

The Pelican Chorus (Edward Lear)

King and Queen of the Pelicans we
Mood III 54; Peng.An 240; Spo I 49; Sto II 94; V.F 96

The Pobble who has no Toes (Edward Lear)

The Pobble who has no toes
Ex.Tro 38; Fab.C.V 91; Fab.N.V 153; G.Tr.P 212; Min III 74; Ox.P.C 16; Ox.V.J II 98; P.F.P I 14; P.Life III 20; Puf.V 80; Scrap 80; Tree III 70

The Quangle Wangle's Hat (Edward Lear)

On top of the Crumpetty Tree
Fab.N.V 59; Mer 219; Mer.Puf 161; Plea III 74; P.Life I 49; Read I 158; Rhyme IV 85; Riv I 79

The Table and the Chair (Edward Lear)

Said the table to the chair
B.P II 15; Fab.N.V 235; G.Tr.P 215; Min III 91; Mood I 14

The Two Old Bachelors (Edward Lear)

Two old bachelors were living in one house

Cor 152; Kal 142; M.M.A 83; Plea III 28; Tree III 15; V.F 92; Wheel I 114

NONSENSE (MILNE)

See also Mil.N.S, Mil.V.Y throughout

Disobedience (A. A. Milne)

James James Morrison Morrison
Mil.V.Y 30

The Dormouse and the Doctor (A. A. Milne)

There once was a dormouse that lived in a bed
Mil.V.Y 66

In the Fashion (A. A. Milne)

A lion has a tail and a very fine tail
Mil.V.Y 95

The Old Sailor (A. A. Milne)

There once was an old sailor my grandfather knew
B.P II 51; Fab.N.V 36; Mil.N.S 36

NOON

Noon (John Clare)

All how silent and how still
Read I 129

Noon (John Clare)

The midday hour of twelve the clock counts o'er
Cla.Wo 42; Read I 128

NOVELISTS

The Novelist (W. H. Auden)

Encased in talent like a uniform
Ten 18

NOVEMBER

See also Guy Fawkes Night

November (part) (John Clare)

The landscape sleeps in mist from morn to noon
Com 65; Flock 266

The shepherds almost wonder where
they dwell
*Bat 14; Cla.Wo 35; G.Tr.P 282; Prel III
34; R.R 88; Sphe 36*

The timid hare seems half its fears to lose
B.B.F 71

November (Hartley Coleridge)

The mellow year is hasting to its close
Com 66

November (Edward Thomas)

November's days are thirty
Tho.Gr 51

November in London (Thomas
Hood)

No sun—no moon—
*All 77; Cher 392; Comp 39; Cor 27;
G.Tr.P 280; Look 8; Ox.P.C 99; Peg I
106; Prel III 35; P.Rem 113; R.R 89;
Shep 56; Six I 16; Speak I 35*

No warmth, no cheerfulness, no
healthful ease
Com 65

November Night, Edinburgh
(Norman MacCaig)

The night tinkles like ice in glasses
Prel III 34

NUCLEAR WAR

See also Hiroshima

Early Warning (George Macbeth)

Lord god of wings, forgive this hand
Kal 95

Finishing Post (John Roscoe)

'Nonsense!' exclaimed the Director of
Defence Research, pressing this button
won't blow up the universe
Tell I 81

Icarus Allsorts (Roger McGough)

A little bit of heaven fell
Chal II 42

The Responsibility (Peter Appleton)

I am the man who gives the word
R.R 58

What have they done to the rain?
(Malvina Reynolds)

Just a little rain, falling all around
Chal III 92

William Empsom at Aldermaston
(Alan Brownjohn)

This is our dead sea, once a guidebook
heath
Fla 201

Your Attention Please (Peter Porter)

The Polar Dew has just warned that
*Cent 95; Chal III 101; D.P.R IV 68; Fla
191; Make IV 45; Man III 32; Sev 141;
Under 110*

NUMBERS

Arithmetic (Carl Sandburg)

Arithmetic is where numbers fly like
pigeons in and out of your head
*A.S.L.A 17; Bird I 3; Chal I 54; Flock
238; J.Vo III 50; Pers 141; Prel II 10;
Six II 62*

Child Margaret (Carl Sandburg)

The child Margaret begins to write
numbers on a Saturday morning
Flock 74

The Question (C. S. Calverly)

And if you asked of him to say
Act III 101

Roman Figures (Anon)

X shall stand for playmates ten
B.L.J II 23; Ox.N.R 112

NUTS

Sweet Chestnuts (John Walsh)

How still the woods were! Not a red-
breast whistled
Them V 43

NYMPHS

Overheard on a Saltmarsh
(Harold Munro)

Nymph, nymph, what are your beads?
*Go.Jo 227; J.Vo I 16; Look 290; Patch
17; Peg I 94; P.F.P I 110; Quest I 81;
This W.D 33; T.P.W 64*

Sabrina Fair (John Milton)

Sabrina fair/Listen where thou art sitting
Ch.Gar 32; Fab.C.V 217

OAKS

The Oak (Alfred Lord Tennyson)

Live thy life
Fuji 44

OBJECTORS

See Conscientious Objectors

OCCUPATIONS

See also Circuses, Whaling

See also Acrobats, Barbers, Blacksmiths, Builders, Burglars, Bushrangers, Butchers, Carpenters, Carters, Charcoal Burners, Chimney Sweeps, Civil Servants, Clergymen, Conjurors, Cowboys, Dentists, Divers, Dressmakers, Editors, Engine Drivers, Engineers, Explorers, Farmers, Farmworkers, Ferrymen, Fiddlers, Financiers, Firemen (Fire-fighting), Fishermen, Fishmongers, Fitters, Foresters, Fowlers, Gamekeepers, Gardeners, Gipsies, Hermits, Highwaymen, Hoboes, Housewives, Judges, Knife-sharpeners, Lighthouse Keepers, Loggers, Lorry Drivers, Magicians, Millers, Miners, Molecatchers, Navvies, Newsboys, Novelists, Outlaws, Pedlars, Pirates, Ploughmen, Poachers, Poets, Postmen, Professors, Psychoanalysts, Prospectors, Rag-and-Bone Men, Reporters, Rickshaw Pullers, Road-builders, Sailors, Schoolmasters, Schoolmistresses, Seamstresses, Smugglers, Spies, Statesmen, Steelworkers, Stonemasons, Swagmen, Tailors, Tatooists, Telephone Operators, Thatchers, Tramps, Weavers, Wheelwrights, Woodmen

Cherry Stones (A. A. Milne)

Tinker, Tailor/Soldier, Sailor
Mil.N.S 19

Psalm of those who go forth before daylight (Carl Sandburg)

The policeman buys shoes slow and careful
Drag 64; Ev.M 60; Flock 129; J.Vo IV 51; Shep 160; Them VI 3

Rob (Olive Dehn)

Would anyone care to/Change with Rob?
B.P I 32; Quest V 55

A Song for Occupations (Walt Whitman)

All music is what awakes from you when you are reminded by the instruments
Pers 145

OCTOBER

October (Edward Thomas)

The green elm with the one great bough of gold
Act III 69; Camb 51; Ten 131; Tho.Gr 50

October (Robert Frost)

O hushed October morning mild
A.D.L 101; Go.Jo 251

October's Song (Eleanor Farjeon)

The forest's afire!
A.D.L 99; Scrap 39

The Shepherd's Calendar (part) (John Clare)

The free horse rustling through the stubble field
Song IV 44

OCTOPUSES

The Octopus (Ogden Nash)

Tell me, O Octopus, I begs
Fab.N.V 78; Key II 84; Weal II 14

OLD AGE

See also Them IV 57–72

See also Age, Youth

An Acre of Grass (W. B. Yeats)

Picture and book remain
Ten 159

The Autumn Wind (Emperor Wu-Ti—trans Arthur Waley)

Autumn wind rises; white clouds fly
Fab.C.V 379

Beautiful Old Age
(D. H. Lawrence)

It ought to be lovely to be old
Them IV 69; Voi III 56

Beauty that has faded
(Kiyotsugu—trans Ezra Pound)

The Old Woman: When I was young I
had pride
D.P.R II 1

Childhood (Frances Cornford)

I used to think that grown up people
chose
*Bird III 36; D.P.R II 1; Six III 60;
Them IV 6*

Danny Murphy (James Stephens)

He was as old as old could be
Prel I 52

A Farewell to Arms (George Peele)

His golden locks Time hath to silver
turned
*By 18; Cher 346; Plea VII 46; P.W 57;
R.R 102*

I Look into my Glass (Thomas
Hardy)

I look into my glass
Iron III 30; Them IV 58

In Oak Terrace (Tony Connor)

Old and alone she sits at nights
Prel I 49

The Looking Glass (Gerald Bullett)

I met an old woman
B.P IV 12

Ninetieth Birthday (R. S. Thomas)

You go up the long track
Under 102

Old (Anne Sexton)

I'm afraid of needles
Exp VI 37

An Old Man (William Wordsworth)

The little hedgerow birds
Fab.C.V 118

The Old Man's Lament (John Clare)

Youth has no fear of ill, by no cloudy
days annoyed
Them IV 59

*The Old Men Admiring Themselves
in the Water* (W. B. Yeats)

I heard the old, old men say
*Bird III 36; Chal I 50; Fab.C.V 379;
Go.Jo 198; Man II 23; Yea.Run 52*

An Old Woman of the Roads
(Padraic Colum)

O, to have a little house!
*Ex.Ch 148; Fun II 106; Kal 34; Look
105; Make I 154; P.F.P I 90; Puf.V 135;
Puf.Y 14; Them IV 57; Trea 320; Tree
IV 90*

Poor Rumble (James Reeves)

Pity poor Rumble: he's growing wheezy
Riv IV 10

The Song of the Old Mother
(W. B. Yeats)

I rise in the dawn, and I kneel and blow
*Ex.Ch 149; Iron I 17; Ox.V.J II 30;
Peg.V 101; Them IV 58; Tree IV 33;
Yea.Run 42*

Sun and Fun (Sir John Betjeman)

I walked into the night-club in the
morning
Com 170

Warning (Jenny Joseph)

When I am an old woman I shall wear
purple
Mod.P 144; Sev 60

When you are Old (W. B. Yeats)

When you are old and grey and full of
sleep
*By 216; Go.Jo 233; Sphe 314; Weal I
43; Yea.Run 34*

OPTIMISTS

See also Pessimists

The Optimist and the Pessimist
(Arnold Silcock)

The optimist, who always was a fool
Act II 103

ORCHARDS

Goodbye and keep cold (Robert
Frost)

This saying goodbye on the edge of the
dark
Ten 77

ORIENTAL POEMS
(BRIEF)

*A.D.L 113; A.S.L.A 27–28; D.P.R I
14; D.P.R II 96; Flock 8, 9, 10, 11,
34, 53, 54, 58, 67, 93, 102, 114, 119,
139, 151, 163, 179, 205, 206, 209,
213, 228, 234, 263, 264, 266, 273,
276; Fuji 46, 66; J.Vo I 10, 67, 72;
J.Vo II 17, 26, 46; J.Vo III 14, 22,
37, 46, 49, 54; J.Vo IV 8, 13, 39, 90;
P.W 262–263; Read I 130; Riv IV
135; S.D 40, 48, 57; Shep 17, 19, 31,
37, 44, 47, 48, 53, 61, 65, 66, 72, 75,
131, 133, 147; T.P.R 71; Voi I 71,
83, 97, 118, 122; Voi II 100; Voi III
83; Weal II 63, 145*

ORPHEUS

Orpheus with his Lute (William
Shakespeare)

Orpheus with his lute
*Henry VIII III i 3; Cher 82; D.P IV 127;
Fab.C.V 36; Fun II 26; Mood IV 46;
P.Bk 87; P.F.P II 130; Riv IV 2; Sphe
263; Spo I 150; Trea 1*

OSTRICHES

Ostrich (Alan Brownjohn)

Large cold farms in sandy places
Bro.B 30

OTTERBOURNE

The Battle of Otterbourne (Anon)

It fell upon the Lammas tide
Fab.C.V 232

OTTERS

An Otter (Ted Hughes)

Underwater eyes an eel's
*Com 51; Exp V 54; Peng.An 227; Song I
53; Sphe 108; Spir.R 45*

(part)
Dawn 66

Otters (Padraic Colum)

I'll be an otter and I'll let you swim
Ark 45

Running lightly over spongy ground
(Theodore Roethke)

Running lightly over spongy ground
J.Vo III 66

OUTLAWS

See also Bushrangers, James (Jesse),
Kelly (Ned), Robin Hood

Pretty Boy Floyd (Woody Guthrie)

Come and gather 'round me, children
F.S.N.A 437; J.Vo IV 37

OUTSIDE & INSIDE

*The Fallow Deer at the Lonely
House* (Thomas Hardy)

One without looks in tonight
*B.B.F 113; F.Feet 148; J.Mod 99;
Ox.P.C 124; Ox.V.J III 62; Rhyme III
43; Tree IV 82*

Who's In (Elizabeth Fleming)

The door is shut fast
*Bits p; Hap 31; Ox.P.C 145; P.Rem 16;
V.F 65*

OWLS

The Barn Owl (Samuel Butler)

While moonlight, silvering all the walls
Look 196; My 122

The Bird of Night or *Owl* (Randall Jarrell)

A shadow is floating through the moonlight
Say 59; Them I 25; Voi II 136

Disturbances (Anthony Thwaite)

After the darkness has come
Sphe 143

Dusk (Frances Cornford)

This is the owl moment I have always known
J.Mod 138

My Grandpa (Ted Hughes)

The truth of the matter, the truth of the matter
B.P IV 20; Yim I 12

Owl (George Macbeth)

is my favourite who flies
Mod.P 150

The Owl (Walter de la Mare)

Owl of the wildwood I
Hap 50; Six VI 50; Them II 30

The Owl (Alfred Lord Tennyson)

When cats run home and light is come
A.D.L 173; B.B.F 60; B.L.J IV 2; B.P II 55; Ch.Gar 61; Choice 87; Fab.C.V 87; Fab.N.V 23; F.Feet 160; Fuji 112; Fun I 68; Go.Jo 73; G.Tr.P 65; Mer 307; Min IV 45; Ox.P.C 65; Ox.V.J II 71; P.F.P I 13; Plea IV 65; P.Life III 74; P.P 6; Rain 52; Riv I 16; R.R 178; Say 28; Sphe 142; Spo I 157; Ten.Fa 35; This W.D 31; Trea 110

The Owl and the Pussy cat
(Edward Lear)

The Owl and the Pussy cat went to sea
All 39; B.P I 16; By 174; Ch.Gar 149; Ex.H 60; Fab.C.V 87; Fab.N.V 250; Fuji 34; Go.Jo 14; G.Tr.P 224; Mer 214; Min III 72; Mood II 49; My 163; Ox.P.C 117; Ox.V.J I 64; P.F.P I 13; Plea III 9; P.Life I 52; P.Rem 37; Puf.V 167; Puf.Y 160; Rhyme II 43; Riv I 75; Sphe 226; Tree II 42; Weal I 94

The Owl-Critic (James Thomas Fields)

'Who stuffed that white owl?' No one spoke in the shop
D.P II 51; Peg V 70; V.F 62

Sweet Suffolk Owl (Thomas Vautor)

Sweet Suffolk owl, so trimly dight
B.B.F 166; Cher 107; Mer 337; Mer.Puf 256; Riv I 15; Tree IV 44

Town Owl (Laurie Lee)

On eves of cold when slow coal fires
Com 67; Quest IV 28; Sphe 155; Them II 32; Wheel III 188

OXEN

The Oxen (Thomas Hardy)

Christmas Eve, and twelve of the clock
B.B.F 228; Cent 15; D.P.R I 68; F.Feet 173; Har.Ch 21; Key III 150; Look 368; Ox.V.J III 82; R.R 165; Song II 142; Sphe 97; Spo II 96; T.P.W 76; Wheel I 122

The Ox-Tamer (Walt Whitman)

In a far-away northern country in the placid pastoral region
B.B.F 69; Key IV 150; Speak II 33; Voi II 47; Wheel III 127

The Twelve Oxen (Anon)

I have twelve oxen that be fair and brown
B.B.F 170; Cher 114; Mer 154; Mer.Puf 113; Ox.V.J I 22; This W.D 93; Tree I 82

OXEN, ARCTIC

The Arctic Ox (or Goat)
(Marianne Moore)

To wear the arctic fox
Liv 145

PAINTING (POEMS FOR PICTURE MAKING)

Animals' Houses (James Reeves)

Of animals' houses
Puf.Q 75

The Dismantled Ship (Walt Whitman)

In some unused lagoon, some nameless bay
Mood IV 64; Prel IV 25; Riv II 17

The Fly (Walter de la Mare)

How large unto the tiny fly
B.B.F 118; By 228; De la M.Ch 37; De la M.Col 74; De la M.S 79; D.P.R I 6; Ex.H 19; F.Feet 186; First III 44; Ox.V.J I 56; Peng.An 119; Plea II 41; Quest II 4; Shep 138; Start 9; Tree I 61; Way 30

Good Taste (Christopher Logue)

Travelling a man met a tiger, so . . .
Cor 118; Dawn 69; Ev.M 83; Hap 63; Say 30

The Little Creature (Walter de la Mare)

Twinkum, twankum, twirlum and twitch—
De la M.Col 153; De la M.S 52; D.P.R I 88; P.F.P I 18; Speak I 116

October's Song (Eleanor Farjeon)

The forest's afire!
A.D.L 99; Scrap 39

The Rime of the Ancient Mariner (part) (S. T. Coleridge)

Beyond the shadow of the ship
Act II 86; D.P III 67; D.P.R III 51; Fab.C.V 310; P.Bk 168; P.F.P II 172; P.Life IV 56; P.W 166; P.W.R 188; Riv IV 160; Weal II 77

A Still Life (Walter de la Mare)

Bottle, coarse tumbler, loaf of bread
De la M.Ch 72

Stopping by Woods on a Snowy Evening (Robert Frost)

Whose woods these are I think I know
Cent 42; Choice 284; D.P.R II 27; Ex.H 82; Fab.C.V 58; First III 29; Flock 276; Fro.You 30; Fun I 37; Go.Jo 257; Hap 38; Iron I 62; Key IV 72; Make II 11; Man II 12; Min II 33; Mood II 66; Ox.V.J II 49; Patch 29; Pers 71; Rhyme IV 15; Riv IV 66; Ten 80; This W.D 156

The Wolf Also (The Bible)

The wolf also shall dwell with the lamb
Isiah XI 6; B.B.F 230; F.Feet 14

Zebra (Isak Dinesen)

The eagles shadow runs across the plain
Go.Jo 88

PAINTINGS (POEMS ABOUT PICTURES)

The Dance (William Carlos Williams)

In Breughel's great picture, The Kermess
Go.Jo 137; Liv 57

Giorno dei Morti (D. H. Lawrence)

Along the avenue of cypresses
Liv 19

Landscape with the Fall of Icarus (William Carlos Williams)

According to Breughel
J.Vo III 89

Musée des Beaux Arts (W. H. Auden)

About suffering they were never wrong
Camb 132; Cent 31; Comp 44; Mod.P 17; Voi III 135

PALM SUNDAY

The Donkey (G. K. Chesterton)

When fishes flew and forests walked
By 221; Look 372; Make II 35; Mood IV 81; P.Bk 41; Plea VII 50; Rain 53; Rhyme IV 118; Six VI 18; Song II 146; Ver II 226

PAN

The God of Sheep (John Fletcher)

All ye woods, and trees, and bowers
Fab.C.V 217

Hymn of Pan (P. B. Shelley)

From the forests and highlands
Fab.C.V 218

151

A Musical Instrument
(E. B. Browning)

What was he doing, the great god Pan
*By 156; G.Tr.P 162; Plea VII 62; Spo I
96; Trea 239; Vic 111*

PANTHERS

The Panther (Rainer Maria
Rilke—trans J. B. Leishman)

His gaze, going past those bars, has got
so misted
Flock 61

(trans Jessie Lemont)

His weary glance, from passing by the
bars
Ark 120.

PARABLES

See Fables

PARACHUTING

Parachute (Stanley Snaith)

He poises a moment and looks at the
earth far under
M.Ver 129

Parachute (Lenrie Peters)

Parachute men say
Them V 48

PARADISE

See also Eden

Paradise (Christina Rossetti)

Once in a dream I saw the flowers
Vic 166

PARENTS

Bringing Him Up (Lord Dunsany)

Mister Thomas Jones
B.B.G.G 15

Discord in Childhood
(D. H. Lawrence)

Outside the house an ash-tree hung its
terrible whips
Camb 69; Pers 32

PARODY

Ancient Music (Ezra Pound)

Winter is icumen in

(Original: see Cuckoos: Sumer is icumen
in)
Flock 273; Kal 137

Baking of Tarts (E. V. Milner)

Today we have baking of tarts.
Yesterday

(Original: See Wars (1939–45) Training:
Naming of Parts)
Sev 118

The Crocodile (Lewis Carroll)

How doth the little crocodile

(Original: see Bees: *How doth the little
busy bee*)
*Car.J 28; Fab.C.V 89; F.Feet 115; Fuji
83; G.Tr.P 70; Ox.P.C 116; Rain 57*

Envoi (R. J. Yeatman & W. C.
Sellar)

So I sprang to a taxi and shouted 'To
Aix!'

(Original: see Horses: *How they brought
the Good News*)
Look 99; Sto I 74

Father William (Lewis Carroll)

'You are old, Father William' the young
man said

(Original: *The Old Man's Comforts*, R.
Southey, *G.Tr.P 206*)
*Cor 159; Ex.Tro 43; Go.Jo 154; G.Tr.P
206; Iron I 62; Mer 366; Mer.Puf 278;
Min IV 30; P.Life IV 84; Rhyme IV 77;
Riv I 99; Tree III 86; Ver 28*

*How I Brought the Good News from
Aix to Ghent* (W. C. Sellar & R. J.
Yeatman)

I sprang to the rollocks and Jorrocks and
me

152

(Original: See Horses: *How they brought the Good News*)
Sto I 73

If Wordsworth had written 'The Everlasting Mercy' (Sir John Squire)

Ever since boyhood it has been my joy
P.Tong II 18

Lessons on Maths (Schoolchild)

Today we have square roots and surds; yesterday

(Original: See Wars (1939–45) Training: *Naming of Parts*)
Wheel IV 204

An Old Song (Edward Thomas)

I was not apprenticed nor ever dwelt in famous Lincolnshire

(Original: See Poachers: *The Lincolnshire Poacher*)
Tho.Gr 63

The Poets at Tea (Barry Pain)

Pour, varlet, pour the water
P.Tong II 109

The Streets of Laredo (Louis MacNiece)

O early one morning I walked out like Agag

(Original: See Cowboys: *The Streets of Laredo*)
Cher 309; Fla 111; Ris 112

'Tis the Voice of the Lobster (Lewis Carroll)

'Tis the voice of the lobster: I heard him declare

(Original: See Laziness: *The Sluggard*)
Car.J 22; Fab.N.V 146; Key II 44; Plea VIII 48; P.Tong I 167

Winter (David Campbell)

When magpies sing in sky and tree

(Original: See Winter: When icicles hang by the wall)
Act II 77

PARROTS

The Parrot (Thomas Campbell)

The deep affections of the breast
Them I 12

Parrot (Stevie Smith)

The old sick parrot
Them I 13

A Parrot: A True Story (Thomas Campbell)

A parrot, from the Spanish Main
Key I 107; P.Bk 332; Ver II 181

The Parrot (Sacheverell Sitwell)

The parrot's voice snaps out
Ver II 204

Parrot (Alan Brownjohn)

Sometimes I sit with both eyes closed
Bro.B 22

The Sailor to his Parrot (W. H. Davies)

Thou foul-mouthed wretch! Why dost thou choose
Riv IV 75

Speak Parrot (John Skelton)

My name is Parrot, a bird of Paradise
B.B.F 67; Peng.An 235

PATHS

The Goat Paths (James Stephens)

The crooked paths go every way
Act III 71; A.D.L 53; Ark 55; Bird I 59; D.P IV 31; Ox.V.J II 46

The Lane (Andrew Young)

Years and years and man's thoughtful foot
M.Ver 40; Ten 166

The Road Not Taken (Robert Frost)

Two roads diverged in a yellow wood
Act III 120; Bird III 4; Cher 314; Fab.C.V 292; Fro.You 91; Look 49; Man III 23; Pat 116; P.Rem 197; P.W.R 285; Quest V 19; Song III 1; Sphe 388; Way 39

The Track (Andrew Young)

Trodden by man and horse
You.Qu 21

The Way through the Woods
(Rudyard Kipling)

They shut the road through the woods
*Act III 67; Bird I 25; D.P IV 64; D.P.R
IV 38; Fab.C.V 387; Isle 81; Look 294;
Ox.V.J IV 63; P.F.P II 223; Plea VII 53;
P.Life IV 26; Rain 80; Rhyme IV 16;
Song I 139; Sphe 86; Start 126; Them II
6; This W.D 163; Weal I 107; Way 52*

PEACHES

Peach (D. H. Lawrence)

Would you like to throw a stone at me?
Law.S 57

PEACOCKS

Truth (part) (William Cowper)

The self-applauding bird, the peacock,
see—
B.B.F 65

PEARS

Study of Two Pears (Wallace
Stevens)

Opusculum paedagogum
Shep 74

PEDLARS

The Huxter (Edward Thomas)

He has a hump like an ape on his back
Voi I 30

Lawn as white as driven snow
(William Shakespeare)

Lawn as white as driven snow
Winter's Tale IV iii 220; *Ox.V.J II 19*

The little woman and the pedlar
(Anon)

There was a little woman
Ox.N.R 169 (fullest version); *Fab.N.V
150; M.G.B 56; Mood I 73; My 78;
Ox.Dic 427; Ox.V.J II 32; Puf.N.R 142;
Tree II 54*

There was an old woman, as I've heard
tell
*B.P II 22; Fun I 89; G.Tr.P 103; M.G.R
63; P.Life III 53*

No Buyers (Thomas Hardy)

A load of brushes and baskets and
cradles and chairs
Har.Ch 51; Wheel III 134

The Pedlar's Caravan
(W. B. Rands)

I wish I lived in a caravan
*Fun I 108; Min III 14; Ox.P.C 145; Tree
I 69*

Will you buy any tape? (William
Shakespeare)

Will you buy any tape
Winter's Tale IV iii 324; *Ox.V.J II 18*

PENGUINS

Peter and Percival (E. V. Rieu)

Peter and Percival lived in a place
Puf.Q 125

PEOPLE

See Portraits

PEOPLES

See Eskimos, Gypsies, Indians
(Red), Negroes, Picts, Romans,
Vikings

PERSEVERANCE

*The Mouse that gnawed the Oak-
tree down* (Vachel Lindsay)

The Mouse that gnawed the oak-tree
down
J.Vo II 6; Mood III 63

PESSIMISTS

See also Optimists

The Pessimist (Ben King)

Nothing to do but work
*Act II 102; B.L.J IV 41; My 92; Ox.P.C
14; R.R 132; Sto II 98; V.F 89; Weal II
13*

PETS

See also Them I 3–18

See also Animals, Birds, Fishes and Sea Creatures

The Diplomatic Platypus
(Patrick Barrington)

I had a duck-billed platypus when I was up at Trinity
Song III 52

Epitaph on a Hare (William Cowper)

Here lies, who, hound did ne'er pursue
Bat 62; B.B.F 143; Ox.P.C 121; Peng.An 138; Puf.V 55; R.R 108; Shep 86

I knew a Black Beetle (Christopher Morley)

I knew a black beetle who lived down a drain
Fab.N.V 172

The Meadow Mouse (Theodore Roethke)

In a shoe box stuffed in an old nylon stocking
Act III 98; Ark 33; Chal II 12; Exp III 4; J.Vo IV 15; Make I 131; Tell I 19; Yim I 34

My Brother Bert (Ted Hughes)

Pets are the Hobby of my Brother Bert
B.B.G.G 27; Cor 61; Rhyme III 23; Them I 3; Wheel I 165; Yim I 11

The Nymph and her Fawn (Andrew Marvell)

With sweetest milk and sugar first
Fab.C.V 67

Pet Shop (Louis MacNiece)

Cold blood or warm, crawling or fluttering
Sev 91; Them I 14; Way 63

Take one Home for the Kiddies (Philip Larkin)

On shallow straw, in shadeless glass
A.S.L.A 83; Liv 101; Them I 14; Way 55

Two and One are a Problem (Ogden Nash)

Dear Miss Dix, I am a young man of half past thirty-seven
Song II 64

PEWITS

Two Pewits (Edward Thomas)

Under the after-sunset sky
Cent 22; Tho.Gr 38

PHEASANTS

Cock-Pheasant (Laurie Lee)

Gilded with leaf-thick paint; a steady
A.S.L.A 51

Pheasant (Sidney Keyes)

Cock stubble-searching pheasant, delicate
M.Ver 64

Windsor Forest (part) (Alexander Pope)

See! from the brake the whirring pheasant springs
Flock 127; G.Tr.P 64; Song III 67

PHOENIXES

See also Cher 99–102

The Phoenix Self-Born (John Dryden—after Ovid)

The cubs of bears, a living lump appear
B.B.F 211; Cher 100

The Visions of Petrarch (part) (Edmund Spenser)

I saw a phoenix in the wood alone
Cher 99

PHOTOGRAPHERS

Waiting for Birdie (Ogden Nash)

Some hate broccoli; some hate bacon
Key I 102

PHYSICAL ACTIVITIES

See Bathing, Bicycling, Birdsnesting, Bouncing Balls, Boxing, Dancing, Diving, Flying, Games, Gardening, Getting Up, Gliding, Golf, Hopping, Housework, Marching, Mountaineering, Mowing, Parachuting, Riding, Sailing, Skipping, Sport, Surfing, Swinging, Tree Climbing, Wrestling

PICNICS

The Delights of a Picnic
(J. A. Lindon)

You are sitting on stones with rheumaticky bones, and a
Prel I 19

Picnic (Hugh Lofting)

Ella, fell a
Go.Jo 4

PICTS

A Pict Song (Rudyard Kipling)

Rome never looks where she treads
J.Vo IV 35

PIGEONS

Mrs Peck-Pigeon (Eleanor Farjeon)

Mrs Peck-Pigeon
F.Feet 72; P.Life I 47

Pigeons (Richard Kell)

They paddle with staccato feet
A.S.L.A 62; Drag 47; My 140

Pitchfork Department
(D. J. Enright)

It was patent in this ancient city, paradise of
Them I 40

PIGS

See also Boars
P (Edward Lear)

P was a pig
P.Life I 53

The Farmer's Boy (part) (Robert Bloomfield)

From oak to oak they run with eager haste
B.B.F 90

The Pigs and the Charcoal Burner
(Walter de la Mare)

The old pig said to the little pigs
De la M.Col 92; De la M.P.P 81; F.Feet 86; Iron II 60; Ox.V.J II 37

The Poor Man's Pig (Edmund Blunden)

Already fallen plum-bloom stars the green
Blu.Mi 28; J.Mod 114; Sphe 102; Under 68

The Site: Choose a dry Site
(Ronald Duncan)

The site: choose a dry site
J.Mod 115

View of a Pig (Ted Hughes)

The pig lay on a barrow dead
Cent 83; D.P.R IV 11; Drag 71; Fla 194; Flock 229; Make IV 93; Peng.An 248; Pers 131; Sphe 103; Them VII 34

PIKE

The Pike (Edmund Blunden)

From shadows of rich oaks outpeer
Blu.Mi 29; Day 69; Peng.An 253; Pers 127; P.F.P I 130; Shep 124; Song II 49; Wheel III 168

And nigh this toppling reed, still as the dead
Ark 173

Pike (Ted Hughes)

Pike, three inches long, perfect
Drag 18; Make IV 204; Mod.P 79; Peng.An 254; Song II 47; Sto III 94; Tell II 23

The Pike (Theodore Roethke)

The river turns/Leaving a place for the eye to rest
Bird IV 51; Exp V 37; Them I 26

PILGRIMS

The Canterbury Tales: Prologue
(part) (G. Chaucer)

When that Aprille with his showres soote
Cher 281; Flock 17; Song IV 39

(trans N. Coghill)

When the sweet showers of April fall and
shoot
Flock 16

Inviting a Friend to Supper
(Ben Jonson)

Tonight, grave sir, both my poor house
and I
P.Rem 139

The Passionate Man's Pilgrimage
(Part) (Sir Walter Ralegh)

Give me my scallop-shell of quiet
*Cher 283; Iron IV 13; Pat 133; Weal II
169; Wheel I 42*

Pilgrim's Song (John Bunyan)

Who would true Valour see
*By 94; Ch.Gar 127; D.P III 155; D.P.R
III 113; Mer 349; Mer.Puf 264; P.Bk
71; Plea VI 49; Rain 94; Riv II 30; R.R
160; Song I 151; Spo I 100*

PINE TREES

The Pine Trees in the Courtyard
(Po Chu-I—trans Arthur Waley)

Below the Hall what meets my eyes?
Act III 110

PIONEERS & THE WEST

See U.S.A: Pioneers and the West

PIPERS

The Pied Piper of Hamelin
(Robert Browning)

Hamelin Town's in Brunswick
*B.P III 18; Dan 89; Ex.Ch 127;
Fab.C.V 160; Fun II 27; G.Tr.P 153;
Make I 67; P.F.P I 70; Riv I 102; Spir.R
85; Spir 111; Sto I 49*

Into the street the piper stept
First III 46

Rats! they fought the dogs and killed the
cats
F.Feet 116; Key I 72; Min IV 91

The Piper (Seumas O'Sullivan)

A piper in the streets today
*B.L.J III 51; Mood I 26; Rhyme III 46;
S.D 124; Six III 8; Speak II 90; Spo I
140; T.P.W 32*

The Piper o' Dundee (Anon)

The piper came to our town
*Fab.N.V 41; Ox.V.J II 82; Peg II 59;
Plea IV 33*

Tom, the Piper's Son (Anon)

Tom, he was a piper's son
*B.L.J II 33; Fab.N.V 31; Fun II 23;
M.G.E 67; M.G.R 64; Ox.Dic 408;
Ox.N.R 164; Puf.N.R 168; Puf.S.B 56;
Rhyme I 13*

Tom, Tom the piper's son
*M.G.R 64; Ox.N.R 56; Puf.N.R 17;
Scrap 40; Tree II 14*

PIRATES

See also Kidd, Captain

Captain Kidd (Anon)

My name is Captain Kidd, as I sailed
Broad 20

The Coasts of High Barbary (Anon)

Look ahead, look astern, look the
weather and the lee
*Key III 113; Ox.P.C 50; Rain 101;
Rhyme IV 57; Riv II 67*

A lofty ship from Salcombe came
*B.L.J III 37; Cher 224; D.P III 52; Sto
III 124*

There were two lofty ships from old
England came
Bal 777; B.B 41

A Dutch Picture (Henry W.
Longfellow)

Simon Danz has come home again
Peg I 58; Spir 18; Spir.R 15

The Flying Cloud (Anon)

My name is Arthur Halandin, as you may understand
Iron I 24; Make II 21; Song III 119

Henry Martin or *Martyn* (Anon)

In merry Scotland, in merry Scotland
Bal 615; Broad 22; Key III 114; Mer 189; Mer.Puf 146; Riv I 69

There were three brothers in merry Scotland
B.B 37

As we were gone sailing five frosty cold nights
Song III 117

The Inchcape Rock (Robert Southey)

No stir in the air, no stir in the sea
Cher 141; Down 19; D.P I 85; D.P.R I 63; Ex.Ch 170; Fun I 137; G.Tr.P 160; Make I 98; Mood III 77; P.Bk 270; Peg I 64; Plea V 29; Spo I 29; Tell I 42

John Polruddon (Charles Causley)

John Polrudden/All of a sudden
Cau.Nar 9; Drag 57

Pirate Don Durk of Dowdee (Mildred Meigs)

Ho, for the Pirate Don Durk of Dowdee
Min III 71; P.Life III 13

Song of the Pirate King (W. S. Gilbert)

Oh, better far to live and die
Sto III 126

The Tarry Buccaneer (John Masefield)

I'm going to be a pirate with a bright brass pivot-gun
P.Life IV 54

PLACES

See also Cities and Towns, Counties, Countries, Town and Country

Bond Street (Norman Nicholson)

'Bond Street' I said, 'now where the devil's that?'
Sto III 62

In Campbell Street (Rosemary Winn)

In Mayfield Way the pavement's clean
Prel I 35

PLANTING

See also Sowing

Rice Planting (Tokiyo Yamada—trans Ngashi Koriyama)

From early morning the cultivator
Shep 19

PLANTS

See Ferns, Flowers, Lad's-Love, Nettles

PLATYPUSES

The Diplomatic Platypus (Patrick Barrington)

I had a duck-billed platypus when I was up at Trinity
Song III 52

The Platypus (Oliver Herford)

My child, the Duck-billed Platypus
Rhyme IV 94

PLOUGHING

All jolly fellows who follow the plough (Anon)

It was early one morning at the break of day
Broad 46; Com 25

Ploughing in Mist (Andrew Young)

Pulling the shoulder-sack
You.Qu 27

Ploughing on Sunday (Wallace Stevens)

The white cock's tail
Go.Jo 52; My 20; Say 35; This W.D 19; Tree IV 37; Voi I 115

Plowboy (Carl Sandburg)

After the last red sunset glimmer
Yim III 26

PLOUGHMEN

See Ploughing

POACHERS

Dick Daring (Anon)

Honest regular work Dick Daring gave
up
Read I 86

The Lincolnshire Poacher
(Thomas Hood)

When I was bound apprentice in famous
Lincolnshire
Peg IV 52; Plea IV 37; Tree IV 85

The Poacher (R. S. Thomas)

Turning aside, never meeting
Choice 307; Read III 30

Poaching in Excelsis
(G. K. Menzies)

I've poached a pickel paitricks when the
leaves were turnin' sere
Spir 8; Spir.R 6

POETRY

*On First Looking Into Chapman's
Homer* (John Keats)

Much have I travell'd in the realms of
gold
Fab.C.V 34; Plea VII 20

Spicer's Instant Poetry
(James Reeves)

On sale everywhere. Spicer's Instant
Poetry
Mod.P 168

Verse (Oliver St John Gogarty)

What should we know/For better or
worse
Fab.C.V 29; Peg II 100

POETS

See also Chaucer, Clare, Hardy,
Keats, Lear, Milton, Shelley,
Wordsworth, Yeats

Aurora Leigh (part) (Elizabeth
Barrett Browning)

I do distrust the poet who discerns
Peg V 80

Constantly Risking Absurdity
(Lawrence Ferlinghetti)

Constantly risking absurdity
Them VI 19; Ver III 82

Madly Singing in the Mountains
(Po Chu—trans Arthur Waley)

There is no one among men that has not
a special failing
A.D.L 213; Voi II 7

A Minor Bird (Robert Frost)

I have wished a bird would fly away
*A.D.L 172; Cor 176; Ex.Tro 22;
Fro.You 58; Song I 6*

If all the pens (Christopher
Marlowe)

If all the pens that ever poets held
Tamburlaine the Great V i; Peg V 68

To the Public (Louis MacNiece)

Why hold that poets are so sensitive?
Day 2

What the Chairman told Tom
(Basil Bunting)

Poetry? It's a hobby
Them VI 62

Wild Strawberries (Robert Graves)

Strawberries that in gardens grow
Man II 14

POLITICAL SLOGANS

Pie in the Sky (Anon)

Long-haired preachers come out every
night
Act IV 164; F.S.N.A 423

POLITICS

After I wake up (Hilary Corke)

After I wake up and before I get up
Sev 121

Emperors of the Island (Dannie Abse)

There is the story of a deserted island
Dawn 87; Day 99; Exp VIII 1; Shad 70

There lived a King (W. S. Gilbert)

There lived a King, as I've been told
Plea VII 96; Sto III 113

POLLUTION

Clear and cool (Charles Kingsley)

Clear and cool, clear and cool
Bird II 24; Key III 77

Cologne (Samuel Taylor Coleridge)

In Köln, a town of monks and bones
Key IV 101; Wheel III 110

In the Cities (D. H. Lawrence)

In the cities/there is even no more any weather
Song IV 106; Them VII 47; Weal II 161

Litter (Jennifer Budden—Schoolchild)

'Come to Britain', the posters say
Chal III 21

On Bungaloid Growth (Colin Ellis)

When England's multitudes observed with frowns
D.P.R II 31; P.Tong II 187

To Iron-Founders and Others (Gordon Bottomley)

When you destroy a blade of grass
P.F.P II 113; Ver III 63

Windscale (Norman Nicholson)

The toadstool towers infest the shore
Sev 130; Them VII 54

PONDS

The Mill-Pond (Edward Thomas)

The sun blazed while the thunder yet
Iron IV 128; Sphe 60

PONIES

See also Horses

Hunter Trials (Sir John Betjeman)

It's awf'lly bad luck on Diana
By 289; Dawn 82; Mod.P 59; Prel II 27; S.D 144; Sto II 73; Them V 14; V.F 23

The Runaway (Robert Frost)

Once when the snow of the year was beginning to fall
A.D.L 186; Bird I 55; B.P III 37; Drag 28; Fab.C.V 79; F.Feet 126; Fro.You 52; Go.Jo 72; G.Tr.P 29; Hap 68; Key II 49; M.Ver 77; Ox.V.J III 48; Prel I 44; Riv IV 32; Six I 24; Start 23

PONIES, PIT

The Ponies (W. W. Gibson)

During the strike the ponies were brought up
Make III 100; Peg III 48

POOLS

The Pool in the Rock (Walter de la Mare)

In this water, clear as air
Iron II 29; Key III 119; P.F.P I 38; P.Life III 9; Start 134

The Rock Pool (Philip Hobsbaum)

My life could have ended then, crouched over the pool
A.S.L.A 10; D.P.R III 2

The Rock Pool (Edward Shanks)

This is the sea. In these uneven walls
Peg IV 101; Sphe 206

Summer Waterfall (Norman MacCaig)

I watch a rock shine black
Yim III 136

POPLARS

Binsey Poplars (Gerard Manley Hopkins)

My aspens dear, whose airy cages quelled
Cher 239; Choice 116; Fla 27; Flock 104; Iron IV 106; Pers 97; Song IV 54; Speak II 20

The Poplar Field (William Cowper)

The poplars are felled, farewell to the shade
Flock 105; P.F.P II 231; P.Tong I 142; Riv II 15; Shep 23; Song IV 53

PORTRAITS

See also Children, Egoists, Occupations, Pessimists

PORTRAITS (CHAUCER)

Canterbury Tales, The Prologue (complete) (Geoffrey Chaucer)

Whan that Aprille with his showres soote
Flock 17

(trans N. Coghill)

When the sweet showers of April fall and shoot
Flock 16

The Knight
(trans Louis Untermeyer)

A knight there was, and that a worthy man
Flock 19; G.Tr.P 86

(trans N. Coghill)

There was a Knight, a most distinguished man
Flock 18

The Miller (Geoffrey Chaucer)

The Miller was a stout carles for the nones
Flock 31; Iron III 58; M.M.A 53; P.Tong 133

(trans N. Coghill)

The Miller was a chap of sixteen stone
Flock 30; M.M.A 54; Ver III 199; Weal I 105

(trans Louis Untermeyer)

The Miller, stout and sturdy as the stones
G.Tr.P 87

The Parson (Geoffrey Chaucer)

A good man was ther of religioun
Flock 29

(trans N. Coghill)

A holy-minded man of good renown
Flock 28; Ver III 198

The Prioress (Geoffrey Chaucer)

There was also a nun, a Prioress
Flock 21; Wheel IV 25

(trans N. Coghill)

There was also a Nun, a Prioress
Flock 20

The Squire (Geoffrey Chaucer)

With him ther was his sone, a yong Squyer
Flock 21; P.W 45; P.W.R 32; R.R 119; Wheel III 35

(trans Louis Untermeyer)

With him there was his son a youthful Squire
G.Tr.P 87

(trans N. Coghill)

He had his son with him, a fine young Squire
Flock 20; Weal II 121

The Wife of Bath (Geoffrey Chaucer)

A good wife was there of beside Bathe
Flock 29; Iron IV 71; Wheel IV 24

(trans N. Coghill)

A worthy woman from beside Bath city
Flock 28

PORTRAITS (COMIC)

See also Nonsense, Nonsense (Carroll), Nonsense (Hughes), Nonsense (Lear)

The Disagreeable Man (Princess Ida) (W. S. Gilbert)

If you give me your attention I will tell you what I am
Sphe 246

The Diverting History of John Gilpin (William Cowper)

John Gilpin was a citizen
Ch.Gar 158; D.P III 119; D.P.R III 88; Min IV 71; P.Bk 226; Plea III 55; Puf.V 66; Ver II 13; V.F 39; Weal I 47

The Duke of Plaza-Toro (The Gondoliers) (W. S. Gilbert)

In enterprise of martial kind
Key II 34; Speak II 15

Edward Lear (Edward Lear)

How pleasant to know Mr Lear!
Cher 463; Cor 52; Fab.C.V 124; G.Tr.P 212; P.Life III 30; Riv IV 6; Sphe 221; V.F 100

Mr Nobody (Anon)

I know a funny little man
Puf.V 150

The Pigtail (William M. Thackeray)

There lived a sage in days of yore
Ex.Tro 42; Fab.N.V 197; G.Tr.P 232; J.Vo II 38; Min IV 51; Mood I 17; Ox.V.J III 17; Plea III 33; P.Life III 44; Tree IV 105

Sir Smasham Uppe (E. V. Rieu)

Good afternoon, Sir Smasham Uppe!
D.P III 139; D.P.R III 97; Ex.Ch 150; Kal 43; Peg I 20; P.Life III 88; Puf.Q 115; Rhyme IV 72; Sto I 13; V.F 121

PORTRAITS (FEMALE)

Aunt Julia (Norman MacCaig)

Aunt Julia spoke Gaelic/very loud and very fast
Mod.P 178

Aunts Watching Television (John Pudney)

The aunts who knew not Africa
Mod.P 65

Business Girls (Sir John Betjeman)

From the geyser ventilators
Weal 167

Elizabeth of Bohemia (Sir Henry Wotton)

You meaner beauties of the night
Fab.C.V 139

Great Aunts (Anne Gould—aged 12)

Laces and frills are what they wear
Start 50

Love Poem (John Frederick Nims)

My clumsiest dear, whose hands shipwreck vases
Peg V 47

Miss Thompson goes Shopping (Martin Armstrong)

In her lone cottage on the downs
D.P IV 133; Weal 153; Wheel III 145

A little further down the way
P.F.P I 45

Mrs Malone (Eleanor Farjeon)

Mrs Malone
Puf.Q 32

Mrs McGinty (Michael Johnson)

Mrs McGinty/has a gallon of milk every day
Prel I 33

My Last Duchess (Robert Browning)

That's my last Duchess painted on the wall
Peg V 50; P.W.R 227

To Mistress Margaret Hussey (John Skelton)

Merry Margaret
Cor 158; Fab.C.V 116; Go.Jo 109; G.Tr.P 88; P.Bk 6; P.W 52; P.W.R 41; Riv IV 28; Song III 89; Spo II 138; This W.D 77; Trea 156

Under Milk Wood (part) (Dylan Thomas)

Now, woken at last by the out-of-bed-sleepy-head
Man II 33

Yorkshire Wife's Saga (Ruth Pitter)

War was her life, with want and the wild air
Sev 68

PORTRAITS (MALE)

Dreaming in the Shanghai Restaurant (D. J. Enright)

I would like to be that elderly Chinese gentleman
Act IV 128; Mod.P 119

Elegy for Alfred Hubbard (Tony Connor)

Hubbard is dead, the old plumber
Mod.P 98; Them VI 8; Voi III 52

John Mouldy (Walter de la Mare)

I spied John Mouldy in his cellar
Camb 67; De la M.Ch 61; De la M.Col 145; Peg I 95; Plea III 12; Puf.Y 49

The Lay Preacher Ponders (Idris Davies)

Isn't the violet a dear little flower? And the daisy too
Comp 46

A Man of Culture
(A. S. J. Tessimond)

He finds that talk of music, books and art is
M.Ver 103

Miniver Cheevy (Edwin Arlington Robinson)

Miniver Cheevy, child of scorn
Cher 467; Fab.C.V 120; Pers 56; R.R 39

Mr Flood's Party (Edwin Arlington Robinson)

Old Eben Flood, climbing alone one night
Ev.M 67; Look 135; Ox.V.J IV 78; Them IV 61

On the University Carrier (John Milton)

Here lies old Hobson, Death hath broke his girt
Fab.C.V 272

Portrait of a Romantic
(A. S. J. Tessimond)

He is in love with the land that is always over
Peg V 92

Richard Cory (Edwin Arlington Robinson)

Whenever Richard Cory went down town
Chal III 51; Them VI 40

Seumas Beg (James Stephens)

A man was sitting underneath a tree
V.F 157

Sir Geoffrey Chaucer (Robert Greene)

His stature was not very tall
Fab.C.V 116; Speak II 23; Weal II 123

Squire Hooper (Thomas Hardy)

Hooper was ninety. One September dawn
Make III 106; Tell II 151

Uncle Cyril (George Rostrevor Hamilton)

Nobody knew whether from East or West
J.Mod 57; Sev 40

POSTMEN

The Postman (John Stallworthy)

Satchel on hip
Drag 38

The Postman (Gordon Challis)

This cargo of confessions, messages
Exp. II 21

POVERTY

An 18th Century Poor House
(George Crabbe)

Theirs is yon house that holds the Parish Poor
Riv IV 31

His Life (Jennifer Webb)

Dirty, damp, dark/Cold, miserable, dull
Man III 44

Pie in the Sky (Anon)

Long-haired preachers come out ev'ry night
Act IV 164; F.S.N.A 423

Poverty (D. H. Lawrence)

The only people I ever heard talk about my Lady Poverty
P.W 254; P.W.R 299

Song of the Poor Man (Zanzibar, Anon)

Give me a chair
Eye 38

The Song of the Shirt (Thomas Hood)

With fingers weary and worn
P.Bk 52; S.D 111; Six III 20; Them VI 41; Trea 36

The Story about the Road (part)

Imagine yourself in a country, poor—
Fla 174

Timothy Winters (Charles Causley)

Timothy Winters comes to school
A.S.L.A 11; Chal I 73; Com 171; Mod.P 67; My 100; Read II 66; Sev 17; Them IV 43; Under 59; Voi II 90; Wheel II 167

PRAISES

The Benedicite (part) (Book of Common Prayer)

O all ye works of the Lord, bless ye the Lord;
D.P II 124; D.P.R II 98; Speak II 130

Glory to Thee (T. Ken)

Glory to Thee, my God, this night
Rhyme III 82

Magnificat (Book of Common Prayer)

My soul doth magnify the Lord;
D.P.R III 116

Morning Worship (Mark van Doren)

I wake and hear it raining
J.Vo IV 4

Pied Beauty (Gerard Manley Hopkins)

Glory be to God for dappled things
A.D.L 203; By 195; Choice 116; D.P IV 184; D.P.R IV 26; F.Feet 194; Flock 101; Go.Jo 47; G.Tr.P 246; Iron II 12; Look 223; Make IV 117; Man I 12; My 182; Peg V 17; Pers 136; P.F.P I 120; Riv II 12; R.R 165; Six V 30; Song II 7; Sphe 81; Sto III 88; Them VII 40; This W.D 112; Ver III 46; Weal II 37

Pleasure it is (William Cornish)

Pleasure it is
Com 29

Praise (George Herbert)

King of Glory, King of Peace
Riv III 56

Praise the Lord (John Milton)

Let us with a gladsome mind
Fab.C.V 352

Psalm 24 (part)

The earth is the Lord's and the fullness thereof
D.P.R III 115; P.W 82

Psalm 95 (part)

O come let us sing unto the Lord
Mer 127; Mer.Puf 96

Psalm 100

Make a joyful noise unto the Lord, all ye lands
D.P.I 109; D.P.R I 97

Psalm 136 (part)

O give thanks unto the Lord for he is good
D.P.R III 114

Psalm 148 (part)

Praise ye the Lord from the Heavens
Mer 134

Praise the Lord from the earth
Mer 217; Mer.Puf 160; Riv I 63

Psalm 150 (part)

O praise God in his holiness
Cher 446; Ch.Gar 118

The Scribe (Walter de la Mare)

What lovely things
De la M.Ch 148; Fab.C.V 33; Man III 14; Song II 4

Thanksgiving for the Body (Thomas Traherne)

O Lord!/Thou hast given me a body
Pers 6

PRAYERS

The Dry Salvages (part) (T. S. Eliot)

Lady, whose shrine stands on the promontory
Day 5

Eight Prayers (Various Authors)

Lord of the World
Man III 51

For Sleep or Death (Ruth Pitter)

Cure me with quietness
A.D.L 273; Man III 45; My 178; Song I 154; Weal I 144

God be in my Head (Anon)

God be in my head
B.L.J I 39; Cher 386; Ch.Gar 141; D.P I 110; D.P.R I 97; Ex.Ch 184; Key I 56; Make I 158; Mer 270; Mer.Puf 201; My 174; Peg V 103; Puf.V 129; Song II 148

God Bless this House (Anon)

God bless this house from thatch to floor
Tree II 23

Hebridean Sea Prayer (Anon)

Blest be the boat
Speak I 91

A House Blessing (William Cartwright)

Saint Francis and Saint Benedight
Cher 167

Moonless darkness stands between (Gerard Manley Hopkins)

Moonless darkness stands between
Weal II 176

Prayer at Bedtime (Anon)

Matthew, Mark, Luke and John
B.L.J I 7; B.P I 21; Ch.Gar 145; Fab.C.V 371; G.Tr.P 23; Key I 109; Mer 134; Mer.Puf 101; M.G.E 115; M.G.R 99; Ox.Dic 303; Ox.N.R 17; Ox.V.J II 17; Plea III 74; Puf.V 269; Rhyme II 66; Scrap 47

Prayer before Birth (Louis MacNiece)

I am not yet born; O hear me.
Com 91; Dan 58; Day 23; D.P.R III 111; Kal 127; Mod.P 43; Peg V 100; Pers 3; S.D 15; Sev 72; Sphe 404; Wheel IV 174

A Prayer for Everest (Wilfrid Noyce)

That I may endure
Pat 135

Prayer to St Catherine (Anon)

St Catherine, St Catherine, O lend me thine aid
Mood IV 19

The Robin's Song (Anon)

God bless the field and bless the furrow
B.B.F 233; Rhyme II 65; Sto I 141

PREDICTION

The New House (Edward Thomas)

Now first, as I shut the door
P.W.R 292

O Where are you going? (W. H. Auden)

'O where are you going?' said reader to rider
Choice 238; Fab.C.V 294; Liv 101; Wheel IV 180

Prognosis (Louis MacNiece)

Goodbye Winter/The days are getting longer
Cent 49; P.F.P II 242; Wheel IV 176

PRIDE

Isabella (part) (John Keats)

With her two brothers this fair lady dwelt
Bat 50

PRIMROSES

To a Primrose (John Clare)

Welcome, pale Primrose! starting up between
Flock 10

PRISONERS

Durham Gaol (Thomas Armstrong)

You'll all have heard of Durham Gaol
Read II 53; Voi II 144

PRISONS

Cells (Rudyard Kipling)

I've a head like a concertina, I've a tongue like a button-stick,
Them III 17

The Commuted Sentence (Stevie Smith)

Shut me not alive away
Them III 16

The Knight in Prison (William Morris)

Wearily, drearily,
J.Vo III 83; P.Rem 96; P.W 219; P.W.R 255; Sphe 348

PROFESSIONS

See Occupations

PROFESSORS

The Purist (Ogden Nash)

I give you now Professor Twist
Go.Jo 111

PROPERTY

Get off this estate! (Carl Sandburg)

'Get off this estate!'
J.Vo IV 43

PROSPECTORS

Sunstrike (Douglas Lawrence)

A solitary prospector/staggered, locked in a vision
Mod.P 159; Prel III 7

PROTESTS

The Fine Old English Gentleman (Charles Dickens)

I'll sing you a new ballad and I'll warrant it first-rate
Fab.Bal 185

For a' that (Robert Burns)

Is there, for honest poverty
D.P IV 96

Letter to 'The Times' (Dannie Abse)

Sir, I have various complaints to make
Pat 112

PSYCHO-ANALYSTS

The Psycho-Analyst
(A. S. J. Tessimond)

His suit is good, his hands are white
Sto III 112

PUCK

See Robin Goodfellow

PYLONS

Pylons (Stanley Snaith)

Over the tree'd upland evenly striding
Six IV 30; Ver III 65

The Pylons (Stephen Spender)

The secret of these hills was stone, and cottages
Day 12; D.P IV 123; D.P.R IV 95; Ev.M 37; P.F.P II 158; P.Tong II 155; Sphe 65; Them VII 53

PYTHONS

Hello Mr Python (Spike Milligan)

Hello Mr Python
Mill.S.V 47

The Python (Hilaire Belloc)

A Python I should not advise—
Bel.C.V 118; Song II 67; Wheel II 134

QUAILS

Quail's Nest (John Clare)

I wandered out one rainy day
B.B.F 83; B.L.J III 36; Ex.Ch 16; Sto I 115; T.P.R 78

QUEENS

See Kings and Queens

QUESTION & ANSWER

Billy Barlow (Anon)

'Let's go hunting' says Risky Rob
Bird I 13

166

Billy Boy (Anon)

Oh where have you been, Billy Boy, Billy
Boy
*Key I 21; Ox.Dic 78; Ox.N.R 189; Song
III 47*

The Croodin' Doo (Anon)

Where hae ye been a' the day
Ox.Dic 77; Ox.N.R 203

Edward, Edward (Anon)

Why does your brand sae drop wi' blude
*Bal 86B; B.B 142, 189; Bun 39; Com
108; Fab.Bal 119; Iron II 20; Key I 19;
Make III 133; Peg III 89; P.F.P I 149;
Plea IV 72; P.W 4; P.W.R 4; Riv IV 92;
Spo II 9; Ver III 178; Wheel III 25*

The False Knight and the Wee Boy
or *The False Knight upon the Road*
or *Meet-on-the-Road* (Anon)

O whare are ye gaun?
*B.P I 70; Bun 84; Fab.C.V 105; Kal 44;
Key IV 92; M.M.A 30; Ox.V.J II 33;
P.Tong I 99*

'Now pray where are you going, child?'
said Meet-on-the-Road
*Bird I 10; Ex.H 29; Mer 122; Mer.Puf
92; Ox.P.C 84; P.F.P I 56; Puf.V 205;
Shad 18; Tree IV 116*

The knight met a child in the road
Bird I 9

A Gentle Echo on Woman
(Jonathan Swift)

Echo, I ween, will in the wood reply
R.R 144

The Hole in the Bucket (Anon)

There's a hole in my bucket, dear Liza,
dear Liza
All 48; Key I 16

The Keys of Canterbury or *my Heart*
or *Heaven* (Anon)

I will give you the keys of heaven
Rhyme III 60

O Madam, I will give to you the keys of
Canterbury
Cor 112; Key III 104; Rhyme II 22

O Madam I will give to you a new lace
cap
Puf.N.R 82

Lord Randall or *John Randall*
(Anon)

Where have you been, Lord Randall my
son?
*Bal 81; Bat 84; B.B 164; Fab.Bal 34;
Fun I 136; Kal 108; Make II 100;
M.M.A 65; Mood III 72; Ox.Dic 76;
Ox.V.J IV 24; P.Bk 135; P.F.P I 147;
Plea IV 74; P.Tong I 101; P.W 16;
P.W.R 14; Read III 23; Riv III 130; R.R
26; Say 73; Song III 146; Voi II 133;
Yim II 8*

My Man John (Anon)

My man John, what can the matter be?
Key III 101

Neglectful Edward (Robert Graves)

Nancy: Edward back from the Indian
Sea
Quest IV 76

O No, John! (Anon)

On yonder hill there stands a creature
Rhyme III 4

Overheard on a Saltmarsh
(Harold Monro)

Nymph, nymph, what are your beads?
*Go.Jo 227; J.Vo I 16; Look 290; Patch
17; Peg I 94; P.F.P I 110; Quest I 81;
This W.D 33; T.P.W 64*

Paper of Pins (Anon)

I'll give to you a paper of pins
*Bird I 28; Broad 76; Ones 104; Song I
60*

The Quarry or *O What is that Sound*
(W. H. Auden)

O what is that sound which so thrills the
ear
*Camb 130; Choice 237; Dawn 42;
D.P.R I 61; Flock 254; Mod.P 15; Mood
IV 54; M.Ver 141; Nar 1; P.F.P I 70;
Say 77; Song II 124; Sphe 356; Them I
32; Wheel III 180; Yim III 6*

Soldier, Soldier (Anon)

O soldier, soldier, won't you marry me?
*Chor 9; D.P I 98; D.P.R I 77; Ex.Tro
74; Mer 142; Mer.Puf 92; M.G.B 186;
Ox.P.C 35; P.Life II 60; Puf.N.R 176;
Puf.S.B 78; Puf.Y 142; Rain 31; Rhyme
III 20; R.R 143*

What's in there? (Anon)

What's in there?/Gold and money
Mer 157; Mer.Puf 116; Tree II 77

Which? (Walter de la Mare)

What did you say?
De la M.Ch 100; J.Vo II 29

QUESTIONS

I keep six honest Servingmen
(Rudyard Kipling)

I keep six honest servingmen
Bird I 2

RABBITS

Done For (Walter de la Mare)

Old Ben Bailey/He's been and done
De la M.Col 87; De la M.S 81; Tree I 24

Myxomatosis (Philip Larkin)

Caught in the centre of a soundless field
Cent 85; Comp 59; Them I 41

The Rabbit (Elizabeth Maddox
Roberts)

When they said the time to hide was mine
Patch 15

The Snare (James Stephens)

I hear a sudden cry of pain!
*Chal II 42; D.P I 20; D.P.R I 10; Ex.Ch
20; F.Feet 129; Fun II 86; Look 180;
Make I 81; My 129; Ox.P.C 130; P.F.P I
95; P.Life II 25; Rhyme III 53; Shep 83;
Song I 52; Spir 45; Spir.R 37; T.P.R 51;
Tree IV 71*

To See the Rabbit (Alan Brownjohn)

We are going to see the rabbit
*Chal I 94; D.P.R I 12; Hap 36; Mod.P
106; Peng.An 261; Sev 125; Six II 10;
Them VII 60; Yim I 139*

The White Rabbit (E. V. Rieu)

He is white as Helvellyn when winter is
well in
My 164; Puf.Q 136

RACEHORSES

At Grass (Philip Larkin)

The eye can hardly pick them out
Cent 85; Song III 31

RACE RELATIONS

See also Foreigners, Negroes,
Peoples, Refugees

Africa's Plea (Roland Tombekai
Dempster)

I am not you/but you will not
Chal I 39; Voi III 24

At the Well (Lawson Trust)

Take me for instance
Exp.IV 1

'Barricadoed Evermore' (George
Miller Miller)

Sophiatown's not far away
Ver III 258

Come Away, My Love (Joseph
Kariuki)

Come away, my love, from streets
Them III 32

The Cypriots (Jean Salisbury)

It's not the place I mean
Prel I 42

The Discardment (Alan Paton)

We gave her a discardment
Ver III 267

The Lament of the Banana Man
(Evan Jones)

Gal, I'm tellin' you, I'm tired fo' true
Act IV 90; Exp IV 23; Mod.P 165

Man, the Man-Hunter (Carl
Sandburg)

I saw Man, the man-hunter
Them I 33

Prayer of a Black Boy (Guy
Tirolien)

Lord I am so tired
Chal II 56; Exp IV 18

Public Bar (Anthony Thwaite)

A foreign man—God knows
Sev 117

Telephone Conversation (Wole Soyinka)

The price seemed reasonable, location
Act IV 91; Exp IV 20; Flock 134; Sev 116; Voi III 26

RACING

At the Races: The Starter (Alan Ross)

'They're off!' and the fat major
Key IV 84

Galway Races (Anon)

It's there you'll see confectioners with sugar sticks and dainties
Mood IV 16

Right Royal (part) (John Masefield)

The horses sparred as though drunk with wine
Key IV 86; Riv III 9; Them V 10

RACING (BETTING)

Lord Hippo (Hilaire Belloc)

Lord Hippo suffered fearful loss
Make III 59

Song of the Boob (J. H. E. Schroder)

I'm the sort of silly boob that chases/Races
Chal III 60

RADIO

Radio (A. S. J. Tessimond)

Here is another dream, another forgetting, another doorway
Man I 58

RAG & BONE MEN

Money for Lumber (Anon)

The above with most respectful feeling
Key III 64

RAGWORT

Rag-wort (Richard Church)

Nobody considers rag-wort a flower
J.Mod 141

The Ragwort (John Clare)

Ragwort thou humble flower with tattered leaves
Cher 255

RAILWAYS

See Engine Drivers, Trains

RAIN

See also Noah

After Rain (Edward Thomas)

The rain of a night and a day and a night
Tho.Gr 49

The Boy with the Cart (part) (Christopher Fry)

That is rain on dry ground. We heard it
A.S.L.A 50; Dan 43; D.P IV 52; Ev.M 78; Peg IV 53; Speak II 126; Ver II 232

A Description of a City Shower (Jonathan Swift)

Now in contiguous drops the flood comes down
D.P.R III 31

Careful observers may foretell the hour
P.W.R 131

Glass Falling (Louis MacNiece)

The glass is going down. The sun
A.S.L.A 49; Bird I 21; B.L.J IV 27; B.P IV 95; Cor 20; Dawn 37; Make II 45; Ox.V.J IV 50; Say 62

I Hear Leaves (W. H. Davies)

I hear leaves drinking rain
Cent 12; Ex.Tro 30; First III 28; Man I 24; Min II 33; Mood I 58; P.Life I 63; Quest III 65

Jardin sous la Pluie (Redwood Anderson)

Tenderly, gently, the soft rain
Peg IV 54

Notes Written on a Damp Verandah
(P. McGinley)

Do they need any rain
Peg III 85

Prayer for Rain (Herbert Palmer)

O God, make it rain!
Prel III 10

Rain (Walter de la Mare)

I woke in the swimming dark
Ox.V.J IV 55; P.Life IV 37; Shep 44

Rain (Norman Nicholson)

Rain/when it falls on land
Prel III 11

Rain (Robert Louis Stevenson)

The rain is raining all around
Fuji 60; Go.Jo 34; Mood I 58; Tree I 29

Rain in Summer (H. W. Longfellow)

How beautiful is the rain!
Bat 79; Fuji 103; Key III 128; Mood III 26; Peg II 3; Sto I 85

A Rainy Scene (Chu Hsiang—
trans Kai-Yu Hsu)

Many a rainy scene I love
Shep 47

The Shower (Richard Church)

So here we stand beneath the dripping trees
Look 9

Signs of Rain (E. Jenner)

The hollow winds begin to blow
Mood IV 40; Tree IV 87

Sudden Shower (John Clare)

Black grows the southern sky,
betokening rain
Riv III 8

The Summer Shower (John Clare)

I love it well o'ercanopied in leaves
D.P.R III 19

Wet Through (Hal Summers)

Being now completely wet through to the skin
M.Ver 34; Prel III 12

Winter Rain (Christina Rossetti)

Every valley drinks
F.Feet 21; Iron I 11; Make I 85; Scrap 43; Tree III 16

RAINBOWS

The Rainbow (Walter de la Mare)

I saw the lovely arch
P.Life II 52

RAINDROPS

Waiting at the Window
(A. A. Milne)

These are two drops of rain
Quest I 25

RAMS

See also Sheep

The Ram of Derby or *Derby Ram*
(Anon)

As I was going to Derby, Sir, 'twas on a summer's day
Mer 173; Mer.Puf 131; Rain 54; Read I 159; Rhyme II 16; Song II 62; Voi I 37

As I was going to Derby, upon a market day
B.L.J IV 23; Fab.N.V 70; M.G.B 144; Ox.Dic 145; Ox.N.R 205; Sto I 104

As I went down to Derby, sir, all on a market day
B.B.F 195

As I went down to Derby town
Bird I 43; Iron I 2; Key III 126; Peg I 46; Riv I 83

As I went to Dalby, upon a market day
Cor 57

As I went to market, 'twas on a market day
Bird I 44

RAT RACE

Ambition (Morris Bishop)

I got pocketed behind 7X-3824
Six IV 8; Wheel IV 162

The Miller's Song (Anon)

There was an old miller and he lived all alone
Bird IV 37

RATS (LYRIC & DESCRIPTIVE)

An Advancement of Learning (Seamus Heaney)

I took the embankment path
Them I 49

A Rat (Baku Yamanoguchi)

Having cast away/This life of death-in-life
Shep 91

The Rat (Andrew Young)

Strange that you let me come so near
Com 50; You.Qu 21

Rats (Frank Eyre)

When dusk is falling
All 30; Key I 42

Song of the Brown Sea Rat (Hamish Maclaren)

Now we are the rodent mariners
All 109; P.Bk 355; Peg I 48; Speak I 95; Spo I 128; Sto I 65

RATS (NARRATIVE)

Bishop Hatto (Robert Southey)

The summer and autumn had been so wet
Cher 130; D.P.I 90; P.Bk 238; Tell I 48

The Pied Piper of Hamelin (Robert Browning)

Hamelin Town's in Brunswick
B.P III 18; Dan 89; Ex.Ch 127; Fab.C.V 160; Fun II 27; G.Tr.P 153; Make I 67; P.F.P I 70; Riv I 102; Spir 111; Spir.R 85; Sto I 49;

Rats!/They fought the dogs and killed the cats
F.Feet 116; Key I 72; Min IV 91

Into the street the Piper stept
First III 46

RATTLESNAKES

Rattlesnake Ceremony Song (North American Indian—trans A. L. Kroeber)

The king snake said to the rattlesnake
J.Vo III 9

RAVENS

Noah's Ark (part) (Anon)

Then, as the lifted land lay upwards
Peng.An 265

The Raven (Edgar Allan Poe)

Once upon a midnight dreary, while I pondered weak and weary
Fab.C.V 190; Go.Jo 165; P.Bk 240; Plea VI 40; Trea 249

The Raven's Nest (John Clare)

Upon the collar of an huge old oak
Voi II 36

The Raven's Tomb (Walter de la Mare)

'Build me my tomb' the Raven said,
Plea VI 87

The Three Ravens (Anon)

There were three ravens on a tree
Bal 111; Bat 30; B.B 170, 193; Cher 165; Song IV 83; Voi II 160

There were two ravens who sat on a tree
Fab.Bal 37; Them I 22

The Twa Corbies (Anon)

As I was walking all alane
Bal 112; B.B 171; Bun 132; Fab.Bal 38; Fab.C.V 266; Flock 256; Kal 1; Make II 52; Mer 241; Mer.Puf 175; Peg II 64; P.F.P I 147; Puf.V 98; P.W 6; P.W.R 6; Riv I 30; Riv IV 58; R.R 170; Shep 107; Song I 47; Ver III 31; Voi II 159; Wheel III 19

RECRUITS

The Misfit (C. Day Lewis)

At the training depot that first morning
Song IV 74

The Recruited Collier (Anon)

'Oh, what's the matter with you, my lass
Song IV 70

RED INDIANS

See Indians, Red

REDWINGS

The Redwing (Patric Dickinson)

The winter clenched its fist
M.Ver 61

REFLECTIONS

Gentleman aged Five before the Mirror (John Wain)

It tells you what you do but never why
J.Mod 73

The Mud (Andrew Young)

This glistening mud that loves a gate
Bird I 25; You.Qu 18

Reflections (Louis MacNiece)

The mirror above my fireplace reflects the reflected
A.S.L.A 38

The River is a piece of Sky (John Ciardi)

From the top of a bridge
Puf.Y 63

Water Picture (May Swenson)

In the pond in the park
Voi II 50

REFUGEES

See also Negroes, Race Relations

REFUGEES (LYRIC & DESCRIPTIVE)

The Evacuee (R. S. Thomas)

She woke up under a loose quilt
Choice 303; Mod.P 28; Under 65

The Little Cart (Ch'en Tsu-Lung—trans Arthur Waley)

The little cart jolting and banging through the yellow haze of dust
Flock 89; Iron I 47; Shep 144; Song II 25; Voi I 28

Refugee Blues (W. H. Auden)

Say this city has ten million souls
Bird IV 14; Cent 31; Chal I 41; Ev.M 58; Exp IV 28; Fla 106; Man II 50; Pers 47; Read III 25; Them III 39; Under 46; Weal I 122

The Refugees (Herbert Read)

Mute figures with bowed heads
Them III 39

REFUGEES (NARRATIVE)

The Companion (Yevgeny Yevtushenko—trans Milner-Gulland)

She was sitting on the rough embankment
D.P.R III 69; Flock 252; Tell I 11

Hiding beneath the Furze (Henry Reed)

Hiding beneath the furze as they passed him by
J.Mod 35

The Italian in England (Robert Browning)

That second time they hunted me
Nar 12; P.Bk 219; Tell II 13; Ver III 216

Refugees (Schoolchild)

'Of course I'll do what I can, but—
Wheel IV 211

RELIGIOUS THEMES

See also Chal III 69–78

See also Booth (General William), Church-going, Judgement (Day of), Praise, Prayers, Saints, Spirituals

RELIGIOUS THEMES
(NEW TESTAMENT)

See also Christ, Christmas (Religious), Crucifixion, Easter, Epiphany, Herod, John the Baptist, Judas, Lazarus, Martha, Palm Sunday

RELIGIOUS THEMES
(OLD TESTAMENT)

See also Abraham & Isaac, Adam, Balaam, Creation, Daniel, Eden, Eve, Goliath, Jacob, Jael & Sisera, Jericho, Jonah, Joseph, Joshua, Moses, Noah, Ruth, Samson

RELIGIOUS THEMES

All but Blind (Walter de la Mare)

All but blind
Bird II 43; B.B.F 29; De la M.Ch 144; De la M.Col 80; De la M.P.P 78; De la M.S 78; D.P.R I 94; F.Feet 190; Ox.V.J I 54; Plea III 35; R.R 168; Weal I 121

Darky Sunday School (Anon)

Jonah was an immigrant, so runs the Bible tale
Tell II 4

Design (Robert Frost)

I found a dimpled spider fat and white
Song II 15

The Destruction of Sennacherib (Lord Byron)

The Assyrian came down like a wolf on the fold
B.L.J IV 49; By 148; Fab.C.V 254; G.Tr.P 143; Mood IV 53; P.Bk 275; Plea VII 21; P.F.P II 66; Sphe 340; Spir 76; Spir.R 60; Spo I 101; Ver II 138

Eddi's Service (A.D. 687)
(Rudyard Kipling)

Eddi priest of St Wilfrid
Key III 148; Mood III 100; Plea IV 55; Speak I 132

In the Cool of the Evening
(James Stephens)

I thought I heard Him calling! Did you hear
By 245

Little Gidding IV (part)
(T. S. Eliot)

The dove descending breaks the air
Fla 71

Peace (Henry Vaughan)

My soul, there is a country
Cher 347; D.P IV 181; Ex.Ch 185; Fab.C.V 368; Ox.V.J III 85; P.F.P II 246; Riv III 55; S.D 65; Song III 170; Sphe 395; Weal II 172

Vice Versa (Christian Morgenstern —trans R. F. C. Hull)

The rabbit sits upon the green
Ark 36

REPORTERS

Girl Reporter (Philip Hobsbaum)

Fact is her fiction. Sitting in the bar
Act IV 81; Bird IV 40; Chal III 84; Exp II 30

REPTILES

See Crocodiles, Pythons, Slow-worms, Snakes, Tortoises, Turtles

REVENGE, THE

The Revenge, A Ballad of the Fleet
(Alfred Lord Tennyson)

At Flores in the Azores Sir Richard Grenville lay
D.P II 106; D.P.R II 59; Fab.C.V 247; Kal 78; Nar 153; Peg II 36; P.F.P II 57; Plea V 56; P.Rem 70; Puf.V 87; Riv III 141; Song II 105; Ver II 143

RHYMES

See Alphabet Rhymes, Counting Rhymes, Counting-Out Rhymes, Cumulative Rhymes, Ruthless Rhymes

RHINOCEROS

The Rhinoceros (Ogden Nash)

The Rhino is a homely beast
G.Tr.P 37

RICKSHAW PULLERS

The Rickshaw Puller (Tsang K'O-Chia—trans Kai-Yu Hsu)

The wind roars and rocks treetops
S.D 40

RIDDLES

See also B.B.F 190, 192–193; B.L.J I 51; Cher 3, 10, 11, 12, 13, 36, 97, 235, 389, 395, 402; Drag 23, 38, 39; Ex.Tra 27; Fab.C.V 62; Fab.N.V 44, 48–54; First I 10–11; Go.Jo 244; J.Vo I 47; J.Vo II 1, 2; J.Vo III 2, 4, 7, 28; J.Vo IV 18, 19; Mer 15, 54, 73, 80, 135–137, 164, 235, 252, 254, 296, 329; Mer.Puf 8, 40, 52, 57, 102–104, 124, 171, 185, 187, 220, 250; M.G.B 154–157, 189, 192; M.G.E 15, 23, 75, 107; M.G.R 49, 99, 136; My 25; Ones 53–58; Ox.Dic 55, 81, 87, 158, 161, 173, 190, 196, 208, 209, 212, 213, 217, 223, 258, 268, 277, 343, 355, 362, 363, 377, 383, 386, 388, 397, 403, 424; Ox.N.R 147–155; Peng.An 81, 229, 256; Plea I 12, 13, 18, 50, 63; Puf.N.R 72, 75, 108–109, 112, 118–119, 159, 160, 179, 182; Rhyme III 55; Rhyme IV 19, 27, 109; Rid throughout; Riv I 101; Scrap 78–79, 97; Start 3; Tree I 54–55; Voi I 7–9, 13–16

RIDDLES

Captain Wedderburn's Courtship (Anon)

The laird of Bristoll's daughter was in the woods walking
Bal 158

Clouds (Christina Rossetti)

White sheep, white sheep
Fuji 107

The Devil's Nine Questions (Anon)

O you must answer my questions nine
F.S.N.A 180

The Fur Coat (James Stephens)

I walked out in my Coat of Pride
Ox.V.J III 30

The Haystack (Andrew Young)

Too dense to have a door
Bits b; Cor 144; Dawn 98; Tree III 94; You.Qu 25

A Head but no Hair (Christina Rossetti)

A pin has a head but no hair
Key II 51

I had four brothers (Anon)

I had four brothers over the sea
Riv I 31

I had four sisters sailed across the sea
Key I 89

I will give my love an apple (Anon) or *O send to me an apple* (Welsh—trans Gwyn Williams)

I will give my love an apple without e'er a core
F.S.N.A 27; Key I 88; Mood III 5; Ox.P.C 34; Riv II 24; Song III 91

O send to me an apple that hasn't any kernel
Fab.C.V 282

A Long-eared Beast (Jonathan Swift)

A long-eared beast and a field house for cattle
Key II 91

Love on the Canal Boat (E. J. Brett)

Why is love like a canal boat?
J.Vo IV 76

The Lover's Gift (Anon)

My love sent me a chicken without e'er a bone
Ox.N.R 197

Moon and Sun (Anglo-Saxon—
trans Gavin Bone)

I saw a creature sally with booty
P.W 31; P.W.R 27; Riv IV 24

(trans Kevin Crossley-Holland)

I saw a strange creature
Rid 17

(trans B. Raffel)

I saw a silvery creature scurrying
Go.Jo 244

On a Pen (Jonathan Swift)

In youth exalted high in air
Key II 50

Riddle (trans K. Crossley-Holland)

This wind wafts little creatures
Drag 38

The Riddling Knight (Anon)

A knight came riding from the east
There were three sisters, fair and bright
*Bal 48, 50; B.P II 71; Bun 94; Fab.Bal
25; Fab.C.V 281; Key I 86; Mer 310;
Mer.Puf 232; Ox.P.C 39; P.Tong I 150;
Spo I 73; Wheel I 23*

Snow and Sun (Anon)

White bird featherless
Mer 329; Mer.Puf 250

There was a lady in the west
(Anon)

There was a lady in the west
Peg II 60

RIDING

The Boy (Rainer Maria Rilke—
trans J. B. Leishman)

I'd like, above all, to be one of those
My 135

The Cavalier's Escape or
The Pursuit (G. W. Thornbury)

Trample! trample! went the roan
*Bird I 48; D.P II 93; Min IV 61; Mood
II 26; P.F.P II 78; Speak I 43*

*How they brought the Good News
from Ghent to Aix*
(Robert Browning)

I sprang to the stirrup and Joris and he
*By 169; Down 35; G.Tr.P 149; Look 95;
Make II 126; Min IV 65; Mood II 14;
P.Bk 254; Peg II 53; P.F.P II 80; P.Rem
89; Sphe 171; Spir 29; Spir.R 24; Sto I
70; Trea 117; Ver II 23; Weal I 66*

Paul Revere's Ride (Henry
Wadsworth Longfellow)

Listen, my children, and you shall hear
*D.P II 87; D.P.R II 44; Ex.Ch 98;
G.Tr.P 184; Spir 162; Spir.R 121*

RIVERS

See also Brooks, Thames

Clear and Cool (Charles Kingsley)

Clear and cool, clear and cool
*Bird II 24; Dan 34; Key III 77; Spo II
108*

Rivers (Thomas Storer)

Fair Danube is praised for being wide
Fab.C.V 129

The Two Rivers (Anon)

Said Tweed to Till
*Bun 83; Cher 165; D.P IV 172; Fab.C.V
268; Plea V 24; Riv IV 2; Shad 69; Tree
IV 32*

Where go the Boats? (Robert
Louis Stevenson)

Dark brown is the river
*A.D.L 158; B.P I 60; Ex.Tra 64; First II
28; Go.Jo 177; Ox.V.J I 68; Start 77;
Ste.C.G 32; Ste.Ho 22*

ROADBUILDERS

Hot Asphalt (Ewan MacColl)

You can talk about your concrete and
the boys who work the train
Song I 20

I'm a Navvy (Anon)

I'm a navvy, you'm a navvy
Voi II 138

Song of the Road Builders (Ewan
MacColl)

Come all you gallant drivers
Rhyme IV 67

175

ROADS

The Rolling English Road
(G. K. Chesterton)

Before the Roman came to Rye or out to Severn strode
D.P IV 79; D.P.R IV 48; Fab.C.V 292; Plea VIII 9; Six V 58; Song III 54

ROBIN GOODFELLOW

Robin Goodfellow (Ben Jonson)

From Oberon in Fairyland
Fab.C.V 206; Mer 313; Mer.Puf 234; P.Bk 85

ROBIN HOOD

See also Bal 334–423

The Birth of Robin Hood (Anon)

O Willie's large of limb and bone
Bun 41

Robin Hood and Allen A Dale
(Anon)

Come listen to me, you gallants so free
Bal 397; B.L.J IV 53; B.P IV 32; Bun 44; Ex.Ch 120; G.Tr.P 115; Mood III 67; P.Bk 142; Peg I 82; P.P 27; Spir 145; Spir.R 109; Sto I 120

As Robin Hood in the forest stood
Min III 49

Robin Hood and the Bishop (Anon)

Come gentlemen all, and listen awhile
D.P I 52; D.P.R I 50; Key II 108; Min IV 92; Ox.P.C 73; P.Bk 146

Robin Hood and the Bishop of Hereford (Anon)

Some they will talk of bold Robin Hood
Bal 411; B.P III 62; Bun 74

Robin Hood and the Bold Pedlar
(Anon)

It's of a pedlar, a pedlar bold
Song II 74; Tell I 102

Robin Hood and the Butcher
(Anon)

Come, all you brave gallants and listen awhile
Bun 62; D.P I 56

Robin Hood and the Curtal Friar
(Anon)

In summer time when leaves grow green
Bal 361; Bun 48

Robin Hood and the Friars
(Thomas Love Peacock)

Bold Robin has robed him in ghostly attire
D.P I 50; D.P.R I 48

Robin Hood and Guy of Gisborne
(Anon)

When shawes beene sheene, and shradds full fayre
Bal 334; Bun 54

Robin Hood and Little John
(Anon)

When Robin Hood was about twenty years old
D.P II 59; D.P.R II 84; P.F.P I 61

Robin Hood and the Monk (Anon)

In somer, when the shawes be skeyne
Fab.Bal 81; Wheel II 16

Robin Hood and the Two Priests
(Anon)

I have heard talk of bold Robin Hood
Bun 66

Robin Hood and the Widow's Three Sons (Anon)

There are twelve months in all the year
B.B 102; Bun 70; D.P II 66; G.Tr.P 118; Peg I 77; P.F.P I 66; Plea IV 26; Tell I 88

Robin Hood's Death (Anon)

When Robin Hood and Little John
B.B 107; Bun 77; Fab.Bal 94; Flock 156

I will never eate nor drinke, Robin Hood said
Bal 349

Robin Hood's Golden Prize (Anon)

I have heard talk of bold Robin Hood
Tree IV 106

Song (Anthony Munday)

Weep, weep, ye woodmen! wail;
B.L.J III 30; Ox.P.C 152; Riv I 68

ROBINS

Cock Robin (Anon)

Who killed Cock Robin?
*All 52; Fab.N.V 114; F.S.N.A 181; Fun
II 5; G.Tr.P 62; Mer 9; M.G.B 60;
M.G.E 84; M.G.R 143; Ox.Dic 130;
Ox.N.R 166; Plea I 41; P.Life I 28;
Puf.N.R 76; Puf.S.B 94; Puf.V 38; Tree
I 40*

Who killed cocky Robin?
Iron I 60

The Red Robin (John Clare)

Cock Robin he got a new tippet in spring
*B.B.F 51; Mer 221; Mer.Puf 163; Scrap
77*

The Robin (Thomas Hardy)

When up aloft/I fly and fly
*B.L.J II 4; Mood I 41; Rhyme IV 108;
Say 31; Scrap 49; Tree III 14*

Robin (Hal Summers)

With a bonfire throat
A.S.L.A 63; Drag 83; Tree III 83

Rural Tales (part) (Robert
Bloomfield)

E'en as the redbreast, sheltering in a
bower
B.B.F 85

ROLLER COASTERS

Flight of the Roller Coaster
(Raymond Souster)

Once more around should do it, the man
confided
*A.S.L.A 36; Chal II 63; Look 310; Peg
V 12; Quest II 76; Way 83*

ROMAN BRITAIN

See also England (History, Roman),
Picts

A Road in the Weald (Richard
Church)

No one would notice that gap between
two fields
M.Ver 29

The Roman Road (Thomas Hardy)

The Roman Road runs straight and bare
Go.Jo 200; Har.Ch 23

Roman Road (A. G. Prys-Jones)

This is the way the Romans came
Spo I 142

The Roman Wall (Andrew Young)

Though moss and lichen crawl
Ten 171

Roman Wall Blues (W. H. Auden)

Over the heather the wet wind blows
*Choice 242; Dawn 43; Eye 25; J.Mod
34; J.Vo IV 37; Kal 36; My 79; Peg V
95; Say 83; Them VI 37; Ver III 67;
Weal I 122*

ROME

See Horatius

ROOKS

Alarm (Joan Prince)

Elms are etched against the clean washed
sky
Man I 42

Rookery (Seamus Heaney)

Here they come, freckling the sunset
Act III 68; Sev 102

ROUNDABOUTS

Roundabout (part) (James Reeves)

At midsummer fair on a galloping pony
Say 39

The Roundabout (Clive Sansom)

Round and round the roundabout
B.L.J II 15; Rhyme I 36

The Roundabout by the Sea (John
Walsh)

The crimson-spotted horses
All 38; B.P II 61; Ex.Tro 30; Min IV 18

RUGBY FOOTBALL

Rugby League Game (James Kirkup)

Sport is absurd, and sad.
Chal III 64; Man II 59; Them V 70; Yim III 147

Under the Goalposts (Arthur Guiterman)

We had battered their weakening rush line till it gave like a wisp of grass
Them V 3

RUTH

Ruth (Thomas Hood)

She stood, breast-high, amid the corn
D.P IV 103; Ver II 92

The Immigrant (Frank Kendon)

When Ruth was old
By 275

SAILING

Sailing to an Island (Richard Murphy)

The boom above my knees lifts, and the boat
Mod.P 129

SAILORS

See also Benbow, Columbus, Cortez, Drake, Grenville (Sir Richard), Nelson, Pirates

SAILORS (LYRIC & DESCRIPTIVE)

Billy in the Darbies (Herman Melville)

Good of the chaplain to enter Lone Bay
D.P.R II 67

Fleet Visit (W. H. Auden)

The sailors come ashore
Peg V 94

The Press-Gang (Anon)

Here's the tender coming
Rhyme IV 52

Psalm 107

They that go down to the sea in ships, that do business in great waters
B.L.J IV 11; Cher 217; D.P III 54; D.P.R III 41; P.Bk 76; P.Life IV 57; Speak I 109; Ver II 105

The Seafarer (J. M. Couper)

And there were, if I spit and speak true
Exp VI 26

The Seafarer (part) (Anglo-Saxon —trans Michael Alexander)

The tale I frame shall be found to tally
Comp 31; Voi I 28

(trans Ezra Pound)

May I for my own self song's truth reckon
D.P.R III 37

Skipper (of the Clipper Ship Mary Ambree) (C. Fox Smith)

A rough old nut/a tough old nut
A.D.L 128

Square-toed Princes (R. T. Coffin)

My ancestors were fine, long men
Peg III 78

SAILORS (NARRATIVE)

The Old Sailor (A. A. Milne)

There was once an old sailor my grandfather knew
B.P II 51; Fab.N.V 36; Mil.N.S 36

Stoker Rock's Baby (Charles Causley)

On a typical night when the stars were alight
Cau.Nar 31

A Truthful Song: II: The Sailor (Rudyard Kipling)

I tell this tale which is stricter true
Plea V 87

SAILOR'S SONGS

See also Sea Shanties

A-Roving (Anon)

At number three Old England Square
Mood III 14

The Fish of the Sea (Anon)

Come all ye young sailormen, listen to
me
F.S.N.A 50

The Gallant Seaman's Sufferings
(Anon)

You gentlemen of England that live at
home at ease
Sto III 122

The Mermaid (Anon)

One Friday morn when we set sail
*All 91; Bal 673; B.P III 72; Ex.Ch 26;
Fun II 173; Min IV 40; P.Bk 75; P.F.P I
57*

Nelson Gardens (Charles Causley)

As I was walking in Nelson Gardens
Cau.Nar 43

Roll down to Rio (Rudyard
Kipling)

I've never sailed the Amazon
Mood I 44; Peg I 57

Song of the Galley Slaves
(Rudyard Kipling)

We pulled for you when the wind was
against us and the sails were low
*Act I 13; Cher 223; J.Vo III 85; Read II
45*

Stephano's Song (William
Shakespeare)

The master, the swabber, the boatswain
and I
The Tempest II ii 45; *Plea VI 84*

A Wet Sheet and a Flowing Sea
(Allan Cunningham)

A wet sheet and a flowing sea
Mood II 25

SAINTS

St Anthony: *The Temptation of St
Anthony* (R. L. Gales)

Goblins came, on mischief bent
Peng.An 247

St Brendan: *St Brendan and the
Fishes* (Ian Serraillier)

St Brendan chanted Mass in voyage
Ser.B 60; Tell I 33

St Bridget: *The Giveaway*

Saint Bridget was/A problem child
Chal III 11: Peg III 83

St Christopher: *St Christopher*
(Eleanor Farjeon)

'Carry me, ferryman, over the ford'
Look 365

St Francis: *St Francis and the Birds*
(Seamus Heaney)

When Francis preached love to the birds
Flock 89

St George: *St George and the
Dragon* (Anon)

Here stand I, Saint George; from
Com 160

St Martha: *St Martha and the
Dragon* (Charles Causley)

In far Provence, where runs the brawny
river
Cau.Nar 65

St Martin: *St Martin and the Beggar*
(Thom Gunn)

Martin sat young upon his bed
Cent 75; Hap 47; Ris 51; Them II 22

St Paul: *In the British Museum*
(Thomas Hardy)

What do you see in that time-touched
stone
J.Mod 32

St Peter: *In the Servants' Quarters*
(Thomas Hardy)

Man, you too, aren't you, one of these
rough followers of the criminal
Tell II 71

St Stephen: *Saint Stephen and King Herod* (Anon)

Saint Stephen was a clerk
Kal 102; Plea V 63; Puf.V 258; Speak II 46; Tell I 100; Wheel I 19

SALMON

Rural Sports (part) (John Gay)

If an enormous salmon chance to spy
Peng.An 269

The Salmon (Anon)

For often at night in a sportive mood
B.B.F 179

SAMSON

Angry Samson (Robert Graves)

Are they blind, the lords of Gaza
Voi III 49

How Samson bore away the gates of Gaza (Vachel Lindsay)

Once, in a night as black as ink
J.Vo III 85; Tell I 76

Samson Agonistes (part) (John Milton)

Occasions drew me early to this city
Flock 173; Nar 92; P.Bk 251; Wheel III 75

SCARECROWS

The Lonely Scarecrow (James Kirkup)

My poor old bones—I've only two—
Dawn 19; Hap 38; Ox.P.C 139; Puf.Y 57; Say 23; Scrap 51; S.D 42; Six V 14; Way 55

The Scarecrow (Walter de la Mare)

All winter through I bow my head
De la M.Ch 67; Ex. Ch 40; P.Bk 84; P.F.P II 27; Ver II 207

SCHOLARS

The Scholars (W. B. Yeats)

Bald heads forgetful of their sins
Liv 26; Peg V 77; P.Rem 230; Yea.Run 68

SCHOOL

The Best of School (D. H. Lawrence)

The blinds are drawn because of the sun
Cent 43; Choice 190; Law.S 62; Them VI 13; Under 100

Bird in the Class-room (Colin Thiele)

The students drowsed and drowned
A.S.L.A 16

'Bus to School (John Walsh)

Rounding the Corner
Cor 82; Key II 18; Mood I 24; Prel II 2

The Dunce (Carla Lanyon Lanyon)

That boy in the seventh row in the secondary modern
Look 106

Exercise Book (Jacques Prevert— trans Paul Dehn)

Two and two four
A.S.L.A 14; Ev.M 11; Kal 31; Six II 30; Weal II 8

Last Lesson in the Afternoon (D. H. Lawrence)

When will the bell ring and end this weariness?
Camb 69; Choice 189; D.P.R II 5; Them III 51; Under 99

Last Lesson of the Afternoon (Susan Ford—aged 14)

Who wants to work
Them III 52

The Moment (Patrick B. Mace)

Right in the middle of the morning
Man II 9

Out of School (Hal Summers)

Four o'clock strikes
Bird I 4; Chal I 53; Cor 2; Dawn 28; Hap 70; Plea II 15; Quest III 8; Six II 6; Them V 65

School Bell (Eleanor Farjeon)

Nine-o'-clock Bell! Nine-o'clock Bell!
Quest I 4

The Schoolboy (William Blake)

I love to rise in a summer morn
Bla.Gr 37; Fab.C.V 102; Flock 136; Key II 20; Pers 9; Wheel II 72

Schoolmaster (Yevtushenko—trans Peter Levi S.J)

The window gives onto the white trees
Ev.M 13; Flock 137; Pers 48

School's Out (W. H. Davies)

Girls scream
B.L.J I 1; Cor 11; Fun I 12; Rhyme I 3; Tree II 61

A Snowy Day in School
(D. H. Lawrence)

All the long school-hours, round the irregular hum of the class
Flock 75

SCHOOLMASTERS

Brainy Teacher (Anon—trans B. Stone)

Brainy teacher, is it your
D.P.R II 42

The Deserted Village (part)
(Oliver Goldsmith)

Beside yon straggling fence that skirts the way
Man II 26; Peg IV 84; Prel II 15; Spo I 117; Wheel III 85

Pedagogue Arraigned (John Wain)

You lay across my childhood like a stone
Peg V 82

Snow-Bound (part) (John G. Whittier)

Brisk wielder of the birch and rule
G.Tr.P 90

SCHOOLMISTRESSES

Schoolmistress (Miss Humm)
(Clive Sansom)

Straight-backed as a Windsor chair
Mod.P 125; Prel II 14

SCIENCE (MISAPPLIED)

James Honeyman (W. H. Auden)

James Honeyman was a silent child
Make IV 12; My 94; Ris 100

The Play Way (Seamus Heaney)

Sunlight pillars through glass, probes each desk
Act V 43

SCIENTISTS

The Microscope (Maxine Kumin)

Anton Leeuwenhoek was Dutch
Chal I 89

SCOTLAND

See also Arran, Bannockburn, Charlie (Bonnie Prince), Claverhouse, Culloden, Flodden, Jacobites, Killiecrankie

Canadian Boat Song (Anon)

Listen to me, as when ye heard our father
Fab.C.V 132

A Highland Lad (Robert Burns)

A highland lad my love was born
Riv II 47

Mary Hamilton (Anon)

Mary Hamilton's to the kirk gane
B.B 111

My Heart's in the Highlands
(Robert Burns)

My heart's in the Highlands, my heart is not here
B.P IV 40; Ch.Gar 76; Com 193; Mood II 29; Ox.P.C 141; P.Bk 39; Peg II 14; Plea IV 58; P.Rem 21; Rhyme III 43; Spo I 101

Scots wha hae (Robert Burns)

Scots, wha hae wi' Wallace bled
Fab.C.V 143; Peg II 58; Wheel I 66

SCYTHING

See Mowing

SEA

See also Anenomes (Sea), Coral, Diving, Fishes & Sea Creatures, Fog, Icebergs, Lighthouses, Pirates, Pools, Sailors, Sea Battles, Sea Birds, Sea Monsters, Sea Shanties, Seagulls, Seaside, Seaweed, Shells, Ships, Shipwrecks, Smugglers, Storms, Tides, Waves

SEA (LYRIC & DESCRIPTIVE)

All Day I hear (James Joyce)

All day I hear the noise of waters
Fab.C.V 330; Man I 28

Dover Beach (part) (Matthew Arnold)

The sea is calm tonight
Com 185

The Eye (Robinson Jeffers)

The Atlantic is a stormy moat, and the Mediterranean
Them VII 65

Harp Song of the Dane Women (Rudyard Kipling)

What is a woman that you forsake her
Act II 97; Peg IV 103; R.R 38; Song IV 142; Them VI 58

The Horses of the Sea (Christina Rossetti)

The horses of the sea
B.L.J I 55; First II 20; Go.Jo 42; Ox.V.J II 79; Rain 48; Rhyme II 42; Tree II 27

The Main Deep (James Stephens)

The long-rolling/steady-pouring
Peg V 23; Quest III 62; Speak I 101

Man Cursing the Sea (Miroslav Holub—trans George Theiner)

Someone/just climbed to the top of the cliff
Voi I 33

The Sea (James Reeves)

The sea is a hungry dog
A.S.L.A 9; Puf.Q 82; Sto I 78

The Sea and the Skylark (Gerard Manley Hopkins)

On ear and ear two noises too old to end
P.W 228; P.W.R 264; Song IV 153; Voi I 116

Storm Tide on Mejit (Marshall Islands—trans A. Kramer & W. Trask)

The wind's spine is broken
J.Vo II 24

Tell me, Tell me, Sarah Jane (Charles Causley)

Tell me, tell me, Sarah Jane, Tell me, dearest daughter
Cau.Fig 40

Under Milk Wood (part) (Dylan Thomas)

What seas did you see
J.Vo II 5; Ox.V.J IV 15

Upon this Beach (Louis MacNiece)

Upon this beach the falling wall of sea
Bird III 4

A Wet Sheet and a Flowing Sea (Allan Cunningham)

A wet sheet and a flowing sea
Fun II 169; Peg IV 102

The Wind has such a rainy Sound (Christina Rossetti)

The wind has such a rainy sound
Patch 24; P.Life I 71; Rhyme I 39

The World below the Brine (Walt Whitman)

The world below the brine
J.Vo IV 49; Peg III 38

Zennor (Anne Ridler)

Seen from these cliffs the sea circles slowly
Pers 94

SEA (NARRATIVE)

The Ballad of Kon-Tiki (parts) (Ian Serraillier)

All day long the plane had searched for them
Look 108; Puf.Q 177; Ser.B 91

Now nothing could stop them. Drawn
Tell I 69

They were not lonely. They found the sea
Puf.Q 180; Song I 112

The Bay of Biscay (Andrew Cherry)

Loud roared the dreadful thunder
Sto I 139

The Blind Rower (Wilfrid Gibson)

And since he rowed his father home
Tell I 73

Flannan Isle (Wilfrid Gibson)

Though three men dwell on Flannan Isle
*Chal II 60; Make III 114; M.M.A 11;
Mood II 89; Ox.P.C 78; P.F.P II 219;
R.R 29; Six II 26; Song I 116; Speak II
55; T.C.N 116; T.P.W 54; Way 41;
Weal I 76; Yim I 93*

The Golden Vanity (Anon)

A ship have I got in the North Country
Fab.C.V 171; Ox.P.C 57

The Last Chantey (Rudyard
Kipling)

Thus said the Lord in the Vault above the
Cherubim
Fab.C.V 323

The Rime of the Ancient Mariner
(Samuel Taylor Coleridge)

It is an ancient mariner
*D.P III 55; D.P.R III 42; Fab.C.V 301;
Key II 63; Make IV 69; P.Bk 159; P.F.P
II 103; P.W 156; P.W.R 179; Riv IV
149; Song I 124; Ver II 118; Weal II 68;
Wheel IV 77*

Down dropt the breeze, the sail dropt
down
Fun II 149; Kal 58

The fair breeze blew, the white foam flew
Bat 80

SEA BATTLES

See also Armada, Lepanto, Revenge
(The), Trafalgar

A Burnt Ship (John Donne)

Out of a fired ship, which by no way
R.R 45

Hervé Riel (Robert Browning)

On the sea and at the Hogue
D.P III 45; P.Bk 265

The Old Navy or
Token of All Brave Captains
(Captain Frederick Marryat)

The captain stood on the carronade:
'First Lieutenant' says he
*Bird I 63; B.P IV 17; D.P II 114; Min IV
39; Mood I 28; Plea IV 24; P.Rem 74;
Puf.V 114; Riv III 37; Spo I 132; Sto II
134*

On the Victory obtained by Blake
(Andrew Marvell)

... The thundering cannon now begins
the fight
Iron III 62

SEA BIRDS

See also Seagulls

The Echoing Cliff (Andrew Young)

White gulls that sit and float
*D.P IV 23; D.P.R IV 9; Kal 60; Sphe
212; You.Qu 19*

The Storm (Walter de la Mare)

First there were two of us, then there
were three of us
*B.B.F 181; B.P III 94; De la M.Ch 40;
De la M.Col 105; De la M.S 165; Look
270; Rain 83; Song IV 144; Spo I 130*

SEA MONSTERS

See also Kraken, Leviathan

Beowulf the Warrior (parts)
(Anon—trans Ian Serraillier)

Angrily Beowulf answered
Ser.B 15

At once Beowulf unslung his battle horn
Ser.B 28

The king saddled his war steed, proud
champion
Ox.V.J IV 10

The Faerie Queene (part)
(Edmund Spenser)

Eftsoons they saw an hideous host arrayed
Cher 207

The waves came rolling and the billowes rose
Peng.An 270

Fastitocalon (J. R. R. Tolkien)

Look, there is Fastitocalon!
Hap 90

Grim and Gloomy (James Reeves)

Oh, grim and gloomy
Puf.Q 88; Speak I 37

Sea Serpent (Alberta Vickridge)

Ten degrees south, a hundred east, at sea
Spo I 160

The Sea Serpent Chantey
(Vachel Lindsay)

There's a snake on the western wave
J.Vo III 24

SEA SHANTIES

See also B.L.A.F 126–153, Fun II 11–17

Away, haul away, boys, haul away
(Anon)

Away, haul away, boys, haul away together
P.Tong I 11; Riv II 56; Speak I 89

Blow the man down (Anon)

Blow the man down, bullies, blow the man down
D.P II 119; D.P.R II 66; Iron IV 5

I sing you a song, a good song of the sea
Fun II 13

Boney was a Warrior (Anon)

Boney was a warrior
P.Tong I 13; P.W 25; P.W.R 21; Riv III 34

The Bullgine Run (Anon)

Oh the smartest clipper you can find
F.S.N.A 56

The Dead Horse (Anon)

They say, old man, your horse will die
Bird I 39

Fire down below (Anon)

Fire in the galley, fire down below
Mer 179; Mer.Puf 138; P.Life III 65; Puf.S.B 123; Rain 19; Rhyme II 6; Tree I 22

Heave away, me Johnny (Anon)

There are some that's bound for New York town
Song IV 143

Leave her, Johnny (Anon)

Oh the work was hard and the wages low
D.P II 118; My 56; Song IV 110

I thought I heard the captain say
Key III 74; Sto II 135

Lowlands (Anon)

I dreamt a dream the other night
Cher 229; Riv II 57

Reuben Ranzo (Anon)

Hurrah! for Reuben Ranzo
Fun II 11

Santy Anna (Anon)

Oh Santy Anna won the day
Riv II 53

Shenandoah (Anon)

Oh Shenandoah, I long to hear you
B.L.A.F 138

Oh Shenandoah, I love your daughter
F.S.N.A 53;

Missouri she's a mighty river
Bird I 38

Spanish Ladies (Anon)

Farewell and adieu to you, fair Spanish Ladies
Fab.C.V 300; Plea VIII 21; P.Tong II 20

A Yankee Ship (Anon)

A Yankee ship came down the river
All 19; Key III 76; Mer 362; Mer.Puf 275; Mood I 29; Riv II 52

SEAGULLS

Gull over Freshwater (M. Willy)

High over his cliff-nest and whitening waves of barley
Spo I 164

The Seagull (Gaelic—Anon)

All day long o'er the ocean I fly
Fuji 91

The Sea-gull (J. Redwood Anderson)

The very spirit of the coast is he
Six VI 32

Thames Gulls (Edmund Blunden)

Beautiful it is to see
Sphe 141; Ver II 225

SEALS

The Great Silkie of Sule Skerrie (Anon)

An earthly nourrice sits and sings
Bal 323; B.B 13; Bun 18; Cher 206; Fab.Bal 69; Fab.C.V 68; Isle 23

In Norway there sits a maid
Bal 321; Voi II 115

Hymn to the Seal (Stevie Smith)

Creature of God, thy coat
Bat 48

Seal (William Jay Smith)

See how he dives
G.Tr.P 68

SEAMSTRESSES

The Song of the Shirt (Thomas Hood)

With fingers weary and worn
P.Bk 52; S.D 111; Six III 20; Them VI 41; Trea 36

SEASIDE

See also Bathing, Diving, Pools (Rock), Shells, Shrimping, Surfing, Swimming

The Arrival (John Walsh)

Our train steams slowly in, and we creep to a stop at last
Key III 98; Them V 65

At the Seaside (Robert Louis Stevenson)

When I was down beside the sea
Bits p; First I 21; Mood I 66; Scrap 102; Ste.C.G 19

The Beach (W. Hart-Smith)

The beach is a quarter of golden fruit
Say 16

The Beach (Robert Graves)

Louder than gulls the little children scream
Prel II 39; Sphe 196; Wheel I 153

Beside the Seaside (Sir John Betjeman)

Green Shutters, shut your shutters! Windyridge
Pers 73

The Black Pebble (James Reeves)

There went three children down to the shore
Patch 5

House of Sand (Philip Hobsbaum)

We knew it wouldn't last, That's why
Bird I 2

Maggie and Milly (e. e. cummings)

Maggie and Milly and Molly and May
A.S.L.A 7; Bits y; Dan 54; Hap 18; Prel II 37

Sand-between-the-toes (A. A. Milne)

I went down to the shouting sea
Mil.V.Y 73

Summer Beach (Frances Cornford)

For how long known this boundless wash of light
Bird III 3

Summoned by Bells (part) (Sir John Betjeman)

Then before breakfast down toward the sea
Start 94

Trippers (Osbert Sitwell)

But these were only a few, there were others too, many others
M.Ver 104

SEASONS

See also Cla.Wo throughout, *Six I* throughout

See also Autumn, Harvest, Months, Spring, Summer, Winter

The Calendar (Barbara Euphan Todd)

I knew when spring was come
Fab.N.V 23; Look 5; Puf.V 24; Six I 58; T.P.W 12

Days and Seasons in London, 1715 (John Gay)

Experienced men, inured to city ways
Iron III 24

The Faerie Queene (part) (Edmund Spenser)

So forth issued the Seasons of the year
P.Bk 46

Seasons (Christina Rossetti)

In Springtime when the leaves are young
Scrap 9

Seasons (Christina Rossetti)

Oh the cheerful budding-time!
Tree III 22

The Year (Coventry Patmore)

The crocus, while the days are dark
This W.D 115

SEAWEED

Seaweed (part) (Henry Wadsworth Longfellow)

When descends on the Atlantic
Shep 29

SEDGEMOOR

The Song of Samuel Sweet (Charles Causley)

As I leaned at my window
Song II 114

SEEDS

In the Fallow Field (Andrew Young)

I went down on my hands and knees
You.Qu 22

The Seed Shop (Muriel Stuart)

Here in a quiet and dusty room they lie
By 283; G.Tr.P 257; Pat 161

SENSES

See Noises, Smells

SERPENTS

See Sea Monsters, Snakes

SHADOWS

In Moonlight (Andrew Young)

We sat where boughs waved on the ground
Ox.V.J IV 97; Say 57; You.Bu 8

My Shadow (Robert Louis Stevenson)

I have a little shadow
Ex.H 72; Fab.N.V 112; Min II 74; Ste.C.G 35

The Shadow (Andrew Young)

Dark ghost/That from treetrunk to treetrunk tost
You.Bu 6

Shadow March (Robert Louis Stevenson)

All round the house is the jet-black night
Ox.V.J II 16; P.Life III 94; Scrap 23; Ste.C.G 66

SHAGS

At Porthcothan (Christopher Middleton)

A speck of dark at low tide on the tideline
D.P.R IV 7; Peng.An 271; Shep 110

SHARKS

The Maldive Shark (Herman Melville)

About the Shark, phlegmatical one
Bat 86; B.B.F 186; Iron III 1; Peng.An 274; P.W.R 236; R.R 177; Shep 123

The Shark (Lord Alfred Douglas)

A treacherous monster is the shark
Key III 100

SHEEP

See also Lambs, Rams

A Child's Pet (W. H. Davies)

When I sailed out of Baltimore
Fun II 80; Key II 56; P.Life III 79; Riv III 54

The Seasons (part) (James Thomson)

They drive the troubled flocks, by many a dog
B.B.F 70

Sheep (W. H. Davies)

When I was once in Baltimore
Ark 76; Chal I 29; D.P.I 21; D.P.R I 10; Fun II 82; Kal 13; Key II 39; Mer 322; Mer.Puf 243; Mood II 47; Peg I 45; P.Life III 78; P.Rem 121; Rhyme IV 117; Riv I 42

A Sheep Fair (Thomas Hardy)

The day arrives of the autumn fair
Bird III 39; Har.Ch 28; Iron II 56; Key IV 37; Shep 50; Voi I 93

Sheep in Winter (John Clare)

The sheep get up and make their many tracks
Cor 26; Flock 280; Peg I 47; Rhyme III 58; Sto II 113

Spraying Sheep (Norman MacCaig)

Old tufts of wool lie on the grass
Bird II 28

SHEEPDOGS

Allendale Dog (Lilian Bowes Lyon)

A lean tyke, supple
J.Mod 112

Rake (Dorothy Una Ratcliffe)

There's no better dog nor Hardcastle's Rake
J.Mod 113

Sheepdog Trials in Hyde Park (C. Day Lewis)

A shepherd stands at one end of the arena
Sphe 98

SHELLEY

The General Public (Stephen Vincent Benet)

Shelley? Oh, yes, I saw him often then
Peg IV 72

SHELLS

Let Me Hear (Linda Whitehead)

A shell, look a shell.
Prel IV 32

The Sea Shell (Amy Lowell)

Sea Shell, Sea Shell
Mood I 59; P.Life III 10

See What a Lovely Shell (Alfred Lord Tennyson)

See what a lovely shell
B.B.F 180; Ch.Gar 179; D.P IV 75; Go.Jo 185; Man I 20; Song II 10; Sphe 207

The Shell (James Stephens)

And then I pressed the shell
A.D.L 77; Bits b; B.P IV 52; Chor 22; D.P IV 76; Flock 43; Kal 57; P.F.P I 113; Rhyme IV 38; Six V 34; Them II 55; Yim I 77

SHIPS

See also Boats, Cutty Sark, Jervis Bay, Submarines, Tugs

SHIPS (LYRIC & DESCRIPTIVE)

Beowulf's Voyage to Denmark (part) (Anon)

He bade a seaworthy wave-cutter fitted out for him
Flock 45

Cargo (Denis Glover)

From the hold they lift the hatches
Chal I 88

Cargoes (John Masefield)

Quinquireme of Nineveh from distant Ophir
D.P IV 49; Look 277; Peg II 42; P.F.P II 12; Six V 40; Trea 144; Ver II 162; Weal I 109

The Dismantled Ship (Walt Whitman)

In some unused lagoon, some nameless bay
Mood IV 64; Riv II 17

Lament for the Great Yachts (Patric Dickinson)

Suddenly into my dream why should they come
M.Ver 125

The Old Ships (James Elroy Flecker)

I have seen old ships sail like swans asleep
Com 109; D.P IV 48; Look 328; Peg III 34; P.F.P II 46; Plea VIII 74; Riv IV 67; Song II 101; Ver III 56

Sailor's Delight (C. Fox-Smith)

Tall raking clipper ships driving hell-for-leather
A.D.L 156

The Ship (J. C. Squire)

There was no song nor shout of joy
Peg II 43; P.F.P II 46

The Ship (Richard Church)

They have launched the little ship
A.D.L 154; B.P III 71; D.P III 28; Drag 35; Make I 66; P.Life III 56

Trawlers (Francis Scarfe)

Red sail on tan sail and black sail by white
Ox.V.J III 26

SHIPS (NARRATIVE)

See also Nabara, Revenge

The Golden Vanity (Anon)

A ship have I got in the North Country
Fab.C.V 171; Ox.P.C 57

The Yarn of the Nancy Bell (Sir William S. Gilbert)

'Twas on the shores that round our coast
D.P.R II 34; Fab.C.V 179; Peg II 26; P.F.P II 62; Sto II 44

SHIPWRECKS (LYRIC & DESCRIPTIVE)

Clarence's Dream (William Shakespeare)

Lord, Lord! methought what pain it was to drown
Richard III I iv 21; Act I 39; Cher 229; Peg V 107; P.W 70; P.W.R 65; Riv III 19; Song I 121

Full Fathom Five (William Shakespeare)

Full fathom five thy father lies
Tempest I ii 394; B.P II 53; Cher 231; Com 187; D.P II 119; D.P.R II 67; Fab.C.V 268; Flock 42; Go.Jo 141; Key III 118; Mer 270; Mer.Puf 200; My 29; Ox.P.C 52; Ox.V.J IV 89; P.F.P I 111; Plea VI 47; P.Rem 202; P.W 65; P.W.R 60; Rhyme IV 56; Riv I 53; S.D 129; Speak I 88; This W.D 83; Ver II 10

An Inscription by the Sea (Greek—trans E. A. Robinson)

No dust have I to cover me
Cher 231

On the Quay (Theodore Roethke)

What they say on the quay is
J.Vo IV 20

She is far from Land
(Thomas Hood)

Cables entangling her
Wheel I 79

Survivors (Alan Ross)

With the ship burning in their eyes
Drag 62; Read III 89; Yim III 22

The Wrecker's Prayer (Theodore
Goodridge Roberts)

Give us a wrack or two, Good Lard,
Look 89; J.Vo IV 20

SHIPWRECKS (NARRATIVE)

The Alice Jean (Robert Graves)

One moonlight night a ship drove in
Drag 56; J.Vo I 31; Shad 40; Them II 7

The Cleggan Disaster (part)
(Richard Murphy)

Five boats were shooting/their nets in the
bay
Make IV 29; Nar 95

Don Juan (part) (Lord Byron)

They counted thirty, crowded in a space
Comp 85

The Inchcape Rock (Robert
Southey)

No stir in the air, no stir in the sea
*Cher 141; Down 19; D.P I 85; D.P.R I
63; Ex.Ch 170; Fun I 137; G.Tr.P 160;
Make I 98; Mood III 77; P.Bk 270; Peg
I 64; Plea V 29; Spo I 29; Tell I 42*

The Lifeboat Mona (Peggy Seeger)

Remember December, fifty-nine
Quest IV 82

The Loss of the 'Royal George'
(William Cowper)

Toll for the brave!
*Chor 26; Com 96; Fun I 145; P.F.P II
61; Plea VI 20; P.W 137; P.W.R 148;
Riv III 107; Spo I 106; Ver II 110*

The Mayblossom (John Masefield)

The ship, Mayblossom, left Magellan
Straits
A.D.L 237

The Rescue (Ted Hughes)

That's what we live on: thinking of their
rescue
Drag 62

Sir Patrick Spens (Anon)

The king sits in Dunfermline town
*All 71; Bal 179; B.B 45, 185; Bun 1; D.P
III 29; D.P.R III 38; Fab.Bal 121;
Fab.C.V 296; Flock 46; Fun I 141;
Go.Jo 159; Make II 36; Ox.P.C 47;
Ox.V.J IV 16; Peg II 32; P.F.P I 142;
Plea V 69; P.Life IV 61; P.Rem 100;
Puf.V 99; P.W 7; P.W.R 7; Riv III 87;
Six III 44; Song I 109; Spir 134; Spir.R
101; Sto II 119; Wheel II 43; Yim I 27*

The Borough (part) (George
Crabbe)

Darkness begins to reign; the louder
wind
D.P.R III 63

The Survivors (R. S. Thomas)

I never told you this
Chal II 49; Make III 151; Sev 33

The Titanic (part)
(E. J. Pratt)

Out on the water was the same display
Look 278

SHOOTING

Dawn Shoot (Seamus Heaney)

Clouds ran their wet mortar
Drag 12

The Deerstalker (L. E. Jones)

The shadow of the mountains lay
Them V 20

Done For (Walter de la Mare)

Old Ben Bailey
*De la M.Col 87; De la M.S 81; Ox.P.C
131; Tree I 24*

First Blood (Jon Stallworthy)

It was. The breach smelling of oil
Drag 13; Them VII 58; Voi II 38

Hi! (Walter de la Mare)

Hi! handsome hunting man
De la M.Ch 132; De la M.Col 87; De la M.S 80

The Hunter (Roy Ferguson)

Nine o'clock on a June evening was his magic hour
Them V 19

The Towerer (John Masefield)

Old Jarge, Hal, Walter and I, the Rector and Bill
T.C.N 107

Windsor Forest (parts)
(Alexander Pope)

See from the brake the whirring pheasant springs
Flock 127

To plains with well-breath'd beagles we repair
Mood IV 78

SHRIMPING

Shrimping (Ian Serraillier)

I take my shrimping net and wade into the pool
Prel II 37

SICILY

The Story about the Road (part)
(Christopher Logue)

Imagine yourself in a country poor
Fla 174

SINGING

See also Love Songs, Sailors' Songs, Sea Shanties, Soldiers' Songs

Everyone Sang (Siegfried Sassoon)

Everyone suddenly burst out singing
A.D.L 214; Cent 21; Dan 65; Man II 19; My 173; Ox.V.J IV 107; P.F.P II 130; Six II 58; Spo I 148; Sto III 102

A Minor Bird (Robert Frost)

I have wished a bird would fly away
A.D.L 172; Cor 176; Ex.Tro 22; Fro.You 58; Song I 6

The Quartette (Walter de la Mare)

Tom sang for joy, and Ned sang for joy, and old Sam sang for joy
Com 39; De la M.Col 169; De la M.P.P 40; De la M.S 171

The Solitary Reaper (William Wordsworth)

Behold her, single in the field
Choice 21; D.P IV 104; D.P.R IV 76; Fab.C.V 119; Iron III 15; Look 113; Ox.P.C 146; P.Bk 16; Peg IV 34; P.F.P II 131; Plea VII 35; P.Rem 61; P.W 149; P.W.R 172; R.R 123; S.D 39; Song III 28; Sphe 57; This W.D 145; Trea 70; Ver III 23; Weal II 142; Wor.So 75

Two Girls Singing (Ian Crichton Smith)

It neither was the words nor yet the tune
Them IV 8

A Wandering Minstrel (*The Mikado*)
(Sir W. S. Gilbert)

A wandering minstrel I
Song III 132

SIRENS

The Sirens' Welcome to Cronos
(Robert Graves)

Cronos the Ruddy, steer your boat
Exp VIII 51

SISTERS

My Sister Jane (Ted Hughes)

And I say nothing—no, not a word
Cent 84; Cor 157; D.P.R I 32; Flock 95; Hap 16; Prel I 11; Rhyme IV 98; Start 49; Yim I 13

SISYPHUS

Sisyphus (Robert Garioch)

Bumpity down in the corrie gaed whud-
dran the pitless whun stane
Comp 41

SIZES

The Fly (Walter de la Mare)

How large unto the tiny fly
*B.B.F 118; By 228; De la M.Ch 37; De
la M.Col 74; De la M.S 79; D.P.R I 6;
Ex.H 19; F.Feet 186; First III 44;
Ox.V.J I 56; Peng.An 119; Plea II 41;
Quest II 4; Shep 138; Start 9; Tree I 61;
Way 30*

A Lilliputian Ode (Alexander Pope)

In amaze/Lost I gaze
Wheel II 68

The Magnifying Glass (Walter de
la Mare)

With this round glass
Ox.P.C 123; Them II 47

Worlds (Wilfrid Gibson)

Through the pale green forest of tall
bracken-stalks
Way 45

SKATES

Skate (Alan Brownjohn)

Flitting the sea-bed, wide and flat
Bro.B 19

SKATING

The Midnight Skaters (Edmund
Blunden)

The hop-poles stand in cones
*Blu.Mi 93; D.P IV 173; D.P.R IV 121;
Go.Jo 235; P.Tong I 133; R.R 28; Sphe
47; Them V 39; Voi III 163; Weal II 145*

The Prelude Book I (part) (William
Wordsworth)

And in the frosty season, when the sun
Choice 23; Fab.C.V 57; G.Tr.P 281;
*Look 116; Man I 66; Peg III 25; Prel II
23; P.W 150; P.W.R 173; R.R 93;
Speak II 35; Sphe 45; Wor.So 16*

The Skater of Ghost Lake (William
Rose Benet)

Ghost Lake's a dark lake, a deep lake,
and cold
Song I 100

Skating (Herbert Asquith)

When I try to skate
Them V 38

The Virtuoso (James Kirkup)

As he stands at the brink
Peg IV 1

SKIPPING

Skipping (Thomas Hood)

Little children skip
*Min II 88; Puf.Y 34; Rhyme II 15; Tree I
58*

Skipping Song (John Walsh)

When bread and cheese
Ox.V.J II 24; Patch 22; T.P.W 14

SKYSCRAPERS

Building a Skyscraper (James S.
Tippett)

They're building a skyscraper
Cor 74

SKYLARKS

See Larks

SLAVE TRADE

The Flying Cloud (Anon)

My name is Edward Holland
Bal 778

Pity for Poor Africans (William
Cowper—1731–1800)

I own I am shocked at the purchase of
slaves
Comp 83; Wheel III 88

The Slave Chase (c. 1850) (Anon)

Set every stitch of canvas to woo the freshening wind
Iron IV 46; Key II 15

SLAVERY

The Masque of Anarchy (part) (P. B. Shelley)

What is freedom? ye can tell
Bat 15

Peter Grimes (part) (George Crabbe)

Now lived the youth in freedom, but debarred
Weal II 65

Old Peter Grimes made fishing his employ
Read II 34

Peter had heard there were in London then
D.P.R I 38; Tell II 60

The Runaway Slave (Walt Whitman)

The runaway slave came to my house and stept outside
Tell I 111

The Slave's Dream (Henry Wadsworth Longfellow)

Beside the ungathered rice he lay
By 158; Mood III 48; Weal I 18

Song of the Galley-Slaves (Rudyard Kipling)

We pulled for you when the wind was against us and the sails were low
Act I 13; Cher 223; J.Vo III 85; Read II 45

SLEEP

See also Dreams, Falling Asleep, Insomnia, Lullabies, Nightmares, Sleepwalking

Nod (Walter de la Mare)

Softly along the road of evening
Ch.Gar 59; G.Tr.P 303; P.F.P II 26; Rhyme III 63

On a Quiet Conscience (Charles I)

Close thine eyes and sleep secure
Plea IV 80; Trea 13

Sleep (William Shakespeare)

How many thousands of my poorest subjects
2 Henry IV III i 4; Act III 136; P.W 73; Song II 135; Trea 170

O sleep, O gentle sleep
2 Henry IV III i 5; D.P IV 84

Sonnet (John Keats)

O soft embalmer of the still midnight
Sphe 432; Voi III 139

Spell of Sleep (Kathleen Raine)

Let him be safe in sleep/As leaves folded together
M.Ver 172

To Sleep (William Wordsworth)

A flock of sheep that leisurely pass by
Shep 153; Song II 136; Sphe 431

The Twin of Sleep (Robert Graves)

Death is the twin of Sleep, they say
Voi III 138

Vesper (Alcman of Sparta—trans F. L. Lucas)

Now sleep the mountain-summits, sleep the glens
Ark 206

(trans Thomas Campbell)

The mountain summits sleep: glens cliffs and caves
Cher 409

SLEEPWALKING

The Sleepwalker (Antun Branko Simic—trans Janko Lavrin)

The god of night/the moon
Them II 41

What, no Sheep? (Ogden Nash)

I don't need no sleepin' medicine
Act IV 27

SLEET

Sleet (Norman MacCaig)

The first snow was sleet. It swished heavily
Drag 88

SLOTHS

The Sloth (Theodore Roethke)

In moving slow, he has no peer
Hap 73; Peng.An 279; Shep 81; V.F 130

SLOWWORMS

Briggflatts (part) (Basil Bunting)

I am neither snake nor lizard
J.Vo III 21

SLUGS

Slug (Theodore Roethke)

How I loved one like you when I was little!
Them I 42; Yim III 64

SMELLS

The Beanfield (John Clare)

A beanfield in blossom smells as sweet
Peg IV 51

Buying Fuel (Richard Church)

Now I come to the farmer about some logs
Prel IV 46

Cologne (S. T. Coleridge)

In Köln, a town of monks and bones
Key IV 10; Wheel III 110

Smells (Christopher Morley)

Why is it that poets tell
D.P IV 46; Man I 65; Peg I 50; P.Life IV 53; Prel IV 46; Quest IV 14; Speak I 24; T.P.W 104

The Song of Quoodle
(G. K. Chesterton)

They haven't got no noses
Act I 108; Go.Jo 107; P.F.P I 19; Them I 11; Weal I 10

SMUGGLERS

Rum Lane (James Reeves)

Gusty and chill
B.L.J IV 18; Key II 96; Ox.V.J II 12; Rhyme IV 53

The Smuggler (Anon)

O my true love's a smuggler and sails upon the sea
B.P IV 28; Make II 40; Mood IV 70; Riv I 19; Song II 103

The Smuggler's Leap
(R. H. Barham)

The fire-flash shines from Reculver cliff
P.Rem 75

A Smuggler's Song (Rudyard Kipling)

If you wake at midnight, and hear a horse's feet
All 43; B.P. IV 47; Chor 16; D.P I 72; D.P.R I 60; Ex.Ch 117; Fun I 120; Key II 94; Look 68; Make I 55; Mood II 18; Ox.P.C 52; Ox.V.J II 10; Peg I 62; Plea IV 20; P.Life III 92; Rhyme IV 54; Spir 22; Spir.R 18

SNAILS

Considering the Snail (Thom Gunn)

The snail pushes through a green
A.S.L.A 78; Bird II 45; Cent 74; Com 46; D.P.R III 18; Drag 23; Flock 211; Peng.An 282; Pers 125; Say 116; Shep 82; Song II 56

The Garden Snail (Robert Wallace)

This backyard/cousin
Hap 77

Hibernating Snails (Andrew Young)

Here where the castle faces south
You.Qu 8

The Housekeeper (Charles Lamb)

The frugal snail, with forecast of repose
Ch.Gar 69; G.Tr.P 79; Peg I 42; Speak II 17

Old Shellover (Walter de la Mare)

'Come!' said Old Shellover
B.B.F 106; Com 46; De la M.Ch 125; De la M.Col 211; De la M.P.P 20; De la M.S 74; Key I 33; Mer 209; Plea II 63; Riv I 15; Song II 56

The Snail (James Reeves)

At sunset, when the night-dews fall
B.L.J IV 33; Key I 32; Ox.P.C 123; P.P 9; Puf.Q 74; Riv I 5; Song II 55

Snail (John Drinkwater)

Snail upon the wall
B.L.J II 32; Fab.N.V 74; Go.Jo 85; Scrap 26

The Snail (William Cowper)

To grass, or leaf, or fruit, or wall
B.B.F 58; Cor 172; G.Tr.P 79; Key I 32

The Snail (William Kean Seymour)

Veined and lustrous, ringed with pearl and azure
Pat 174

The Snail (John Gay)

When bordering pinks and roses bloom
Tree II 21

Starry Snail (Vasko Popa—trans Anne Pennington)

You crept out after the rain
J.Vo III 11

Upon the Snail (John Bunyan)

She goes but softly, but she goeth sure
Cher 116; R.R 173; Ver II 178; Voi I 97

SNAKES

See also Rattlesnakes

The Colubriad (William Cowper)

Close by the threshold of a door nail'd fast
Key IV 134; P.F.P II 103; Sto II 33

Coverings (Stella Gibbons)

The snake had shed his brindled skin
J.Mod 83

In the Snake Park (William Plomer)

A white-hot midday in the Snake Park
Ev.M 20

Little Boys of Texas (Robert Tristram Coffin)

The little boys of Texas prance
Peg III 75

A Narrow Fellow in the Grass (Emily Dickinson)

A narrow fellow in the grass
A.D.L 163; Ark 136; F.Feet 107; Flock 210; Go.Jo 65; G.Tr.P 68; J.Mod 85; Key IV 135; Make III 30; P.W.R 249; Riv IV 34; Song III 59; Sto III 88

Rokeby (part) (Sir Walter Scott)

Thus circled in his coil the snake
B.B.F 213

The Serpent (Theodore Roethke)

There was a serpent that had to sing
V.F 128

The Serpent (Percy Bysshe Shelley)

Wake the serpent not—lest he
F.Feet 65; Tree IV 110

Snake (D. H. Lawrence)

A snake came to my water-trough
Bird II 47; Cent 44; D.P IV 38; D.P.R IV 18; Kal 19; Key IV 130; Law.S 18; Make IV 101; P.F.P I 126; P.Rem 214; Riv IV 35; Six VI 24; Song III 60; Sphe 120; T.C.N 110

The Viper (Ruth Pitter)

Barefoot I went, and made no sound
A.D.L 163; B.P IV 49; Dawn 68; Ex.Tro 19; Six VI 22; Sto III 89

SNARES

See Traps

SNOW

See also Sleet, Thaw

SNOW (LYRIC & DESCRIPTIVE)

Cat and the Weather (May Swenson)

Cat takes a look at the weather
Chal II 15; J.Vo II 50

A Dog in Snow (Margaret Stanley-Wrench)

Overnight the world has become delft china
Shep 97

The Father's Song (Eskimo—trans Peter Freuchen)

Great snowslide/Stay away from my igloo
Prel III 45; Voi I 129

First Sight (Philip Larkin)

Lambs that learn to walk in snow
Act IV 108; Ark 186; By 303; Chal II 18

The First Snow (Robert Frost)

From the pit's mouth men pour, a stream of black
Bird II 16

Late Snow (J. C. Squire)

The heavy train through the dim country went rolling, rolling
Sphe 41

On a Night of Snow (Elizabeth Coatsworth)

Cat, if you go outdoors, you must walk in the snow
F.Feet 187; G.Tr.P 48; Ox.V.J III 56; Patch 18; P.Life IV 17; Quest II 58; Say 50; Shad 105; Song I 71

A Patch of Old Snow (Robert Frost)

There's a patch of old snow in a corner
A.S.L.A 43; Bird II 18; Fro.You 32

Snow (Edward Thomas)

In the gloom of whiteness
Make II 93; Prel III 40; Song I 72; Tho.Gr 55; Voi III 157

The Snow (Emily Dickinson)

It sifts from leaden sieves
G.Tr.P 248

Snow (Walter de la Mare)

No breath of wind/No gleam of sun
Bird I 22; De la M.Col 160; De la M.P.P 105; De la M.S 153; D.P II 9; D.P.R II 26; Ex.Ch 38; Peg II 9; Scrap 8; Shep 49; Song II 19

Snow (Andrew Young)

Ridged thickly on black bough
You.Bu 26

Snow Harvest (Andrew Young)

The moon that now and then last night
B.P III 79; You.Bu 25

Snow in the Suburbs (Thomas Hardy)

Every branch big with it
A.D.L 119; Bird II 17; Com 75; D.P IV 61; D.P.R IV 35; Go.Jo 254; Har.Ch 52; Look 4; Man I 32; P.F.P II 44; P.Life IV 29; Prel III 40; Riv IV 43; R.R 67; Say 95; Shep 48; Six I 30; Song I 74; Sphe 31; This W.D 129; Weal I 127

The Snow-Storm (Ralph Waldo Emerson)

Announced by all the trumpets in the sky
Peg III 24; Prel III 45; Shep 45

Snowstorm (John Clare)

What a night! The wind howls, hisses and but stops
Prel III 44

Snow towards Evening (Melville Cane)

Suddenly the sky turned grey
B.L.J III 15; B.P I 35; Ox.V.J III 81; Peg III 23; Quest III 63

Velvet Shoes (Elinor Wylie)

Let us walk in the white snow
B.P II 73; Go.Jo 255

White Fields (James Stephens)

In the winter time we go
B.L.J II 17; Ex.H 81; Patch 20; P.Life II 59; Say 14; Six I 26; T.P.W 93; Tree III 30

Winter Morning (Ogden Nash)

Winter is the king of showmen
Puf.Y 76

Winter Snowstorm (John Clare)

Winter is come in earnest, and the snow
Cla.Wo 37; Iron II 87; Prel III 44

Winter World (Roy Fuller)

Behind the city the unmoving mist
Com 74

SNOW (NARRATIVE)

At nine of the Night I opened my Door (Charles Causley)

At nine of the night I opened my door
Cau.Fig 38

The Drove Road (Wilfrid Gibson)

'Twas going to snow—'twas snowing!
Curse his luck!
Tell I 62

London Snow (Robert Bridges)

When men were all asleep the snow came flying
A.D.L 63; Bird III 43; Cher 308; Dan 30; P.Bk 25; Peg III 54; P.F.P II 43; Song I 73; Sphe 42; Weal I 126

The Runaway (Robert Frost)

Once when the snow of the year was beginning to fall
A.D.L 186; Bird I 55; B.P III 37; Drag 28; Fab.C.V 79; F.Feet 125; Fro.You 52; Go.Jo 72; G.Tr.P 29; Hap 68; Key II 49; M.Ver 77; Ox.V.J III 48; Prel I 44; Riv IV 32; Six I 24; Start 23

Stopping by Woods on a Snowy Evening (Robert Frost)

Whose woods these are I think I know
Cent 42; Choice 284; D.P.R II 27; Ex.H 82; Fab.C.V 58; First III 29; Flock 276; Fro.You 30; Fun I 37; Go.Jo 257; Hap 38; Iron I 62; Key IV 72; Make II 11; Man II 12; Min II 33; Mood II 66; Ox.V.J II 49; Patch 29; Pers 71; Rhyme IV 15; Riv IV 66; Ten 80; This W.D 156

SNOWDROPS

The Snowdrop Walter de la Mare

Now—now, as low I stooped, thought I
Ten 55

SNOWFLAKES

The Snowflake (Walter de la Mare)

Before I melt
A.D.L 116; B.P IV 14; Dan 30; De la M.S 147; Peg I 111; P.Life IV 30; Prel III 43

The Snowflake (Walter de la Mare)

See, now, this filagree: 'tis snow
De la M.Ch 52

To a Snowflake (Francis Thompson)

What heart could have thought you?
A.D.L 116; D.P IV 115; G.Tr.P 248; Peg V 43; Say 95; Six I 32; Song II 11; This W.D 113; Trea 290; Ver II 195

SOLDIERS

See also Riv III 25

See also Claverhouse, Deserters, Hannibal, Horatius, Napoleon

Danny Deever (Rudyard Kipling)

'What are the bugles blowin' for?' said Files-on-Parade
Fab.Bal 195; Make III 57; Nar 62; Peg IV 92; Plea VIII 96; Song IV 175; T.C.N 58

Gunga Din (Rudyard Kipling)

You may talk o' gin and beer
Make II 136; Weal I 69

Johnny has gone for a Soldier (Anon)

Sad I sit on Butternut Hill
B.L.A.F 117; F.S.N.A 47

An Old Soldier of the Queen's (Anon)

Of an old soldier of the Queen's
Key IV 58; P.W 21

Old Timers (Carl Sandburg)

I am an ancient reluctant conscript
Them VI 15

The Quarry or O What is that Sound (W. H. Auden)

O what is that sound which so thrills the ear
Camb 130; Choice 237; Dawn 42; D.P.R I 61; Flock 254; Mod.P 15; Mood IV 54; M.Ver 141; Nar 1; P.F.P I 170; Say 77; Song II 124; Sphe 356; Them I 32; Wheel III 180; Yim III 6

SOLDIERS' SONGS

All the Hills (Charles Sorley)

All the hills and vales along
Fab.C.V 261

Ballad of the Soldier (Bertolt
Brecht—trans H. R. Hays)

The trigger will shoot and the dagger will
strike
Them VI 74

Boots (Rudyard Kipling)

We're foot slog-slog-slog-sloggin' over
Africa—
Read II 47; Six IV 46

Chant before Battle (Maori—
trans Allen Curnow, Roger
Oppenheim)

Let fog fill the skies
Voi I 67

Fife Tune (John Manifold)

One morning in spring
Go.Jo 193; Liv 103

Johnny I hardly knew ye (Anon)

While going the road to sweet Athy
Fab.Bal 212; Peg III 97; P.Tong II 198

Mandalay (Rudyard Kipling)

By the old Moulmein Pagoda, lookin'
lazy at the sea
Nar 64; Song IV 71

Men who march away (Thomas
Hardy)

What of the faith and fire within us
Spo II 95

Mrs McGrath (Anon)

'Oh Mrs McGrath' the sergeant said
Fab.Bal 211

Over the hills and far away
(Anon)

Hark! now the drums beat up again
Chor 5; Riv III 26

Pibroch of Donuil Dhu
(Sir Walter Scott)

Pibroch of Donuil Dhu
*Fab.C.V 231; J.Vo III 78; Song II 126;
Trea 81*

Roman Wall Blues (W. H. Auden)

Over the heather the wet wind blows
*Choice 242; Dawn 43; Eye 25; J.Mod
34; J.Vo IV 37; Kal 36; My 79; Peg V
95; Say 83; Them VI 37; Ver III 67;
Weal I 122*

A Song to Mithras (Rudyard
Kipling)

Mithras, God of the Morning, our
trumpets waken the Wall!
Plea V 92

Tommy (Rudyard Kipling)

I went into a public 'ouse to get a pint o'
beer
Read II 46; Wheel IV 140

War Song of the Saracens (James
Elroy Flecker)

We are they who come faster than fate
D.P IV 82; Nar 32; Ver II 158

We be soldiers three (Anon)

We be soldiers three
Cher 87

We be the King's men (Thomas
Hardy)

We be the King's men, hale and hearty
*B.P IV 24; Chor 8; Ex.Ch 105; Mer 346;
Mer.Puf 263; Min I 67; Mood I 27; Riv
II 45*

What did the Soldier's Wife receive?
(Bertolt Brecht)

And what did the soldier's wife receive
D.P.R IV 57; Them VI 59

SONGS

The Fall of Songs (Robert Louis
Stevenson)

Bright is the ring of words
Ste.Ho 67

SONG THRUSHES

The Song Thrush (W. MacGillivray)

Dear, dear, dear/Is the rocky glen
Key I 52

SONS

See also Fathers and Sons

A Parental Ode to my Son, aged Three Years and Five Months (Thomas Hood)

Thou happy, happy elf
Prel I 2; V.F 87; Wheel I 84

SOUNDS

See also Bells, Noises

All Sounds have been as Music (part) (Wilfred Owen)

All sounds have been as music to my listening
A.D.L 207

Bed Time (Ruth Squires—aged 11)

I am in bed
Prel IV 28

Midnight's Bell (Thomas Middleton)

Midnight's bell goes ting, ting, ting, ting, ting
B.B.F 104; Key I 103; Min II 91; Ox.P.C 140; Ox.V.J I 27; P.Rem 26

Pleasant Sounds (John Clare)

The rustling of leaves under the feet in woods and under hedges
B.B.F 76; Key I 104; Man I 62; P.W 185; P.W.R 206; Song III 40; Sphe 82; Way 28; Yim I 75

Sounds in the Night (Coventry Patmore)

How strange the distant bay
B.L.J IV 30

Tortoise Shout (part) (D. H. Lawrence)

I remember, when I was a boy
Prel IV 27

Village Sounds (James Reeves)

Lie on this green and close your eyes—
All 94; Puf.Q 83; T.P.W 28

SOUP

Beautiful Soup (Lewis Carroll)

Beautiful Soup, so rich and green
All 34; Ex.Tro 41; Man I 27; Mer 340; Mer.Puf 259; Min III 9; My 160; Ox.P.C 12; Plea VIII 24; P.Life II 28; P.Tong I 12; Riv I 90; V.F 30

SOUTH AFRICA

See Africa (South)

SOWING

See also Planting

Putting in the Seed (Robert Frost)

You come to fetch me from my work tonight
Iron IV 70

Sowing (Edward Thomas)

It was a perfect day
A.D.L 264; Chal I 83; Choice 175; Iron III 33; Man I 47; Ox.V.J IV 84; Pat 27; Peg IV 49; Read II 68; Six I 46; Sphe 56; Them VII 30; Tho.Gr 29; Voi I 114

SPACE TRAVEL

See also Exp VII 27–42

The Astronaut (James Kirkup)

Star-sailor, with your eyes on space
Sphe 192

Heel and Toe to the end (William Carlos Williams)

Gagarin says in ecstasy
Exp VII 33; Sto II 33

Love in a Space-Suit (James Kirkup)

Dear, when on some distant planet
Mod.P 116

Moon Landing (W. H. Auden)

It's natural the Boys should whoop it up for
Sto II 48

Off Course (Edwin Morgan)

The golden flood, the weightless seat
J.Vo IV 56

Report Back (John Cotton)

Galactic probe seven thousand and four
Tell II 163

Science Fiction Cradle Song
(C. S. Lewis)

By and by Man will try
Sev 137

Southbound on the Freeway
(May Swenson)

A tourist came in from Orbitville
Chal I 93; J.Vo IV 54

Space Travellers (James Nimmo)

There was a witch hump-backed and
hooded
*B.P II 47; Dan 26; Exp VII 27; Min IV
83; Ox.V.J III 79; P.Life IV 95; Quest II
57; Speak I 120; Sto II 27; T.P.W 19*

Tea in a Space-Ship (James
Kirkup)

In this world a tablecloth need not be laid
*Dan 29; Exp VII 40; Mod.P 115; Peg V
12; Sto II 40; Ver III 76*

SPARROWS

The Book of Philip Sparrow
(parts) (John Skelton)

It had a velvet cap
Com 45; Peng.An 286

It was so pretty a fole
P.Bk 19

To weep with me look that ye come
Peng.An 41

When I remember again
*B.B.F 135; Fab.C.V 84; Kal 2; Tree IV
16*

The Dead Sparrow (William
Cartwright)

Tell me not of joy: there's none
P.Bk 15

The Thresher's Labourer (part)
(Stephen Duck)

Thus have I seen on a bright summer's
day
B.B.F 84

SPEED

Swift Things are Beautiful
(Elizabeth Coatsworth)

Swift things are beautiful
Man I 63

SPELLS

See Charms & Spells

SPIDERS

The Image (Roy Fuller)

A spider in the bath. The image noted:
Them I 47

Little City (Robert Horan)

Spider, from his flaming sleep
Under 90

No Jewel (Walter de la Mare)

No jewel from the rock
Mer 300; Mer.Puf 224; P.Life III 89

The Spider (Kenneth Mackenzie)

Just as my fingers close about the pen
Voi II 53

The Spider and the Fly (Anon)

'Will you walk into my parlour?'
Ex.Tra 26; M.G.E 151; Tree II 68

The Study of a Spider (John
Leicester Warren, Lord de Tabley)

From holy flower to holy flower
Peng.An 293; Shep 132

A Web early in the morning
(P. Williamson—aged 10)

It stood there in the grass
Say 24

SPIES

My Neighbour Mr Normanton
(Charles Causley)

My neighbour Mr Normanton
Cau.Fig 75

Secret Police (G. Rostrevor
Hamilton)

They follow me, left right, left right
Make IV 63

SPIRITUALS

See also B.L.A.F 328–377, F.S.N.A 448–486

Amazing Grace (Anon)

Amazing grace, how sweet the sound
B.L.A.F 344

The Battle of Jericho (Anon)

Joshua fit de battle ob Jericho
B.L.A.F 374; J.Vo III 96; Riv II 48

Dem Bones Gona Rise Again (Anon)

In come de animals two by two
Chor 37

Go Down Moses (Anon)

Go down Moses
B.L.A.F 372; J.Vo IV 35; Riv II 49

I got a Robe (Anon)

I got a robe, you got a robe
Key II 16; Mood III 11; Puf.S.B 58

Nobody Knows (Anon)

Nobody knows the trouble I've seen
Puf.S.B 74

Spiritual (Michael Thompson—aged 15)

Long before Genesis, long before Man
Song IV 174

Swing Low, Sweet Chariot (Anon)

Swing low, sweet chariot
Puf.S.B 10

When the Saints go Marchin' in (Anon)

O when the Saints go marchin' in
F.S.N.A 454

When the Stars begin to fall (Anon)

My Lord, what a mornin'
F.S.N.A 454

SPORT

See also Boxing, Bullfighting, Fishing, Shooting

The Sportsman (Clive Sansom)

Nature he loves, and next to Nature—death
Them V 72

SPRING

See also April, March, May Day, Months, Weather

Atalanta in Calydon (part) (A. C. Swinburne)

When the hounds of spring are on winter's traces
Pat 36; Trea 276

By chance I walk (Yuan Mei)

By chance I walk into the Western courtyard
Flock 7

Chanson Innocente or
In Just-spring (e. e. cummings)

In Just-spring when the world is mud-
Ev.M 93; Fab. N.V 25; G.Tr. P 272; Hap 67; Look 333; This W.D 69; T.P.W 16

Coming (Philip Larkin)

On longer evenings/Light, chill and yellow
Ev.M 79

The Computer's Spring Greeting (Gary Lewis—aged 9)

Spring gling
J.Vo II 25

Diffugere Nives (part) (Horace—trans Maurice Baring)

The snows have fled, the hail, the lashing rain
A.D.L 88

Early Spring (Alfred Lord Tennyson)

Once more the Heavenly Power
Com 206

The Georgics (part) (Virgil)

Then are the trackless copses alive with the trilling of birds
Flock 11; Georgics II 328

I thank you God (e. e. cummings)

I thank you God for most this amazing
A.S.L.A 89; Song III 35

The Prologue (part) (Geoffrey Chaucer)

Whan that Aprille with his shoures sote
Cher 281; Flock 17; Song IV 39

The Song of Solomon (part) (Bible)

For lo, the winter is past
Song of Solomon II, 2; Fuji 98; Puf.V 21

The Spirit of Spring (Liu Ta-Pai— trans Kai-Yu Hsu)

A little open-top boat
Shep 60

Spring (Gerard Manley Hopkins)

Nothing is so beautiful as Spring—
A.D.L 89; Choice 115; Ox.V.J IV 67; Song of Solomon II, ii; Fuji 98; Puf.V 21

The Spring (part) (Thomas Carew)

Now that the winter's gone, the earth hath lost
Pat 33; Peg IV 51; Shep 61; Sphe 4

Spring (Henry Howard Earl of Surrey)

The soote season, that bud and bloom forth brings
B.B.F 48; Flock 6

Spring (William Blake)

Sound the Flute!
Fab.C.V 50; Fuji 99

Spring (Thomas Nashe)

Spring, the sweet spring, is the year's pleasant king
By 26; Com 206; Flock 6; Fun II 122; Key I 51; Mer 331; Mer.Puf 251; Min IV 25; Mood IV 47; Ox.P.C 102; Pat 31; P.Bk 12; P.F.P I 117; Riv I 2; Trea 157; Wheel III 67

Spring Comes (John Clare)

Spring comes and it is May. White as are sheets
Iron II 49; Song I 7

Spring is like (e. e. cummings)

Spring is like a perhaps hand
Flock 7; Shep 59

Spring Quiet (Christina Rossetti)

Gone were but the Winter
Key IV 110; Puf.V 31

Sumer is icumen in (Anon)

Sumer is icumen in
By 13; Cher 48; Com 57; Flock 34; Kal 137; Key I 51; P.Bk 11; Song IV 39

When daffodils begin to peer (William Shakespeare)

When daffodils begin to peer
Winter's Tale IV iii 1; Cher 42; Fab. C.V. 52

When daisies pied (William Shakespeare)

When daisies pied and violets blue
Love's Labour's Lost V ii 902; Mood I 40; P.Life II 45; Six I 42; This W.D 72

SQUIRRELS

The First Sights of Spring (part) (John Clare)

The squirrel sputters up the powdered oak
B.B.F 92

The Grey Squirrel (Humbert Wolfe)

Like a small grey
Bird III 18; F.Feet 19; Go.Jo 65; Peng.An 294

The Mountain and the Squirrel (Ralph Waldo Emerson)

The mountain and the squirrel
Ark 91; Fuji 27; Go.Jo 26; G.Tr.P 57; Plea III 69

The Squirrel (Ian Serraillier)

Among the fox-red fallen leaves I surprised him. Snap
A.D.L 164; Ox.V.J IV 28; Puf.Q 175

The Squirrel (William Cowper)

The squirrel, flippant, pert and full of play
G.Tr.P 57; Sto I 117

The Squirrel emulates the Bird
(Charlotte Smith)

Though plumeless he can dart away
B.B.F 92

The Squirrel's Nest (John Clare)

One day, when all the woods were bare
and bled
*B.B.F 95; Cla.Wo 77; Make I 38; Sto I
116; Yim I 32*

The Task (part) (William Cowper)

Drawn from his refuge in some lonely
elm
B.B.F 92; Sto I 117

To a Squirrel at Kyle-na-no
(W. B. Yeats)

Come play with me
Key II 40; Puf.Y 108; This W.D 45

Whisky Frisky (Christina Rossetti)

Whisky, frisky
*B.L.J I 52; Dan 98; Fab N.V 77; J.Vo I
58; Tree I 51*

STAGS

A Runnable Stag (John Davidson)

When the pods went pop on the broom,
green broom
*Ark 177; Key III 88; P.Bk 328; Peng.An
295; P.F.P II 84; Ver II 213; Wheel I
125*

STARLINGS

In the Lane (L. A. G. Strong)

All the starlings in the world
M.Ver 60

The Starling (John Heath-Stubbs)

The starling is my darling, although
Flock 91; Mod.P 111

The Starlings in George Square
(Edwin Morgan)

Sundown on the high stonefields!
J.Vo IV 10

STARS

See also Exp VII 1–10

At the Bottom of the Well (Louis
Untermeyer)

Something befell
Go.Jo 218

Blue Stars and Gold (James
Stephens)

While walking through the trams and
cars
Act I 65

Daisies (Andrew Young)

The stars are everywhere tonight
Say 47; You.Qu 18

Escape at Bedtime (Robert Louis
Stevenson)

The lights from the parlour and kitchen
shone out
*A.D.L 268; B.P III 60; G.Tr.P 13; Min
III 61; P.Life II 80; P.Rem 42; Rain
118; Scrap 42; Ste.Ho 23; Ste.C.G 39*

The Falling Star (Sara Teasdale)

I saw a star slide down the sky
B.L.J IV 3; Ox.V.J III 72

I stood and stared (Ralph
Hodgson)

I stood and stared; the sky was lit
Act I 52

Names (Roy Fuller)

A skein of suns, the uncut stones of night
Voi III 141

The Starlight Night (Gerard Manley
Hopkins)

Look at the stars! look, look up at the
skies!
*A.D.L 13; Camb 5; Choice 117; Com
130; Shep 155; Speak II 22; Spo II 99;
This W.D 105; Ver III 101*

The Stars (Andrew Young)

The stars rushed forth to-night
By 251

Star-Talk (Robert Graves)

'Are you awake, Gemelli
*A.D.L 16; Exp VII 4; Go.Jo 242; Key III
136*

Waiting Both (Thomas Hardy)

A star looks down at me
Sphe 393

STATELY HOMES

The Grand Houses at Lo-Yang
(Po Chu-I)

By woods and water, whose houses are
these
Act IV 123

Verses on Blenheim (Jonathan
Swift)

See, here's the grand approach
Shep 148

STATESMEN

See Churchill, Jackson, Lincoln

STEAM SHOVELS

Steam Shovel (Charles Malam)

The dinosaurs are not all dead
Chal I 87; J.Vo IV 93

STEELWORKERS

Steel: the Night Shift (Charles
Tomlinson)

Slung from the gantries crane
D.P.R IV 77; J.Vo IV 50

STOCKDOVES

The Stockdoves (Andrew Young)

They rose in a twinkling cloud
J.Mod 137; Ten 163

STOCKMEN

How the Sailor rode the Brumby
(Anon)

There was an agile sailor lad
Act III 104

STONEMASONS

The Old Workman (Thomas Hardy)

'Why are you so bent down before your
time
Riv III 52; Song III 111

STORMS

See also Thunder & Lightning,
Wind

The Ballad of the Kon-Tiki (part)
(Ian Serraillier)

And the trade wind swept them
northwards
Ser.B 94

The Bay of Biscay (Andrew Cherry)

Loud roared the dreadful thunder
Sto I 139

Big Wind (Theodore Roethke)

Where were the greenhouses going
*Act I 86; Go.Jo 213; J.Vo IV 66; Look
11*

Blow Winds (William Shakespeare)

Blow winds, and crack your cheeks!
rage! blow!
King Lear III ii 1; Flock 272

Description of a Thunderstorm
(John Clare)

Slow boiling up, on the horizon's brim
Iron II 47

I sit up here (Robert Louis
Stevenson)

I sit up here at midnight
Ste.Ho 30

Night Wind (John Clare)

Darkness like midnight from the sobbing
woods
Voi II 136

Patrolling Barnegat (Walt
Whitman)

Wild, wild the storm and the sea high
running
Key IV 88; Riv IV 41; Shep 36

Resolution and Independence (part)
or *After the Storm*
(William Wordsworth)

There was a roaring in the wind all night
*Act I 115; Flock 36; Fun II 126; Iron II
72; Key III 130; Min I 16; Mood III 26;
Ox.V.J IV 31; P.Life IV 34; Prel III 32;
P.Rem 178; Rain 86; Rhyme IV 9;
Wor.So 71*

Storm (Theodore Roethke)

Against the stone breakwater
Under 60

The Storm (Emily Dickinson)

An awful tempest mashed the air
Dan 33; Key III 130; Ox.V.J III 74

The Wind begun to rock the Grass
(Emily Dickinson)

The wind begun to rock the grass
J.Vo III 74

STREET CRIES

See also Street Songs, *Ox.N.R
72–73*

Hot Cross Buns! (Anon)

Hot cross buns! Hot cross buns!
B.L.J III 26; Ox.N.R 73

STRIKES

The Case for the Miners (Siegfried
Sassoon)

Something goes wrong with my synthetic
brain
Bird IV 13; Day 45; Them VI 45

SUBMARINES

Diesel and Shale (Cyril Tawney)

On the fifth of November in '53
Wheel I 162

Elegy for a Lost Submarine
(Ewart Milne)

Would you talk to Davy Jones in his
locker
Fla 89

SUCCESS

Kindly unhitch that star, buddy
(Ogden Nash)

I hardly suppose I know anyone who
wouldn't rather be a success than a
failure
Day 121

What Then? (W. B. Yeats)

His chosen comrades thought at school
Cent 61; Liv 42; Yea.Run 79

SUMMER

See also August, July, June, Sun

A Hot Day (A. S. J. Tessimond)

Cottonwool clouds loiter
A.S.L.A 48; Bits g (part); *J.Mod 118;
Make II 78; Prel III 7; Quest IV 5; Song
I 17*

Raging Noon (James Thomson)

'Tis raging noon; and, vertical, the sun
Key IV 145

Smelling the End of Green July
(Peter Yates)

Smelling the end of green July
Man I 57

Summer (Christina Rossetti)

Winter is cold-hearted
*A.D.L 92; Cor 29; F.Feet 137; Iron I 59;
Key I 77; Ox.V.J III 28; Plea III 21;
P.W 215; P.W.R 250; Riv III 7; Say 64;
Shep 62; Sphe 13; Voi I 118*

Summer Fountains (Eleanor
Farjeon)

Now the mid-May brings
Peg III 14

Thyrsis (part) (Matthew Arnold)

Soon will the high midsummer pomps
come on
Peg III 16

SUN

Riddle: The Moon and the Sun
(Anglo-Saxon—trans Gavin Bone)

I saw a creature sally with booty
P.W 31; P.W.R 27; Riv IV 24

(trans Burton Raffel)

I saw a silvery creature scurrying
Go.Jo 244

(trans K. Crossley-Holland)

I saw a strange creature
Rid 17

Summer Sun (Robert Louis
Stevenson)

Great is the sun and wide he goes
Fuji 15

SUNRISE

See Dawn (City), Dawn (Country)

SUPERNATURAL

See also Exp VIII throughout, *Shad*
throughout, *Them II 3–22*

See also Charms and Spells,
Dwarfs, E'ves, Fairies, Fauns,
Ghosts, Giants, Goblins, Magic,
Mystery, Nymphs, Pan, Robin
Goodfellow, Trolls, Witches

The Feckless Dinner-Party
(Walter de la Mare)

'Who are we waiting for?' 'Soup burnt?'
. . . Eight—
De la M.Ch 108; Pers 68

'Fight with a Demon' (W. B. Yeats)

. . . He slowly turned
Key IV 41

The Neckan (Matthew Arnold)

In summer, on the headlands
Ex.Ch 61

The Paphian Ball (Thomas Hardy)

We went our Christmas rounds once
more
T.C.N 121

SUPERSTITION

Superstition (Minji Ateli)

I know/that when a grumbling old
woman
Exp VIII 35

SURFING

The Surfer (Judith Wright)

He thrust his joy against the weight of
the sea
Look 123

The Surf-Rider (Zulfikar Ghose)

Out in the Golfe de Gascogne, on the far
Them V 38

SURGEONS

A Correct Compassion (James
Kirkup)

Cleanly, sir, you went to the core of the
matter
Flock 141

SWAGMEN

The Dead Swagman (Nancy Cato)

His rusted billy left beside the tree
*Act II 45; Song III 114; Ver III 302; Voi
II 122*

The Old Bark Hut (Swagman's
Song) (Anon)

My name is Bob the Swagman, and I'll
have you understand
Tell II 80

The Swagless Swaggie (Edward
Harrington)

This happened in the years gone by
before the bush was cleared
Act II 42

The Swagman's Rest
(A. B. Paterson)

We buried old Bob where the
bloodwoods wave
Iron III 70

Waltzing Matilda (A. B. Paterson)

Once a jolly swagman camped by a
billabong
*Act II 44; Bird II 21; Cher 138; Key I
98; Mer 344; Riv II 58; Song III 114;
Ver III 284*

SWALLOWS

Anglo-Saxon Riddle III (Anon)

This air beareth little beings
B.B.F 192

The Swallow (Christina Rossetti)

Fly away, fly away, over the sea
First II 17

The Swallow (Ogden Nash)

Swallow, swallow, swooping free
Puf.Y 127

The Swallows (Andrew Young)

All day—when early morning shone
Read I 144; Sphe 152; You.Qu 20

SWANS

Anglo-Saxon Riddle I (Anon)

My robes are silent when I roam the earth
B.B.F 192

(trans K. Crossley-Holland)

Silent is my dress when I step across the earth
Drag 23; Rid 31

The Silver Swan (Anon)

The silver swan, who living had no note
Fab.C.V 89; Key IV 80

The Swan Bathing (Ruth Pitter)

Now to be clean he must abandon himself
Look 222

The Wild Swans at Coole (W. B. Yeats)

The trees are in their autumn beauty
Act II 50; Camb 26; Cent 58; Cher 97; Com 177; Ev.M 42; F.Feet 197; Fla 30; Flock 260; Look 237; Man I 16; Pat 165; P.Rem 150; Shep 109; Sphe 136; Ver II 222; Ver III 62; Weal II 128; Yea.Run 63

SWEDES

Swedes (Edward Thomas)

They have taken the gable from the roof of clay
Ten 128

SWEET PEAS

Sweet Peas (John Keats)

Here are sweet peas, on tiptoe for a flight
B.P III 30; First III 13; Fuji 60; Look 186; Min IV 25

SWIMMING

The Swimmers (Edward Shanks)

The cove's a shining plate of blue and green
Them V 35

SWINGING

The Swing (Robert Louis Stevenson)

How do you like to go up in a swing
Ex.Tra 52; Go.Jo 25; Min I 90; Six V 20; Ste.C.G 55; T.P.R 16

Swing Song (A. A. Milne)

Here I go up in my swing
Mil.N.S 77

A Swing Song (William Allingham)

Swing, swing,/Sing, sing
Fuji 111

SYMPATHY

On Another's Sorrow (William Blake)

Can I see another's woe
Bl.Gr 69

TAILORS

The Old Tailor (Walter de la Mare)

There was once an old tailor of Hickery Mo
De la M.Col 135; Fab.N.V 41; Fun I 83; Tree III 66

Tailor (Eleanor Farjeon)

I saw a little Tailor sitting stitch, stitch, stitching
B.P I 20; Puf.Q 24; Tree III 67

TALES, CAUTIONARY

The Boy who laughed at Santa Claus (Ogden Nash)

In Baltimore there lived a boy
B.B.G.G 16; Key III 85; Rhyme IV 74; V.F 105

Going Too Far (Mildred Howells)

A woman who lived in Holland, of old,
Fab.N.V 203

Greedy Richard (Jane Taylor)

I think I want some pies this morning
Puf.V 136

Harriet and the Matches (Dr Heinrich Hoffman)

It's really almost past belief
Fab.N.V 157

Johnny-Head-in-Air (Dr Heinrich Hoffman)

As he trudged along to school
B.B.G.G 78; Ex.H 26; Fab.N.V 162; Mood I 71

TALES, CAUTIONARY (BELLOC)

See also Bel.C.V 15–87

About John (Hilaire Belloc)

John Vavasour de Quentin Jones
Bel.C.V 70

Charles Augustus Fortescue (Hilaire Belloc)

The nicest child I ever knew
Bel.C.V 48; Puf.V 138

George (Hilaire Belloc)

When George's Grandmamma was told
Chor 51; Fab.N.V 159; G.Tr.P 216; M.M.A 8; Rhyme III 22; Wheel II 132

Godolphin Horne (Hilaire Belloc)

Godolphin Horne was nobly born
Bel.C.V 34; Yim I 3

Henry King (Hilaire Belloc)

The Chief Defect of Henry King
B.B.G.G 48; Fun II 51; Peg I 9; P.Life II 16; Song I 33

Jim (Hilaire Belloc)

There was a Boy whose name was Jim
A.D.L 239; B.B.G.G 70; Bel.C.V 15; Cher 22; Ex.Ch 89; Fab.N.V 161; Mer 284; Peg I 10; Quest II 79; Riv I 94; Spir 6; Spir.R 5

Lord Lundy (Hilaire Belloc)

Lord Lundy from his earliest years
P.Tong I 83

Matilda (Hilaire Belloc)

Matilda told such Dreadful Lies
Bel.C.V 26; D.P I 34; D.P.R I 24; Ex.Tro 59; Fab.C.V 96; Mood II 30; Ox.P.C 30; Peg I 12; P.Life IV 90; Puf.V 152; Rhyme IV 79; Sphe 216; V.F 18; Wheel I 129

Peter Goole (Hilaire Belloc)

Young Peter Goole, a child of nine
Bel.C.V 79

Rebecca (Hilaire Belloc)

A Trick that everyone abhors
Bel.C.V 42; D.P II 40; D.P.R II 33; Ex.Ch 93; Fab.N.V 156; Fun II 52; Mood II 31

Sarah Byng (Hilaire Belloc)

Some years ago you heard me sing
Bel.C.V 55; Go.Jo 112

Tom and his Pony Jack (Hilaire Belloc)

Tom had a little pony—Jack
Bel.C.V 66

Jack had a little pony—Tom
Bel.C.V 62; Fab.N.V 173; F.Feet 178; V.F 19

William Shand (Hilaire Belloc)

There was a man called William Shand
M.M.A 79

TALES, TALL

Adventures of Isabel (Ogden Nash)

Isabel met an enormous bear
A.D.L 241; All 62; Ex.Ch 78; Fab.N.V 105; Make I 77; Ox.V.J IV 73; P.Life II 10; Quest III 80; Sphe 218; Spir.R 10; T.P.W 96; Yim I 5

Derby Ram or *The Ram of Dalby*
(Anon)
See under Rams

The Heroes of the Sea
(A. P. Graves)
I'll tell you a wonder that will stiffen up
your hair
Key I 44

*The Man put green spectacles on
his cow* (Carl Sandburg)
The man put green spectacles on his cow
and fed her sawdust
J.Vo IV 30

*The Merchant's Tale of the Trapper
and the Bears* (W. K. Connell)
Outside the window howled the storm
Key I 113

The Old Sailor (A. A. Milne)
There was once an old sailor my grand-
father knew
B.P II 51; Fab.N.V 36; Mil.N.S 36

The Priest and the Mulberry Tree
(T. L. Peacock)
Did you hear of the curate who mounted
his mare
Key I 105

A Snake Yarn (W. T. Goodge)
'You talk of snakes' said Jack the Rat
Make II 94

The Stage Driver's Story (Bret
Harte)
It was the stage driver's story, as he
stood with his back to the wheelers
Key III 124; Nar 57; Sto II 25

Tall Stories (American Anon)
A farmer, tired of dry farming in desert
country
J.Vo IV 30

Yarns (Carl Sandburg)
They have yarns of a skyscraper so tall
G.Tr.P 196

TATTOOISTS
Blackie, the Electric Rembrandt
(Thom Gunn)

We watch through the shop front while
Flock 130; Liv 153

TEA
On Making Tea (R. L. Wilson)
The water bubbles
J.Vo III 36

One to Seven (Lo Tung)
The first cup moistens my lips and throat
Act III 19

TEACHERS
See Schoolmasters,
Schoolmistresses

TELEPHONE OPERATORS
Manual System (Carl Sandburg)
Mary has a thingamajig clamped on her
ears
Chal I 86; Voi II 140

TELEVISION
Death at Suppertime (Phyllis
McGinley)
Between the dark and the daylight
Chal III 80

TeeVee (Eve Merriam)
In the house
J.Vo II 72

Viewing Time (E. V. Milner)
What is this life if, freed from care
Chal III 82

The Winning of the T.V. West
(John T. Alexander)
When twilight comes to Prairie Street
Chal III 80

TERMITES
See Ants

THAMES

The Frozen Thames (John Gay)

Then hoary Thames, with frosted oziers crowned
Key IV 71

The River's Tale (Rudyard Kipling)

I walk my beat before London Town
Key III 78

THATCHERS

Thatcher (Seamus Heaney)

Bespoke for weeks, he turned up some morning
Read III 29

THAW

February—a Thaw (John Clare)

The snow is gone from cottage tops
D.P.R I 15

A Hillside Thaw (Robert Frost)

To think to know the country and not know
Fro.You 26

Last Snow (Andrew Young)

Although the snow still lingers
A.D.L 120; Bird II 17; B.P III 86; Prel III 48; P.W 258; P.W.R 302; Read I 127; Riv IV 46; Sphe 3; Ten 169; You.Bu 18

Sudden Thaw (Andrew Young)

When day dawned with unusual light
Bird I 23; Bits p (part); Read I 126; You.Qu 6

Thaw (Edward Thomas)

Over the land freckled with snow half-thawed
Act III 69; Bird IV 51; Choice 171; D.P IV 59; D.P.R IV 34; Flock 10; Iron I 39; Make II 84; M.Ver 31; Prel III 48; R.R 83; Sphe 3; Tho.Gr 56

To the Thawing Wind (Robert Frost)

Come with rain, O loud southwester
A.D.L 108; J.Mod 116; P.P 38

THISTLES

Thistledown (Andrew Young)

Silver against blue sky
Way 86; You.Bu 18

Thistles (Ted Hughes)

Against the rubber tongues of cows and the hoeing hands of men
A.S.L.A 49; Bird II 35; Drag 68; Mod. P 173; Read II 74; Voi III 171

THRUSHES

See also Missel Thrushes

The Darkling Thrush (Thomas Hardy)

I leant upon a coppice gate
B.B.F 110; Choice 134; Har.Ch 60; P.F.P I 88; P.Rem 162; R.R 89; Ten 93; Ver III 43

The Throstle (Alfred Lord Tennyson)

Summer is coming, summer is coming
Pat 38

The Thrush's Nest (John Clare)

Within a thick and spreading hawthorn bush
A.D.L 171; B.B.F 34; B.P III 46; By 153; Cla.Wo 64; Cor 168; F.Feet 42; Flock 12; Go.Jo 91; G.Tr.P 64; Man I 32; Mood III 57; My 118; Ox.P.C 67; P.F.P I 121; Riv II 8; Song I 52; Sphe 153; This W.D 117

THUNDER & LIGHTNING

An African Thunderstorm (David Rubadiri)

From the west/Clouds come hurrying with the wind
Prel III 19

Giant Thunder (James Reeves)

Giant Thunder, striding home
My 120; Pat 182; Quest II 28

Storm in the Black Forest
(D. H. Lawrence)

Now it is almost night, from the bronzy soft sky
Dan 33; D.P.R III 27; Iron IV 39; Peg IV 57; Prel III 32; R.R 85; Say 63; Way 56

Struck by Lightning (James Thomson)

Down comes a deluge of sonorous hail
Key III 17

Thunder (Walter de la Mare)

Call the cows home!
De la M.Ch 39; De la M.Col 27; Iron I 6

Thunder and Lightning (James Kirkup)

Blood punches through every vein
J.Vo III 96; Peg II 10; Shep 63

TIDES

Caught by the Tide (George Crabbe)

Sometimes a party, rowed from town, will land
Tell II 78

The High Tide on the Coast of Lincolnshire 1571 (Jean Ingelow)

The old mayor climbed the belfry tower
P.Bk 210; P.F.P II 50; P. Tong I 135; P.W 201; Riv III 99; Spir 150; Spir.R 112

The Sands of Dee (Charles Kingsley)

'O Mary go and call the cattle home
B.P IV 31; Look 63; Mood III 99; Ox.P.C 153; P.Bk 270; P.F.P II 49; Plea V 24

The Tide in the River (Eleanor Farjeon)

The tide in the river
Bits b; My 10; Ox.P.C 136

The Tide rises, the Tide falls (H. W. Longfellow)

The tide rises, the tide falls
Cher 191; Make I 63; Ox.V.J III 53;

Rain 86; Say 64; Shep 31; Sto II 63; Way 58

TIGERS

India (W. J. Turner)

They hunt the velvet tigers in the jungle
Bird II 50; Cor 177; Hap 63; Ox.P.C 112; Peg II 108; Quest IV 29

The Tigress (Clifford Dyment)

They trapped her in the Indian hills
Chal II 20; Eye 18; J.Mod 111

The Tyger (William Blake)

Tyger! Tyger! burning bright
Act II 87; Ark 118; B.B.F 18; Bird I 58; Bla.Gr 59; B.P IV 44; By 109; Cher 115; Ch. Gar 48; Choice 43; D.P IV 114; D.P.R IV 85; Fab.C.V 64; G.Tr.P 36; Ox.P.C 111; P.Bk 111; Peg IV 15; Peng.An 301; P.F.P I 92; Plea V 52; P.Life IV 15; P.Rem 47; Puf.V 52; P.W 140; Riv IV 39; Shep 79; Song I 66; Sphe 118; Spo I 95; Them I 21; Weal II 171; Yim I 137

TIME

See also Mortality, Weekdays

Cities and Thrones and Powers (Rudyard Kipling)

Cities and thrones and powers
Act II 88; By 210; D.P IV 185; Go.Jo 197; Iron III 24; Plea VII 103; Song IV 156; Them VII 64

Clock (Harold Munro)

When first you learn to read a clock
P.F.P II 118

Even such is Time (Sir Walter Ralegh)

Even such is time which takes in trust
Cher 381; Com 97; Man III 59; Ox.V.J IV 91; Plea VIII 124; R.R 100; S.D 92; Song III 171; Sphe 448; Trea 163; Weal II 169

How Time consumeth All Earthly Things (Thomas Proctor)

Ay me, ay me, I sigh to see the scythe afield
Cher 243

Latter-Day Geography Lesson
(R. A. K. Mason)

This, quoth the Eskimo master
Ver III 319

Lines in a Clock in Chester Cathedral (Henry Twells)

When, as a child, I laughed and wept
B.P IV 87; Chal II 34; Puf.V 214

The Slow Starter (Louis MacNiece)

A watched clock never moves, they said
Mod.P 76

Sonnet No 64 (William Shakespeare)

When I have seen by Time's fell hand defaced
Peg V 55; Ver III 87

Time, Gentlemen, Time!
(O. St J. Gogarty)

O would not life be charming
P.F.P II 116

Time's Glory (William Shakespeare)

Time's glory is to calm contending kings
Rape of Lucrece 939; Cher 322

Time, you old Gipsy Man (Ralph Hodgson)

Time, you old gipsy man
By 223

Virtue (George Herbert)

Sweet day, so cool, so calm, so bright
Iron I 42; P.Bk 60; P.F.P II 233; P.W 98; Riv IV 128; R.R 158; Song IV 157; Sphe 375; Spo I 119; Trea 182

TIMES PAST

All that's Past (Walter de la Mare)
Very old are the woods
Act I 53; Camb 59; De la M.Ch 145; De la M.S 128; D.P IV 65; D.P.R IV 39; Go.Jo 202; Song III 157; Ten 52; This W.D 107

At Castle Boterel (Thomas Hardy)

As I drive to the junction of lane and highway
Ten 107

Gone (Walter de la Mare)

Where's the Queen of Sheba?
Go.Jo 205

The House of Hospitalities
(Thomas Hardy)

Here we broached the Christmas barrel
Iron I 13

In the British Museum (Thomas Hardy)

What do you see in that time-touched stone
J.Mod 32

The Old Ships (J. E. Flecker)

I have seen old ships sail like swans asleep
Com 109; D.P IV 48; Look 328; Peg III 34; P.F.P II 46; Plea VIII 74; Riv IV 67; Song II 101; Ver III 56

The Roman Road (Thomas Hardy)

The Roman Road runs straight and bare
Go.Jo 200; Har.Ch 23

Then (Walter de la Mare)

Twenty, forty, sixty, eighty
Cent 13; Com 107; De la M.Col 33; De la M.P.P 35; De la M.S 125; Ex.H 15; First III 38; Fun I 65; Ox.V.J II 9; Plea III 80; P.Life I 69

Up on the downs (John Masefield)

Up on the downs the red-eyed kestrels hover
Isle 82

TITMICE

Indomitable (Mark van Doren)

The chickadee the cat clawed
J.Vo III 19

TOADS

Lullaby for a Baby Toad
(Stella Gibbons)

Sleep my child/The dark dock leaf
A.D.L 165; J.Mod 82

TOES

An Exchange between the Fingers and the Toes (John Fuller)

Cramped, you are hardly anything but fidgets
Quest V 8; Sev 74

TONGUE-TWISTERS

Act I 62–63; Act II 51, 52, 54; Cher 3; Fab.N.V 188; Fuji 61, 113; M.G.B 182, 194, 197; M.G.E 74; M.G.R 42; Ox.Dic 73, 150, 347, 366, 418; Ox.N.R 156–157; Puf.N.R 170, 171

TOOTHACHE

See also Dentists

A Charm against Toothache (John Heath-Stubbs)

Venerable Mother Toothache
Dawn 53; Flock 231; My 159

TORTOISES

Baby Tortoise (D. H. Lawrence)

You know what it is to be born alone
Bird IV 65; Choice 194; Fla 47; J.Mod 79; Under 117

Meditations of a Tortoise (E. V. Rieu)

One cannot have enough
Puf.Q 130

So far as I can see
Puf.Q 123

The world is very flat
Puf.Q 137

Tortoise Family Connections (D. H. Lawrence)

On he goes, the little one
Law.S 44; M.Ver 90

TOWNS

See Cities & Towns

212

TOWN & COUNTRY

See Them VII throughout

The Londoner in the Country (Richard Church)

Exiled to bowers of beauty
M.Ver 47; Song I 22

On Bungaloid Growth (Colin Ellis)

When England's multitudes observed with frowns
D.P.R II 31; P.Tong II 187

To a Young Lady (Alexander Pope)

As some fond virgin, whom her mother's care
Weal II 124

Up at the Villa—Down in the City (Robert Browning)

Had I plenty of money, money enough and to spare
Peg III 60; P.Rem 211; Riv IV 77; Them VII 18; Vic 82

TRACKS

See Paths

TRACTORS

Cynddylan on a Tractor (R. S. Thomas)

Ah you should see Cynddylan on a tractor
Bird III 22; Chal I 84; Choice 307; Dawn 78; D.P.R IV 79; Hap 26; Liv 18; Make IV 37; Mod.P 54; Sev 101; Six IV 28; Song III 17; Speak II 110; Sto III 59; Them VII 53; Wheel IV 188

New Farm Tractor (Carl Sandburg)

Snub nose, the guts of twenty mules are in your cylinders and transmission
Exp II 36; Peg III 51

TRADES & PROFESSIONS

See Occupations

TRAFALGAR

The Night of Trafalgar (Thomas Hardy)

In the wild October night-time when the wind raved round the land
A.D.L 251; Cher 340; Fab.C.V 258; Har.Ch 19; P.Tong II 66; Riv II 50; Spo I 118

TRAINS

See also Accidents (Railway), Engine Drivers & Firemen, U.S.A.: Railroads

As we rush in the train (James Thompson)

As we rush, as we rush in the train
Mood II 13; Peg IV 99

The Bridge (part) (J. Redwood Anderson)

Here with one leap
Key IV 50; P.F.P II 151; Spir 62; Spir.R 50; Wheel III 153

Out of the silence grows
D.P.R II 69; Plea II 157; P.Life IV 38; Song I 28

The Express (Stephen Spender)

After the first powerful plain manifesto
A.D.L 147; Com 176; Dan 46; Day 11; D.P IV 125; Go.Jo 210; Liv 17; Mod.P 3; Pat 156; Peg IV 98; P.F.P II 153; Six IV 22; Song III 7; Sphe 186

The Flying Gang (A. B. Paterson)

I served my time, in the days gone by
Sto I 63

From a Railway Carriage (Robert Louis Stevenson)

Faster than fairies, faster than witches
A.D.L 149; All 104; Ex.Tro 32; Mer 185; Mer.Puf 143; Min III 19; Mood I 65; Ox.V.J II 48; P.Life II 49; Riv I 6; Six IV 20; Sphe 183; Spo I 152; Ste.C.G 60; Ste.Ho 25; T.P.W 41

I Like to see it Lap the Miles (Emily Dickinson)

I like to see it lap the miles
Bird I 32; B.L.J III 64; D.P III 92; D.P.R II 69; J.Mod 124; Peg II 83; Pers 142; P.W.R 248; Riv IV 27; R.R 70; S.D 48; Song III 5

Locomotive (Shigeharu Nakano—trans Takamichi Ninomiya & D. J. Enright)

He has a giant's frame
Rhyme IV 68; Yim III 13

Morning Express (Siegfried Sassoon)

Along the windswept platform pinched and white
Bird II 10; D.P IV 124; D.P.R II 70; M.Ver 128; P.F.P II 151; Riv IV 25; R.R 68; Song II 26; Sphe 176; Sto II 55; T.P.W 45; Weal II 165

Night Journey (Theodore Roethke)

Now as the train bears west
D.P.R II 73; Peg II 82

Night Mail (W. H. Auden)

This is the night mail crossing the border
A.D.L 147; All 24; Bird I 34; B.P IV 92; Cher 407; Cor 124; D.P III 90; D.P.R II 71; Ex.Ch 160; Kal 64; Key IV 120; Mood II 22; Ox.V.J III 23; Peg II 86; P.F.P II 154; P.Life IV 40; P.Rem 52; S.D 50; Six IV 14; Song I 26; Sphe 177; Spir 60; Spir.R 48; Sto II 56; T.P.W 42; Ver II 47; Weal I 132; Wheel II 157; Yim II 5

Puffing Billy (Christopher Hassall)

Oh the grand approach at Euston
Key II 22; Song I 23

Sic Transit (J. K. R. Thorne—aged 14)

In the vast and gloomy precincts of the ancient engine-shed
Key II 27

Skimbleshanks the Railway Cat (T. S. Eliot)

There's a whisper down the line at 11.39
Ch.Gar 52; D.P II 30; D.P.R II 21; El.O.P 40; Ex.Ch 156; Fab.C.V 285; J.Mod 107; Mood II 51; Plea V 74; Read I 152; Song I 31; T.P.W 36; V.F 58; Wheel I 149

Sleeping Compartment (Norman MacCaig)

I don't like this, being carried sideways
Sev 92; Sphe 180

Song of a Train (John Davidson)

A monster taught/To come to hand
Peg II 84; Spo I 108; Sto II 53

Song of the Railway Train
(Australian Aboriginal—trans G. Taplin)

You see the smoke at Kapunda
J. Vo II 15

The Train (Mary Coleridge)

A green eye—and a red—in the dark
B.P II 68; Peg II 81; P.Life IV 39; T.P.W 40

Train in Ireland (Kenneth Hopkins)

The train has stopped—it was going only slowly
Read III 64

The Train to Glasgow (Wilma Horsburgh)

Here is the train to Glasgow
B.P I 9; Fab.N.V 251

The Train will fight to the Pass (Ruth Pitter)

The train will fight to the pass and pierce the mountains or perish
M.Ver 127

TRAINS, UNDERGROUND

In the Tube (Richard Aldington)

The electric car jerks
Them VII 11; Weal I 128

The Subway in New York (Tsutomu Fukuda)

Here forests of skyscrapers
S.D 53

Underground (Rose Macaulay)

A sultry, small, perpetual breeze drives sickly-sweet and warm and thin
Man I 45

The Underground (Guy Boas)

The underground
V.F 25

TRAMPOLINES

The Trampoline (John Pudney)

Miss Pleak of the woolshop folded her hands
Speak I 15

You can weigh what you like for a trampoline
Them V 64

TRAMPS

See also Hoboes

On the Swag (R. A. K. Mason)

His body doubled
Make III 91; Them III 34; Ver III 318; Voi II 121

On their Own (Bessie Bobtail)

As down the street she wambled slow
Act II 68

Tramp (R. S. Thomas)

A knock at the door
Choice 301; Liv 15; Them III 33

The Vagabond (Robert Louis Stevenson)

Give to me the life I love
Sto I 60

The Vagabond (John Drinkwater)

I know the pools where the grayling rise
D.P III 23; Mood III 52; P.Life IV 21

TRAMS

The Tram (Leila Berg)

When I was younger
Tree I 45

TRANSFORMATIONS

The Great Silkie of Sule Skerrie
(Anon)

An earthly nourrice sits and sings
Bal 323; B.B 13 (part)*; Bun 18; Cher
206; Fab.Bal 69; Fab.C.V 68; Isle 23*

In Norway there sits a maid
Bal 321; Voi II 115

The Griesley Wife (John Manifold)

Lie still my newly married wife
Act I 71; Ris 25

Little Fan (James Reeves)

I don't like the look of little Fan, Mother
*J.Mod 54; Make II 19; Puf.Q 87; Quest
II 71; Rhyme IV 50; Scrap 32; Shad 82;
Sto II 12; V.F 112*

The Milk-White Dove (Anon)

Pew, pew/My Minny me slew
Cher 159

Snake into Woman (John Keats)

Left to herself, the serpent now began
Iron II 35

Tree Disease (Ted Hughes)

On the moon with great ease
J.Vo II 29

The Twa Magicians (Anon)

The Lady stands in her bower door
Bal 152

O she looked out of the window
*Cher 68; Mer 341; Mer.Puf 260; Min III
84; Pat 169; P.Tong I 98; Speak I 124*

TRANSPLANTING

Transplanting (Theodore Roethke)

Watching hands transplanting
J.Vo IV 84; Yim III 30

TRANSPORT

See also Accidents, Bicycling,
Buses, Lorries, Motor Cycles,
Motoring, Motorways, Roads,
Ships, Trains, Trams, U.S.A.:
Railroads

Jamaican Bus Ride
(A. S. J. Tessimond)

The live fowl squatting on the grapefruit
and bananas
J.Mod 124; Sev 30; Song III 55

Whitman on Wheels (Adrian
Mitchell)

Fanfare: in transports over transport
A.S.L.A 34

TRANSPORTATION

Botany Bay (Anon)

Come all young men of learning and a
warning take by me
Mood IV 98; Song IV 90

Farewell to Old England (Anon)

Farewell to old England for ever
All 13

The Female Transport
(Australian Convicts' Song)

Come all young girls, both far and near,
and listen unto me
Tell II 32

Jim Jones (Anon)

O listen for a moment lads, and hear me
tell my tale
Eye 15; Them III 11; Ver III 278

Ten Thousand Miles Away (Anon)

Sing ho for a brave and gallant ship
Song IV 94

Van Dieman's Land (Anon)

Come all ye boys of Liverpool I'd have
you to beware
Bal 708; Fab.Bal 224

You rambling lads of Liverpool
*Bird II 23; Iron III 21; Key II 13;
Rhyme IV 59*

TRAPS

A Fellow Mortal (John Masefield)

I found a fox, caught by the leg
Tell I 26

215

A Joyous Revelling Song
(Anon—trans W. Colenso)

Oh, Rat, O let us descend the tree
J.Vo I 59

The Rabbit (W. H. Davies)

Nor even when the early birds
Riv II 29

The Snare (James Stephens)

I hear a sudden cry of pain!
Chal II 42; D.P I 20; D.P.R I 10; Ex.Ch 20; F.Feet 129; Fun II 86; Look 180; Make I 81; My 129; Ox.P.C 130; P.F.P I 95; P.Life II 25; Rhyme III 53; Shep 83; Song I 52; Spir 45; Spir.R 37; T.P.R 51; Tree IV 71

TRAVEL

See Exploring, Roads, Space Travel

TRAVEL, IMAGINARY

The Golden Journey to Samarkand
(James Elroy Flecker)

Away, for we are ready to a man!
Chor 67; Riv III 131

Travel (Robert Louis Stevenson)

I should like to rise and go
Cor 131; D.P I 48; D.P.R I 46; Fab.C.V 100; G.Tr.P 263; Mood III 21; Peg I 52; Riv I 38; Sphe 163; Start 78; Ste. C.G 27; T.P.W 49

Walking Song (Charles Williams)

Here we go a-walking, so softly, so softly
A.D.L 137

TRAVELLING

Dr Fell and Points West (Ogden Nash)

Your train leaves at eleven-forty-five and it is now eleven-thirty-nine-and-a-half
Song III 9

The End of the Road (Hilaire Belloc)

In these boots and with this staff
Cor 127; Dan 109; P.F.P I 12; Puf.V 179; Rhyme III 36

The Long Trail (Rudyard Kipling)

There's a whisper down the field where the year has shot her yield
P.Rem 125

Travellers' Choice (Jon Stallworthy)

Counsel yourself that traveller
J.Vo IV 89

TREACHERY

The Castle (Edwin Muir)

All through that summer at ease we lay
Day 50; Fla 57; Nar 94; Song IV 65; Sphe 346; Spir.R 21; T.C.N 18; Under 76

TREE-CLIMBING

Birches (parts) (Robert Frost)

When I see birches bend from left to right
Bird II 33; Choice 281; D.P.R IV 28; Fro.You 36; Hap 55; M.Ver 35; Sev 20; Six V 44; Ten 81

Every Time I climb a Tree
(David McCord)

Every time I climb a tree
G.Tr.P 253

The Rescue (Hal Summers)

The boy climbed up into the tree
Bird I 18; Chal I 32; Cor 104; Dawn 58; D.P.R I 42; J.Mod 26; Make I 102; Prel I 16; Quest V 75; Six VI 62; Song I 64; Sto I 11; Tell I 10; T.P.R 64

Wild Grapes (Robert Frost)

What tree may not the fig be gathered from?
T.C.N 95

Windy Boy in a Windswept Tree
(Geoffrey Summerfield)

The branch swayed, swerved
A.S.L.A 21; Quest IV 22; Them V 51

TREES

See also Apple Trees, Aspens, Birches, Cherry Trees, Christmas Trees, Firewood. Firs, Foresters, Oaks, Pine Trees, Poplars

TREES

Child's Song in Spring (E. Nesbit)
The silver birch is a dainty lady
Ch.Gar 85

The Faerie Queene (part)
(Edmund Spenser)
The laurel, meed of mighty conquerors
Faerie Queene I v 9; *Bat 20*

The Hollow Tree (John Clare)
How oft a summer shower hath started me
Bird I 7

In a Wood (The Woodlanders)
(Thomas Hardy)
Pale beech and pine so blue
Iron II 43

The Old Tree (Andrew Young)
The wood shakes in the breeze
Look 242

Pruning Trees (Chinese—trans Arthur Waley)
Trees growing—right in front of my window
Bird III 49; Flock 107; Them VII 55

Throwing a Tree: New Forest
(Thomas Hardy)
The two executioners stalk along over the knolls
Bird II 32; Drag 75; Fla 26; Har. Ch 56; Iron III 63; J.Mod 144; Key IV 24; Song IV 56; Sphe 63

Trees (Walter de la Mare)
Of all the trees in England
De la M.Ch 38; De la M.Col 77; De la M.P.P 99; Ox.V.J IV 56; Sphe 83; Tree IV 76

Trees (Sara Coleridge)
The Oak is called the King of Trees
Cor 148; Fuji 26; Rhyme II 53

A Withered Tree (Han Yu—trans A. C. Graham)
Not a twig or a leaf on the old tree
J.Vo III 9

TROLLS

Troll sat alone (J. J. R. Tolkien)
Troll sat alone on his seat of stone
Key IV 42

TROUT

Trout (Seamus Heaney)
Hangs, a fat gun-barrel
Drag 17

TROY

The Entry into Troy (John Masefield)
King Sthenelus, my father, has often told me
T.C.N 13

TUGS

Tugs (George R. Hamilton)
At noon three English dowagers ride
Peg III 33; P.F.P II 145; Six IV 56

TURKEYS

Turkeys (John Clare)
The turkeys wade the close to catch the bees
B.B.F 66

TURPIN, DICK

Dick Turpin's Ride (Alfred Noyes)
The daylight moon looked quietly down
Bird I 49; D.P II 76; D.P.R II 89; Min IV 57; Ver II 33

My Bonny Black Bess (Anon)

Dick Turpin bold! Dick hie away
Read I 139

Uncle Tom (John Cotton)

I'll tell you what we'll do boy
Prel I 39

TURTLES

The Little Turtle (Vachel Lindsay)

There was a little turtle
*B.L.J. II 38; Fab.N.V 85; Go.Jo 79; J.Vo
I 69*

Living Tenderly (May Swenson)

My body is a rounded stone
J.Vo II 57

Tony the Turtle (E. V. Rieu)

Tony was a turtle
*D.P I 37; D.P.R I 23; Ex.Tro 17;
Fab.N.V 85; Min IV 33; P.Life III 75;
Puf.Q 124*

Turtle City (Kevan Hall)

Let turtles' patterned shells break the
surface of the shining water
J.Vo IV 46

TWINS

The Twins (H. S. Leigh)

In form and feature face and limb
D.P.R I 34; Prel I 9; Sto I 95

UNCLES

*Incidents in the Life of my Uncle
Arly* (Edward Lear)

O my agéd Uncle Arly
*A.D.L 242; Comp 92; Min III 69; Pers
50; Plea V 44; P.Life II 33; Prel I 39;
V.F 94*

Uncle Albert (Vernon Scannell)

When I was almost eight years old
Prel I 37

Uncle Cyril (George R. Hamilton)

Nobody knew whether from East or
West
J.Mod 57; Sev 40

UNEMPLOYMENT

A Carol (C. Day Lewis)

O hush thee, my baby
Sphe 406

Labour Exchange (Clifford
Dyment)

These men clutching cards, stand in
slack groups
D.P.R IV 83

Moving through the Silent Crowd
(Stephen Spender)

Moving through the silent crowd
Mod.P 4

The Unemployed (T. S. Eliot)

No man has hired us
Peg III 64; Riv IV 124

UNICORNS

A Dublin Unicorn
(B. S. Johnson)

Not by nature simple, as his end might
Peng.An 309

Fantasy in a Forest (Leam Bodine
Drake)

Between two unknown trees I stood
Exp V 11

The Late Passenger (C. S. Lewis)

The sky was low, the sounding rain was
falling dense and dark
Tell I 23

The Unicorn (George Darley)

Lo! in the mute mid wilderness
B.B.F 219; Cher 116

Unicorn (William Jay Smith)

The Unicorn with the long white horn
Puf.Y 111

The Unicorns (Nicholas Moore)

What use to shoot off guns at unicorns
Say 115

UNITED STATES OF AMERICA

See U.S.A.

UNKNOWN CITIZENS

The Ascent of F6 (part)
(W. H. Auden & Christopher
Isherwood)

Life-Patterns: No, nothing that matters
will ever happen
Chal III 13

Mr A.: Has anything happened?
Kal 50

Mrs A.: Evening. A slick and unctuous
time
Day 6

For the Record (George Jones)

I think that I live in a street
Them III 56

How Beastly the Bourgeois is
(D. H. Lawrence)

How beastly the Bourgeois is
Law.S 74

Life Cycle of Common Man
(Howard Nemerov)

Roughly figured, this man of moderate
habits
Mod.P 117

Little Boxes (Malvina Reynolds)

Little boxes on the hillside
Chal II 24

The Man in the Bowler Hat
(A. S. J. Tessimond)

I am the unnoticed, the unnoticeable
man
*Dan 52; Exp II 11; Man III 29; M.Ver
105; Pat 110; Sev 25; Them III 54*

Spring Voices (Louis MacNiece)

The small householder now comes out
warily
Weal II 45

The Unknown Citizen
(W. H. Auden)

He was found by the Bureau of Statistics
to be
*Camb 135; Choice 244; Day 10; Man
III 30; Pers 46; R.R 130; Wheel IV 181*

U.S.A.

See also Buffaloes, Chicago, Colum-
bus, Cowboys, Freedom Songs,
Hoboes, Indians (Red), Slavery,
Slave Trade, Spirituals, Trains
(Underground)

American Names (Stephen Vincent
Benet)

I have fallen in love with American
Names
Peg V 66; S.D 24

U.S.A.: CIVIL WAR

See also Brown (John), Lincoln

Barbara Frietchie (John
Greenleaf Whittier)

Up from the meadows rich with corn
*D.P I 88; D.P.R I 65; Ex.Ch 106; G.Trp
190; Min IV 68; Mood II 96; P.Bk
223; Peg II 47*

Battle-Hymn of the Republic
(Julia Ward Howe)

My eyes have seen the glory of the com-
ing of the Lord
G.Tr.P 311

Jake Diefer (S. V. Benet)

Jake Diefer, ploughing, a day of the early
spring
Tell II 82

John Brown's Body (Anon)

John Brown's body lies a-mouldering in
the grave
B.L.A.F 120; Iron II 39

Luke Breckinridge (S. V. Benet)

Luke Breckinridge woke up one
sunshiny morning
Tell II 96

The Rebel Soldier (Anon)

One morning, one morning, one morning
in May
Say 82; Tree III 53

U.S.A.: PIONEERS & THE WEST

See also F.S.N.A 75–99

See also James (Jesse)

The Ballad of William Sycamore
(Stephen Vincent Benet)

My father he was a mountaineer
*Look 131; Mood IV 117; Peg III 79;
Spir 39; Spir.R 31*

Betsy from Pike (Anon)

Did you ever hear tell of sweet Betsy
from Pike
B.L.A.F 176; Fab.Bal 239; F.S.N.A 335

Do you remember sweet Betsy from
Pike?
Tree III 12

Oh, don't you remember sweet Betsy
from Pike
Bal 750; Iron IV 107

The Shooting of Dan McGrew
(Robert Service)

A bunch of boys were whooping it up in
the Malamute saloon
Mood IV 113

*Starving to death on a Government
Claim* (Anon)

My name is Tom Hight, an old Bach'lor I
am
B.L.A.F 238; Wheel IV 127

Western Wagons (Stephen Vincent
Benet)

They went with axe and rifle when the
trail was still to blaze
Peg II 71

U.S.A.: PRESIDENTS

See Jackson, Lincoln

U.S.A.: RAILROADS

*See also B.L.A.F 244–281, F.S.N.A
406–425*

The American Railway (Anon)

In eighteen hundred and eighty-one
*B.L.A.F 270; Cor 106; Dan 47; Key I
60; Rhyme III 37; Song I 25*

Casey Jones (Anon)

Come all you rounders listen here
*All 9; B.B 93; Bird I 33; B.L.A.F 266;
Chor 32; D.P II 34; D.P.R II 75; Ex.Ch
164; F.S.N.A 564; Iron IV 6; Key I 84;
Make I 122; M.M.A 23; Mood II 20;
Ox.P.C 76; Ox.V.J IV 25; Peg II 78;
P.F.P I 156; Plea VIII 68; P.Tong I 17;
Riv III 39; Sphe 181; Spir 58; Spir.R 47*

Coal for Mike (Bertolt Brecht)

I have heard how in Ohio
D.P.R II 77

Drill, Ye Tarriers (Anon)

Every morning at seven o'clock
F.S.N.A 417

I am a Railroad (Richard G. Esler)

In the San Francisco yards
Read III 64

John Henry (Anon)

John Henry was a little baby (or boy)
*Bal 756; B.L.A.F 258; Fab.Bal 243;
F.S.N.A 562; Peg II 76; Read II 55; Tell
I 114*

Well, it's honey and it's darlin' when I'm
here
F.S.N.A 560

Landscape as Metal and Flowers
(Winfield Townley Scott)

All over America railroads ride through
roses
Go.Jo 209; Look 169

Night Journey (Theodore Roethke)

Now as the train bears west
D.P.R II 73; Eye 9; Peg II 82

Rhyme of the Rail (A Period Piece)
(John Saxe)

Singing through the forests, rattling over
ridges
Speak I 12

Song of the Freight Car (Strickland
W. Gillilan)

I'm a bumped and battered freight car on
a sidetrack
Read II 33

Southern Recipe (Carl Sandburg)

Huntington sleeps in a house six feet long
Bird II 11

To a Locomotive in Winter
(Walt Whitman)

Thee for my recitative
Peg IV 47; Song II 29

The Wabash Cannonball (Anon)

From the great Atlantic Ocean to the wild Pacific shore
F.S.N.A 421

From the waves of the Atlantic to the wild Pacific shore
Song II 27

What the Engines said (Bret Harte)

What was it the engines said
Key IV 122

Zack, the Mormon Engineer (Anon)

Old Zack he came to Utah, way back in Seventy-three
Chor 35

U.S.A.: WAR OF INDEPENDENCE

Paul Revere's Ride (Henry Wadsworth Longfellow)

Listen my children and you shall hear
D.P II 87; D.P.R II 44; Ex.Ch 98; G.Tr.P 184; Spir 162; Spir.R 121

VEGETABLES

See Celery, Swedes

VERSES

See Poetry

VIKINGS

Beowulf the Warrior (trans Ian Serraillier)

Hrothgar, King of the Danes, glorious in battle
Ser.B 9

Harp Song of the Dane Women
(Rudyard Kipling)

What is a woman that you forsake her
Act II 97; Peg IV 103; R.R 38; Song IV 142; Them VI 58

O'er the Wild Gannet's Bath
(George Darley)

O'er the wild gannet's bath
Cher 222; Peg III 26

VILLAGES

See also Cities & Towns, Dunwich, Grantchester

Our Village—By a Villager
(Thomas Hood—1799–1845)

Our village, that's to say not Miss Mitford's village, but our village of Bullock Smithy
Plea VII 98; Read III 53; Riv III 123; R.R 79; Them VII 41; Wheel II 90

VIOLINS

At the Railway Station, Upway
(Thomas Hardy)

There is not much that I can do
Flock 71; Har.Ch 50; Key III 36; Read III 35; Say 72; Voi I 36; Way 49

The Fiddler of Dooney
(W. B. Yeats)

When I play on my fiddle in Dooney
A.D.L 127; Ex.Ch 154; Fab.C.V 41; Fun II 25; Mood IV 10; Ox.V.J II 26; Peg II 99; P.F.P I 86; P.Life III 42; Riv II 33; R.R 167; Sphe 258; Spo I 166; Sto I 59; Them VI 18; Yea.Run 47

The Fiddlers (Walter de la Mare)

Nine feat fiddlers had good Queen Bess
P.Life II 18

The Penny Fiddle (Robert Graves)

Yesterday I bought a penny fiddle
J.Vo I 32; Mer 133; Mer.Puf 101; Puf.Y 126; Quest II 25; Rhyme II 21; T.P.R 111

Old Zip Coon (David Stevens)

There was once a man with a double chin
Tree III 98

VIPERS

See Snakes

VOWELS

A E I O U or *Vowels* (Jonathan Swift)

We are little airy creatures
Fab.N.V 53; Ox.P.C 21; Wheel I 54

We are very little creatures
Mer 252; Mer.Puf 185; P.Rem 38; Rain 16; Rhyme II 2; Tree IV 81

VULTURES

Vulture (Douglas Livingstone)

On ragged black sails
Peng.An 314

The Vulture (Hilaire Belloc)

The vulture eats between his meals
Bits p; B.L.J II 28; Fab.N.V 77; P.Life III 74

WAGTAILS

Little Trotty Wagtail (John Clare)

Little Trotty Wagtail, he went in the rain
B.B.F 72; B.P II 28; Cla.Wo 61; Ex.H 18; Fab.N.V 32; Mer 202; Min III 95; Mood I 42; Ox.P.C 65; Ox.V.J I 54; P.Bk 40; P.F.P I 35; P.Life II 26; P.Rem 18; Puf.V 43; Rhyme III 49; Riv I 11; Spo I 106; Tree II 39

WAKING

Getting up Early on a Spring Morning (Po Chu-I—trans A. Waley)

The early light of rising sun shines on the beams of my house
Flock 9

WALES

Welsh Landscape (R. S. Thomas)

To live in Wales is to be conscious
Mod.P 52

WAR

See also Kal 69–96, Voi III 108–133

See also Battles, Drums, Frontiers, Nuclear War, Recruits, Refugees, Treachery

As the Team's Head-Brass (Edward Thomas)

As the team's head-brass flashed out on the turn
Tell II 101

At Fifteen I went with the Army (Chinese—trans Arthur Waley)

At fifteen I went with the army
D.P.R III 75; Read III 92; Song III 103

The Ballad of Mulan (Arthur Waley)

Click, click, for ever click, click
J.Mod 36; Tell I 94

Bayonet Charge (Ted Hughes)

Suddenly he awoke and was running—raw
Man II 51

Carentan O Carentan (Louis Simpson)

Trees in the old days used to stand
Mod.P 40

Channel Firing (Thomas Hardy)

That night your great gun unawares
Fla 22

Conquerors (Henry Treece)

By sundown we came to a hidden village
Chal II 55; Man II 43; Mod.P 42; Read III 79; Song III 103; Under 85; Yim III 23

The Destruction of Sennacherib (Lord Byron)

B.L.J IV 49; By 148; Fab.C.V 254; G.Tr.P 143; Mood IV 53; P.Bk 275;

P.F.P II 66; Plea VII 21; Sphe 340; Spir 76; Spir.R 60; Spo I 101; Ver II 138

For the Record (R. S. Thomas)

What was your war record, Prytherch?
Mod.P 34

In Time of the Breaking of Nations (Thomas Hardy)

Only a man harrowing clods
Cent 16; Har.Ch 33; Song III 156; Ten 95

Lament (F. S. Flint)

The young men of the world
Fla 41

Lament of the Frontier Guard (Rihaku—trans E. Pound)

By the North Gate, the wind blows full of sand
D.P.R III 68

The Man He Killed (Thomas Hardy)

Had he and I but met
Bird IV 59; Key IV 17; S.D 59; Sto III 107

Men in Green (David Campbell)

Oh, there were fifteen men in green
Chal II 44; Drag 70

My Brother was a Pilot (Bertolt Brecht)

My brother was a pilot
D.P.R III 65

The Old Man with the Broken Arm (Po Chu-I—trans Arthur Waley)

At Hsin-feng an old man four-score-and-eight
Tell II 6

A Protest in the Sixth Year of Ch'ien Fu (Ts'ao Sung—trans A. Waley)

The hills and rivers of the lowland country
Chal III 37; Key III 68; Song II 110; Voi II 75

The Shield of Achilles
(W. H. Auden)

She looked over his shoulder
Fla 108; Liv 115; Say 155

Six Young Men (Ted Hughes)

The celluloid of a photograph holds them well
Song IV 75; Them VI 75

The Soldier's Death (Anne Finch Countess of Winchilsea)

Trail all your pikes, dispirit every drum
By 95; D.P.R IV 59; R.R 46

The Unconcerned (Thomas Flatman)

Now the world is all in a maze
Fab.C.V 263

War (Miguel Hernandez)

Old age in the towns
Look 364

Where have all the flowers gone? (Pete Seeger)

Where have all the flowers gone?
Quest V 22

The White Horse (Tu Fu—trans Rewi Alley)

Out of the Northeast
Cher 343

WAR: AFTERMATH

Grass (Carl Sandburg)

Pile the bodies high at Austerlitz and Waterloo
S.D 66

The Horses (Edwin Muir)

Barely a twelvemonth after
Cent 90; M.Ver 158; Pers 128; Read III 86; R.R 185; Ten 120

Ultima Ratio Regum (Stephen Spender)

The guns spell money's ultimate reason
Mod.P 19; Under 85

Vergissmeinnicht (Keith Douglas)

Three weeks gone and the combatants gone
Mod.P 31

Will it be so again? (C. S. Lewis)

Will it be so again?
Sphe 367

WAR:
CONSCIENTIOUS OBJECTORS
Dooley is a Traitor (James Michie)

'So then you won't fight?'
D.P.R IV 60; Them III 67

Undivided Loyalty (James Kirkup)

Nothing is worth dying for
Them III 70

WARS: BOER
Drummer Hodge (Thomas Hardy)

They throw in Drummer Hodge to rest
*Camb 23; R.R 46; Song IV 73; Sphe
355; Ten 93; Wheel IV 138*

WARS: CRIMEAN
See also Balaclava

The Kerry Recruit (Anon)

One fine morning in May I was tilling the
land
P.W 26

WARS: SPANISH CIVIL
See Nabara

WARS: VIETNAM
Condemnation (Thich Nhat Nanh)

Listen to this:
Chal III 38

Norman Morrison (Adrian Mitchell)

On November 2nd 1965
Chal III 36

What were they like? (Denise
Levertov)

Did the people of Viet Nam
Voi III 108

WARS: 1914–18 (AIR)
An Irish Airman foresees his Death
(W. B. Yeats)

I know that I shall meet my fate
*Camb 30; Cent 57; D.P IV 88; D.P.R IV
60; Fab.C.V 270; Go.Jo 191; P.W.R
276; R.R 48; S.D 57; Song IV 78; Sphe
353; Ten 148; Ver III 51; Yea.Run 66*

Over the Lines (Anon)

We were flying in formation and con-
tinued to keep station
Kal 72

When the Plane Dived (Wilfrid
Gibson)

When the plane dived and the machine-
gun spattered
Chal I 35; Cor 117; Peg IV 94

WARS:
1914–18 (FALSE PATRIOTISM)
'Next to of course God
(e. e. cummings)

'Next to of course God America I
Iron III 35; Song IV 86

WARS: 1914–18 (GAS)
Dulce et Decorum est (Wilfred
Owen)

Bent double, like old beggars under sacks
*Cent 19; Choice 156; Kal 69; Make IV
176; Man II 53; Peg IV 94; R.R 47;
Them III 64; Wheel III 163*

WARS: 1914–18 (GENERAL)
Anthem for Doomed Youth
(Wilfred Owen)

What passing-bells for those who die as
cattle?
*Camb 122; Cher 349; Choice 158; Flock
250; Make IV 220; P.W.R 319; Song IV
78; Sphe 359; Under 73; Ver III 103*

The Chances (Wilfred Owen)

I mind as 'ow the night afore that show
Bird IV 34

224

Concert Party (Siegfried Sassoon)

They are gathering round
Bird III 12

Editorial Impressions
(Siegfried Sassoon)

He seemed so certain 'all was going well'
D.P.R III 36

The Enlisted Man (Robert Graves)

Yelled Corporal Punishment at Private
Reasons
Voi III 132

Futility (Wilfred Owen)

Move him into the sun—
Cent 20; Choice 161; Liv 87; P.W.R 317; Song III 106; Voi III 127

In Memoriam (Edward Thomas)

The flowers left thick at nightfall in the wood
Song IV 75

Lost in France (Ernest Rhys)

He had the plowman's strength
Chal I 35; Peg IV 87; Song III 105

Memorial Tablet (Siegfried Sassoon)

Squire nagged and bullied till I went to fight
Song IV 77

The Parable of the Old Men and the Young (Wilfred Owen)

So Abram rose, and clave the wood, and went
By 275; Voi III 127

The Send Off (Wilfred Owen)

Down the close, darkening lanes they sang their way
Song II 131

Sonnet (Wilfred Owen)

Be slowly lifted up, thou long black arm
Voi III 126

Stretcher Case (Siegfried Sassoon)

He woke; the clank and racket of the train
Bird IV 35

WARS: 1914–18 (MISSING)

A Private (Edward Thomas)

This ploughman dead in battle slept out of doors
Make IV 129

This is no case of petty right or wrong (Edward Thomas)

This is no case of petty right or wrong
Tho.Gr 83

WARS: 1914–18 (SEA)

Mine-Sweeping Trawlers
(E. Hilton Young)

Not ours the fighter's glow
Peg II 44; Spir 89; Spir.R 67

WARS: 1914–18 (TRENCHES)

Attack (Siegfried Sassoon)

At dawn the ridge emerges massed and dun
Bird IV 32; Them VI 39

The Battle (Louis Simpson)

Helmet and rifle, pack and overcoat
Chal I 36; Drag 90

Bombardment (Richard Aldington)

Four days the earth was rent and torn
Chal I 37; Kal 70

Break of Day in the Trenches
(Isaac Rosenberg)

The darkness crumbles away—
Camb 114

Breakfast (Wilfrid Gibson)

We ate our breakfast lying on our backs
Kal 71

Exposure (Wilfred Owen)

Our brains ache in the merciless iced east winds that knive us
Camb 123; D.P.R IV 54; Ev. M 75; Them VI 38

The General (Siegfried Sassoon)

'Good-morning: good-morning!' the General said
Peg IV 93; Riv IV 117; Six IV 49; Song III 105

Into Battle (Julian Grenfell)

The naked earth is warm with spring
D.P IV 92; D.P.R IV 65; Ver III 190

The Rear-Guard (Siegfried Sassoon)

Groping along the tunnel, step by step
Bird IV 32

Strange Meeting (Wilfred Owen)

It seemed that out of battle I escaped
*Camb 121; Cent 17; Choice 160; Fla 80;
Liv 63; S.D 60; Sphe 370; T.C.N 60;
Them II 20; Voi III 129*

Winter Warfare (Edgell Rickword)

Colonel Cold strode up the line
D.P.R IV 56

WARS: 1939–45 (AIR)

The Bomber (B. R. Gibbs)

White moon setting and red sun waking
Sto III 105

For Johnny (John Pudney)

Do not despair
*Day 75; Make IV 47; Mood III 42;
M.Ver 157; Weal I 24; Wheel IV 183*

Missing (John Pudney)

Less said the better
Day 77; M.Ver 142; Weal I 24

Night Bombers (Fl. Lt. O. C. Chave)

Eastward they climb, black shapes
against the grey
Kal 73; Spir 92; Spir.R 69; Sto III 104

Reported Missing (John Bayliss)

With broken wing they limped across the
sky
Man II 32

Revelation (William Soutar)

Machines of death from east to west
M.Ver 158; Spir 92

Thoughts in 1932 (Siegfried
Sassoon)

Alive and forty-five I jogged my way
Under 39

WARS: 1939–45 (BLITZ)

The Air Raid (Francis Scarfe)

All night we stood out on the terrace
Yim III 21

Five Minutes after the Air Raid
(Miroslav Holub—trans I. Milner &
G. Theiner)

In Pilsen/Twenty-six Station Road
D.P.R III 66

Fire Watch ('Sagittarius')

'We came on watch at the third shift' he
said
Speak II 122

Homage to Wren (Louis MacNiece)

At sea in the dome of St Paul's
Under 73

Still Falls the Rain (Edith Sitwell)

Still falls the rain—
Ver III 71

The Streets of Laredo (Louis
MacNiece)

O early one morning I walked out like
Agag
Cher 309; Fla 111; Mod.P 36; Ris 112

Unseen Fire (R. N. Currey)

This is a damned inhuman sort of war
Mod.P 26

WARS: 1939–45 (BOMBING)

Swing Song (Louis MacNiece)

I'm only a wartime working girl
Chal I 38; Day 31; Ver III 68

Target Area (Peter Roberts)

Just ahead/Streams of orange tracer,
streams of red
Chal II 46; Make II 79; Mood III 32

WARS: 1939–45 (GENERAL)

All Day it has Rained (Alun Lewis)

All day it has rained, and we on the edge
of the moors
Cent 87

The Misfit (C. Day Lewis)

At the train depot that first morning
Day 20

1st September 1939 (W. H. Auden)

I sit in one of the dives
Ten 23

WARS: 1939–45 (HOME FRONT)

Watching Post (C. Day Lewis)

A hill flank overlooking the Axe valley
A.D.L 254; Mod.P 22

WARS: 1939–45 (SEA)

Dunkirk, 1940 (Idris Davies)

The little ships, the little ships
Spir 89

Night Patrol (Alan Ross)

We sail at dusk. The red moon
A.S.L.A 31; Yim 319

WARS: 1939–45 (TRAINING)

Judging Distances (Henry Reed)

Not only how far away, but the way that
you say it
Ev.M 54

Naming of Parts (Henry Reed)

Today we have naming of parts.
Yesterday
Go.Jo 189; Kal 76; Mod.P 24; P.F.P II 112; R.R 53; Six IV 17; Song IV 81; Sphe 363; Spir 90; Spir.R 68; Weal II 148; Wheel IV 184

WASHING (CLOTHES)

Dashing away with a Smoothing Iron
(Trad)

'Twas on a Monday morning
Mer 93; Mer.Puf 70; P.Life III 66; Tree III 28

The Laundry Song (Wen I-To—
trans Kai-Yu Hsu)

(One piece, two pieces, three pieces)
S.D 114

Stocking and Shirt (James Reeves)

Stocking and shirt/can trip and prance
Dan 101; T.P.R 101

Wash Day (Anon)

They that wash on Monday
B.L.J III 1; Ex.Tra 12; Fab.N.V 228; Ox.P.C 145; Plea I 38; Puf.N.R 90; Scrap 41; Voi I 55

Washing Day (D. H. Thomas)

The chalk-lined tub, like a coral basin, is
choked with soap and water
Shep 143; Them VI 10

The Washing Machine (Jeffrey Davies)

It goes fwunkety
A.S.L.A 34

WASPS

The Wasps' Nest (George Macbeth)

All day to the loose tile behind the
parapet
Drag 15

WATCHES

The Watch (May Swenson)

When I
J.Vo IV 61

WATER

See also Brooks, Pools (Rock),
Rivers, Sea, Waterfalls, Wells

Green, Green is El Aghir
(Norman Cameron)

Sprawled on the crates and sacks in the
rear of the truck
Ris 114

WATERFALLS

The Cataract of Lodore (Robert Southey)

How does the water
All 27; Dan 40 (part); D.P I 43; D.P.R I 27; Key III 28; Ver II 50

WATER-LILIES

Water-Lilies (John Clare)

The water-lilies white and yellow flowers
Patch 12

WATERLOO

Childe Harold (part) or
The Eve of Waterloo (Lord Byron)

There was a sound of revelry by night
*Bat 18; Fab.C.V 259; P.Bk 293; P.F.P
II 75; Plea VII 41; Song IV 67*

The Field of Waterloo (Thomas
Hardy)

Yea, the coneys are scared by the thud of
hooves
Fab.C.V 260; Song IV 69

The Plains of Waterloo (Anon)

Come all courageous Britons brave, of
honour and renown
Broad 28

WAVES

The Horses of the Sea (Christina
Rossetti)

The horses of the sea
*B.L.J I 55; First II 20; Go.Jo 42; Ox.V.J
II 79; Rain 48; Rhyme II 42; Tree II 27*

The Main Deep (James Stephens)

The long-rolling/Steady-pouring
Peg.V 23; Quest III 62; Speak I 101

There are Big Waves (Eleanor
Farjeon)

There are big waves and little waves
*B.L.J I 56; B.P I 18; P.Life I 59; Puf.Y
66*

WEASELS

Winter: East Anglia (Edmund
Blunden)

In a frosty sunset
Bird IV 49; Peg I 110; Riv IV 45

WEATHER

See also Cla.Wo throughout, *Cor
18–30, Look 2–24, Ox.N.R 117*

See also Clouds, Drought,
Earthquakes, Floods, Fog, Frost &
Ice, Hail, Mist, Monsoon, Months,
Rain, Rainbow, Seasons, Snow,
Storms, Sun, Thaw, Thunder &
Lightning, Wind

Glass Falling (Louis MacNiece)

The glass is going down./The sun
*A.S.L.A 49; Bird I 21; B.L.J IV 27; B.P
IV 95; Cor 20; Dawn 37; Make II 45;
Ox.V.J IV 50; Say 62*

Weather (Anon)

Whether the weather be fine
Fun II 114; Rhyme I 40

Weather Ear (Norman Nicholson)

Lying in bed in the dark, I hear the bray
Dawn 105; D.P.R III 18; Mod.P 62

Weathers (Thomas Hardy)

This is the weather the cuckoo likes
*A.D.L 112; Bird II 15; B.P IV 19; By
194; Choice 133; Fab.C.V 59; First III
36; Fun I 117 (part); Mer 347; My 121;
Ox.P.C 96; P.Bk 22; P.F.P I 43; Plea V
15; Prel III 2; Puf.V 165; Riv II 20; Six I
6; Song I 17; Sphe 78; Weal I 30*

WEATHERCOCKS

Weathercock (Clive Sansom)

High in the stream
B.L.J III 42

WEAVERS

The Poor Cotton Weaver (Anon)

I'm a poor cotton weaver as many a one
knows
Tell II 76

The Wark o' the Weavers (Anon)

We're a' met thegither here to sit and to
crack
Song IV 101

WEDDINGS

See also Marriage

A Ballad upon a Wedding (part)
(Sir John Suckling)

I tell thee, Dick, where I have been
Riv IV 47

WEEKDAYS

Birthdays (Anon)

Born on a Monday
B.L.J II 1

Finger Nails (Anon)

Cut them on Monday, you cut them for
health
Fab.N.V 228; Ox.N.R 16

Monday for health
Plea I 22

Monday's Child (Anon)

Monday's Child is fair of face
*B.P I 18; G.Tr.P 22; M.G.B 16; M.G.E
30; M.G.R 79; Min III 10; Ox.Dic 309;
Ox.N.R preface*

Round the Town (Charles Causley)

Round the town with Billy
Cau.Fig 92

Sneeze on Monday (Anon)

Sneeze on Monday, sneeze for danger
*B.P I 57; Fab.N.V 228; M.G.E 122;
M.G.R 91; Plea I 32*

Washdays (Anon)

They that wash on Monday
*B.L.J III 2; Ex.Tra 12; Fab.N.V 228;
Ox.P.C 145; Plea I 38; Puf.N.R 90;
Scrap 41; Voi I 55*

WELLINGTON, DUKE OF

See also Waterloo

*Ode on the Death of the Duke of
Wellington* (Alfred Lord Tennyson)

Bury the Great Duke
Trea 265; Vic 56

All is over and done
Spo I 157

WELLS

Personal Helicon (Seamus Heaney)

As a child, they could not keep me from
wells
Man II 47

WHALES

See also Jonah

Physiologus (part) (Anglo-Saxon—
trans Charles W. Kennedy)

Now I will fashion the tale of a fish
Ark 151

(trans Gavin Bone)

To explain the nature of fishes in a craft
of verse
P.W 32; P.W.R 27; Riv IV 22

*The Whale (The Progress of the
Soul)* (John Donne)

At every stroke his brazen fins do take
Cher 210; Key IV 111; P.Tong II 5

The Whale (Erasmus Darwin)

—warm and buoyant in his oily mail
G.Tr.P 69

WHALING

The Bonny Ship the 'Diamond'
(Anon)

The *Diamond* is a ship, my lads
Broad 36

Farewell to Tarwathie (Anon)

Farewell to Tarwathie, adieu Mormond
Hill
Song II 43

Greenland Fishery or
The Greenland Whale Fishery or
The Whale or
Whaling in Greenland (Anon)

In eighteen hundred and forty-nine
F.S.N.A 61

In seventeen hundred and ninety-four
*Eye 35; Make I 31; P.F.P I 152; Sto III
130*

It was in the year of forty-four
B.B 43

It was in the year of ninety-four
P.Tong I 70

They signed us weary whaler men
Song III 122

'Twas eighteen hundred and twenty-four
Wheel II 83

'Twas in eighteen hundred and fifty-three
Tree III 100

'Twas in the year of forty-nine
Cher 208

We may no longer stay ashore
All 85; Bal 707; Broad 34; Iron III 72

WHEELWRIGHTS

Wheelwright (R. C. Scriven)

For the hub, elm.
T.P.W 30

WILDERNESS

Inversnaid (Gerard Manley Hopkins)

This darksome burn, horseback brown
A.D.L 69; Choice 113; Iron II 76; Man I 14; Pers 96; P.F.P I 120; P.Rem 235; Shep 25; Song I 14; Them VII 40; Ver III 47; Wheel IV 139

Landscape as Werewolf (William Dunlop)

Near here, the last grey wolf
D.P.R IV 51

The Last Mowing (Robert Frost)

There's a place called Far-Away Meadow
Fro.You 41

Rocky Acres (Robert Graves)

This is a wild land, country of my choice
D.P.R IV 49; Them VII 39

WILDFLOWERS

The Idle Flowers (Robert Bridges)

I have sown upon the fields
Cher 247

A Widow's Weeds (Walter de la Mare)

A poor old Widow in her weeds
De la M.Col 75; De la M.P.P 59; Iron I 1; Song I 12

The Wild-Flower Nosegay (part) (John Clare)

From the sweet time that spring's young thrills are born
Song I 13

WILTSHIRE

Wiltshire Downs (Andrew Young)

The cuckoo's double note
A.D.L 69; Cor 135; Riv IV 44; Ten 170; You.Qu 14

WIND

See also Storms

WIND
(LYRIC & DESCRIPTIVE)

And it was Windy Weather (James Stephens)

Now the winds are riding by
Ex.Ch 30; Ox.V.J III 73

Arthur O'Bower (Anon)

Arthur O' Bower has broken his band
Cher 389; Fab.C.V 62; Ox.Dic 57; Ox.N.R 148; Plea I 63; Puf.N.R 179

A Boisterous Winter Evening (Dorothy Wordsworth)

What way does the wind come? What way does he go?
B.L.J I 6; Mer 355; Ox.P.C 100; Pat 22; Prel III 23; Tree III 88

Child on Top of a Greenhouse (Theodore Roethke)

The wind billowing out the seat of my britches
A.S.L.A 21; Bird II 38; Hap 22; J.Vo III 90; Ox.V.J IV 100; Say 26; Them III 3; Them V 64; Voi I 132; Weal I 110

Gale Warning (Michael Roberts)

The wind breaks bound, tossing the oak and
Drag 66

Mid-Country Blow (Theodore Roethke)

All night and all day the wind roared in the trees
Act I 87; Bird III 2; Eye 7

The North Wind doth blow (Anon)

The north wind doth blow
B.B.F 108; Ex.Tra 58; Fab.N.V 29; Fun I 15; Mer 54; Mer.Puf 41; M.G.B 20; M.G.R 86; Min I 68; My 2; Ox.Dic 426; Ox.N.R 50; Ox.P.C 97; P.Life I 72; Prel III 37; Puf.N.R 178; Puf.V 28; Scrap 44

Ode to the West Wind (Percy Bysshe Shelley)

O wild West Wind, thou breath of Autumn's being
By 133; Peg III 20; P.F.P II 35; P.W 182; P.W.R 203; Riv IV 85; Song III 44; Sphe 26; Trea 63; Ver III 144

Praise Song of the Wind (Siberian—trans W. Radloff & W. R. Trask)

Trees with weak roots
J.Vo II 21

A Song to the Wind (Taliessin—trans A. P. Graves)

Guess who is this creature
Fab.C.V 59

The Sound of the Wind (Christina Rossetti)

The wind has such a rainy sound
Mood I 56; Ox.P.C 58; Ox.V.J II 79; Patch 24; P.Life I 71; P.Rem 26; Rhyme I 39; Tree I 29

The Three Winds (Laurie Lee)

The hard blue winds of March
Act IV 103

When the wind is in the East (Anon)

When the wind is in the east
Ex.Tra 58; Fab.N.V 230; G.Tr.P 23;

M.G.B 152; M.G.E 14; M.G.R 91; Ox.N.R 117; P.Life II 52; Puf.V 166

When the wind is in the north
Tree I 27

Who has seen the Wind? (Christina Rossetti)

Who has seen the wind?
B.P I 23; Ex.Tra 61; First II 27; Fuji 50; Fun I 13; Go.Jo 33; Mer 242; Mer.Puf 176; Min II 78; Ox.P.C 96; Ox.V.J I 42; P.Life I 71; P.P 39; Prel III 31; Tree I 16

The Wind (James Reeves)

I can get through a doorway without any key
Key I 22; Puf.Q 91; Puf.Y 59

The Wind (Robert Louis Stevenson)

I saw you toss the kites on high
Min I 75; Ste.C.G 43

Wind (Ted Hughes)

This house has been far out at sea all night
A.S.L.A 36; Bird III 1; D.P.R III 26; Drag 36; Flock 37; J.Vo IV 69; Mod.P 78; Prel III 24; Sev 96; Song III 42; Sphe 30; Under 50

Wind (Leonard Feeney)

Wind is to show/How a thing can blow
G.Tr.P 260

The Wind and the Moon (George MacDonald)

Said the Wind to the Moon
Fun I 18; Go.Jo 35; G.Tr.P 258

Wind on the Hill (A. A. Milne)

No one can tell me
Mil.N.S 93; T.P.R 100

The Wind Rises (S. C. Evernden)

The wind rises . . .
All 107; Key I 23

The Wind tapped like a Tired Man (Emily Dickinson)

The wind tapped like a tired man
Prel III 27; Shep 145

A Windy Day (Andrew Young)

This wind brings all dead things to life
Bird II 38; B.L.J III 25; B.P IV 74; Cor 19; Drag 37; G.Tr.P 259; Peg II 6; P.F.P I 35; Prel III 25; Riv II 3; This W.D 116; Way 86; You.Bu 15

Windy Nights (Robert Louis Stevenson)

Whenever the moon and stars are set
A.D.L 190; Com 128; Ex.Tra 62; Fab.N.V 241; First III 42; Fun I 64; Go.Jo 35; Look 2; Min III 40; Mood I 54; Ox.V.J II 78; P.Life I 70; Puf.V 218; Shad 49; Ste.C.G 26

WIND (NARRATIVE)

Brown's Descent (Robert Frost)

Brown lived at such a lofty farm
Fro.You 73

Daybreak (Henry Wadsworth Longfellow)

A Wind came up out of the sea
Pat 178; Sto I 77

The Wind in a Frolic (William Howitt)

The wind one morning sprang up from sleep
All 105; B.P IV 62; D.P II 10; Ex.Ch 34; Mer 243; Mer.Puf 177; Min IV 53; Tree IV 104 (part)

Windy Boy in a Windswept Tree (Geoffrey Summerfield)

The branch swayed, swerved
A.S.L.A 21; Quest IV 22; Them V 51

WINDMILLS

The Windmill (Henry W. Longfellow)

Behold! a giant am I!
D.P I 40; Ex.Ch 44; Min IV 12; Rhyme II 54; Tree II 46

The Windmill (Robert Bridges)

The green corn waving in the dale
Ch.Gar 185

The Windmill (E. V. Lucas)

If you should bid me make a choice
Ex.Ch 52

The miller stands before his door
Fun I 41

WINE

Wine and Water (G. K. Chesterton)

Old Noah he had an ostrich farm and fowls on the largest scale
Peg II 41

WINTER

See also Frost & Ice, Months, Snow, Snowflakes, Thaw

Christmas Landscape (Laurie Lee)

Tonight the wind gnaws
Pat 58

Hiawatha (part) (H. W. Longfellow)

Oh! the long and dreary winter!
Speak II 37

Hot Cake (Shu Hsi—trans Arthur Waley)

Winter has come; fierce is the cold
Act I 76; A.D.L 101; Flock 280; Iron III 82; Prel IV 24; Read I 127

The Land (part) (Victoria Sackville-West)

Now in the radiant night, no men are stirring
Com 75

The Last Word of a Bluebird as told to a Child (Robert Frost)

As I went out a crow
Fab.N.V 33; Fro.You 61; Go.Jo 13; Puf.Y 79

A Litany (Thomas Nashe)

Autumn hath all the summer's fruitful treasure
Ver III 4

Old Winter (T. Noel)

Old Winter sad in snow yclad
Fun II 140; Key III 52; Peg I 108

Sheep in Winter (John Clare)

The sheep get up and make their many tracks
Cor 26; Flock 280; Rhyme III 58; Sto II 113

Shine out Fair Sun (Anon)

Shine out fair sun with all your heat
Read I 128

Summer is Gone (trans Kuno Meyer)

My tidings for you: the stag bells
Fab.C.V 55

To Winter (William Blake)

O Winter! bar thine adamantine doors
Bla.Gr 30; Peg V 42; R.R 94

Up in the morning's no' for me (Robert Burns)

Up in the morning's no' for me
B.P III 40; D.P IV 60; D.P.R I 15; Fun II 135; Iron I 7; Mood III 28; Ox.P.C 98; Peg I 110; P.Life IV 34; Prel III 38; R.R 92; Song I 59

When Icicles Hang (William Shakespeare)

When icicles hang by the wall
Love's Labour's Lost V ii 920; *Bat 64; B.B.F 109; Bird I 22; Cher 392; Ch.Gar 20; Com 76; Cor 30; D.P I 106; D.P.R I 19; Fab.C.V 56; Fun II 137; Go.Jo 252; Iron I 57; Key I 75; Mer 348; Min IV 29; Mood II 6; Ox.P.C 98; Ox.V.J II 59; Pat 21; P.F.P I 44; Plea IV 78; P.Life II 58; Puf.V 128; Rain 32; Riv I 8; Say 93; Song I 71; Sphe 36; Them VII 36; This W.D 72; Ver II 2*

Winter (Walter de la Mare)

Clouded with snow
Wheel I 135

Winter (Alfred Lord Tennyson)

The frost is here
B.L.J IV 16; Cor 21; Mood I 53; Peg I 104; Tree III 40

Winter (Walter de la Mare)

Green Mistletoe! Oh, I remember now
Cher 394; De la M.Ch 51; P.Rem 44

Winter (Richard Hughes)

Snow wind-whipt to ice
This W.D 140

Winter: East Anglia (Edmund Blunden)

In a frosty sunset
Bird IV 49; Peg I 110; Riv IV 45

Winter in the Fens (John Clare)

So moping flat and low our valleys lie
Flock 4

Winter's Beauty (W. H. Davies)

It is not fine to walk in spring
Ch.Gar 98

Winter's Troops (Charles Cotton)

Like an invader, not a guest
Cher 390

Winter with the Gulf Stream (Gerard Manley Hopkins)

The boughs, the boughs are bare enough
Camb 3

The Words of Finn (Old Irish)

My words for you
Cher 389

WITCHES

See also Exp VIII 17–28, Isle 37–49, Speak I 112–128

See also Charms and Spells, Halloween

WITCHES (LYRIC & DESCRIPTIVE)

The Broomstick Train (O. W. Holmes)

Look out! Look out, boys! Clear the track
Fuji 45

The Hag (Robert Herrick)

The Hag is astride
Chor 30; Com 178; Fab.C.V 221; G.Tr.P 107; Her.Mu 27; Mood III 8; My 38; Ox.P.C 85; Ox.V.J II 71; Shad 91; Speak I 118; Voi I 68

The Hare (Walter de la Mare)

In the black furrow of a field
First III 43; Ox.V.J III 66

Her Kind (Anne Sexton)

I have gone out, a possessed witch
Exp VIII 28

I Saw Three Witches (Walter de
la Mare)

I saw three witches
*De la M.Col 148; De la M.Ch 87; Isle
47; Ox.V.J III 77; Plea VI 37*

Kitchen Song (Edith Sitwell)

Grey as a guinea fowl is the rain
*Dawn 50; Isle 49; Ox.V.J III 76; Scrap
9; Shad 93*

The Little Creature (Walter de
la Mare)

Twinkum, twankum, twirlum and
twitch—
*De la M.Col 153; De la M.S 52; D.P.R I
88; P.F.P I 18; Speak I 116*

Mother Maudlin the Witch (Ben
Jonson)

Within a gloomy dimble she doth dwell
Cher 160

My Cats (A Witch speaks)
(Stevie Smith)

I like to toss him up and down
Shep 97

The Ride-by-Nights (Walter de
la Mare)

Up on their brooms the Witches stream
*Dan 21; De la M.Col 150; De la M.P.P
90; De la M.S 162; Mer 312; Mood I 11;
Ox.V.J III 75; P.Life III 96; P.P 7; Riv I
89*

Space Travellers (James Nimmo)

There was a witch hump-backed and
hooded
*B.P II 47; Dan 26; Exp VII 27; Min IV
43; Ox.V.J III 79; P.Life IV 95; Quest II
57; Speak I 120; Sto II 27; T.P.W 19*

Three Poor Witches (Edith
Sitwell)

Whirring, walking/On the tree top
Exp VIII 21; Ox.V.J II 73

The Three Witches (William
Shakespeare)

First Witch: When shall we three meet
again
Macbeth I i 1; *Dan 24*

The Witch (Gillian Pursey—
aged 12)

The witch is an ugly creature
Them II 12

WITCHES (NARRATIVE)

Alison Gross (Anon)

O Alison Gross that lives in yon tow'r
*Bal 128; Bun 108; Fab.C.V 222; Shad
101*

As Lucy went a-Walking (Walter
de la Mare)

As Lucy went a-walking one morning
cold and fine
De la M.Col 151; My 40

A Country Witch (William
Barnes)

There's that old hag, Moll Brown
G.Tr.P 106; Song II 92

The Two Witches (Robert Graves)

O sixteen hundred and ninety-one
*Dawn 51; D.P.R I 87; Hap 41; Shad
103; Voi I 51*

The Witch (Mary E. Coleridge)

I have walked a great while over the
snow
Cor 93; Ox.V.J III 53; Speak I 122

WOLVES

*The Hunting Song of the Seeonee
Pack* (Rudyard Kipling)

As the dawn was breaking the sambhur
belled
A.D.L 26

WOOD

Buying Fuel (Richard Church)

Now I came to the farmer about some logs
Prel IV 46

Fifty Faggots (Edward Thomas)

There they stand, on their ends, the fifty faggots
Choice 172

Woodworker's Ballad (Herbert Palmer)

All that is moulded of iron
Spo II 121

WOODLARKS

The Woodlark (Gerard Manley Hopkins)

Teevo cheevo cheevio chee:
B.B.F 2; Key I 53

WOODMEN

The Bushfeller (Eileen Duggan)

Lord, mind your trees today!
Chal I 44

Throwing a Tree: New Forest (Thomas Hardy)

The two executioners stalk along over the knolls
Bird II 32; Drag 75; Fla 26; Har.Ch 56; Iron III 63; J.Mod 144; Key IV 24; Song IV 56; Sphe 63

The Woodman's Dog (The Task) (William Cowper)

Shaggy, and lean and shrewd, with pointed ears
A.D.L 176; D.P III 23; Kal 5; Speak I 19

Forth goes the woodman, leaving unconcerned
D.P.R III 19

WOODPECKERS

Upon Appleton House (part) (Andrew Marvell)

He walks still upright from the root
B.B.F 93; Cher 96

The Woodpecker (Richard Church)

Tread softly here
Cor 179; M.Ver 63

WOODS

See also Foresters, Trees, Woodmen

An English Wood (Robert Graves)

This valley wood is pledged
Peg V 35; Wheel III 167

The Way through the Woods (Rudyard Kipling)

They shut the road through the woods
Act III 67; Bird I 25; D.P IV 64; D.P.R IV 38; Fab.C.V 377; Isle 81; Look 294; Ox.V.J IV 63; P.F.P II 223; Plea VII 53; P.Life IV 26; Rain 80; Rhyme IV 16; Song I 139; Sphe 86; Start 126; Them II 6; This W.D 163; Way 52; Weal I 107

WORDS

See also Language

Conundrums (D. H. Lawrence)

Tell me a word
Law.S 71

Hints on Pronunciation for Foreigners (T. S. W.)

I take it you already know
Flock 237; Yim II 142

The Siouxs (Charles Adams)

A wandering tribe called the Siouxs
Act I 102

Skinflint (H. S. Mackintosh)

How delectable is the word 'skinflint'
Pat 191

Words (Edward Thomas)

Out of us all
D.P IV 15; D.P.R IV 1; Iron II 41; Song II 2; Sphe 264; Ten 136; Tho.Gr 91; Under 56; Weal II 4

WORDSWORTH

The Prelude (part) (William Wordsworth)

One summer evening (led by her) I found
Song IV 41

There was a Boy (William Wordsworth)

There was a boy; ye knew him well, ye cliffs
D.P.R IV 43; Fab.C.V 103

William Wordsworth (Sidney Keyes)

No room for mourning: he's gone out
D.P IV 73; D.P.R IV 45; Peg IV 69; Ver III 176

WORK

Toads (Philip Larkin)

Why should I let the toad work
Day 95; D.P.R IV 86; Exp II 8; Liv 159; Them VI 28

Toads Revisited (Philip Larkin)

Walking around in the park
Them VI 29

Will consider situation (Ogden Nash)

These here are words of radical advice for a young man looking for a job

D.P.R IV 84; Exp II 1

Work (D. H. Lawrence)

There is no point in work
D.P.R IV 72; J.Mod 22; Man II 58; Them VI 27

WORKERS

All these trust to their hands (Ecclesiasticus 38)

The wisdom of a learned man cometh by opportunity of leisure
D.P.R IV 71

As I came Home from Labour (F. C. Boden)

As I came home from labour
Sphe 382

The Case for the Miners (Siegfried Sassoon)

Something goes wrong with my synthetic brain
Bird IV 13; Day 45; Them VI 45

Questions of a Studious Working Man (Bertolt Brecht)

Who built Thebes of the seven gates?
My 184

WORK SONGS

See also Cowboys, Sea Shanties

Pick a Bale of Cotton (Anon)

You got to jump down, turn around
B.L.A.F 234

This old hammer (Anon)

This old hammer
J.Vo I 42

WORMS

Worms and the Wind (Carl Sandburg)

Worms would rather be worms
Ark 92; Quest V 44

WRENS

The Cutty Wren (Anon)

'Oh where are you going?' says Milder to Malder
Bird I 15; Ones 117

Jenny Wren (Walter de la Mare)

Of all the birds that rove and sing
B.B.F 7; De la M.Ch 38; De la M.S 146; D.P II 17; D.P.R II 10; Ex.Ch 17; Mood IV 79

Netted Strawberries (Gordon Bottomley)

I am a willow-wren
D.P II 16

WRESTLING

All-in Wrestlers (James Kirkup)

These two great men battling like lovers
D.P.R II 48; Sev 14; Wheel IV 194

WRITING

Essay on Criticism (parts)
(Alexander Pope)

True ease in writing comes from art, not
chance
Peg V 74

Words are like leaves, and where they
most abound
Peg V 75

YAKS

The Yak (Hilaire Belloc)

As a friend to the children commend me
the Yak
D.P I 24; Fab.N.V 166; Ox.P.C 117

Yak (William Jay Smith)

The long-haired yak has long black hair
G.Tr.P 55

YEATS, W. B.

In Memory of W. B. Yeats
(W. H. Auden)

He disappeared in the dead of winter
Camb 128

YELLOWHAMMERS

The Yellowhammers (Andrew
Young)

All up the grassy many-tracked sheep-
walk
You.Qu 28

YORK

York, York for my Money
(William Elderton)

As I went through the North Country
Riv I 54

YOUTH & AGE

About Crows (John Ciardi)

The old crow is getting slow
Chal I 72

Variations on a Theme (Peter
Champkin)

I spent my youth by a harbour where the
sun was caught
Sev 27

ZEBRAS

Zebra (Isak Dinesen)

The eagle's shadow runs across the plain
Go.Jo 88

The Zebras (Roy Campbell)

From the dark woods that breathe of
fallen showers
Day 133; Peg V 18

ZOOS

See also Exp III

See also Aquaria

Au Jardin des Plantes (John
Wain)

The gorilla lay on his back
*Exp III 14; Flock 220; Make IV 217;
Sphe 119; Them I 71; Yim III 58*

The Black Ape (Leo Aylen)

The black ape's principal food is fruit
Make IV 197; Yim II 78

The Dromedary (A. Y. Campbell)

In dreams I see the dromedary still
Exp III 17; Kal 9; P.F.P I 94; Way 23

Exile (Verna Sheard)

Ben-Arabie was the Camel
*Kal 10; Look 189; Make I 36; P.Life III
76*

The Jaguar (Ted Hughes)

The apes yawn and adore their fleas in
the sun

Bird III 28; Exp III 15; Them I 71; Ver III 79

Our Visit to the Zoo (Jessie Pope)

When we went to the Zoo
B.P II 34; Plea II 14

The Panther (Rainer Maria Rilke—trans Jessie Lemont)

His weary glance, from passing by the bars
Ark 120

(trans J. B. Leishman)

His gaze, going past those bars, has got so misted
Flock 61

Recognition (W. J. Turner)

One Sunday in Regent's Park, sheltering, I saw
Kal 7

Riverdale Lion (John Robert Colombo)

Bound lion, almost blind from meeting their gaze and popcorn
Exp III 12

The Tigress (Clifford Dyment)

They trapped her in the Indian hills
Chal II 20; Eye 18; J.Mod 111

The Zoo (Boris Pasternak)

The zoo lies in the parkland thickets
Flock 221

Books to which reference is made

Explanation of symbols used for books

The symbol used for a book of poems by a single author begins with the first three letters of the poet's name: e.g. *Bro.B*, Alan Brownjohn's *Brownjohn's Beasts*, *You.Qu*, Andrew Young's *Quiet as Moss*.

Anthologies are coded by title: e.g. *Hap, Happenings*; *Ris, Rising Early*. When there is a series of volumes graded for classroom use, the volumes are indicated by Roman figures, the pages by Arabic numbers: e.g. *Voi II 21* is *Voices*, volume II, page 21. When the series is not numbered on the cover, an indication of the main title is given, followed by a different symbol for each volume: *Ex.Ch* and *Ex.H* belong to the *Exploring Poetry* series, and are respectively *Treasure Chest* and *Treasure Hunt*.

Such indications as *Fab*, Faber; *Peng*, Penguin; *Ox*, Oxford; are easily recognisable.

A very brief description of each book gives some indication of its type and the age-range for which it is designed.

Act
Active Anthologies I–V (by A. W. Rowe)
Blond Educational n.d.
> Mixed poetry and prose, serious and trivial, grouped by theme. Chosen by a most experienced secondary headmaster, author of *English through Experience*.

A.D.L
All Day Long (comp. Pamela Whitlock)
Oxford 1954 4th imp. 1963
> Unusual unanthologised poems, often rather difficult, arranged by subject. Useful book for the teacher.

All

All Together! (comp. David J. Aitken)

Blond Educational 1968

    Verses specifically chosen for juniors to speak aloud; good selection, many familiar favourites, for many purposes.

Ark

Out of the Ark (comp. Gwendolyn Reed)

Longman Young Books 1968 repr. 1970

    Distinguished by the number of poems *not* met in other anthologies of animal poetry. Much American verse.

A.S.L.A

as large as alone (chosen Christopher Copeman & James Gibson)

Macmillan 1969 repr. 1971

    Remarkable selection of very recent unfamiliar poetry which is yet within the understanding of many secondary children.

Bal

The Ballad Book (ed. MacEdward Leach)

A. S. Barnes (New York) Thomas Yoseloff (London) 1955

    Comprehensive collection of 370 English, Scottish and American ballads, with notes, glossary, bibliography and discography. Very good source book for school and classroom libraries.

Bat

The Batsford Book of Children's Verse (ed. Stevie Smith)

Batsford 1970

    A poet's very individual selection of unusual poems by well-known poets. Beautifully produced, magnificent photographs as illustrations.

B.B

A Book of Ballads (comp. Alan Bird)

Longmans (Heritage of Literature) 1967

> Seventy 'ballads', old and recent, serious and merry. Very convenient collection for classroom use.

B.B.F

Birds, Beasts and Fishes (ed. R. Manning-Sanders)

Oxford University Press 1962

> One of the best anthologies of animal poetry; amazing variety, including Anglo-Saxon riddles, passages from Isiah and Whitman, and nonsense poems. Many short extracts from little-known works.

B.B.G.G

Beastly Boys and Ghastly Girls (sel. William Cole)

Methuen 1970

> Self-explanatory title: appropriate spidery drawings by Tomi Ungerer. Useful for children who think poetry is solemn and goody-goody, but the humour is sometimes strained.

Bel.C.V

Selected Cautionary Verses (1930) (by Hilaire Belloc)

Puffin 1940 repr. 1968

> The immortal Jim, Matilda and many others of Belloc's children, beasts and peers. Most enjoyable light verse, easily memorised.

Bird

The Golden Bird I–IV (ed. Frank Whitehead)

Oliver & Boyd 1969

> Beautifully produced. Poems of real quality, chosen to be spoken, and arranged so that neighbouring poems enhance each other. Secondary. L.P. records of ballads from the books are available.

Bits
Bits and Pieces (chosen P. Blakeley)
A & C Black Ltd 1970
> Very short poems and fragments of poems, printed in large type on coloured, unnumbered pages (y, yellow; p, pink; b, blue; g, grey). Meant for the youngest, but much would appeal to any juniors.

B.L.A.F
Best Loved American Folk Songs (coll. John & Alan Lomax)
Grosset & Dunlap (New York) 1947
> Admirable selection for children: invaluable for the teacher who wants ample background material. Good simple piano accompaniments and guitar chords.

Bla.Gr
A Grain of Sand (by William Blake, chosen R. Manning)
The Bodley Head 1967
> Good introduction to a major poet.

Bl.J
Blackwell's Junior Poetry Books I–IV (chosen Evan Owen)
Blackwell 1960 repr. 1964
> A fresh selection, clearly set out and skilfully graded, for the junior school. Great emphasis on rhythm. Rather disappointing illustrations.

Blu.Mi
The Midnight Skaters (by Edmund Blunden chosen C. Day Lewis)
The Bodley Head 1968
> Readers still enjoy Blunden's combination of 'gentleness and toughness'. Poems by a true countryman.

242

B.P
Birthright Poetry I–IV (sel. W. T. Cunningham)
Hamish Hamilton 1963 repr. 1966
> Pleasant set, graded for juniors. Mainly but not entirely traditional poems for schools.

Broad
Ballads and Broadsides (ed. Michael Pollard)
Pergamon 1969
> Chosen to give readers 'the sound of voices from the past'. The editor has omitted ballads usually anthologised and presented an unusual selection, deliberately 'unpoetic', with historical notes.

Bro.B
Brownjohn's Beasts (by Alan Brownjohn)
Macmillan 1970
> Delightfully illustrated by Carol Lawson; a well-known modern poet gaily impersonates many creatures.

Bun
A Bundle of Ballads (comp. R. Manning-Sanders)
Oxford University Press 1959
> Well-chosen selection for schools: tactfully modernised spelling where necessary for easy reading.

By
By Heart (chosen Francis Meynell)
Nonesuch Press 1965
> Poems specially chosen because memorable, easily memorised. Mostly rhyming, all rhythmic, shapely and direct, from all periods. Beautifully produced book, ideal for browsing.

Camb
Cambridge Book of English Verse 1900–1939 (ed. Allen Freer &
John Andrew)
Cambridge University Press 1970
> Substantial selections from the eleven 'most important'
> modern poets. Perhaps rather over-weighted by notes oc-
> cupying more than a quarter of the book. Upper forms and
> students.

Car.J
Jabberwocky and Other Poems (by Lewis Carroll)
Faber & Faber 1968
> Eleven nonsense poems illustrated by Gerald Rose.

Cau.Fig
Figgie Hobbin (by Charles Causley)
Macmillan 1970
> New poems for juniors, in many moods, but all attractively
> rhythmical and musical, by a Cornish schoolmaster-poet.

Cau.Nar
Figure of Eight: Narrative Poems (by Charles Causley)
Macmillan 1969
> Varied stories in verse: useful to have *new* narrative poems for
> children.

Cent
Poems of this Century (ed. C. B. Cox & A. E. Dyson)
Edward Arnold 1968
> Poems chosen both as 'excellent by any standard' and as like-
> ly to appeal to school and college readers. Brief notes. A
> useful introduction to the better-known twentieth century
> poets for upper forms.

Chal

World of Challenge I–III (ed. Marie Sweeney)
Hodder & Stoughton 1970 repr. 1971

Lively and unusual poems; in II and III many very recently written. Arranged by themes which are of real concern to teenagers.

Cher

The Cherry Tree (chosen G. Grigson)
Phoenix House London 1959

Invaluable for the teacher and for school and class libraries. Over 500 poems of every imaginable kind, most helpfully arranged to enhance each other, in 29 sections. Much not found anywhere else. For all ages.

Ch.Gar

A Child's Garland (gathered Jane Carton)
Faber & Faber 1942 8th imp. 1962

A personal selection of fine quality made for an absent daughter. Poetry not verse: good for reading aloud to children. Sentiments naturally tinged by date of compilation.

Cla.Wo

The Wood is Sweet (by John Clare chosen David Powell)
Bodley Head 1966

The clarity and vividness of Clare's descriptions of nature delight children. A good selection for young readers.

Choice

A Choice of Poets (chosen and ed. R. P. Hewett)
George G. Harrap 1968

Fourteen poets from Wordsworth to R. S. Thomas chosen by an experienced teacher for readers from 14 to 16. Rather heavily annotated, but the reader is invited to use only what he needs.

245

Chor

Choral Verse (comp Alexander Franklin)

Oliver & Boyd 1962 repr. 1965

> Pieces chosen for 11–13 years, but appealing to a far wider age-range. Each accompanied by detailed notes suggesting methods of presentation. Record of some poems available.

Com

Common Ground (sel. L. Clark)

Faber 1964

> An unusual selection, well-grouped and attractively set out. Useful for top juniors and throughout the secondary school.

Comp

Compass (ed. S. Bolt, P. Mansell & J. J. Lewis)

Hutchinson Educational 1969

> A really unusual and original anthology for older pupils, with an excellent introduction, simple, clear and profound. Some striking sets of contrasted poems.

Cor

Poet's Corner (ed. Barbara Ireson)

Nelson 1969

> Nominally for 9 year olds upwards, this delightfully produced collection of varied adult poems will appeal to people of all ages. A lovely book for children browsing.

Dan

That Way and This (ed. Frances Baldwin & Margaret Whitehead)

Chatto & Windus 1972

> Unique collection of poetry specially chosen for creative dance, with helpful introduction and notes.

246

Dawn

Dawn and Dusk (ed. Charles Causley)
Brockhampton Press Ltd Leicester 1962

>   Ninety-one poems by fifty modern poets; unusual 20th century choices for older children, made by schoolmaster-poet who writes an interesting introduction.

Day

This Day and Age (sel. Stanley Hewett)
Edward Arnold 1960

>   Poems written mainly in the 1930s and 1940s, a good proportion by American and Commonwealth poets not well-known here. For secondary children, with simple, helpful notes 'placing' each poem.

De la M.Ch

A Choice of De La Mare's Verse (sel. with introduction by W. H. Auden)
Faber & Faber 1963

>   Contains many later poems rarely found in anthologies.

De la M.Col

Collected Rhymes and Verses (by Walter de la Mare)
Faber & Faber 1944 repr. 1967

>   Poet *par excellence* for gentle and imaginative children. Many selections are available; this contains all his verses specifically written for children.

De la M.P.P

Peacock Pie (by Walter de la Mare)
Faber & Faber 1913, this edn. 1946 repr. 1969

>   A particularly attractive edition, illustrated by Edward Ardizzone, of favourite de la Mare poems.

De la M.S
Secret Laughter (by Walter de la Mare)
Puffin 1962 revised 1970
> A well-chosen selection for the younger readers of poetry.

Down
All Along Down Along (comp. Leonard Clark)
Longmans 1971
> Ten popular stories in verse, gaily and lavishly illustrated.

D.P
Discovering Poetry I–IV (chosen E. W. Parker)
Longmans 1953
> A popular well-graded series which ran into 16 impressions before revision (See *D.P.R*). I The Journey Begins; II The Way Opens; III The Road Ahead; IV Fresh Fields. Many long story poems, often historical.

D.P.R
as *D.P* above, revised by Michael Marland 1971
> Revised by an expert, and attractively recovered and printed.

Drag
Dragonsteeth (ed. Eric Williams)
Edward Arnold 1972
> For ages 13–15 primarily. A vital and well-organised collection strikingly presented with many photographs.

El.O.P
Old Possum's Book of Practical Cats (by T. S. Eliot)
Faber & Faber 1939 5th imp. 1963.
> A distinguished modern poet writes for his friends' children. *Skimbleshanks the Railway Cat* (after Kipling) is especially popular.

Ev.M

Every Man will Shout (comp. R. Mansfield, ed. I. Armstrong)
Oxford University Press 1964
> Poems on themes which should appeal especially to teenagers: deliberately 'unpoetic' in manner and style.

Ex.Ch, Ex.H, Ex.Tra, Ex.Tro

Exploring Poetry: Treasure Chest, Treasure Hunt, Treasure Trail, Treasure Trove (ed. E. W. Parker)
Longmans Group 1961 repr. 1970
> Children's poems both traditional and modern, grouped by subject and graded for juniors.

Eye

An Eye on Things (ed. Esmor Jones)
Pergamon 1969
> Poems and (unconnected) photographs, to encourage readers to see 'ordinary' things more vividly.

Exp

Themes to Explore I-VIII (comp. T. H. Parker & F. J. Teskey)
Blackie 1970
> Eight books of contemporary prose, poetry and photographs, with suggestions for further reading. For upper forms. I The Adolescent; II And so to Work; III Animals in Captivity; IV Discrimination; V Inland Waters; VI On Being Alone; VII Pathway to the Stars; VIII The Supernatural

Fab.Bal

The Faber Book of Ballads (ed. Matthew Hodgart)
Faber 1965
> Ballads and broadsides from country and town, mainly for older children. Some Australian ballads for tough boys, and verses from Ireland and America.

Fab.C.V
The Faber Book of Children's Verse (ed. Janet Adam Smith)
Faber & Faber 1953 repr. 1968
>Admirably wide-ranging selection for children already interested in poetry, including many classic poets—Marvell, Milton, Pound. Grouped under imaginative headings: Night and Day, Marvels and Riddles, History and Time, etc. All ages from top juniors upwards.

Fab.N.V
The Faber Book of Nursery Verse (ed. Barbara Ireson)
Faber & Faber 1958
>Splendid collection for younger children—well beyond nursery age—with much that top juniors appreciate. Emphasis on nonsense jingles and rhythmic verse easy to speak aloud.

F.Feet
Four Feet and Two (comp. Leila Berg)
Puffin 1960 repr. 1970
>The best collection of animal poems for juniors, it includes some unusual and stimulating choices.

First
First Poems I–III (comp. N. Grisenthwaite & J. H. Wheeler)
Schofield & Sims Ltd 1968 repr. 1970
>Sturdy, gay books with rhymes, poems and jingles. Carefully graded with much for the very youngest in I, but many poems to which children will return for years, and plenty in III which adults will appreciate.

Fla
Flashpoint (comp. Robert Shaw)
E. J. Arnold 1964
>Adult poems, mainly modern, chosen to interest top forms. Brief survey of recent poetry and biographical notes.

Flock

A Flock of Words (coll. David Mackay)
Bodley Head 1969

> An expert and sympathetic teacher's commonplace book, wide-ranging in every way. Surprising choices and juxtapositions, a splendid collection to return to again and again.

Fro.You

You Come Too (by Robert Frost)
The Bodley Head 1964

> The poet's own choice for younger readers, dedicated to his wife, 'who knew as a teacher that no poetry was good for children that wasn't equally good for their elders'. A valuable book.

F.S.N.A

The Folk Songs of North America (comp. Alan Lomax)
Cassell 1960

> The most comprehensive and authoritative collection, with ample accounts of the general historical and geographical background of each group of songs, and particular notes on each song. Invaluable for school libraries.

Fuji

A Child's Book of Poems (pictures by Gyo Fujikawa)
Collins 1969, 1970

> Large attractively illustrated book containing a wide assortment of poems and fragments of poems, verses and jingles (many too brief to itemise) for juniors to browse in.

Fun

Fun and Fancy I, II (comp. W. R. S. McIntyre)
Macmillan 1957 repr. 1966

> Designed for secondary children who are poor readers. Both format and introductions to the poems in Book I would suit juniors. Mainly strongly rhythmical verses with fairly simple vocabulary; also snatches of verse grouped by subject.

251

Go.Jo

The Golden Journey (comp. Louise Bogan & William Jay Smith)
Evans Bros Ltd 1967

Beautifully produced and distinctive anthology compiled by two poets. Great variety and some unusual poems.

G.Tr.P

The Golden Treasury of Poetry (sel. Louis Untermeyer)
Collins 1961

Valuable collection for all ages—the American format makes it appear to be for younger children. Contains useful unhackneyed American poems.

Har.Ch

A Choice of Thomas Hardy's Poems (made by Geoffrey Grigson)
Macmillan 1969

Excellent introduction to a major poet.

Her.Mu

The Music of a Feast (by Robert Herrick chosen by Eleanor Graham)
The Bodley Head 1968

Here may be found lyrics by the author of the popular *The Hag*. Children can enjoy the sweetness and good humour of Herrick and so sample the 17th century.

Iron

Iron, Honey, Gold I–IV (ed. David Holbrook)
Cambridge University Press 1961 repr. 1967

Interesting individual anthology, arranged rather erratically. Adolescents quickly appreciate many of the poems and can be helped to enjoy those that are more difficult.

Isle

The Isle of Gramarye (ed. Jennifer Westwood)
Rupert Hart-Davies 1970

Poetry of magic and enchantment.

J.Mod

Harrap's Junior Book of Modern Verse (comp. M. Wollman & D. M. Hurst)

Harrap 1961 repr. 1970

Well-chosen selection for middle schools and above, on topics of special interest to children.

J.Vo

Junior Voices I–IV (ed. Geoffrey Summerfield)

Penguin 1970

Four excitingly illustrated collections of songs, riddles, jingles, haikus *and* poems, which are refreshingly different from most anthologies, if sometimes trivial.

Kal

Kaleidoscope (comp. Roy Smith)

E. J. Arnold 1968

Secondary headmaster's choices: with good relevant illustrations; many popular poems, conveniently grouped by subject. Tape recordings of the poems available.

Key

Poetry I–IV: The Key of the Kingdom (chosen R. O'Malley & D. Thompson)

Chatto & Windus 1961–63

Excellent set of anthologies for secondary pupils. All moods, periods and styles. Non-specialists will be helped by arrangement of poems in groups. Rich collection of very, very short poems.

Law.S

D. H. Lawrence: Poems selected for Young People (by William Cole)

Macmillan 1968

Well-chosen collection, with rapturous introduction.

Liv
The Living Stream (comp. Janet Adam Smith)
Faber & Faber 1969

> Twentieth century verse primarily for sixth forms. Helpful suggestions for grouping poems. An interesting collection for the more academic.

Look
Look through a Diamond (comp. Joan Forman)
Holt, Rinehart & Winston 1971

> Ample, wide-reaching, intelligently-chosen anthology, with a rather heavy apparatus of notes and questions, directing the readers' responses very firmly. Upper forms.

Make
The Poetry Makers I–IV (chosen J. McGrath)
Bodley Head 1968

> Graded set of secondary anthologies: good variety of poems with 'tough' verses for boys. Small books (160 pp.) and therefore rather small type.

Man
Man I–III (ed. C. Gardiner, J. Glen & R. Scully)
Harrap 1971

> Three volumes, *His Senses, Looking around Him, Looking at Himself,* with many new and unusual poems, accompanied by good but irrelevant photographs. For older children.

Mer and **Mer.Puf**
The Merry-Go-Round (chosen James Reeves)
Heinemann 1955 repr. 1969
Puffin 1967 repr. 1969

> Excellent anthology for all juniors, chosen by a poet. Many rhymes, jingles and traditional nursery ballads.

M.G.B
The Mother Goose Treasury (ed. Raymond Briggs)
Hamish Hamilton 1966 repr. 1967
> Large lavish book, containing over 400 rhymes (mainly those in *Ox.N.R* and *Puf.N.R*) and nearly 900 brightly coloured illustrations.

M.G.E
Mother Goose Nursery Rhymes (illus. by Esmé Eve)
Blackie, n.d.
> A big, very brightly illustrated collection of old favourites.

M.G.R
Mother Goose Nursery Rhymes (illus. by Arthur Rackham)
Heinemann 1913 repr. 1969
> The traditional favourites. A period piece by the most popular illustrator of children's books of his time. Beautifully produced.

Mil.N.S
Now we are six (by A. A. Milne)
Methuen 1927 repr. 43 times by 1969
> See *Mil.V.Y*

Mil.S.V
Silly Verse for Kids (by Spike Milligan)
Puffin 1968 repr. 1970
> New nonsense verses for Milligan fans.

Mil.V.Y
When we were very young (by A. A. Milne)
Methuen 1924 repr. 66 times by 1968
> Chosen with discrimination, some of Milne's lively verses still delight younger children.

Min

The Merry Minstrel I–IV (comp. Haydn Perry)

Blackie & Son 1948 revised 1967 repr. 1968

> I, *Rhymes and Roundelays*; II, *Music and Mime*; III *Jest and Jollity*; IV, *Song and Story*. Jolly collection for primary children; deliberate exclusion of 'unhappiness . . . any cruelty direct or implied.' Aim, enjoyment. Sometimes a little twee.

M.M.A

Mystery Magic and Adventure (chosen John A. Cutforth)

Blackwell, Oxford 1955

> A pleasantly robust collection, splendid for reading aloud. Great diversity: includes admirable extracts from Shakespeare, as well as limericks and music-hall songs.

Mod.P

Modern Poetry (sel. J. R. Townsend)

Oxford University Press 1971

> Varied poems, adult in tone, arranged to picture many aspects of life in the last forty years. Relevant reproductions of modern works of art increase the reader's interest and enlightenment.

Mood

Mood and Rhythm I–IV (chosen Esmé Mears)

A & C Black 1963

> Very helpfully arranged and indexed selection, fitting the sub-titles: I, *Feeling the Tempo*; II, *On the Beat*; III, *A Handful of Stars*; IV, *Changes of Mood*. Middle school.

M.Ver

The Harrap Book of Modern Verse (comp. M. Wollman & K. B. Parker)

Harrap 1958 repr. 1969

> Popular collection of good poems, chosen by teachers for pupils of 14–15 years; helpful juxtapositions. Many poems too complex to classify in this index.

256

My

My Kind of Verse (comp. John Smith)

Burke 1965

> Poems selected by the English Speaking Board for Junior Examinations. Gentle, even a little sentimental, in general tone, but contains a variety of verse, both familiar and unusual, for speaking aloud.

Nar

Narrative Verse (sel. S. C. Paterson)

Longmans (Heritage of Literature) 1967

> Mainly modern verse with 'a few old favourites'; meant for fourteen year olds, but could be used with a wide range of ages and abilities. Extraordinary variety in style, story, kind and quality. Many tales of bad men from Australia and Canada.

Nev

Never Till Now (ed. Edith Cope & Norman Stephenson)

Oxford University Press 1968 repr. 1970

> Unfamiliar examples of contemporary writing 'exploring the young person's search for understanding of himself and others through love and work'. Mainly prose with some poems and pictures.

Ones

One's None (chosen James Reeves)

Heinemann 1968

> Mainly for infants; many little-known traditional brief rhymes, songs and fragments; lively and vigorous.

Ox.Dic

The Oxford Dictionary of Nursery Rhymes (ed. I. and P. Opie)

Oxford University Press 1951 revised 1952 repr. 1966

> Fascinating for the teacher interested in the history and sources of the best 500 rhymes and songs for youngest

children. Children reading for themselves should have *Ox.N.R* or *Puf.N.R*.

Ox.N.R
The Oxford Nursery Rhyme Book (ed. I. and P. Opie)
Oxford University Press 1955 repr 1963
> The most complete collection available—800 rhymes and songs. Invaluable for teachers of younger children. Delightful tiny woodcut illustrations.

Ox.P.C
The Oxford Book of Poetry for Children (ed. E. Blishen)
Oxford University Press 1963
> Very well-produced: illustrated by Brian Wildsmith. An excellent choice of real poems, designed for younger children but appropriate at many ages. Should be in every class library.

Ox.V.J
The Oxford Books of Verse for Juniors I–IV (ed. James Britton)
Oxford University Press 1957 repr. 1958
> Admirable set for class use: attractively printed poems, often modern, sometimes unusual in anthologies.

Pat
The Pattern of Poetry (ed. W. K. Seymour & J. Smith)
Burke Publishing Co 1963
> Specially good for reading aloud, because the poems are those chosen for the verse-speaking examinations of the Poetry Society. Ranging over four centuries and many moods and styles. Many rarely anthologised. Twelve years upwards.

Patch
The Patchwork Quilt and Other Poems (sel. Joan Cass)
Longmans Green & Co 1968
> Gay picture book illustrating relevantly the accompanying poems. For top juniors.

P.Bk

A Poetry Book for Boys and Girls (chosen Guy Pocock)
J. M. Dent & Sons 1963 repr. 1967

Rather conventional selection of lyric and narrative poems. Useful book for children to explore, to meet traditional favourites.

Peg

Pegasus I–V (ed. N. Grisenthwaite)
Schofield & Sims Ltd 1962 repr. 1967

An excellent and lively collection. Carefully graded for use as secondary class books. Mainly traditional but many unexpected choices and pleasures in later volumes.

Peng.An

The Penguin Book of Animal Verse (intro. and ed. George Macbeth)
Penguin 1965

Poems on animals, alphabetically arranged, in widest variety of style, mood, period and sophistication. Some complete poems, and parts of many others, will delight children, but it is primarily for adults and top forms.

Pers

Persons Places and Things II (coll. Allen Freer)
Cambridge University Press 1969

Companion volume of poems, mainly twentieth century, to a prose collection with the same title. Most intelligently and sensitively arranged to be read in succession and so illuminate one another. Top forms.

P.F.P

Poems for Pleasure I, II (ed. A. F. Scott)
Cambridge University Press 1955 repr. 1969

Useful for any age from top juniors to adults, and very well arranged under such headings as Rhythm in Verse or Scenes

259

of the Machine Age. A third volume advises the teacher about presentation of the poems.

Plea
Poetry for Pleasure I–VIII (chosen Ian Parsons)
Ginn 1952 repr. 1966
> Eight admirable graded volumes for juniors; the first two rich in memorable jingles; the selection widens and deepens in each succeeding volume.

P.Life
Poetry and Life I–IV (ed. N. Grisenthwaite)
Schofield & Sims Ltd 1961 repr. 1969
> Poems both attractive to children and of real quality. One of the best sets for the junior classroom; much traditional material attractive to the ear. Expertly graded.

P.P
Poems and Pictures (planned by Ian Serraillier)
Heinemann 1958
> Unique workbook by a poet, encouraging both creative painting and writing as well as appreciation of poetry. When completed by the child, an individual anthology.

Prel
Preludes I–IV (ed. Rhodri Jones)
Heinemann Educational 1971
> I, *Families*, II *Work and Play*, III *Weathers*, IV *Five Senses*. Well chosen groups of poems to match these titles, mainly modern. For middle schools upwards. Good relevant photographs which really illustrate, and with the poems (in IV particularly) inspire good writing.

P.Rem
Poetry to Remember (comp. P. Dickinson & Sheila Shannon)
Harvill Press 1958 repr. 1966
> Useful for teachers of top juniors upwards. Varied poems of merit, chosen often for rhythmical quality.

P.Tong
The Poet's Tongue I, II (ed. W. H. Auden & John Garratt)
Bell 1935 repr. 1962
> First rate book for the teacher; poems for all ages. Lots of traditional verses in varied moods for both lowbrows and highbrows, also poetry by Donne, Milton, Shakespeare. Interesting introduction.

Puf.N.R
Puffin Book of Nursery Rhymes (ed. I. & P. Opie)
Puffin 1963
> Selected from *Ox.N.R* some 150 standard rhymes, plus 200 others. An admirable collection for the youngest children, very attractively presented.

Puf.Q
A Puffin Quartet of Poets (by E. Farjeon, J. Reeves, E. V. Rieu & I. Serraillier)
Puffin 1958 repr. 1970
> Delightful new poems by four poets who excel in writing for younger children.

Puf.S.B
The Puffin Song Book (comp. Leslie Woodgate)
Puffin 1956 repr. 1970
> Traditional songs from many countries, grave and gay. Also familiar carols; for unusual carols see the two Penguin Books of Christmas Carols.

Puf.V
A Puffin Book of Verse (ed. Eleanor Graham)
Puffin 1953 repr. 1970
> A rather conventional, but wide, selection.

Puf.Y

The Young Puffin Book of Verse (comp. Barbara Ireson)
Puffin 1970

> Enjoyable verses for the youngest children, arranged in helpful sequences so that successive poems enrich each other. Many memorable jingles.

P.W

The Poet's World (ed. James Reeves)
Heinemann 1948 reset 1963

> A poet's selection from a thousand years of English poetry, including particularly well-chosen passages from the Old Testament. Adult poetry for upper classes of academic ability. See *P.W.R.*

P.W.R

as *P.W* above, revised 1972

> Still admirable.

Quest

Poetry Quest I–V (comp. T. H. Parker and F. J. Teskey)
Blackie & Son 1970

> I, *All Around You*; II, *Magic Question, Magic Answer*; III, *It Could Happen to You*; IV, *Through the Five Senses*; V, *It Makes You Think*. Contemporary verses of many genres and of varying merit. The useful 'follow-up' questions and suggestions might be considered by some children slightly patronising in tone. Much better than its format.

Rain

The Swinging Rainbow (sel. Howard Sergeant)
Evans Bros 1969

> Poems of very varied difficulty, from nursery rhymes to adult poems, grouped by subjects. Attractive extra book for juniors own reading.

Read
Readings I–III (ed. R. Doubleday)
Heinemann Educational 1970

> Tough modern prose and verse chosen for secondary boys, grouped by theme. Variety, and unusual thought-provoking juxtapositions.

Rhyme
Rhyme and Rhythm I–IV (comp. J. Gibson & R. Wilson)
Macmillan 1965 repr. 1970

> Red, I; Blue, II; Green, III; Yellow, IV. Four lively, well-graded, well-produced collections for juniors, with excellent recordings available. Recommended.

Rid
Storm and other Old English Riddles (trans. Kevin Crossley-Holland)
Macmillan 1970

> Unique book; ancient riddles with Miles Thistlethwaite's pictorial answers. Excellent for inspiring children's writing of riddling descriptions. Introduction and notes help to give vivid pictures of Anglo-Saxon life.

Ris
Rising Early (chosen Charles Causley)
Brockhampton Press 1964

> Poet's choice of twentieth century poems and ballads, mainly for older children. A few have a slightly sick flavour, but it is a useful, unusual collection.

Riv
The Rhyming River I–IV (chosen James Reeves)
Heinemann Educational 1959 repr. 1966

> Supposedly secondary, but very good for middle schools too. Wide choice of fairly well-known poems, all of high poetic quality. Good set for class-work.

R.R
Rhyme and Reason (chosen R. O'Malley & D. Thompson)
Chatto & Windus 1957 repr. 1966
> For the oldest children, a particularly good selection of 175 sensitively chosen poems of every period and style, grouped by subject. Interesting introduction and helpful notes.

Say
First I Say This (ed. Alan Brownjohn)
Hutchinson Educational 1969
> Poems chosen by a popular modern poet, for the Poetry Society, to give special pleasure when read aloud.

Scrap
Scrap Box (chosen Margaret Greaves)
Methuen Educational 1969
> 'Precision, zest, unsentimentality' are the compiler's criteria. Poems to be read (allegedly) to the very young, but many admirable for all juniors.

S.D
Songs and Dreams (chosen James Kirkup)
Blackie 1970
> A poet's collection of poems which he knows children have enjoyed, including translations of Oriental verse not available elsewhere. Grouped interestingly by subject.

Ser.B
The Windmill Book of Ballads (by Ian Serraillier)
Heinemann Educational 1962 repr. 1966
> Stories from Beowulf to Kon-Tiki told in straightforward modern verse.

264

Sev

Seven Themes in Modern Verse (sel. M. Wollmann)
Harrap 1968 repr. 1970

Poems rarely found in anthologies; often difficult, but rewarding for teacher and upper forms. Very skilfully chosen and arranged in groups.

Shad

Shadows and Spells (ed. Barbara Ireson)
Faber & Faber 1969

Eerie poems for all ages, but primarily for readers of 8 to 12. Poems about ghosts and witches written over a period of 350 years.

Shep

Shepherding Winds (chosen James Kirkup)
Blackie 1969

Poems from east and west, mainly modern, which have been enjoyed by a poet's pupils. Secondary age. Grouped loosely by themes.

Six

Six Anthologies I–VI (chosen Helen Riley)
Ginn & Co 1968 repr. 1969

I, *The Seasons*; II, *Story Poems*; III, *About People*; IV, *Men and Machines*; V, *Look Around You*; VI, *About Animals*. Six little books (64 pp.) where children can search for poems on a theme. Each poem followed by suggestions for further writing, talking and doing, which may overwhelm the poem itself. Contains lists of related poems.

Song
Poetry and Song I–IV (chosen by James Gibson)
Macmillan 1967 repr. 1971
>Valuable and most varied secondary selections, having as an integral part recordings of poems and songs. Volume IV is sixth form material. Very attractive volumes.

Speak
Speaking Together I, II (ed. Maisie Cobby & Rona Laurie)
Pitman 1964
>Chosen by experts in speech and drama for secondary children. Part I grouped by style, Part II by subject. Instructions for group speaking of poems in rather elaborate ways.

Sphe
The Poet's Sphere (comp. C. F. Bricknell Smith)
Wheaton (Pergamon) 1969
>Nearly 350 poems, mostly well-known, of all periods and genres. A useful reference book for secondary teachers.

Spir
Poems of Spirit and Action (sel. W. M. Smyth)
Edward Arnold 1957 16th imp. 1968
>Vigorous straightforward poems, mainly narrative, popular with younger secondary children.

Spir.R
as *Spir* above, revised second edition 1971

Spo
An Anthology of Spoken Verse and Prose I, II (sel. G. Johnson, J. Byrne & C. Burniston)
Oxford University Press 1957
>A widely-ranging selection, chosen for choral speaking by schoolchildren, with suggested arrangements.

Start
Come Down and Startle (chosen Jeffrey Aldridge)
Oxford University Press 1968 repr. 1969
>Poems (and some prose) of quality, with particularly good photographs. Meant for youngest secondary pupils, but much for older readers too.

Ste.C.G
A Child's Garden of Verses (1885—by Robert Louis Stevenson)
Puffin 1948 repr. 1969
>Still attractive to many younger children: as the author says, the reader hears 'a child's voice'.

Ste.Ho
Home from Sea (by R. L. Stevenson chosen Ivor Brown)
Bodley Head 1970
>Poetry of childhood: Ardizzone illustrations in perfect accord with the verse.

Sto
Story and Rhythm I–III (chosen G. F. Lamb)
Harrap 1966
>Rather simple poems for lower secondary forms, with stress on narrative and rhythm. Very useful for less academic forms.

T.C.N
Twentieth Century Narrative Poems (comp. M. Wollman)
Harrap 1954 repr. 1970
>Very popular collection of 35 longer modern poems for secondary schools. Useful list of further titles.

Tell
tell I, II (chosen Denys Thompson & Raymond O'Malley)
Heinemann Educational 1971
>   Two very useful books of narrative poems (often un-anthologised) with a teacher's book packed with further titles and suggestions.

Ten
Ten Twentieth Century Poets (ed. Maurice Wollman)
Harrap 1957 repr. 1969
>   Very popular collection for top forms, with helpful notes on each poet.

Ten.Fa
The Falling Splendour (by Alfred Lord Tennyson sel. George Macbeth)
Macmillan 1970
>   A very modern poet tries to rehabilitate a neglected Poet Laureate who, he thinks, had 'the sharpest eye and clearest ear of all the great poets'.

Them
themes I–VII (ed. Rhodri Jones)
Heinemann Educational 1969
>   I *Men and Beasts*; II *Imagination*; III *Conflict*; IV *Generations*; V *Sport and Leisure*; VI *Men at Work*; VII *Town and Country*. Excellent slim books (70 pp.) with poems, mainly recent, grouped thematically. Much unusual material, closely relevant to modern ways of life.

This W.D
This Way Delight (sel. Herbert Read)
Faber & Faber 1957 repr. 1970
>   Poems mainly lyrical and fantastical. Some unexpected modern poets. Many poems impossible to classify.

Tho. Gr
The Green Roads (by Edward Thomas chosen Eleanor Farjeon)
Bodley Head 1965
> Pleasant selection of country poems with interesting introduction by a personal friend, telling how Thomas began to write poetry.

T.P.R, T.P.W
A Time for Poetry: Ring of Rhyme
A Time for Poetry: Words take Wing
E. J. Arnold & Son 1963
> Sometimes verse rather than poetry, but many useful and quite unusual pieces which interest juniors.

Trea
A Treasury of Verse (sel. M. Edgar revised D. M. Stuart)
Harrap 1925 revised 1959
> Handy reference book for the teacher. Many well-known poems by standard authors, once popular, and rarely found in modern school anthologies, but still worth introducing to children.

Tree
The Tree in the Wood I–IV (chosen R. O'Malley & D. Thompson)
Chatto & Windus 1966
> I, *The Egg in the Nest*; II, *The Nest on the Twig*; III, *The Twig on the Bough*; IV, *The Bough on the Tree*. Outstanding junior series, well set out for easy reading. Wide variety of poems of quality, each good of its kind, grave or amusing, homely or fantastic, sense or nonsense.

Under

Modern Poems Understood (ed. C. W. Gillam)

Harrap 1965 repr. 1967

Poems written between 1914 and 1964: a really useful introduction to modern poetry for secondary pupils. Notes perhaps a little trite.

Ver

Verse for You I–III (made by J. G. Brown)

Longmans (Heritage of Literature) 1958 repr. 1965

Traditional material plus much rare verse from the Commonwealth. Useful as a sampler for upper forms exploring 'Eng. Lit.'. Book III has sections of 'Lyric', 'Ode', etc.

V.F

Verse that is Fun (ed. Barbara Ireson)

Faber 1962 repr. 1967

Humorous poems and jingles, long and short, credited and anonymous. For occasional light relief.

Vic

Victorian Poetry 1830–1890 (sel. C. & H. Tennyson)

Ginn 1971

A change from the ultra-modern. Much to interest secondary children, with brief helpful notes on poems and poets.

Voi

Voices I–III (ed. Geoffrey Summerfield)

Penguin 1968

Extremely varied poems, lavishly and strikingly illustrated. The third volume is almost adult. All are individual and thought-provoking. See also *J.Vo*.

Way
A Way of Looking (comp. Lorna & Derek Brown)
Harrap 1969
> Modern verses for secondary schools, intended to stimulate
> creative writing. Classified by subject.

Weal
A Wealth of Poetry I, II (comp. Winifred Hindley & John
Betjeman)
Blackwell Oxford 1963
> An anthology of high quality. Over 250 poems, many of them
> very popular with children, and over a quarter by living poets.
> Widely ranging, arranged by theme. Dazzling illustrations by
> Bridget Riley.

Wheel
The Wheel of Poetry I–IV (comp. Jerome Hanratty)
University of London Press 1963
> For rather academically-inclined secondary classes; poems
> chronologically arranged in each volume; a few notes. Sec-
> tions of poems by children are interesting.

Wor.So
The Solitary Song (by William Wordsworth chosen Edmund
Blunden)
Bodley Head 1970
> A poet of nature chooses for young readers many well-known
> pieces by Wordsworth. Only likely to be popular with the
> already converted, I fear.

Yea.Run
Running to Paradise (by W. B. Yeats sel. K. Crossley-Holland)
Macmillan 1967
> Samples of Yeats in many moods which may whet young
> readers' appetites.

Yim

Young Impact I–III (ed. R. H. Poole & P. J. Shepherd)
Heinemann Educational 1972

Prose, poetry and photographs grouped thematically. Much new and striking material at middle school level.

You.Bu

Burning as Light (by Andrew Young chosen Leonard Clark)
Rupert Hart-Davies 1967

Delicate precise observation of nature in wiry, spare poems. Recommended for use in part or entire to teach children to look closely and describe accurately.

You.Qu

Quiet as Moss (by Andrew Young chosen Leonard Clark)
Rupert Hart-Davies 1967

The poet's keen vision and sharp economical language create birds, animals, scenes most vividly. Wonderful evocations of natural scenes. Very well chosen selection.

Index of Poets

Graves, Robert *contd.*
73, 74, 78, 88, 108, 112, 116, 118, 119, 120, 124, 132, 136, 137, 139, 159, 180, 185, 189, 190, 192, 202, 221, 225, 230, 234, 235
Gray, Alexander, 28
Gray, Thomas, 29, 67
Gray, William, 102
Greenaway, Kate, 29
Greene, Robert, 33, 163
Grenfell, Julian, 91, 226
Gridley, Gordon, 103
Griffiths, Ian, 46
Griffiths, Mervyn, 29
Grimble, Sir Arthur, 62
Guiterman, A., 132, 178
Gunn, Thom, 2, 3, 27, 36, 95, 115, 179, 193, 208
Guthrie, Woody, 149

Hale, Robert B., 72
Hall, Donald, 81, 134
Hall, Kevin, 218
Hamburger, Michael, 8, 19, 27, 28, 125
Hamilton, G. Rostrevor, 133, 163, 199, 217, 218
Handle, Johnny, 127
Hankin, St John, 133
Hardy, Thomas, 10, 17, 25, 30, 37, 41, 54, 66, 72, 74, 86, 87, 90, 94, 108, 115, 120, 135, 138, 148, 149, 150, 154, 163, 177, 179, 187, 195, 197, 203, 205, 209, 211, 213, 217, 221, 222, 223, 224, 228, 235
Harrington, Edward, 24, 205
Harris, Max, 9
Harrison, Keith, 54
Hart, H. H., 96
Hart, Henry, 24
Harte, Bret, 1, 46, 208, 221
Hart-Smith, W., 185

Harvey, F. W., 61
Hassall, Christopher, 24, 86, 133, 213
Hawker, Robert S., 66
Hawkshawe, A., 96
Hay, Sara H., 70
Hayes, Evelyn, 28
Hayes, Robert, 3
Hayman, Robert, 59
Hays, H. R., 78, 197
Hays, Lee, 84
Heaney, Seamus, 2, 3, 18, 25, 54, 55, 57, 75, 84, 124, 171, 177, 179, 181, 189, 209, 217, 229
Heath-Stubbs, John, 32, 118, 141, 202, 212
Hennell, Thomas, 126
Henri, Adrian, 117, 142
Henry VIII, King, 102
Herbert, A. P., 2, 47, 80
Herbert, George, 32, 62, 116, 164, 211
Herford, Oliver, 158
Hernandez, Miguel, 223
Herrick, Robert, 19, 32, 33, 37, 38, 44, 50, 54, 70, 91, 112, 125, 131, 132, 233
Hesketh, Phoebe, 19, 22, 61
Heyrick, Thomas, 48, 101
Heywood, Thomas, 16, 53
Hill, F. E., 41, 83
Hill, R. F. C., 102
Hillyer, Robert, 7, 132
Hobsbaum, Philip, 19, 21, 35, 160, 173, 185
Hodgson, Ralph, 5, 17, 23, 67, 68, 94, 202, 211
Hoey, Edwin A., 12
Hoffman, Dr Heinrich, 207
Holbrook, David, 133
Hollo, Anselm, 34
Holmes, O. W., 233

Holub, Miroslav, 21, 57, 80, 103, 135, 136, 182, 226
Homer, 20
Hood, Thomas, 14, 24, 57, 66, 75, 100, 108, 137, 146, 159, 163, 178, 185, 189, 191, 198, 221
Hooley, Teresa, 24
Hopkins, Gerard Manley, 18, 37, 93, 111, 125, 160, 164, 165, 182, 201, 202, 230, 233, 235
Hopkins, Kenneth, 214
Horace, 200
Horan, Robert, 199
Horner, Frances, 81
Horsburgh, Wilma, 49, 214
Housman, A. E., 15, 34, 48, 51, 93, 120, 124, 134
Howard, Henry, 201
Howe, Julia Ward, 84, 219
Howell, Russell, 90
Howells, Mildred, 207
Howitt, Mary, 71
Howitt, William, 232
Hsiang, Chu, 170
Hsu, Kai-Yu, 170, 174, 201, 227
Hsü, Pên, 96
Hubbell, Patricia, 23
Hudson, Flexmore, 9, 60
Hughes, Betty, 23
Hughes, Jabez, 88
Hughes, Langston, 19, 45, 98, 138
Hughes, Linda, 82
Hughes, Richard, 233
Hughes, Ted, 6, 23, 27, 73, 95, 99, 102, 105, 143, 144, 149, 150, 155, 156, 189, 190, 209, 215, 222, 223, 231, 237
Hull, Richard, 173
Hulme, Thomas E., 9, 130
Hutchinson, M. M., 44
Huxley, Aldous, 107

Ingelow, Jean, 210
Isherwood, Christopher, 219
Ives, Charles E., 39

Jackson, Ada, 85
Jackson, K., 8
Jammes, Francis, 58
Janosco, Beatrice, 86
Jardine, Tony, 82
Jarrell, Randall, 13, 150
Jeffere, John, 33
Jeffers, Robinson, 95, 182
Jeffery, Gordon, 83
Jenner, E., 170
Jennings, Elizabeth, 3, 13, 78, 79, 103, 111, 140
Jesse, ?Michael or Baldwin, 77
Johnson, B. S., 116, 218
Johnson, Geoffrey, 21, 47, 109
Johnson, James Weldon, 47
Johnson, Lionel, 31
Johnson, Michael, 162
Jones, Brian, 54, 80
Jones, Evan, 11, 105, 168
Jones, George, 219
Jones, L. E., 189
Jones, T. H., 109
Jonson, Ben, 32, 33, 56, 70, 92, 157, 176, 234
Joseph, Jenny, 81, 84, 148
Joseph, M. K., 3
Joseph, Rosemary, 11
Joyce, James, 182
Justice, Donald, 122

Kariuki, Joseph, 168
Keats, John, 10, 14, 21, 28, 90, 92, 128, 140, 159, 165, 192, 206, 215
Keene, D., 128
Kell, Richard, 156
Keller, Martha, 105
Ken, T., 163

Kendall, John, 88
Kendon, Frank, 44, 178
Kennedy, Charles W., 132, 229
Kenward, Jean, 59
Kernahan, Coulson, 47
Keyes, Sidney, 107, 155, 236
King, Ben, 28, 154
King, Henry, 132
Kingsley, Charles, 60, 78, 109, 121, 160, 175, 210
Kipling, Rudyard, 5, 7, 12, 23, 37, 63, 64, 65, 66, 67, 75, 93, 101, 122, 124, 126, 129, 136, 138, 154, 156, 165, 168, 173, 178, 179, 182, 183, 192, 193, 196, 197, 209, 210, 216, 221, 234, 235
Kirkconnell, Watson, 29
Kirkup, James, 23, 25, 27, 37, 60, 61, 82, 90, 97, 105, 117, 121, 178, 180, 191, 198, 199, 205, 210, 224, 237
Kiyotsugu, 148
Knight, Max, 26, 103
Knox, E. V., 8
Koriyama, Naoshi, 40, 158
Kotewall, R., 14
Kramer, A., 182
Kroeber, A. L., 103, 171
Kuba, 53
Kumin, Maxine, 181

Lamb, Charles, 193
Landor, Walter S., 66
Lang, Andrew, 134
Lanyon, Carla L., 180
Larkin, Philip, 38, 99, 110, 116, 124, 125, 155, 168, 195, 200, 236
Lauren, Joseph, 69
Lavrin, Janko, 192
Lawrence, D. H., 12, 13, 16, 19, 34, 39, 63, 79, 87, 101, 108, 128, 130, 132, 133, 139, 148, 151, 152, 154,
160, 163, 180, 181, 194, 198, 210, 212, 219, 235, 236
Lawrence, Douglas, 166
Lawson, Henry, 9, 60
Layton, Irving, 23
Lear, Edward, 29, 112, 144, 145, 150, 156, 162, 218
Lee, Laurie, 7, 8, 10, 38, 74, 127, 150, 155, 231, 232
Lefebvre, Denys, 60
Lehrer, Tom, 134
Leigh, H. S., 218
Leishman, J. B., 152, 175, 238
Lemont, Jessie, 152, 238
Lennon, John, 115
Leonard, William E., 69
Lerner, Laurence, 87
Leslie, Shane, 139
Levertov, Denise, 133, 224
Levi, Peter, 39, 76, 105, 119, 181
Lewis, Alun, 128, 226
Lewis, C. S., 124, 141, 199, 218, 223
Lewis, Cecil Day, 3, 10, 14, 24, 38, 39, 83, 94, 111, 113, 116, 129, 137, 139, 171, 187, 218, 226, 227
Lewis, Gary, 42, 200
Li Po, 85
Lindley, Roger, 96
Lindon, J. A., 156
Lindsay, Norman, 45
Lindsay, Vachel, 20, 22, 24, 25, 28, 52, 70, 77, 103, 113, 127, 131, 154, 180, 184, 218
Lipsitz, Lou, 40
Liu, Ta-Pai, 201
Livingstone, Douglas, 222
Lofting, Hugh, 156
Logan, John, 3, 76, 91
Logue, Christopher, 37, 52, 151, 190
Longfellow, Henry W., 18, 52, 69, 89, 97, 157, 170, 175, 186, 192, 210, 221, 232

Plath, Sylvia, 11, 14, 91, 104, 122, 135
Plomer, William, 67, 114, 134, 194
Po, Chu-I, 25, 41, 52, 75, 81, 82, 95, 101, 102, 112, 157, 159, 203, 222, 223
Poe, Edgar Allen, 14, 62, 109, 171
Ponchon, Raoul, 37
Popa, Vasco, 5, 194
Pope, Alexander, 44, 70, 89, 123, 155, 190, 191, 212, 237
Pope, Jessie, 141, 238
Porter, Kenneth, 58
Porter, Peter, 146
Pound, Ezra, 75, 92, 115, 117, 148, 152, 178, 223
Pratt, E. J., 189
Press, John, 25, 36, 85
Prevert, Jacques, 16, 101, 128, 180
Prince, Joan, 177
Pringle, Thomas, 3
Probert, W., 105
Proctor, Thomas, 210
Prys-Jones, A. G., 177
Pudney, John, 56, 86, 94, 162, 214, 226
Purcell-Buret, Theobald, 57
Pursey, Gillian, 234

Radloff, W., 231
Raffel, Burton, 131, 175, 205
Raine, Kathleen, 47, 192
Ralegh, Sir Walter, 116, 157, 210
Ramsey, Alan, 69
Ramsey, T. W., 16
Randall, Celia, 96, 103
Rands, William B., 141, 154
Ratcliffe, Dorothy U., 92, 187
Read, Herbert, 172
Reed, Alastair, 137
Reed, Henry, 172, 227

Reeves, James, 5, 6, 11, 14, 30, 33, 41, 57, 78, 88, 89, 100, 126, 137, 142, 148, 150, 159, 177, 182, 184, 185, 193, 194, 198, 209, 215, 227, 231
Reid, Alastair, 33
Renton, William, 79
Reynolds, Malvina, 146, 219
Reznikoff, Charles, 12
Rhys, Ernest, 56, 128, 225
Richards, Laura, 142
Rickword, Edgell, 226
Ridler, Anne, 47, 182
Rieu, E. V., 14, 28, 54, 79, 100, 154, 162, 168, 212, 218
Rilke, Rainer Maria, 152, 175, 238
Roberts, Elizabeth Madox, 96, 127, 168
Roberts, Michael, 231
Roberts, Peter, 226
Roberts, Sally, 135
Roberts, Theodore G., 189
Robinson, Edwin Meade, 52, 100, 163, 188
Robinson, S., 21
Rodgers, W. R., 13, 48
Roethke, Theodore, 10, 12, 13, 34, 56, 80, 96, 126, 133, 149, 155, 156, 188, 193, 194, 203, 204, 213, 215, 220, 230, 231
Rogers, Samuel, 77
Roscoe, John, 146
Rosenberg, Isaac, 225
Ross, Alan, 47, 78, 83, 169, 189, 227
Ross, W. W. E., 57
Rossetti, Christina, 17, 26, 34, 36, 40, 41, 42, 52, 67, 76, 82, 85, 88, 90, 99, 106, 110, 111, 121, 130, 131, 152, 170, 174, 182, 186, 201, 202, 204, 206, 228, 231
Rossetti, Dante Gabriel, 64, 129
Rowlands, Samuel, 59, 110

286

Wilbur, Richard, 21, 36, 58, 77, 91, 103
Wilde, Oscar, 11, 42, 93
Williams, Charles, 216
Williams, Gwyn, 174
Williams, Hugo, 23
Williams, William Carlos, 7, 28, 34, 50, 72, 81, 99, 137, 151, 198
Williamson, P., 199
Willy, M., 185
Wilson, R. L., 208
Winchelsea, Countess of, 56, 223
Winn, Alison, 21
Winn, Rosemary, 158
Wolcot, John, 79
Wolfe, Charles, 43
Wolfe, Humbert, 18, 77, 87, 100, 122, 201
Wordsworth, Dorothy, 230
Wordsworth, William, 25, 30, 33, 57, 72, 82, 109, 114, 115, 124, 127, 148, 190, 191, 192, 204, 236
Wotton, Sir Henry, 90, 162
Wright, Judith, 22, 73, 131, 205
Wu, General Su, 124
Wu-Ti, Emperor, 148
Wyatt, Sir Thomas, 120

Wylde, A. E., 124
Wylie, Elinor, 195

Yamada, Tokiyo, 158
Yamanoguchi, Baku, 171
Yates, Peter, 115, 204
Yeatman, R. J., 152
Yeats, William Butler, 27, 29, 70, 71, 73, 75, 76, 88, 90, 94, 96, 104, 116, 118, 120, 130, 132, 148, 180, 202, 204, 205, 206, 221, 224
Yevtushenko, Yevgeny, 119, 172, 181
Yin, Lo, 14
Young, Andrew, 8, 10, 16, 19, 30, 37, 46, 48, 49, 50, 53, 61, 64, 85, 94, 95, 99, 100, 110, 123, 129, 130, 153, 158, 171, 172, 174, 177, 183, 186, 193, 195, 202, 203, 206, 209, 217, 230, 232, 237
Young, Duncan, 14
Young, E. Hilton, 225
Young, F. B., 25
Young, Geoffrey W., 133
Yu, Han, 217
Yuan, Mei, 200